Loredana Filip
Self-Help in the Digital Age

Vigilanzkulturen /
Cultures of Vigilance

Herausgegeben vom / Edited by
Sonderforschungsbereich 1369
Ludwig-Maximilians-Universität München

Editorial Board
Erdmute Alber, Peter Burschel, Thomas Duve,
Rivke Jaffe, Isabel Karremann, Christian Kiening and
Nicole Reinhardt

Band / Volume 12

Loredana Filip

Self-Help in the Digital Age

TED Talks, Speculative Fiction, and the Role of Reading

DE GRUYTER

Funded by the Deutsche Forschungsgemeinschaft (DFG, German Research Foundation) – Project-ID 394775490 – SFB 1369

This book is a revised version of a doctoral dissertation written at the University of Munich (Ludwig-Maximilians-Universität München) that was defended in July 2023.

ISBN 978-3-11-138826-7
e-ISBN (PDF) 978-3-11-138992-9
ISBN (EPUB) 978-3-11-139009-3
ISSN 2749-8913
DOI https://doi.org/10.1515/9783111389929

This work is licensed under the Creative Commons Attribution 4.0 International License. For details go to https://creativecommons.org/licenses/by/4.0/.

Creative Commons license terms for re-use do not apply to any content (such as graphs, figures, photos, excerpts, etc.) that is not part of the Open Access publication. These may require obtaining further permission from the rights holder. The obligation to research and clear permission lies solely with the party re-using the material.

Library of Congress Control Number: 2024938441

Bibliographic information published by the Deutsche Nationalbibliothek
The Deutsche Nationalbibliothek lists this publication in the Deutsche Nationalbibliografie; detailed bibliographic data are available on the Internet at http://dnb.dnb.de.

© Copyright 2024 the author(s), published by Walter de Gruyter GmbH, Berlin/Boston
The book is published open access at www.degruyter.com.

Cover illustration: Weißes iPad auf weißer Oberfläche. Photo: Leone Venter, Unsplash, https://unsplash.com/de/fotos/weisses-ipad-auf-weisser-oberflache-pVt9j3iWtPM

www.degruyter.com

Acknowledgments

A book about confessions ought to start with one: I always dreamed of being an author, but I never would have guessed my first book would be an academic one. I am deeply grateful to all the people, places, and circumstances that have played a part in its creation. Its long journey began with the shelves of my father's library and the first books I eagerly devoured there. I owe a debt of gratitude to my parents, my partner, and all the teachers who inspired in me a love for knowledge.

In particular, I wish to express my heartfelt appreciation to Antje Kley, who has been a guiding light and mentor to me throughout these years. Her seminar *Literature and Science* was pivotal in shaping my academic trajectory. Antje recognized my potential, believed in me, and offered unwavering support during crucial moments in my journey.

I am also indebted to Bärbel Harju and Klaus Benesch for opening doors that seemed out of reach and for providing me with their invaluable feedback. I am thankful to all the participants in the doctoral colloquiums at Friedrich-Alexander-University of Erlangen-Nuremberg and Ludwig Maximilian University of Munich for sharing with me their meaningful thoughts. Being part of the CRC "Cultures of Vigilance" has been an enriching experience, and I extend my gratitude to all those involved in the research group. Special thanks go to Alina Enzensberger for her continuous support, Kira Hentschel for her helpful assistance, and John Barrett for his careful copy-editing.

To the editors who have collaborated with me over the years, the colleagues I have met at conferences, and my close circle of friends, I owe a debt of gratitude. Each of you has contributed to my growth and learning in ways both seen and unseen.

Finally, I acknowledge with sincere gratitude all the inanimate companions that have accompanied me on this journey—laptops, rooms, papers, books, pens, cups of coffee, and more. To those who may find this acknowledgment peculiar, I invite you to discover the significance of these seemingly mundane things by reading this book.

To everyone mentioned and to those unnamed but nonetheless essential to this endeavor, I offer my heartfelt thanks once again.

Contents

1 Introduction: What Do We Expect? —— 1

I Happy Confessions: Context, Theory, Approach

Introduction —— 15

2 Confessional Culture and American Self-Help —— 17
2.1 Autobiography and America —— 19
2.2 Self-Vigilance and the Redemptive Self —— 26

3 Confessions and Science Communication —— 32
3.1 The Intimization of Science —— 32
3.2 TED Talks: History, Genre, Culture —— 39

4 Confessions and Reading: From Self-Writing to Life Writing —— 59
4.1 From "Critical Vigilance" to "Critical Solace" —— 59
4.2 Literary Synesthesia and the Affect of Aliveness —— 68

II Self-Improvement: Finding Success in a Digital Age

Introduction —— 81

5 TED Talks on "How to Be a Better You" and Social Media Influencers —— 83
5.1 Digital Culture Meets Self-Help: Building Confidence Online —— 83
5.2 Self-Surveillance, the Quantified Self, and the "Power of Posing" —— 93
5.3 The Mission of Saving Humanity and the Duty to Be Alive —— 101

6 Gary Shteyngart's *Super Sad True Love Story* and the Privilege of "Merely Existing" —— 106
6.1 Self-Help Culture: "You've Got to Sell to Live" —— 106
6.2 Self-Descriptive Reminiscence: "Dear Diary" —— 116
6.3 Literary Synesthesia: "That Thing Smells like Wet Socks" —— 121

7 Literature and Scanning: "A Burble of Warm White Spray" —— 130

III Mindfulness and Self-Vigilance in the Anthropocene

Introduction —— 143

8 TED Talks on Mindfulness and the "Second Sight" —— 144
8.1 Mindfulness and Self-Help: Restoring Vigor in the Age of Anxiety —— 144
8.2 The "Inner Scientist" Is Noticing the Body —— 156
8.3 Mindfulness and the Survival of the Species —— 163

9 Margaret Atwood's *MaddAddam* Trilogy and the "Insight of Interbeing" —— 171
9.1 Self-Help Culture: "What People Want Is Perfection" —— 172
9.2 Self-Descriptive Reminiscence: Jimmy's Autobiography —— 180
9.3 Literary Synesthesia: "A Songbird Made of Ice" —— 189

10 Literature and Storytelling: "These Stories Are Real as Kitchens" —— 200

IV Self-Transcendence in the Age of Empathy

11 TED Talks on "What Makes You Happy?" and the Science of Happiness —— 214
11.1 Science Meets Self-Help: "Where Do You Go to Find Happiness?" —— 214
11.2 Self-Compassion and "Looking at it Outside of Yourself" —— 222
11.3 Flow and Out-of-Body Experiences —— 227

12 Richard Powers' *Generosity: An Enhancement* and the "Small Shared Joy" of Reading —— 237
12.1 Self-Help Culture: "Dangerous Altruism" —— 237
12.2 Self-Descriptive Reminiscence: Russell Stone's "Creative Nonfiction" —— 245
12.3 Literary Synesthesia: "A Sharp Blue Filament of Need" —— 251

13 Literature and Compositing: "The Secret Quickening in the Hands" —— 261

14 Conclusion: A Kinship of Posthumanity —— 270

Bibliography —— 279

List of Figures —— 304

Index —— 305

1 Introduction: What Do We Expect?

> Today, we have so little darkness. *Our world is lit up 24 hours a day. It's transparent with blogs and social networks* broadcasting the buzz of a whole new generation of people that have made a choice to live their lives in public. It's a much more noisy world. So one challenge we have is to remember, *oversharing*, that's not *honesty*. Our manic tweeting and texting can blind us to the fact that the subtleties of *human decency—character integrity*—that's still what matters, that's always what's going to matter.[1]

In February 1984, designers Harry Marks and Richard Saul Wurman founded TED as a one-off conference about technology, entertainment, and design, hence the acronym TED. In 2011, American author Pamela Meyer delivered a TED talk titled "How to Spot a Liar," which has since become one of the most popular talks of all time. During the talk, Meyer addressed several contemporary issues related to individual privacy, including the problem of oversharing.[2] This phenomenon has also become a significant focus of surveillance studies,[3] for it seems to threaten notions of intimacy and authenticity.[4] In our current "confessional society," individuality has been transformed into a public spectacle, and the very notion of individuality has become an "effort towards conformism."[5] As Bauman and Tester argue, what we tend to display on public media are merely "approved photocopies of individual emotions."[6] Happiness is one such commonly approved emotion.

The culture of self-help and the "happiness duty"[7] in North America has prioritized certain types of confessions over others, particularly those which are positive and happy. Positive psychology has even turned happiness into a measurable

---

[1] Meyer, How to Spot, 00:17:13; emphasis added. As of 13 September 2022, the talk had amassed over thirty million views.
[2] In this respect, she echoes Abraham Maslow's words that "secrecy, censorship, dishonesty, blocking of communication threaten *all* the basic needs" (*Motivation*, p. 47, emphasis in original). However, in this case, dishonesty is associated with oversharing rather than censorship.
[3] Sociologist David Lyon has famously described our society as a "surveillance society" (Zappe/Gross, *Surveillance*, p. 10). In surveillance studies, the "post-panoptic theoretical shift tries to capture the moment when disciplinary institutions are supplemented—and sometimes supplanted by—over-sharing, consumerism, and indifference" (ibid., p. 15).
[4] At the same time, "[a]uthenticity is making a comeback, in the guises of memory, ethics, religion, the new sincerity, and the renewed interest in 'real things'" (Haselstein et al., Introduction, p. 19). The "value placed on authentic or 'natural' feeling has increased dramatically with the full emergence of its opposite—the managed heart" (Hochschild, *Managed Heart*, p. 190).
[5] Tommasi, Technology and Privacy, p. 252.
[6] Ibid.
[7] Ahmed, *Promise of Happiness*; Paul, Tacit Knowledge; Freitas, *Happiness Effect*; Cabanas/Illouz, *Manufacturing Happy Citizens*.

ə Open Access. © 2024 the author(s), published by De Gruyter. [CC BY] This work is licensed under the Creative Commons Attribution 4.0 International License. https://doi.org/10.1515/9783111389929-002

commodity, while new media such as the Happify app encourage consumption of this emotion.[8] Amid a capitalist environment that relies on "emotional labor" and "deep acting," happiness has become an important emotional good that the self is invited to continuously produce and consume.[9] However, this intense focus on happiness could lead to a lack of vigilance, as Barbara Ehrenreich suggests in attributing the American failure to prevent the 9/11 terrorist attacks to the "reckless optimism" of an "invulnerable nation."[10] Thus, it is possible that capitalism promotes "willful blindness," "political paralysis,"[11] and thereby creates "happy slaves with slavish happiness."[12]

This monograph aims to explore the intersection of science communication, self-help culture, and various media platforms. It will examine not only how self-help culture uses science to justify its narrative of happiness, but also how this cultural and historical context can influence science communication. The analysis will consider online media, including podcasts, online courses, and social media content, but will primarily focus on TED talks and their aesthetics of individualism. This investigation will also include contemporary speculative novels with the view to reflect on the role of literature in an age dominated by science and technology.

The popularity of self-help, the emergence of new digital communication avenues for science, and the so-called crisis of humanities should be considered as interrelated phenomena. In order to address the methodological challenge of incorporating these various genres, this book employs multiple approaches including image analysis, word clouds, text analysis, and discourse analysis. Adopting the

---

[8] Following Eva Illouz, this thesis assumes that capitalism does not promote only cold rationality, but it actually mobilizes and relies on a commodification of feelings, hence the term "emotional capitalism." In this context, happiness can be grasped as an emotional commodity or "emodity" (Cabanas/Illouz, *Manufacturing Happy Citizens*, p. 12).
[9] Hochschild defines "emotional labor" as the "management of feeling to create a publicly facial and bodily display," so it "requires one to induce or suppress feeling in order to sustain the outward countenance that produces the proper state of mind in others" (*Managed Heart*, p. 7). Thus, it can lead to a form of alienation from one's own body, like the workers who "spoke of their smiles as being *on* them but not *of* them" (p. 8, emphasis in original). Furthermore, Hochschild's distinction between surface and "deep acting" (p. 47) is also interesting. If surface acting means one pretends for others but privately or inwardly knows better, "deep acting" is pretending for one's own self, trying to change how one feels inwardly.
[10] Ehrenreich, *Bright-Sided*, p. 11.
[11] Paul W. Harland makes this argument in his reading of Margaret Atwood's *MaddAddam* trilogy. See Ecological Grief, p. 593.
[12] Borrowing Fukuyama's words, Marie Aline Ferreira refers to the Crakers in *MaddAddam* as "happy slaves with slavish happiness" ("Toward a Science," p. 411), which seems to capture this tension at the core of the American idea of happiness.

concept of research as assemblage, this book does not merely observe and document "a river and its contents from a fixed point on the bank" but rather becomes a part of the flow to comprehend it.[13] Research as assemblage reveals that all research designs, methods, and techniques are permeated with affective relations that connect events, researchers, and data.[14]

The research maintains a clear focus by concentrating on the following questions: How are confessions used in various cultural products? As argued by Bärbel Harju, confessions can be used in politically progressive ways in order to create spaces of autonomy or as performative tools that obscure rather than reveal, leading to the paradox of privacy.[15] Self-help culture uses confessions in a distinct way, for they become part of its sentimentalist aesthetic. Confessions serve as didactic tools to persuade, inspire, and discipline the audience by cultivating a sense of human connection and trust, based on honesty, intimacy, and empathy. Facebook ads and webinars also utilize confessions as a marketing strategy to promote and sell their products or services. If empathy is regarded as an "ability that makes us truly human,"[16] adopting confessional speech in scientific discourse could highlight an effort to "rehumanize" the scientific field, often criticized for its cold and rational methods.[17]

Returning to Meyer's TED talk, her use of the personal plural "we" suggests a call for a shared humanity based on empathy. "Through TED, experts contribute to the 'humanisation' of knowledge, establishing an interpersonal proximity with the audience, which feels part of the knowledge dissemination."[18] However, as Shannon Howard argues, "while empathy and connection to audience members is nothing to scoff at, the overabundance of showmanship characteristic of the single TED speaker has *emotional pull* with some of us, and such pull is substantial enough to

---

13 Fox/Alldred, New Materialism, p. 10. The minor science of Deleuze and Guattiari is famous for this new materialist approach. For an overview of new materialist strands of thought, including Deleuze and Guattiari's microphysics of becoming, Karen Barad's materialist onto-epistemology, Rosi Braidotti's posthumanism, and Bruno Latour's actor-network theory, see Fox/Alldred.
14 Ibid., p. 12.
15 For instance, Hasan's project aims to overwhelm agencies with too much information. Bärbel Harju's essay offers a genealogy of confession, tracing its development from the 13th-century to Puritan practices, from Enlightenment autobiography to 20th-century therapy. See Harju, Too Much Information.
16 S. Taylor, Empathy.
17 Throughout the centuries, claims of scientific coldness resurfaced repeatedly in science and literature debates. Examples include the Thomas-Huxley debate of the 19th-century, C.P. Snow's "two cultures" debate, and the more recent "Science Wars." For a more in-depth analysis of these debates, see Jan D. Kucharzewski's *Propositions about Life*.
18 Cf. Scotto di Carlo, Patterns of Clusivity, p. 140.

give us pause."[19] Meyer's TED talk also reveals the irony of her confession, as her speech contributes to the very phenomenon she criticizes. TED talks are an example of intimate media where individuals confess on stage and live their lives publicly.

Furthermore, Meyer's concept of "liespotting" aims to promote transparency and presupposes the body's readability—"we all chatter with our fingertips."[20] The second important research question pursued by this thesis concerns the role of the body: more specifically, how does technology interpret the senses? It also acknowledges that a book "is a technology for engaging the human sensorium as much as it is a vehicle for the transmission of information,"[21] an aspect often overlooked in literary debates.[22] This engagement extends beyond the book's physical properties, such as its cover and smell, to include the quality of the writing itself. The physical book creates "intimacy and reciprocity with readers,"[23] as does the act of reading itself, regardless of whether the book is read in print or as an e-book.

In a digital society focused on the transmission of information, attending to bodily senses becomes increasingly urgent. Psychologists and philosophers have traditionally treated sensations as mere elements of knowledge, disregarding their importance.[24] Even though society is seemingly obsessed with our bodies,[25] the focus tends to be on the datafied body—the body as genetic data and statistics.[26] TED talks are an example of where information and the visual sense take

---

19 Howard, Ideas Worth Spreading?, p. 67; emphasis added.
20 Meyer, How to Spot a Liar, 00:08:31. According to Meyer, honesty can be found in the body—only by reading bodies can truth be accessed. "We rehearse our words, but we rarely rehearse our gestures. We say 'yes,' we shake our heads 'no.' We tell very convincing stories, we slightly shrug our shoulders. We commit terrible crimes, and we smile at the delight in getting away with it" (00:11:23). Someone deceptive "may be withdrawn, look down, lower their voice, pause, be kind of herky-jerky" (00:10:48). However, at the same time, Meyer describes a lack of self-confidence that may come across as deception. In other words, it is confidence *par excellence* which becomes a sign of truth.
21 Silverman, Reading in the Flesh, p. 451.
22 Although the advent of postcritique could be grasped as an attempt to attend to the "human sensorium" while reading. See also chapter four in this book.
23 Silverman, Reading in the Flesh, p. 452.
24 They have been "so obsessed with the problem of knowledge that they have treated 'sensations' as mere elements of knowledge" (Dewey, *Art as Experience*, p. 21).
25 Cf. Grace, Cognition, p. 9.
26 See also Jean Baudrillard's discussion of the body as the "finest consumer object" or "the representation of the body as capital and as fetish" (*Consumer Society*, p. 129).

center stage, and vision remains "the noblest of the senses."[27] Western societies demand individuals to shape themselves in terms of their capacity for "paying attention," as Jonathan Crary argues.[28] Following his ideas, this book assumes that society prioritizes vision and that attention is an essential element of this process.

In this case, it is important to consider the preference for "visuality" as the primary "model of perception,"—one that is "cut off from richer and more historically determined notions of 'embodiment,' in which an embodied subject is both the location of operations of power and the potential for resistance."[29] As Crary explains, the body is not limited to vision alone, but is also subject to various external techniques that shape and control it. Therefore, it is crucial to recognize that perception extends beyond the single-sense modality of sight, and also includes hearing and touch, as well as mixed modalities that are not typically analyzed in the context of visual studies.[30]

Through my analysis of the uses of literary synesthesia in contemporary novels, I aim to demonstrate that literature has the potential to challenge the dominance of vision and its humanist worldview. This book is concerned with exploring the interconnection between emotion and technology,[31] as well as examining the ways in which aesthetics and politics are closely intertwined. To accomplish this, I employ an interdisciplinary approach that incorporates insights from the sociology of emotions, affect theory, reception theory, and other relevant fields. By doing so, I hope to investigate the emotional effects that various texts can have and explore how form and content co-produce each other, leading to different receptions of texts based on their media, genre, or other factors.

The concept of a "horizon of expectations"[32] is particularly relevant to this discussion. A text can evoke in the reader/listener expectations and rules that are familiar from previous texts, which can then be varied, corrected, changed, or reproduced.[33] For example, both watching a TED talk and reading a speculative novel may create similar expectations, as both deal with science and its future applications. One such expectation is to be amazed by new discoveries. However, while

---

[27] Jay, *Downcast Eyes*, p. 21. "Vision, it bears repeating, is normally understood as the master sense of the modern era, variously described as the heyday of Cartesian perspectivalism, the age of the world picture, and the society of the spectacle or surveillance" (ibid., p. 543).
[28] Crary, *Suspensions*, p. 1.
[29] Ibid., p. 3.
[30] Ibid.
[31] See also Marlin Brenton for an analysis of the "consequences of various rhetorics of emotion and technology," such as the technological sublime in 19th-century America (*Feeling Mediated*, p. 10).
[32] "Horizon of expectation" is a key term in the reception theory of Hans Robert Jauss.
[33] See Benzinger/Jauss, Literary History, p. 13.

reading fiction often involves a "suspension of disbelief" and the abandonment of considerations of factual or conceptual accuracy,[34] then TED talks are usually perceived as truthful and factual.

TED talks are a newly born genre that negotiates the meeting of the "two cultures."[35] They capture what I refer to as an *intimization of science*, using confessional speech acts or life writing alongside statistics and factual knowledge to communicate "ideas worth spreading."[36] This book explores the interplay between authority and authenticity in TED talks. While authenticity is typically characterized as "a rebellion against authority, linked to pathos and feeling, and expressed primarily in the first-person,"[37] TED talks update this view by revealing their powerful coexistence. Instead of being mutually exclusive, authority and authenticity feed off each other, as the speakers' authenticity depends on their image as experts and their authority is in turn strengthened by their confessions. As Michel Foucault argues, "truth [...] is produced and transmitted under the control of a few great political and economic apparatuses (university, army, writing, media)," meaning that specialist knowledge provides power and control because the specialist's word is regarded as authoritative.[38] TED talks are an example of such a discourse that relies on expert knowledge and thus warrant closer investigation.[39]

Embedded within the US-American culture of self-help, TED talks not only convey scientific knowledge, but they also play a role in shaping "individual" and "community" identity.[40] However, the dissemination of knowledge through these talks is influenced by other discursive practices, such as "self-promotion," in line with the norms of a knowledge-based and professional culture.[41] This raises important questions about how TED talks shape audience perspectives of themselves and their society. Specifically, do these talks reinforce a "technoliberal model of

---

34 Abbott, Autobiography, p. 613.
35 A TED conference is "showcasing important research and ideas from all disciplines and exploring how they connect" (Conferences). C.P. Snow is famous for drawing attention to the gap between science and the humanities as far back as the 1950s. However, he also conceived of science as a homogenous and inherently ethical culture, and he superimposed his "technocratic definition" over the meaning of science as a whole. See also Kucharzewski, *Propositions about Life*, p. 105.
36 The slogan "ideas worth spreading" is also mentioned under "Programs and Initiatives," where an overview of TED's main work is visible. It includes TED Courses, TED Masterclass, TED Talks in the English Classroom, TED Audio Collective, TED Partnerships, TED-Ed, TED Fellows Program, TEDx Program, TED Conferences, and TED Talks—which constitute the main focus of this book.
37 Haselstein et al., *The Pathos of Authenticity*, p. 9.
38 Rua, Manipulative Power, p. 151.
39 TED's history, genre, and culture will be further investigated in chapter three.
40 Ludewig, TED Talks, p. 3.
41 Cf. Compagnone, Reconceptualization of Academic Discourse, p. 66.

civic attention" that prioritizes the familiar and the private over a "democratic model" that emphasizes the "common and the stranger"?[42] These questions are particularly pressing given that TED talks are seen as a continuation of the "lyceum tradition of translating academic ideas to public audiences through speeches by charismatic rhetors."[43] Furthermore, there are concerns that these talks reinforce a "dominant vision of digital culture," one structured by "large corporate entities that *monetize attention.*"[44]

The critical lenses of posthumanism and new materialism are further employed to frame these investigations, as this book endeavors to shift the focus away from humans as the central point of attention, even within literary studies. Many contemporary narratives of human enhancement perpetuate an anthropocentric perspective, which I see as problematic. For example, Michael Hauskeller claims that the "radical transformation" of the human should occur because we have to stay true to our "nature."[45] On the other hand, Marjorie Garber argues that nowadays only science grapples with the question of "human nature," which had been the primary concern of literature for centuries.[46] However, this book suggests that literary studies remain in crisis precisely due to an approach that is still too humanist. The relevance of the humanities may lie in their perception as "posthumanities."[47]

Critical posthumanism sheds light on the connections between speciesism, racism, and sexism, exposing how the humanist subject has historically excluded and marginalized those who are different. According to this perspective, the "others" who occupy the "slot of devalued difference" have been subjected to violent and belligerent exclusions, and were "reduced to the subhuman status of disposable bodies."[48] In this context, literature can serve as a powerful tool to challenge the anthropocentric discourse that characterizes contemporary technoliberalism. This book will explore the role of literature in this context through the analysis of the following novels: Gary Shteyngart's *Super Sad True Love Story* (2010), Mar-

---

42 Cf. Pfister, Technoliberal Rhetoric, p. 184. Damien Smith Pfister understands neoliberalism as a "a governing rationality that privileges market logics, individualism, and private profit," pushing civil inattention to extremes: "attention to others is valued only insofar as it is useful or monetizable, relations with others are seen as zero-sum and competitive, friends and family are to be preferred over strangers, and time is just another commodity that should be efficiently spent" (ibid., p. 183).
43 Ibid.
44 Ibid., p. 185 f; emphasis added.
45 Hauskeller, *Better Humans?*, p. 79.
46 Garber, *Manifesto*, p. 17.
47 Braidotti, Contested Posthumanities.
48 Ibid., p. 16.

garet Atwood's *MaddAddam* trilogy (2003–2013), and Richard Powers' *Generosity: An Enhancement* (2009).

The selected novels share several essential characteristics. They uniquely blend speculative fiction with fictionalized life writing, and all protagonists practice some form of journal writing. These dystopian[49] novels critically reflect upon the ways in which contemporary self-help culture influences scientific practice. They offer a vigilant perspective on the TED phenomena instead of taking its truthfulness for granted, which is crucial in a culture that prioritizes entertainment value above scientific truth.[50] Moreover, these novels act as a cautionary commentary on the uses of science in the present age, where future scenarios need to be anticipated with "added *vigilance*" due to the greater potential applications of new technologies.[51] They become tools for raising awareness as they contribute to a transdisciplinary dialogue about bioethics and science policy. For example, these novels explore the ethical implications of genetic engineering, which has become the primary lens through which identity and humanity are perceived over recent decades. Additionally, they all focus on America[52] and its cultural myths, which circulate globally and can have a significant impact on how humanity and its future are envisioned.

Thirdly, these novels also contemplate the significance of literature in a "postfictional" era. While their scientific plots tend to steal the limelight, even in their academic reception, these novels make a compelling case for the importance of

---

49 "Traditionally, dystopias are cautionary tales, giving the readers a pessimistic alternative to their present-day reality from a sharper, more *vigilant* perspective (Gheluwe 2015, p. 145)" (Ringo/Sharma, Reading, p. 112; emphasis added). Dystopias usually involve the themes of surveillance, control, and social stratification, see also Sutherland/Swan, Margaret Atwood, p. 223. So, "the writer attempts to *awaken* in the public the need for personal *vigilance* and engagement in a contemporary world that has become unmoored from moral categories and in which our very humanity is under threat" (Bosco, Apocalyptic Imagination, p. 161; emphasis added).
50 Or, in a "culture in which entertainment value is the highest value, [and] all things—including scientific truth—must be hyped for mass consumption" (Charles, Book World).
51 Ferreira, "Toward a Science," p. 414; emphasis added.
52 Following Winfried Fluck, "we often speak of America but then we sometimes correct ourselves and speak of the United States" (Surface Readings, p. 61). In this book, whenever I use the term "America," I aim to refer to the "idea of America" as an imaginary construct. For this reason, I include Margaret Atwood in my analysis. Even if she is Canadian, her trilogy is set, for the most part, in the United States. As a Canadian, she also brings the perspective of an "intimate outsider" in her writing. An intimate outsider is "a member of the society who is in some ways separate from the more powerful elements of the society and not fully convinced of the society's views" (Sutherland/Swan, Margaret Atwood, p. 224). Sutherland and Swan use this term to also designate the position of Canada in relation to the US: "an intimate outsider [is] directly affected by the political choices being made, yet largely powerless to impact the decisions" (ibid., p. 220).

reading and writing. In addition to their inquiries into science and scientific practices, the novels pose even deeper questions about the role of fiction and human survival. By doing so, they offer more than just an observation of the intersection of science and culture. They also allow access to the ordinary knowledge of literature that often goes unnoticed—the "unknown known" of life. This knowledge encompasses not only the struggle for survival but also the different ways of being alive. As John Dewey argues, "the work of art enhances and intensifies what is characteristically valuable in things of everyday experience."[53]

The experience of feeling alive may seem obvious and trivial, so it is often overlooked in discussions of literature. To explore this idea, this book draws on Toril Moi's concept of the "spirit of the ordinary"[54] and focuses on practices of reading and writing. Rather than emphasizing higher passions and emotions, which is what the cultural canon prefers,[55] this analysis seeks to highlight the value of ordinary experiences.[56] In this sense, literature can be viewed as a "life science" that illuminates the meaning of being alive. This perspective is in line with Ottmar Ette's critique of the life sciences' appropriation of the term "life."[57]

The selected novels introduce what I refer to as "survival scenes" that employ literary synesthesia to challenge and subvert the typical science fictional expectation of the human mind's power of vision.[58] Rather than focusing solely on the intellectual aspects of reading, these scenes highlight the material and sensory di-

---

53 Dewey, *Art as Experience*, p. 11.
54 Moi, *Revolution of the Ordinary*, p. 3.
55 Ngai, *Ugly Feelings*, p. 11.
56 Dewey, *Art as Experience*, p. 11.
57 In "Literature as Knowledge for Living," Ottmar Ette claims that the humanities should engage in a dialogue with the biosciences. He argues that the concept of life should not be the topic of biotechnological disciplines only, as literature also produces knowledge about/of life: for instance, it "shapes blueprints for how to live" (p. 986). However, his normative assumption that there is a right way to live means literature has mainly a mimetic function and didactic purpose. In this case, literature teaches sympathy to the reader, a position that this thesis also aims to question. Furthermore, Jan Kucharzewski also claims that "Where applied science asks 'how,' literature asks 'why' and sometimes proposes an 'if'" (*Propositions about Life*, p. 112). Yet, besides these ethical and speculative interventions, literature also provides an ordinary knowledge of life, which is less considered in academic debates.
58 Even if science fiction has been apprehended as a "posthuman literary mode" (cf. Clarke/Rossini, *The Cambridge Companion*), and science fiction and posthumanism are "entwined discourses that ask similar questions about what it means to be human" (cf. Vint, *Science Fiction and Posthumanism*), a humanist focus still looms largely in this genre due to the expectation that science fiction offers visionary knowledge and thought-provoking future scenarios. Nevertheless, they also comment on the contemporary social reality (see Haraway, *A Cyborg Manifesto*), and the importance of reading, as this study aims to show.

mensions of the experience, emphasizing human-nonhuman interactions. Despite resembling fictionalized life writing, these scenes do not reinforce a transformation from a "thing" into an "I am." Rather, they depict a shift from "I am" to "thing,"[59] drawing attention to mortality and the physical body. As J. Paul Narkunas suggests, "Mortality itself is the *thingness* of the human," and transhuman immortality is often sought as a way to avoid confronting the fear of our finite existence and the limits of our bodies' "cellular regeneration."[60] The novels offer a fresh perspective on these topics, reframing the terms in which we understand the body, life, and their vulnerabilities while also subverting the fear of being a mere "thing."

In my selection of texts and media, I choose the year 1985 as a starting reference point for various reasons: in science, the mid 1980s marked the origins of the Human Genome Project, which sparked a new era that promised to deliver "the molecular instruction book of human life."[61] This is also the time TED was born. In the cultural sphere, the year 1985 marks the transition to the third wave of cybernetics, which illustrates a conceptual shift toward virtuality: the cultural perception that "material objects are interpenetrated by information patterns, from DNA code to the global reach of the World Wide Web."[62] The "late Eighties and early Nineties" also saw the birth of both transhumanism and posthumanism.[63] And this period shifts attention to "radically changed modes of knowledge production, including digitization."[64]

Each analytical section focuses on one main topic at a time, though they intersect in meaningful ways. The first part of each section focuses on TED talks and other media—on how self-help culture influences contemporary understandings of success, mindfulness, and happiness. This part aims to show the pervasiveness of self-help, which stretches beyond canonical self-help books[65] and influences acts of science communication. This is particularly visible in the kind of expectations

---

[59] I borrow these terms from Klaus Benesch's essay "From a *Thing* into an *I Am*: Autobiographical Narrative and Metahistorical Discourse in Contemporary African-American Fiction" (1998). This transition from *I am* into a *thing* challenges the very logic of humanization and dehumanization, as *things* begin to speak and be heard, while the *I* exists in a concert of voices only. In other words, the "I" is a thing and the thing is an "I."
[60] Narkunas, Between Words, p. 17; emphasis added.
[61] Gannett, Human Genome Project.
[62] Hayles, *How We Became Posthuman*, p. 14.
[63] Ferrando, Posthumanism, p. 26.
[64] Kloeckner et al., *Knowledge Landscapes*, p. 9.
[65] In this respect, my book aims to close a gap in the research on self-help, too. Most of the research has been done on the works of Samuel Smiles, Tony Robbins, Dale Carnegie, Napoleon Hill, Martin Seligman, and others.

that these texts create, which "are part and parcel of what we see, and in the same way they are part of what we feel."⁶⁶ For instance, "in the American middle class, there may be an 'optimism norm' so that *what we realistically expect* and what we think is ideal are closer together than they are in other classes and other cultures."⁶⁷ Besides, this first part also explores various forms of "self-fashioning"⁶⁸ and culminates with an investigation of the ways in which these expressive acts shape responsibilities.

The second part of each section focuses on one of the novels in a bid to expand and reframe the discussion introduced in the first part. The analysis begins with self-help culture and the fictional uses of life writing; it focuses on acts of "self-descriptive reminiscence"⁶⁹ and investigates the ways in which literary synesthesia challenges previously established expectations. As such, each section ends with a third subchapter that focuses on the relevance of literature and argues for its vitality, even in an Internet age governed by science and technology. This fractal-like makeup can be identified throughout the chapters and subchapters and reestablishes the three main red threads of this book: self-help culture, life writing, and the senses. They are introduced in the following chapter too, which offers a cultural, historical, and theoretical dive into these topics.

---

66 Hochschild, *Managed Heart*, p. 231.
67 Ibid., p. 61; emphasis added.
68 Greenblatt, *Renaissance Self-Fashioning*. In this case, I aim to engage in a cultural analysis that pushes "beyond the boundaries of the text, to establish links between the text and values, institutions, and practices elsewhere in the culture," and yet remains indebted to the practice of close reading (Greenblatt, Culture, pp. 226 f). This new historicist approach serves my purpose of reading the present moment as a particular social and cultural configuration where multiple perspectives coexist, a moment that is also continuously shaped by competing forces and changing power relations. Furthermore, this will also allow me to underline the "cultural work" (see Tomkins, *Sensational Designs*) that literary texts perform, since they do not merely reflect the outside world. They actively negotiate and comment on contemporary social debates.
69 James, Critical Solace, p. 494.

I **Happy Confessions: Context, Theory, Approach**

Introduction

> Listening to other people's stories can make us feel *vulnerable*. Stories open us up and *empower* us to talk about things we normally might never tell another soul. I think that's why, whenever I teach my memoir class, it always ends up hitting students at a *deep level*. When we are in the presence of others who have shown us their best and also their worst, their successes and failures, their joys and their deepest moments of pain, their stories call forth the same in us, they stir up the good and the bad, they ask us to look at love and loss, its presence and absence, our greatest triumphs and our darkest moments. *They humanize us and call forth empathy.*[1]

Confessions can be highly persuasive because they establish a foundation of trust between the speaker and the listener. Typically, confessions involve a conversation with a confidant, a friend, or a trustee, someone who is perceived as safe and trustworthy enough to share one's secrets with. To facilitate such an intimate exchange, trust must be established and further nurtured by the belief in the authenticity of the confession.[2] Confessions also elicit an empathic response, as the listener is called upon to feel with the speaker.[3] Donna Freitas has also emphasized the empathic function of confessions, noting that they can elicit a sympathetic identification from the listener.

While Freitas emphasizes the empathic function of confessions, she does not critically reflect on how this empathic approach can also be used to discipline rather than empower. This same approach is used in contemporary self-help culture, which invokes the ideas of vulnerability, empowerment, personal transformation, and humanity to inspire its readers.[4] However, sympathetic identification has its limits. As several critics have pointed out, these texts often run the risk of negating differences "for the sake of embracing the idea of a common humanity, and at potentially great cost to the 'objects' of compassion."[5] "Humanizing" can

---

1 Freitas, *Happiness Effect*, p. xix; emphasis added.
2 Ezra Waldman took a first step in establishing privacy not only as an abstract right, but as an affective category too. By focusing on the notion of privacy as trust, she underscores the ways in which trust "reflects a behavioral exchange between two people" (Privacy as Trust, p. 171).
3 The obligation to hear confessions out complements the voyeurism of confessional culture. If the interlocutor fails to engage with compassion, the confessant may feel ashamed, compelled to retreat, disengage, or remain silent. Thus, it is not enough to simply confess; there is also a responsibility to listen attentively and empathetically to the confession.
4 This book is mainly concerned with self-help as a literary genre and way of thinking. For an analysis of self-help organizations and support groups, see Matthew E. Archibald's *The Evolution of Self-Help* (2007).
5 Gerund/Paul, Sentimentalism, p. 19.

also mean civilizing, instructing, enlightening, or educating. Self-help culture relies on this didacticism to promote its ideas.

This first part of the book aims to provide a conceptual framework for understanding the relationship between American self-help culture, science communication, and the relevance of literary studies. Donna Freitas' book also employs confessions as a rhetorical tool, revealing her experience as a teacher. This highlights how confessions can become part of science dissemination. Additionally, Freitas emphasizes the power of stories to create empathy, which is a vital aspect of literature and practices of reading.

2 Confessional Culture and American Self-Help

Christopher Grobe has identified the confessional mode as "America's favorite genre of performance,"[1] characterized by eye-to-eye talk. This genre can be seen in various forms of public discourse, including poetry readings, stand-up comedy, performance art, or theatrical confession. Preaching, presidential addresses, and even internet-born genres like blogs, podcasts, and social media can further illustrate how public confessions maintain a compelling presence not only in US society but also globally. Confessions are a *"sine qua non* of modern power,"[2] hence the need to investigate the contemporary use of confessions in self-help culture. Self-help gurus, content creators, motivational speakers, and social media influencers have all embraced confessions as a means of persuading their audience or readership. Confessions have become a popular advertising strategy on webinars and social media platforms, emphasizing their persuasive potential.

However, as Michel de Certeau suggests, consumers of cultural products have agency and autonomy and can use these products in unintended ways.[3] Confessional writing has been used throughout history as a tool for social justice, from slave narratives to the MeToo movement. Thus, it is essential to investigate the contemporary use of confessions not only for their persuasive potential but also as a means of challenging power and carving out spaces of agency.

Furthermore, understanding the power of confessions in self-help culture is particularly important in America, where marginalized groups such as women and ethnic minorities have long been silenced. As Klaus Benesch argues, the question of "Who is speaking?"[4] is particularly relevant in a society where "the hell of being the *unseen* object" is prevalent.[5] For these groups, the struggle for visibility and voice is ongoing, and confessional writing has been used to fight for social jus-

---

[1] Grobe, *Art*, p. 191.
[2] Tell, Rhetoric and Power, p. 98. Dave Tell also argues that "Foucault's confession should be understood in rhetorical terms, not because it is a means of persuasion or an act of human expression [...] but because its basic movement is metonymical. Moreover, it is precisely this metonymical function of confession that earns it a central place in Foucault's account of modern power – thus are rhetoric and power intertwined" (ibid., p. 97). By metonymical function, Tell understands the act of "substituting an 'artificial unity' for discontinuous somatic sensations" (ibid., p. 111).
[3] De Certeau, *The Practice of Everyday Life*, p. xiii. In this context, the theory of encoding and decoding proposed by sociologist Stuart Hall also challenges the idea of media consumers who simply absorb messages without second thoughts. The messages are not transparent and the audience is not just some passive recipient of meaning.
[4] Benesch, From a *Thing*, par. 7.
[5] Ibid., par. 4; emphasis in original.

tice. This also sheds new light on the power and limits of empathy: while it can be used to disempower when it obscures individual struggles and focuses only on a common humanity, empathy is also "among the essential conditions for knowing others."[6] As such, it is important to be aware of the limits of empathy and the risks of sentimentalism, which can lead to the erasure of individual struggles and perpetuate the status quo.

In the context of self-help culture, confessions have primarily been used as a sentimental rhetorical mode. Sentimentalism is a term used to describe popular literature from the 19th century that relied on rhetorical and literary devices to "generate compassion" and "contribute to the moral education" of readers.[7] Similarly, the most visible and popular confessions in America rely on a sentimentalist aesthetic and are part of its culture of self-help. These confessions hinge on "rhetorical empathy,"[8] which can make them particularly persuasive. To gain a more detailed understanding of their persuasive potential, it is necessary to examine the wider historical and cultural context, including the origins of autobiography and America.

Confession has undergone a transformation from religious rituals to cultural practices that shape individual identities, social interactions, and power relations. This cultural shift can be traced back to the tradition of the autobiography in America, where figures like Benjamin Franklin used self-reflection and confession to construct an idealized version of themselves and conform to society's expectations. Today, with the rise of social media and the advent of transhumanism, confessional culture has become more complex. Confessions can now be used as tools of control and surveillance, training us to monitor ourselves and others. However, they can also be a source of empowerment and solidarity, enabling us to connect with others who share our struggles. The ethical implications of confession are now more relevant than ever, and the work of philosophers like Jean Paul Sartre and Michel Foucault helps us to better understand the complexities of this phenomenon. By examining the complexities and implications of confessional culture, this chapter seeks to provide a nuanced understanding of the role of confession in contemporary society.

---

6 Harel, Constructing the Nonhuman, p. 902.
7 Gerund/Paul, Sentimentalism, p. 19.
8 See Jessica Edens McCrary's review published in the *South Atlantic Review* (2021).

2.1 Autobiography and America

Autobiography has played a crucial role in shaping America, as it is one of the oldest and most vibrant forms of American writing.[9] At the same time, autobiography has been commodified,[10] becoming an industry and a type of confessional speech that authors use to promote their public image.[11] However, autobiographical writing is marked by its inherent failure, given that it can never fully capture an individual's identity, which is continually evolving: "The identity it seeks to express is always blurred, for the narrative can only bring the autobiographer to that continual 'passing' in which he writes."[12] The genre of autobiography has shifted over time, from a focus on *bios* (the life of an achieved person) to *autos* (the troubling issue of self in modernity) and then to *graphè* (the linguistic foundations of identity construction in postmodernism).[13]

In America, autobiography has also "encouraged certain kinds of expression at the expense of others."[14] It has played a crucial role in shaping the American myth of progress, which emphasizes the journey from imperfection to perfection.[15] As a result, becoming the "ideal-common man"[16] has become the central narrative arc of many autobiographies, contributing to the connections between confessional culture and self-help. This emphasis on emulation has a long history in American

---

9 Sayre, Autobiography, p. 1.
10 Ibid., p. 2.
11 Benesch, Auto/Biography, p. 563f. For a more in-depth analysis of "the topic of auto/biographical mediation" as well as "the recent history and transformation of the field of life writing from its marginal position within literary criticism and historiography to the mainstream of what is now widely known as cultural studies" (ibid., p. 564), see also Alfred Hornung's *Auto/Biography and Mediation* (2010).
12 Abbott, Autobiography, p. 609.
13 Benesch, Auto/Biography, p. 564f. As Benesch adds: "Though laudable for its attempt to historicize the form and its obvious changes over time, Olney's proposition falls short, however, of explaining the performative and discursive character of all of auto/biographical writing" (ibid., p. 565).
14 Sayre, Autobiography, p. 9.
15 Spengemann/Lundquist, Autobiography, p. 503. This pilgrimage can take many forms: "[f]or the Puritans, imperfection meant the natural depravity of human nature as exemplified by Adam; perfection referred to ultimate salvation through God's grace. For the Rationalists of our eighteenth century, the two terms meant, respectively, intellectual backwardness and worldly happiness through reason. For the Transcendentalists, they meant separation from and union with the spirit that is alive in Nature. For some later nineteenth-century reformers they denoted predatory individualism and collective utopian harmony. For all of these groups the two terms were absolutely inseparable from the belief in America as a moral idea" (ibid.).
16 Sayre, Autobiography, p. 12.

autobiography, exemplified by Benjamin Franklin's *Autobiography*, which is considered a milestone in the art of self-help.[17] Franklin, an autodidact, sought "the means of improvement by constant study."[18] His confessions not only communicate his personal knowledge but also function as a didactic tool, reflecting the traditional notion of fathers passing on their wisdom to their sons. Building on the theme of autobiography as a means of self-help, Franklin's *Autobiography* illustrates how the genre has been instrumental in shaping the American myth of progress. Franklin's didacticism is evident from the beginning of his work, where he writes:

> Having emerged from the poverty and obscurity in which I was born and bred, to a state of affluence and some degree of reputation in the world, [...] the conducing means I made use of, which with the blessing of God so well succeeded, my posterity may like to know, as they may find some of them suitable to their own situations, and therefore *fit to be imitated.*[19]

This paragraph introduces the myth of the self-made man who shares his "secret recipe" for success or, in Franklin's case, a virtuous life. This narrative lies at the core of the American Dream and the myth of individualism. American individualism is often associated with individual success, which is usually understood in economic terms: "The myth of the self-made man and the idea of expressive individualism [...] are part of a utopian narrative that promises a better life to all those who come to the US, and thus also is very much an immigrant myth."[20]

Autobiography is seen as having greater authority than novels or theater due to its "assumed accuracy and authenticity." [21] Autobiographies are engaged in writing lives,[22] not only in a biographical sense, but also as a "medium through which life is seen."[23] This includes not only the personal history[24] of the protagonist, but also life in general: life as animation, spirit, energy, soul, enthusiasm, and being. For example, in the 19th century, Henry David Thoreau sought to "purify" his

---

17 Anderson, Benjamin Franklin.
18 Franklin, *Autobiography*, p. 128.
19 Ibid., 8f; emphasis added.
20 Paul, *Myths*, p. 16.
21 Sayre, Autobiography, 17.
22 As such, the term "life writing" has begun to gain traction: "Life writing is a broad term encompassing many varieties of personal narrative, including autobiography, biography, memoir, diary, travel writing, autobiographical fiction, letters, collective biography, poetry, case history, personal testimony, illness narrative, obituary, essay, and reminiscences – testimony to its flexible and vibrant format, with an outward-facing as well as introspective purpose" (Sanders, Life Writing). All aspects of auto/biography have been "renamed summarily as life writing" (Hornung, *Auto/Biography*, p. xi).
23 Abbott, Autobiography, p. 599; emphasis added.
24 Cox, Autobiography, p. 254.

"flesh" into "pure spirit" through his writing, aiming for a "resurrection of the body."[25] Similarly, Walt Whitman was also interested in the immortality of the flesh.[26] In addition, Benjamin Franklin intentionally turned his body into "dead, mechanically reproducible matter."[27] Thus, even though the body deteriorates, "the epic unity of life and work – as it is inscribed on paper – will provide the possibility of survival by way of another, more perfect printing."[28]

The journey from imperfection to perfection is one of the most powerful American stories, embodied by the pilgrimage from life to death and back to life. This journey has both ancient and modern roots, from Christian stories of redemption, rapture, and Paradise to contemporary visions of Singularity, life extension, and immortality.[29] The boom in confessions and growing popularity of transhumanist philosophy can be seen as a response to the same urgency to survive, a rejection of the ancient *memento mori*, and a desire for life to continue indefinitely despite its precariousness. According to Hannah Arendt, this intense focus on the self and the pursuit of survival stems from our earth alienation. Modern science and technology have spurred us to "search for ways to overcome our earth-bound condition" by exploring space, recreating life under laboratory conditions, or attempting to extend our lifespan.[30]

Benjamin Franklin is an influential figure for transhumanists, who admire him as a prime example of a "citizen scientist." This term, popularized in contemporary times, refers to ordinary people who voluntarily engage in scientific activ-

---

25 Ibid., p. 269.
26 Ibid., p. 268.
27 Benesch, *Romantic Cyborgs*, p. 36.
28 Ibid.
29 These are the visions of transhumanism. "Transhumanism is a class of philosophies of life that seek the continuation and acceleration of the evolution of intelligent life beyond its currently human form and human limitations by means of science and technology, guided by life-promoting principles and values" (More, The Extropian Principles). In a hypothetical point in the future, the "Singularity" will occur: the life-changing event that will bring about a new reality and superhuman intelligence in "the blink of an eye," and it will thus inaugurate the "post-human era" (Vinge, Coming Technological Singularity, p. 12). The individual self is on a perpetual quest for improvement, motivated by the desire to overcome aging: transhumanists, thus, advance a belief in mind-uploading (Kurzweil), while the body is secondary and may be disposed of. Stories of human enhancement have a transhumanist provenance and are inspired by a "human desire to overcome death" (Humanity+). The website Humanity+ offers more information on transhumanist philosophy. See also Stefan Herbrechter and Ivan Callus' essay "What's Wrong with Posthumanism?" or my book chapter on "Vigilance to Wonder."
30 Cf. d'Entreves, Hannah Arendt, p. 5.

ities that help advance the field. For instance, the Zooniverse project[31] is an excellent example of citizen science in action. Sally Shuttleworth and her team have looked for similar models in which "a large distributed community" contributes to "top-quality professional science" in the 19th century.[32] However, the idea of citizen science is not limited to community-based science. It has also been used to describe and justify the transhumanist philosophy and practices of biohacking. In this case, the focus is on individual genius rather than community involvement, with the citizen scientist using scientific methods to investigate themselves or their environment.[33] This notion of the citizen scientist resembles Ralph Waldo Emerson's American scholar, who is not only self-reliant but also embodies the essence of all professions, stating that "Man is not a farmer, or a professor, or an engineer, but he is all."[34] Franklin's life and works serve as a "singular instance" where "technological expertise and literary authorship meet with natural ease,"[35] making him a model for both citizen science and transhumanist philosophy.

In the context of American culture's emphasis on the display of emotions and "therapeutic sensibilities,"[36] the act of confession can actually be seen as reinforcing the belief in an "autonomous, rational subject."[37] As people increasingly share their most intimate thoughts and feelings online, concerns about the "death of pri-

---

[31] The Zooniverse "is the world's largest and most popular platform for people-powered research." Here, "anyone can be a researcher" (About, Zooniverse).
[32] Belknap et al., Citizen Science, p. 3.
[33] Lightman, Rise of the Citizen Scientist, p. 14.
[34] Emerson, American Scholar, p. 1135. According to Ralph Waldo Emerson, the American scholar finds solace in "exercising the highest functions of human nature," transcending private considerations to live on "public and illustrious thoughts" (1142). He adds: "He is the world's eye. He is the world's heart." Walt Whitman has also introduced himself as an average American who is at the same time a genius. His portrait featured in *The Leaves of Grass* shows a common man wearing a hat, in a posture of ease, much like an American farmer. In the Preface, he also writes: the greatest poet "is a seer... he is individual... he is complete in himself... *the others are as good as he, only he sees it and they do not*" (46; emphasis added), which captures once again this tension between the common man and the genius. Interestingly enough, the president also needs to display "both exceptionality and commonness" (Heinke, Hillary & Bill, p. 156). See also Karsten Fitz on "'Privatizing' the White House: American Presidents and the Visual Aesthetics of Privacy" (2015).
[35] Benesch, *Romantic Cyborgs*, p. 35.
[36] Harju, Too Much Information, p. 58.
[37] Ibid., p. 64. "During the 18th century the American colonies witnessed the systematic implementation of techniques of self-monitoring. The emergence of journals, diaries and virtue catalogues can be described as a secularized version of the Puritan ideology of control. [...] Self-monitoring and collective nation-building converge in autobiographies, memoirs, journals and letters, and have been framed as important forms of expression of the autonomous, rational subject" (ibid.).

vacy" have emerged.[38] The privacy paradigm is "the most widely spread model of individual self-design"[39] and notions of privacy usually "reflect the primacy of the individual as distinct from his social or community self."[40] However, the boundaries between public and private are becoming increasingly porous, with the privacy paradigm shifting toward "the individual's right to *an autonomous choice of life.*"[41] Birgit Wetzel-Sahm has identified a departure from the traditional paradigm of familial privacy in favor of this individualistic approach. Thus, in the age of digital self-disclosure, confessions may serve as a means of mitigating privacy concerns, rather than exacerbating them.

While confessions in the digital age raise concerns about the death of privacy, they may actually serve as tools for self-monitoring. Autobiography, as Samantha Matthews suggests, can be seen as a response to spiritual crises of the past, revealing an "inward turn"[42] rather than just a loss of privacy.[43] However, Richard Sennett warns of the "tyrannies of intimacy," which suggest that society is increasingly measured in psychological terms.[44] Furthermore, the use of confessional practices in self-help culture highlights a desire for authenticity. As individuals strive for self-improvement and personal transformation, they turn to confession as a means of revealing their true selves. Acting as tools to improve the self, confessional practices do not only promise control, but they also presumably have the power to mediate self-awareness and bring about happy and satisfying feelings. This view relies on a belief that self-revelation is a "transcultural human need or psychological compulsion" which "stems from the observation that the act of confession, painful and excruciating as it may be, promises a sense of relief, considerable compensation, catharsis even."[45] This pursuit of authenticity has many names: personal transformation from the inside out, the act of breaking free (from fear all the

---

[38] Such worries have been intensified by "the NSA scandal, the proliferation of surveillance technologies, the accumulation of 'big data' or novel techniques of invasion used by both governments and corporations" (ibid., p. 58).
[39] Fitz/Harju, Cultures of Privacy, p. 3. At the same time, the privacy crisis of the Cold War was also a "metaphor for the crisis of masculine self-sovereignty" (Nelson, *Pursuing Privacy*, p. xvii).
[40] Waldman, Privacy as Trust, p. 167.
[41] Wetzel-Sahm, Negotiating, p. 197; emphasis added. Interestingly enough, this emphasis on choosing life is another undercurrent in transhumanist philosophy, too.
[42] McGee, *Self-Help, Inc.*, p. 47.
[43] Matthews, Autobiography.
[44] Sennett, *Fall of Public Man*, p. 338.
[45] Harju, Too Much Information, p. 60f.

way to faith), self-actualization and the idea of limitless potential,[46] the inner reservoir, the trope of waking up, awakening the self within or tuning in.

The dawning of the "age of authenticity"[47] has led to the proliferation of confessional culture. Confessional writing has a long history, from *The Confessions* of Saint Augustine and Jean-Jacques Rousseau's *Les Confessions* to more contemporary examples, and has served as a means of self-expression and for asserting one's uniqueness. However, critics such as Christopher Lasch and Allan Bloom express concerns about the self-centeredness and narcissism of the "culture of authenticity" and its potential threat to morality and political coherence.[48] Nevertheless, Charles Taylor argues that the development of "an ideal of inwardly generated identity" underscores the importance of "recognition" and "dialogical relations with others,"[49] which are crucial to forming one's identity.

Jared Michelson argues that the ethics of authenticity may lead to a "pseudo-confession," where individuals share their struggles in a bid to meet societal expectations on social media and are celebrated for their courage rather than for seeking forgiveness and absolution.[50] However, the historical context and etymology of "confession" suggest a redemptive approach. Christine Rosen links confessional culture to the American "fascination with personal reinvention," and how narratives of addiction and recovery are tied to the desire for "personal transformation."[51] Confessions were originally associated with disclosing one's sins in a religious context or acknowledging guilt in a legal statement.[52] Despite potentially

---

[46] Abraham Maslow's humanistic psychology introduced self-actualization as the top need in the human pyramid of needs. His model has been adopted and popularized in self-help industry, marketing, and public relations. Advertisements are usually designed and geared toward certain human needs. See, for instance, Rajnerowicz's post on "Nine Types of Advertising Appeals That Actually Work."

[47] C. Taylor, *Ethics of Authenticity*, p. 48.

[48] Guignon/Varga, Authenticity. The social ideal of authenticity has been further criticized for its essentialist approach to identity formation. Poststructuralist views and notions of performativity (Butler) have challenged the term. And yet, rather than rendering it obsolete, the notion of authenticity continues to thrive and reinvent itself, even in or especially in a culture that values performance.

[49] C. Taylor, *Ethics of Authenticity*, p. 47 f.

[50] "Whether performed by a celebrity on Oprah or anyone on Instagram, such a 'confession' reveals one's struggle to, for example, be the sort of parent or attain the body image which society expects. [...] rather than receiving forgiveness and absolution, the pseudo-confessor is celebrated for their courage and society's toxic standards are condemned. [...] what this pseudo-confession achieves [...] is a sense of human solidarity and sympathy" (Michelson, Preaching as Confession).

[51] Rosen, Confessional Culture, p. 5.

[52] Confess, *Merriam-Webster*. Confessions have sacramental, legal, and therapeutic qualities, which Christopher Grobe identifies in Lowell's poetry (*The Art*, p. 13).

conjuring feelings of guilt or shame, confessions can also offer a sense of resolution and absolution.

Jean-Paul Sartre's phenomenology of shame highlights the importance of the gaze in the formation of the self.[53] Shame arises when one becomes aware of oneself as an object of someone else's gaze, and this gaze has an internalizing effect that makes one conscious of their own vulnerability.[54] At the same time, the gaze enables a form of acknowledgement that is crucial to the existence and life of the self.[55] Sartre's famous scene of a lover looking through a keyhole who is then also watched in return emphasizes the importance of the audience in identity formation and suggests that our sense of self is shaped by the responses we get from others, both real and imagined.[56] This also points to the potential for surveillance and the ways in which our identities may be constructed in relation to the gaze of others.[57]

The panopticon is the "most powerful metaphor for official surveillance,"[58] yet it is also a "comforting fiction because it falsely suggests that networks are overseen and rationally controlled" whereas they may be "blind" or "without a cause."[59] Surveillance has also "gone beyond the limits of the visual" and it became an "implicit feature of the structure of liberal society, which maintained their hegemony by encouraging citizens to monitor themselves."[60] In other words, surveillance "is not only a matter of other people watching us; it shapes identity by train-

---

[53] "[In shame] in the first place there is a relation of being. I am this being. I do not for an instant think of denying it; my shame is a confession. I shall be able later to use bad faith so as to hide it from myself, but bad faith is also a confession since it is an effort to flee the being which I am. But I am this being" (Sartre, *Being and Nothingness*, p. 350 f.).
[54] See also Wasihun, Surveillance and Shame, p. 3.
[55] Toril Moi gives another interesting summary of Sartre's play of gazes: "In his famous analysis of shame, Sartre imagines a jealous lover looking through a keyhole in an empty hotel corridor: 'But all of a sudden I hear footsteps in the hall. Someone is looking at me!' Sartre's I isn't autobiographical or empirical. Sartre isn't confessing that he himself ever spied on a lover in this way [...] His I is *exemplary*. It encourages us, Sartre's readers, to see the scene from the I's point of view, to think with and through the example, to imagine what we would feel in the same situation. Would I freeze in shame if I heard footsteps in a similar situation? Sartre's I is dialogic, *open to response*" (*Revolution of the Ordinary*, p. 19; emphasis in original). Thus, she points to the importance of recognition and acknowledgement, rather than only shame.
[56] Since "we are unable to understand or express ourselves except in relation to an audience, to a counterpart, the way in which we define our identity continually is shaped by the real or imagined responses we get" (Benesch, From a *Thing*, par. 6).
[57] "I am seen, therefore I am" (Tommasi, Technology and Privacy, p. 248).
[58] Vincent, Privacy and Surveillance, p. 29.
[59] Ramirez, Contemporary Cultures, p. 284.
[60] Zappe/Gross, Introduction, p. 11, 13.

ing us to look at ourselves in certain ways."[61] This highlights the idea that surveillance is not just a matter of external monitoring, but it also shapes our internal sense of self and our behavior. The pressure to conform to idealized images and to constantly present a certain version of oneself online can lead to self-policing and self-censorship. The act of confession, therefore, may be seen as a way to navigate and negotiate these pressures and to establish a sense of authenticity and individuality within the constraints of online surveillance.

Michel Foucault stressed the "obligation to confess."[62] He believed that the power of the listener in the confession is not only to extract information but also to shape the very identity of the confessant. The listener becomes a kind of authority figure who evaluates and assesses the confession, and the confessant internalizes the listener's judgment of their behavior. At the same time, the listener is also disciplined by the act of listening, as they are expected to remain attentive and non-judgmental, and to offer guidance or feedback in a supportive and non-coercive manner. In this way, the confession becomes a dialogical process in which power relations are constantly negotiated and contested.

2.2 Self-Vigilance and the Redemptive Self

The body plays a crucial role in American self-help culture, as it is considered a repository of stories and an active participant in auto/biography.[63] One common narrative template in self-help culture is that of "the body that speaks," which suggests that confronting and confessing secret sins and traumas can lead to physical healing.[64] Confessional speech acts are used as redemptive tools, exemplified by the famous example of Oprah Winfrey, who has been called the "high priestess of confession" for offering redemption on her talk show.[65] The concept of redemption through confession is integral to the "American neoconfessional," as identified by Gilmore Leigh, contributing to the prevalence of the "redemptive self" in American culture, a notion explored by Dan McAdams.

> Here is a personal story—a biographical script of sorts—that many very productive and caring American adults see as their own: In the beginning, I learn that I am blessed, even as oth-

---

[61] Ibid. 14.
[62] Harju, Too Much Information, p. 58.
[63] Cf. Hornung, Auto/Biography, p. xiii.
[64] Harrington, Cure Within, p. 140. In other words, this is the secular version of the Christian belief that "the first step to healing lies in open confession" (ibid., p. 69).
[65] Harju, Too Much Information, p. 70.

ers suffer. When I am still very young, I come to believe in a set of simple core values to *guide me through a dangerous life terrain*. As I move forward in life, many bad things come my way—sin, sickness, abuse, addiction, injustice, poverty, stagnation. But bad things often lead to *good outcomes—my suffering is redeemed*. Redemption comes to me in the form of atonement, recovery, emancipation, enlightenment, upward social mobility, and/or the actualization of my good inner self. As the plot unfolds, I continue to grow and progress. I bear fruit; I give back; I offer a unique contribution. I will make a *happy ending*, even in a *threatening* world.[66]

This narrative, pervasive in American self-help culture, portrays life's challenges as opportunities for positive transformation, emphasizing agency-as-control over one's inner self. However, it glosses over identity markers and simplifies redemption as something that spontaneously occurs. The script perpetuates the idea that personal happiness is a continual pursuit, forever deferred.[67]

To summarize, this biographical script emphasizes individual responsibility for achieving the social goal of happiness. Self-help culture reinforces this message with "feeling rules," which guide individuals in managing their own emotions. "Acts of emotion management are not simply private acts; they are used in exchanges under the guidance of feeling rules. Feeling rules are standards used in emotional conversation to determine what is rightly owed and owing in the currency of feeling."[68] This notion of personal responsibility has been present throughout history, from Benjamin Franklin's autobiography to modern-day confessional self-help culture exemplified by Oprah Winfrey. According to this script, individual behavior is the main determinant of success or failure, and both happiness and suffering are seen as outcomes of individual choices.

The idea of habit formation as a means to a virtuous life can be traced back to Benjamin Franklin's "conducing means." "While my care was employ'd in guarding against one fault, I was often surprised by another; *habit* took the advantage of *inattention*; [...] I concluded [...] that the contrary habits must be broken, and good ones acquired and established, before we can have any dependence on a steady, uniform rectitude of conduct."[69] Franklin believed that breaking bad habits

---

66 McAdams, American Identity, p. 20; emphasis added.
67 Although calls to be happy now abound in self-help culture, they might have the opposite effect. The deferral of happiness is reminiscent of the Christian ideal: "And so in the dominant Christian worldview, happiness is not something we can obtain in this life. It is not our natural state. On the contrary, it is an exalted condition, reserved for the elect in a time outside of time, at the end of history. This is the opposite of today's egalitarian, feel-good-now conception of happiness." (McMahon, Happiness, the Hard Way).
68 Hochschild, *Managed Heart*, p. 18.
69 Franklin, *Autobiography*, p. 133.

and acquiring good ones was crucial to maintaining a steady, uniform rectitude of conduct. This idea resonates with contemporary motivational speakers such as James Clear, who emphasizes the four stages of habit formation: cue, craving, response, and reward. Clear divides these stages into the "problem phase" and the "solution phase"[70] and argues that with a practical framework, individuals can design good habits and eliminate bad ones. While we may "slip into patterns of thinking and action,"[71] Clear echoes Franklin's belief that the individual will and mind can set the body free from immoral, unsuccessful lives.

Self-help culture views habit formation as both the problem and solution to achieving self-fulfillment. It presents a dichotomous approach that pits habitual behavior against volitional control. According to this approach, losing weight or starting a side business is a matter of rational control over the temptations of bad habits inscribed in the body, like automatisms. This reinforces the "mind over matter" ideology that lies at the core of self-help.[72] The "denigration" of habit is not a new development; it can be traced back to Cartesian dualism and the philosophies of Kant and Descartes, who rejected the notion of "habit" because it belonged to a naturalistic and empirical worldview that identified human beings as just one more object within the natural world.[73]

However, examples from John Dewey and Maurice Merleau-Ponty presented by Crossley offer a more sophisticated approach to habits. According to them, habits emerge in interactions between human actors, nonhuman elements, and the wider physical environment, which invites contingencies and undermines the mastery of habit.[74] Habits "take shape in the to and fro of social interaction" and belong to the collective life of human beings.[75] In fact, Dewey himself wrote that the

---

[70] Clear, *Atomic Habits*, p. 48. On a rhetorical level, Clear's text follows the same logic—it identifies a problem which then it tries to solve. The logic of capitalism, of marketing, and sales-pitches is used to describe all behavior: "All behavior is driven by the desire to solve a problem" (ibid., p. 49). Abraham Maslow's pyramid of needs has been adopted by the field of marketing to explain consumer behavior and advertising strategies. Even if Maslow aimed to counter the behaviorist approach which emphasized only physiological drives, his humanistic psychology approaches behavior following the same logic of 'hunger.'
[71] Ibid., p. 50.
[72] Cf. McGee, *Self-Help, Inc.*, p. 60. In contrast, Sianne Ngai's analysis of the body's plasmaticness emphasizes not only its automatisms, but also its capacity to function as a source of agency. This topic will be further explored in the next chapter.
[73] Cf. Crossley, Habit and Habitus, p. 144.
[74] Ibid., p. 150.
[75] Ibid., p. 152.

"career and destiny of a living being are bound up with its interchanges with its environment, not externally, but in the most intimate way."[76]

Self-help culture simplifies the idea that the self can control its habits by paying attention and remaining self-aware. Robert Wright mentions journalist Samuel Smiles' popular book, *Self-Help*, published in 1859, which did not emphasize "getting in touch" with one's emotions, extracting oneself from negative relationships, "tapping into harmonic cosmic forces," or any other things that have since given self-help books a "sense of self-centeredness and facile comfort."[77] Instead, it "preached Victorian virtues such as civility, integrity, industry, perseverance, and, undergirding them all, *iron self-control*."[78] Smiles believed that a man could achieve almost anything, but he must always be "armed against the temptation of low indulgences" and must not "defile his body by sensuality, nor his mind by servile thoughts."[79] Benjamin Franklin also wrote:

> My intention being to acquire the habitude of all these virtues, I judg'd it would be well not to distract my attention by attempting the whole at once, but to fix it on one of them at a time; and, when I should be *master* of that, then to proceed to another, and so on, till I should have gone thro' the thirteen; [...] Temperance first, as it tends to procure that *coolness and clearness of head*, which is so necessary where *constant vigilance* was to be kept up, and *guard* maintained against the unremitting attraction of ancient habits, and the force of perpetual temptations.[80]

Franklin's approach to developing virtues involved acquiring habits through a focused and deliberate approach. He believed it was best to concentrate on one virtue at a time before moving on to the next. He started with temperance, recognizing its importance in maintaining a clear head to guard against the pull of old habits and temptations. Franklin's practice of creating a list of virtues, daily self-examination, and written confessions reflected a "Puritan ideology of self-control"[81] and vigilance. His emphasis on rational effort to resist bodily temptations reinforced the idea of "mind over matter" at the core of self-help culture. Today, this practice has been expanded and modernized by the Quantified Self move-

---

76 Dewey, *Art as Experience*, p. 13.
77 Wright, *Moral Animal*, p. 11.
78 Ibid.
79 Ibid.
80 Franklin, *Autobiography*, p. 135; emphasis added.
81 Harju, Too Much Information, p. 64.

ment, which uses digital tools and self-tracking devices to gain "self-awareness"[82] and self-knowledge through numbers.

Mindfulness meditation is a popular self-help technique that promises the kind of "clearness of head" espoused by Franklin.[83] The image of the mindful self, whether in the yogi posture or the calm and anchored self detached from the surroundings, suggests Romantic notions of solitude, introspection, and self-reliance. Romantic individualism has been updated to suggest the importance of self-control, which usually means a mental effort to escape bodily constraints. Self-help practices, such as the power of suggestion or the power of positive thinking, have been scrutinized by Anne Harrington in her history of American mind-body medicine. These practices reinforce the belief in the power of the mind over the trivial body, as they promise mind-control.

The self-help approach has unintended consequences, such as the problem of "self-rumination,"[84] which psychologists are investigating. To counter this issue, motivational speakers offer techniques that combat overthinking and apathy. For instance, some self-care challenges suggest indulgent behavior, like taking a bubble bath or eating chocolate cake, to escape constant thinking. But paradoxically, the same self-vigilance that these challenges aim to overcome is reinforced by creating rules, routines, and lists. This constant planning can undercut spontaneity and improvisation, as involuntary reactions are seen as undesirable and in need of control. The focus on self-vigilance can heighten the desire to control everything, including (and especially) the body, while neglecting other social factors.

Autobiographical writing can offer a way to raise self-vigilance by reflecting on the past and envisioning the future.[85] The speculative aspect inherent in confes-

---

[82] Wolf, Quantified Self, 00:04:00. "Commercially available technology like Apple watches, fitbits and pebbles make it increasingly easy to track and quantify bodily functions in the service of health" (Haase, Death by Data, p. 92). See also the statistic bodies of the quantified selves (Abend/Fuchs, *Digital Culture and Society*) or the notion of biofeedback, which emerged as an attempt to combat stress and "to extend the scope of conscious control over physiological processes of which people are normally unaware." (Harrington, *Cure Within*, p. 167).

[83] Motivational speakers such as Jay Shetty continue to make mindfulness widely popular. The Headspace mobile application (and others, such as Calm) promise a relief from stress and anxiety with the help of mindfulness. For a more in-depth analysis of mindfulness, see chapter eight.

[84] Rumination appears in psychology studies where it has been described as "negative, chronic, and persistent self-focus motivated by perceived threats, losses, or injustices to the self; neurotic self-attentiveness" (Morin, Toward a Glossary, p. 2).

[85] In other words, autobiographical writing is not just retrospective, which is the common perception when we think of Augustine and his emphasis of memory: "The mind, through memory—and in the *Confessions* Augustine will say that mind and memory are one and the same thing—can recall experiences of the past, but it can also, in the present, recall itself to itself" (Olney, Memory, p. 870). Autobiographies can also be prospective, as self-help culture shows.

sional writing deserves a more thorough examination, particularly in the context of its role in science communication. An intriguing comparison emerges when considering works like *The Education of Henry Adams*, a departure from the well-known example set by Franklin. In Adams' text, a remarkable ability to "mediate between different disciplines,"[86] including science, is evident.[87] This early instance exemplifies how confessions can be integrated "within a field of scientifically acceptable observations."[88] Consequently, the subsequent section delves into contemporary examples within our digital era, focusing on emerging platforms like TED Talks as an illustrative case. This exploration sheds light on the evolving landscape of communicating scientific discoveries through the strategic use of confession.

---

[86] Hornung, *Auto/Biography*, p. xii.
[87] At the beginning of the 20th century, Henry Adams remained skeptical toward Charles Lyell's theory of geological uniformity, nor was he a "true Darwinian"—"all he could prove was change" (*Education of Henry Adams*, p. 230 f).
[88] "Combining confession with examination, the personal history with the deployment of a set of decipherable signs and symptoms; the interrogation, the exacting questionnaire, and hypnosis, with the recollection of memories and free association: all were ways of reinscribing the procedure of confession in a field of scientifically acceptable observations" (Foucault, *History*, p. 65).

3 Confessions and Science Communication

North American culture places great value on scientific advice as being "impartial," "sound," and "evidence-based."[1] As Antje Kley notes, "scientific notions of depersonalized objectivity, empirical verifiability, and quantification" continue to dominate North American knowledge landscapes.[2] However, despite this emphasis on objectivity, confessional speech acts have come to dominate contemporary scientific discourse. This paradox can be explained by understanding the confession as a ritual that Western societies rely on for the "production of truth."[3] In this chapter, I will explore the intimization of science, with a particular focus on TED talks. Through this analysis, I aim to shed light on the intersection of science communication and confessional culture, and the implications of this intersection for our understanding of science as a field of knowledge.

3.1 The Intimization of Science

Confessional speech acts have become commonplace in the fields of psychology, popular science, and new media such as TED talks and podcasts. This recalls the debate about scientific objectivity which emerged in the latter half of the 19th century. At the heart of this debate was not only the issue of accuracy, but also of morality: scientists were duty-bound to "restrain" themselves from imposing their own biases and expectations on "the image of nature."[4] The ideal of objectivity was closely tied to the belief that visual images, such as atlases, could "eliminate suspect mediation."[5] Objectivity was seen as a sign that science had achieved professional autonomy and was often associated with the philosophy of scientific realism. Traditional connotations of objectivity include disinterest, universality, and

---

1 Cf. Kley, Literary Knowledge, p. 157.
2 Ibid.
3 Cf. Foucault, *History*, p. 58.
4 Cf. Daston/Galison, Image of Objectivity, p. 81. Lorraine Daston also outlines "the ascendance of the ideal of [...] 'a perspectival objectivity' in nineteenth century science" (Objectivity, p. 599), arguing that aperspectival objectivity is only one component of a layered concept of objectivity. It became "a scientific value when science came to consist in large part of communications that crossed boundaries of nationality, training and skill. Subjectivity became synonymous with the individual and solitude; objectivity, with the collective and conviviality" (ibid., p. 609). As such, impersonal autobiographies also became the norm among scientists, exemplified by figures such as Darwin or Huxley.
5 Daston/Galison, Image of Objectivity, p. 81.

independence from any particular perspective or viewpoint, "which are commonly associated with knowledge of a mind-independent world."[6]

Feminist critiques and postmodernism have challenged traditional views of objectivity in science, particularly during the so-called Science Wars[7] of the 1990s. These movements highlighted how science has often been used to legitimize certain power structures and ways of knowing, while excluding others. Additionally, scientific developments such as quantum mechanics and chaos theory have underscored the inherent uncertainty and complexity of the natural world.[8] The "myth of the unbiased observer" has been debunked, for it has become clear that observation is already theory-laden and shaped by our social and cultural context.[9] The very act of observation can potentially change the qualities of what is being observed, further challenging the belief in a neutral and detached perspective.[10] As such, the idea of objectivity as an "escape from perspective"[11] has lost traction even among scientists.

Peter Ellerton emphasizes the importance of viewing science as a dynamic and collaborative process, rather than a mere attempt to record "dry facts about the world."[12] For Ellerton, the word "evidence" reflects not only his training in science and philosophy, but also his ongoing conversations with others.[13] He acknowledges that the nature of evidence is not fixed, but can vary depending on the specific circumstances and perspectives involved. Ellerton's reference to his education suggests that personal experience and background can shape one's scientific practices and beliefs, highlighting the entanglement of biography and scientific inquiry.[14]

---

6 Chakravartty, Scientific Realism.
7 The cultural critique of science initiated by the works of Thomas Kuhn and Bruno Latour has changed the contemporary understanding of science: its claim to objectivity has been challenged by an emphasis on its narrative quality. The "Science Wars," thus, had at the core the same problem of objectivity: "two major 'cultures' that face each other in the 'Science Wars': empiricism, positivism, rationalism, realism on the one side, and any kind of postmodern or contemporary antifoundationalism or relativism on the other" (Kucharzewski, Propositions about Life, p. 136).
8 See for instance Heisenberg's Uncertainty Principle, Gödel's Incompleteness Theorems, or Chaos Theory.
9 See also French, Science, p. 69.
10 For instance, the Quantum Zeno Effect explains how "under constant watching, the atoms behaved very differently" than it was expected (Al-Khalili, Paradox, p. 40).
11 Daston, Objectivity, p. 604.
12 Ellerton, Listen and Learn.
13 Evidence is also "the product of many discussion" and they "have also alerted me to the fact this nature changes in certain circumstances and through certain worldviews" (ibid.).
14 Peter Ellerton has been offering an online course titled "Philosophy and Critical Thinking" on the edX platform.

In addition to valuing the establishment of an "intimate public,"[15] North American culture has also witnessed a shift toward more intimate science communication.[16] The role of intimacy in science has been debated in the psychoanalytic tradition, which has given rise to a "therapy culture" that "normalizes the public exposure of intimate thoughts."[17] According to Eva Illouz, modern power has assumed the benevolent face of psychoanalysis, which is a "political technology of the self" aimed at emancipating individuals, while at the same time making them more manageable and disciplined.[18] Anne Harrington has also identified a new therapeutic self-help culture, in which "scientific experts trained in psychology or medicine" tell people "how to live happier, healthier, and more productive lives."[19]

Psychoanalysis is often seen as an intimate, confessional process between the patient and analyst. However, the controversy between Sigmund Freud and Sándor Ferenczi shows that this has not always been the case. Freud rejected an intimate approach, emphasizing objectivity, neutrality, and disinterestedness as essential to analytic technique.[20] Ferenczi, on the other hand, believed that Freud's approach lacked emotional warmth and proposed an empathic approach instead. This "rage to heal"[21] through empathy aligns with the redemptive narrative of self-help culture. Ferenczi believed that feelings humanize the self and that empathy, rather than hindering observation, mediates it by helping to focus attention. In contrast, Freud's "evenly-suspended attention" amounted to "no attention at all."[22]

Empathy, then, goes beyond mere sympathetic identification found in self-help culture. It assumes a psychoanalytic mode of observation where attentive engagement reflects genuine care. Heinz Kohut further elucidated this notion, regarding empathy as a "controlled tool of observation"[23] that enables the analyst to gain pro-

---

15 Berlant, Queen, p. 4.
16 Berlant also shows how national power relies on both impersonality and intimacy (Queen, p. 1).
17 Harju, Too Much Information, p. 66. "Impacted by Freud, Americans embraced psychoanalysis and the 'transfer of the therapeutic mode into everyday life' (Burkart 23). 'Therapy culture,' a term sociologist Frank Furedi used in his eponymous study to describe Western societies in which therapeutic discourse reigns, is predicated on processes of individualization and the valuation of individualism prevalent in 19th century US culture" (ibid., p. 65).
18 Illouz, Saving, p. 3.
19 Harrington, Cure Within, p. 249.
20 Lunbeck, Empathy, p. 261.
21 Ibid., p. 262.
22 Ibid., p. 258.
23 Ibid., p. 266. The notion of empathy as a "controlled tool of observation" prepared the ground for the emergence of new jobs and new research methods, such as the so-called user personas of UX Design. The design thinking process "starts with empathy. Empathy is absolutely essential to UX

found insights. Surprisingly, he even discussed the emergence of a "new kind of objectivity," one that incorporates subjective elements.[24] As such, it seems that the principle of empathy, as a "specific cognitive process,"[25] has replaced the ideal of "aperspectival objectivity."[26] However, rather than revealing the limits of knowledge and making the author's presence more visible, empathy operates as a new form of objectivity that legitimizes and validates scientific understanding.

While the "view from nowhere" traditionally associated with science aimed to eliminate biases, dehumanize, and detach knowledge from personal experiences,[27] there has been a recent shift toward rehumanizing the scientific realm through the use of confessions. In the realm of positive psychology, confessions have emerged as scientific tools, such as gratitude letters and journals used to explore happiness.[28] They are treated as objects of analysis, exemplified by interviews or confessions from creative individuals, which Mihalyi Csikszentmihalyi utilized to develop the concept of flow. Similarly, Dan Gilbert relies on confessions in order to elucidate the "surprising science of happiness,"[29] and Harvard's longest happiness study involves the examination of the monitored lives of 724 men. This trend reflects a departure from detached objectivity, showcasing a renewed emphasis on personal narratives within scientific discourse.

Furthermore, confessions can serve as rhetorical tools in science communication, fulfilling not only an empathetic role but also providing inspiration and insight. Rather than highlighting the limitations of shared knowledge,[30] the inclusion of confessions in science amplifies its authority. Scientific theories thereby gain enhanced persuasiveness and appeal because they are not only grounded in factual evidence but also subjectively tested. The etymology of "confess" suggests both "to

---

design. In fact, without empathy, UX design simply doesn't exist" (Tutorial 2). This is because "great user experiences come from listening and understanding the needs of the people who will use or engage with the product you're designing" (ibid.). For instance, the research method of user personas "take what might seem like lifeless, overwhelming, or 'boring' research and turn it into something more personal and engaging. [...] they're a useful research when it comes to cultivating empathy and keeping your users at the forefront of design decisions [...] [and] one of the most widely used solutions for humanizing the design process" (ibid.).

24 Lunbeck, Empathy, p. 267.
25 Ibid.
26 Daston, Objectivity, p. 599.
27 Kley, Literary Knowledge, p. 158.
28 See also chapter eleven in this book.
29 Gilbert, Surprising Science.
30 For instance, when teachers use TED talks in their classroom, they never think to "stress the limitations of the knowledge shared," which "raises some questions about how well students recognize what Benjamin Bratton referred to as the 'American Idol' quality of the videos themselves" (Howard, Ideas Worth Spreading?, p. 72).

tell or make known" and "to give evidence of."[31] The latter connotation is particularly relevant in the legal context, where confessions serve as proof in legal cases. Similarly, confessions can be employed as testimonies to validate scientific knowledge, offering an alternative avenue for legitimizing scientific discourse.[32]

The utilization of confession in science extends beyond the realm of psychology or the "talking cure," although its prominence is most notable in those areas. The emergence of new media platforms for science communication, such as TED talks, online courses, and podcasts, contributes to a process of personalizing science. Historical accounts of scientific findings in the seventeenth and eighteenth centuries, even in empirical sciences and mathematics, often presented reports in the first-person singular. The credibility and value of such reports relied not only on the content but also on the skills, character, and "occasionally social status" of the reporter.[33] A similar trend can be observed in TED talks, where the intertwining of the "cult of personality" and advertising objectives has become increasingly prevalent in academia.[34] This tendency is also evident in other web-mediated genres like academia.edu, LinkedIn, X, commonly referred to by its former name Twitter, and Facebook, which are employed by academics to engage with scientific communities and the general public.

Embedded within the American culture of self-help and self-improvement, TED talks go beyond the mere dissemination of facts; they strive to share personal narratives and evoke emotional responses. Similarly, podcasts embody qualities of being "cheap, niche, idiosyncratic, weird, and highly personal."[35] Their style often prioritizes "authenticity over authority," and suggests "a wide open eye avidly searching the world for *wonder* under an ever so slightly arched eyebrow."[36] Adam Sternbergh's choice of words underscores both the skepticism, doubt, and objectivity of science, represented by the "slightly arched eyebrow," as well as the awe-inspiring and astonishing discoveries it unveils. Although podcasts primarily involve listening and hearing, Sternbergh's emphasis on the eye highlights the visual aspect, metaphorically capturing the sense of wonder that science instills.

---

31 Confess. *Merriam-Webster.*
32 These three uses of confession in science are not necessarily new. For instance, Sigmund Freud's *Psycho-Analytic Notes on an Autobiographical Account of a Case of Paranoia* use confessions as an object of scientific analysis and scrutiny, but also as evidence or proof to build up or validate his theory. Freud even uses the personal pronoun "I" to explain and legitimate some of his choices.
33 Cf. Daston, Objectivity, p. 610.
34 Compagnone, Reconceptualization of Academic Discourse, p. 66.
35 Sternbergh, How Podcasts Learned to Speak. Alyn Euritt's recently published book on *Podcasting as an Intimate Medium* (2022) also draws attention to the role of intimacy in podcasting.
36 Sternbergh, How Podcasts Learned to Speak; emphasis added.

Consequently, it is their visionary dimension that takes center stage, showcasing the pervasive influence of visual metaphors in Western culture. The "power of the optical" resonates not only in religious discourse[37] but also within the realm of science. Whether it is the "view from nowhere"[38] or the illuminating moments of insight, both objectivity and wonder are portrayed through ocular-centric imagery in scientific practice. Scientific breakthroughs, often experienced as epiphanies, eureka moments, or aha-moments, are predominantly conceptualized in visual terms. Insight is understood as "the power or act of *seeing* into a situation"[39] and is typically associated with "a bright, happy, emotional spot in any person's life."[40]

In summary, both TED talks and podcasts rely on the coexistence of a skeptical or rational mode (symbolized by the "slightly arched eyebrow" and the authoritative delivery of facts and data) and the evocation of wonder within an intimate context. In science communication, confessions are employed to describe moments of insight that often carry an element of wonder. The "sense of wonder" is an iconic element of science fiction, serving as "the emotional heart"[41] of the genre. The perpetuation of wonder reinforces a stereotypical view of science prevalent in American culture, where science (including fiction) is often evaluated based on its ability to speculate and prophesize visions of the future.[42] The belief that wonder facilitates "a sudden opening of a closed door in the reader's mind"[43] underscores its role in stimulating both visionary and cognitive capacities.

One of the iconic openings of a TED talk features an explosive eye, symbolizing a creative moment akin to the Big Bang, where the eye transforms into a universe

---

37 Jay, *Downcast Eyes*, p. 13.
38 Kley, Literary Knowledge, p. 158.
39 Insight, *Merriam-Webster*. For a more in-depth analysis of the underlying meanings of insight and its various uses in scientific, mystical, or psychological contexts, check my blog post: "InSight: Making a Case for Self-Vigilance?" (2022).
40 Maslow, *Motivation and Personality*, p. 50.
41 Mendlesohn, Introduction, p. 3.
42 Wonder may carry different connotations, though it is more than "simple admiration of super-technology" (Sawyer, Science Fiction, p. 89). Andy Sawyer points to the many qualities of wonder in science fiction: first, the importance of the setting, since one may experience "awe at the vastness of space and time" (ibid., p. 88). Second, he mentions the appeal of the alien element, since one may be "*attracted* by Otherness, *seduced* by strangeness" (ibid., p. 90; emphasis in original). Finally, the sense of "conceptual breakthrough" (ibid., p. 89) is also essential to feeling wonder—challenging hypotheses, opening doors to new possibilities.
43 Ibid., p. 89 f.

adorned with nebulas and stars.[44] This visual representation elicits a sense of wonder on various levels, encompassing amazement at scale, awe at vastness, and the concept of insight. Interestingly, twenty-five percent of the talks delivered at each conference never make it to the TED website due to their lack of the sought-after "wow" factor.[45] The emphasis on vision may also arise from a desire for control. In Sergey Brin's TED talk, touch is portrayed as feminine and disempowering, while vision, associated with masculinity and control, is deemed the primary modality of Glass: "for Brin, hands are meant to be free so they can manipulate the world that the eyes see."[46]

The reliance on vision and the sense of wonder plays a pivotal role in ensuring the inspirational quality of TED talks. Lorraine Daston's research has demonstrated that the "unwavering" and "penetrating attention" required by scientific investigation is fueled by curiosity, which in turn is triggered by wonder.[47] Andy Sawyer has also noted the connection between desire, knowledge, dreaming, and thinking that underpins the wonder found in science fiction.[48] Wonder, therefore, can function as a motivational force. However, the emphasis on vision also reflects a humanistic celebration of individual imagination. This correlation between visual perception and the power of imagination is evident even in dictionary definitions of vision, which encompass both "the act or power of seeing" and "the act or power of imagination."[49] Such associations highlight a humanistic and Western tradition that places the eye at the apex of a sensory hierarchy.

The power of visualization has long been associated with describing the creative endeavors of geniuses. William James famously stated that genius "means little more than the faculty of perceiving in an unhabitual way,"[50] a quote that circulates widely online. Visualization has been embraced as a secret ingredient for success in self-help culture, often linked to The Law of Attraction.[51] Mind-power consistent-

---

[44] Other iconic openings include the water pond: "TED's introductory image of a water drop falling into a pond, making ripples as its effects are felt outward from the center, is not telling the full story of how things spread over time. The concentric circles moving out from the center suggest a clean, purposeful process uninterrupted by other events or forces" (Howard, Ideas Worth Spreading?, p. 77). The pond is also reminiscent of Thoreau's *Walden*.
[45] Trost, AMA: TED's Chris Anderson Answers.
[46] Pfister, Technoliberal Rhetoric, p. 189.
[47] Daston qtd. in Crary, *Suspensions*, p. 18.
[48] Sawyer, Science Fiction, p. 90.
[49] Vision, *Merriam-Webster*.
[50] Paddington, On the Hand-Crafting of Genius.
[51] From Norman Vincent Peale's practical guide to positive thinking published in the fifties to Rhonda Byrne's *The Secret* (2006), and the most recent "Lucky Girl Syndrome" on TikTok (Teitell, Lucky Girl Syndrome)—the same belief in the power of visualization is perpetuated.

ly incorporates a visual component, and vice versa. In TED's most popular science talks, the playlist features an image of a microscope. The microscope serves as a visual tool of observation, reinforcing notions of objectivity and the ability to zoom in. This choice is likely deliberate, as many talks touch upon visions in some capacity, whether it is "liespotting,"[52] "underwater astonishments,"[53] or visions of the future, such as Elon Musk's future cities or Stephen Hawking's vision of space colonization. Images, camera footages, MRI brain scans,[54] graphs—the visual aids employed in these talks act as "lenses" [55] through which the audience explores the unknown and invisible world.

Visions possess a certain allure and desire-inducing quality, as their power to captivate and fascinate can be "hypnotic."[56] This may explain their popularity in the motivational industry, where they are employed to evoke inspiring ideas. TED's slogan, "ideas worth spreading," encapsulates this desire to not only communicate knowledge but also persuade through inspiration. Incorporating visions into science communication serves to make science more appealing to the public by infusing it with excitement and exhilaration. However, this approach sometimes blurs the boundaries between science communication, speculation, and science fiction. It seems that the ongoing need for a professional body to justify its existence to the public can perpetuate a prolonged period of "compromise" in the process of legitimization.[57] This influence shapes the practice and communication of any discipline, including science in a broader sense.

3.2 TED Talks: History, Genre, Culture

The inaugural TED conference included a demonstration of the compact disc presented by Mickey Schulhof of Sony. Nicholas Negroponte predicted the invention of e-books and mathematician Benoit Mandelbrot illustrated his fractal geometry. The event lost money, but Harry Marks and Richard Wurman tried again six years later, in 1990. This time round, the event was more successful and the TED conference became an annual event in Monterey, California. With the acquisition, in 2001, and ongoing curation of TED by media entrepreneur Chris Anderson, the

---

52 Meyer, How to Spot a Liar.
53 Gallo, Underwater Astonishments.
54 Fisher, Brain in Love.
55 Achor, Happy Secret, 00:06:02.
56 Jay, *Downcast Eyes*, p. 13.
57 Daniels, Process of Professionalization, p. 78, 63.

popular science and technology enterprise became a fixture of the digital landscape, too.

In 2006, a selection of six TED talks were posted online for the first time on the websites of TED, YouTube, and iTunes. They quickly reached one million views and their popularity led to the launching of the new TED.com. TED videos are provided with a transcription, translation into several languages, a blog area, and a comment section. Since 2006, many talks have succeeded in attaining millions of views and TED became one of the most famous disseminators of scientific knowledge on a global level. Probably one of the most popular cultural mediums in which the implications of future technologies have been debated, TED may also contribute to a "cultural export of American mythic narratives across the globe."[58]

In "TED's Nonprofit Transition," Anderson discusses his vision for TED and the idea of happiness keeps recurring in his talk. From his initial confession that describes how his personal happiness got tied up with his business to his humorous comment on Madame de Gaulle's desire for "a penis": "When you think about it, it's very true: what we all most desire is a penis—or 'happiness' as we say in English."[59] His play on words incites laughter from the audience, but the comic reference also suggests a link between being male and being happy. It is uncertain whether he proposes maleness as an aspiration or whether he is aware of the patriarchal implications of his pun. He goes on to talk about how happiness can be approached in TED via various angles: offering biochemical, psychological, computational, geopolitical or evolutionary perspectives.

In the end, attending or listening to TED talks seems to bring about happy feelings: "your brain is humming and you feel energized, alive and excited, and it's because all these different bits have been put together. It's the total brain experience."[60] Even if "do[ing] nothing" is the first thing Anderson lists in his vision for TED, his focus on happiness proves the opposite. He promises two qualities at the same time: the "truth" of scientific objectivity and the happiness of feeling inspired —both authority and authenticity.

Truth and curiosity should also prevail over any corporate agenda, and yet many presenters use this opportunity to make their products or services more popular, so the informational and promotional aims overlap. For instance, academics make use of language on the TED stage "to achieve their 'private intentions' as professionals (Bhatia 2012), e.g., building up their identity as experts as well as promoting their research and scholarship, rather than training a group of novices

---

58 Paul, *Myths*, p. 13.
59 Anderson, TED's Nonprofit Transition, 00:05:25.
60 Ibid., 00:08:33.

in their discipline or merely informing mass audiences."[61] Jonathan Elmer also pointed out how "both TED and the world of design are pulled gravitationally toward the iterable commodity."[62]

Julia Ludewig's analysis of TED talks as a hybrid and emergent genre reveals their heavy reliance on three parent genres: the sales-pitch, the memoir, and the academic lecture. The hybridity of TED talks could be traced back to other genres as well. Rhetorically, their reliance on humorous stories, jokes or one-liners is reminiscent of stand-up comedy. Their didacticism can be traced back not only to the genre of academic lecture. At times, their pedagogical tone comes across as sermonizing, which is evocative of the American jeremiad, a "motivational sermon in the Puritan tradition."[63] In other words, speakers may sometimes resemble self-help gurus—experts preaching their own truths.

The American jeremiad encompasses a rhetoric that combines elements of hope and fear, incorporating both the ideal of community and its shortcomings. It propels forward with "prophetic" certainty towards a "resolution."[64] This rhetoric can function as a tool of social control, diverting attention away from potential flaws within institutions or systems and redirecting it toward "considerations of individual sin."[65] Redemption is presented as attainable through the "efforts of the American people" rather than through systemic change itself.[66] Similarly, TED talks promote narratives of redemption, emphasizing the transformative power of the individual self in achieving justice, success, and happiness.

Science fiction is a genre from which TED draws inspiration. Many talks conclude on a utopian note, offering glimpses into the future. This futuristic and speculative dimension is acknowledged in "TED Science Standards" and "TED Content Guidelines." These guidelines state, "At TED, we aim to explore the potential implications of new scientific findings. This stimulates further exploration and discovery. Therefore, we welcome scientists to *speculate* on the potential implications and applications of their work."[67] During these acts of speculation, speakers may assume the role of inspired geniuses, sharing their visionary knowledge. TED's slogan, "ideas worth sharing," also aims to fuel the desire to contribute to

---

61 Compagnone, Reconceptualization of Academic Discourse, p. 65.
62 Elmer, Public Humanities, p. 111.
63 Paul, *Myths*, p. 30.
64 Bercovitch, *American Jeremiad*, p. 16.
65 Cf. Murphy, "Time of Shame and Sorrow," p. 402.
66 Ibid. Or, as Foucault argues: "The statement of oppression and the form of the sermon refer back to one another; they are mutually reinforcing" (*History*, p. 8).
67 TED Science Standards, *TED*.

a better future.[68] Attendees often describe the TED experience as a "journey into the future."[69] The conclusion of a talk is typically crafted as a call to action or as an optimistic vision for the future.

Although TED appears to operate with a hybrid blend of genres, they all share a common emphasis on the individual. Whether it is the teacher, the charismatic preacher, the memoirist, the comedian, the genius, or the businessperson, all these figures highlight the knowledge and personal experiences of individuals. They contribute to the cultivation and perpetuation of an aesthetics of individualism, which is also visually manifested: TED talks feature an individual speaker elevated on a stage, often occupying the center of attention. The focus on creativity and innovation further celebrates the power of the human mind. Similarly, the strong belief in the "power of mind over matter" exemplifies the tradition of "classic American self-improvement."[70]

Much of the scholarly analysis of TED revolves around teaching or linguistic approaches to the genre.[71] Known as the nonprofit "Hollywood of education,"[72] TED talks have been extensively incorporated into educational contexts.[73] The integration of TED talks into educational settings is evident not only through partnerships with textbook publishers but also through initiatives like TED-ED, which actively promotes and shares online lessons built around TED talks.[74] Often, the emphasis is on how these talks can enrich self-directed learning and bolster students' self-confidence.[75]

---

68 How TED Works, *TED*.
69 Conferences, *TED*.
70 McGee, *Self-Help*, p. 60.
71 Gavenila et al., Using TED Talks; Nadeem, Stories; Kung, Critical Theory of Technology; Nguyen/Boers, Effect of Content Retelling; García-Pinar, Influence of TED Talks; Wingrove, How Suitable are TED Talks; Compagnone, Reconceptualization of Academic Discourse.
72 Yuksel, TED Talks Complement, p. 96.
73 TED talks are used to teach students academic thinking and writing skills (see Yuksel), and many language institutions began to use TED talks as a way of fostering academic listening skills (Nguyen/Boers, Effect, p. 11). They inform the ways in which public presentations are taught (Kedrowicz/Taylor). Euodia Inge Gavenila together with Mega Wulandari and Willy A. Renandya investigate the language learning benefits of TED talks for a group of students in Indonesia. Aránzazu García-Pinar considers the ways in which multimodal pedagogy that draws on TED talks could help with motivation or "have an effect on learners' linguistic self-confidence" (Influence, p. 232). Pinar tackles TED talks as "authentic material that can contribute to making language teaching more meaningful and interesting" (Getting Closer, p. 13). And others even consider the ways in which teachers could use their discourse markers in the classroom (Uicheng/Crabtree).
74 Cf. Wingrove, How Suitable, p. 79.
75 García-Pinar; Gavenila et al; Yuksel.

Shannon Howard adopts a more skeptical stance toward the use of TED talks in the classroom, emphasizing the importance of translating ideas into action rather than merely disseminating them.[76] She observes that the enthusiasm for TED talks is often passed on from instructor to instructor, without a thorough understanding of TED's mission. While acknowledging the power of these narratives to captivate audiences, forge personal connections, and inspire "deep reflection"[77] on the topic at hand, Howard raises concerns about the potential lack of follow-through on the ideas presented.

This book specifically examines TED talks as a contemporary expression of American self-help culture. The emphasis on the potential of TED talks to foster self-directed learning further suggests their connection to the self-help movement. Despite the widespread popularity of TED talks, there is a noticeable gap in research that explores their relationship to self-help or conducts a comprehensive analysis of specific playlists or the most popular talks. It is important to note that TED talks not only convey knowledge but also play a role in shaping individuals' identities. The audience has the option to select "personal growth" and "self-improvement" categories to receive tailored recommendations for talks. TED actively encourages viewers to uncover their potential, expand their horizons, acquire new knowledge, shift their perspectives, or explore what's possible.[78]

The optimistic and enthusiastic attitude expressed in TED talks underscores a firm belief in progress and the potential for a better future. TED's mission statement reflects this sentiment, stating, "We firmly believe in the transformative power of ideas to change attitudes, lives, and ultimately, the world."[79] Consequently, TED talks often exhibit an upbeat tone, incorporating redemptive narratives or delivering positive messages. T.J. Tsai's research suggests that the ability of TED talk speakers to maintain a consistently "high-energy" presentation contributes to their success as public speakers.[80] The connections between TED talks and American self-help culture can be observed not only in its origins within Silicon Valley, where technological advancements and innovation are highly revered, but also in its adherence to genre conventions.

An exploration of TED talks reveals the inherent connection between their form and content. The formal aspects of these talks significantly influence the interpretation and reception of scientific and informational content. Pat Kelly's

---

76 Howard, Ideas Worth Spreading?, p. 63.
77 Nadeem, Stories, p. 435.
78 These messages keep hovering at the top of the webpage while browsing through TED talks.
79 This is TED's mission statement that used to appear on their website, but it is now listed only on their LinkedIn profile (TED Conferences, *LinkedIn*).
80 Uicheng/Crabtree, Macro Discourse Markers, p. 3f.

comic parody titled "'Thought Leader' Gives Talk that Will Inspire Your Thoughts" humorously encapsulates some of the most prevalent formal features found in TED talks.[81] Despite Kelly's speech being devoid of substance, the use of presentation techniques and devices manages to impart a sense of significance to the empty discourse.[82] This underscores the significance of rhetoric, form, and performance, often surpassing the importance of content itself. In essence, the delivery of the talk becomes "fetishized" as the primary rhetorical ingredient that has a profound impact on the audience.[83]

It becomes evident that the content or subject matter of the talks takes a backseat to their presentation, which is what ultimately instills inspiration in the audience. Kelly adeptly captures the multitude of elements that contribute to the persuasive nature of these speeches. These elements include body language and vocal tone (such as entering and returning to the center of the stage, modulation of voice volume and pace, maintaining eye contact, hand gestures and counting on fingers), effective rhetoric (utilizing repetition and posing questions), incorporation of science and technology (having a laptop on stage, employing graphs, pie charts, statistics, and visually engaging slides), attention to physical appearance (selecting clothing and fashionable accessories like glasses), as well as the use of personal anecdotes and humor (such as sharing an "unremarkable context about how I became a thought leader").

In "TED's Secret to Great Public Speaking," Chris Anderson challenges the caricatured views of TED talks. He refutes the notion of a predictable "formula" associated with TED speeches, such as revealing personal secrets, sharing childhood stories, or concluding with an inspirational call to action. According to Anderson, relying too heavily on these devices can make speakers appear clichéd or "emotionally manipulative."[84] Instead, he presents a different perspective on TED talks, emphasizing the ways in which they connect: "Your number one task as a speaker is to *transfer* into your listeners' minds an extraordinary gift—a strange and beautiful object that we call an idea."[85] To support this perspective, he cites the example of Haley Van Dyck's talk, where the brains of the audience members become "in sync" with hers, forming a "pattern" that involves "millions of neurons" being "teleported" into the minds of 1200 individuals through voice and fa-

---

81 Other parodies of TED talks (like those of John Oliver on HBO's "Last Week Tonight" and comedian Will Stephen) are addressed in Shannon Howard's essay, p. 66.
82 Strange, This Fake TED Talk.
83 Howard, Ideas Worth Spreading?, p. 67.
84 Anderson, TED's Secret, 00:00:14.
85 Ibid., 00:00:44.

cial expressions.[86] Anderson's choice of words accentuates the idea of transfer, synchronization, and telepathic communication, which could potentially be perceived as emotionally manipulative.[87]

Furthermore, according to him, ideas are essentially patterns of information that exist within the brain and shape individual worldviews. The field of cognitive science has led to a mechanistic understanding of consciousness as a brain process and the mind as an information processor,[88] which underlies these perspectives. Chris Anderson also shares a similar technoliberal assumption found in Sergey Brin's "Why Google Glass?" that views people as mere "stores of information," composed of genetic and cultural material easily converted into "manipulable units of data."[89] Techno-liberals often perceive social problems as primarily technical issues and believe that increasing communication capacity, symbolized by the metaphor of "bandwidth," will improve individuals.[90]

Both the bandwidth metaphor and the teleported patterns in Anderson's talk rely on a technoliberal assumption of "sensation without mediation," promoting the ideal of a "fully transparent citizen."[91] This view disregards multi-sensorial input, favoring vision[92] as the dominant sense. It aligns with a humanist celebration of imagination and a self-help conviction in the power of the mind, where positive thinking and suggestion are seen as the most effective tools for self-improvement. Anderson asserts that properly communicated ideas are capable of forever changing how someone perceives the world and shaping their actions, making ideas the most influential force in shaping human culture.[93]

---

[86] Ibid., 00:02:11.
[87] Nadeem also considers the ways in which Guy Winch's TED talk, his "passionate self-disclosure and multi-modal delivery of the narrative helped to *transfer* his subjective perspective of the narrated events to the audience" (Stories, p. 445). Additionally, the subconscious power of advertisements has also been compared to telepathy. See Brenton, *Feeling Mediated*, p. 52.
[88] Gossin, *Encyclopedia of Literature and Science*, p. 258.
[89] Pfister, Technoliberal Rhetoric, p. 188.
[90] Ibid.
[91] Ibid., p. 190, 188.
[92] And it is also the vision behind Google: "My *vision* when we started Google fifteen years ago was that eventually you wouldn't have to have a search query at all. You'd just have information come to you as you needed it. And this is now, fifteen years later, sort of the first form factor that I think can deliver that *vision* when you're out and about on the street talking to people and so forth" (ibid., p. 190).
[93] Anderson, TED's Secret, 00:04:30. The power of suggestion refers to a "process in which an idea is accepted in such a way as to lead to 'ideomotor and ideosensory automatisms'—i.e., patients feel and behave in a way consistent with an implanted idea without reflecting on its sense or plausibility," so "it often worked better if a patient could be lulled into a state of *reduced vigilance*" (Har-

Anderson believes that TED talks have the potential to change the world by influencing thoughts and behaviors. In his guidelines for crafting ideas within the minds of the audience, he emphasizes focusing on a single idea, arousing curiosity through intriguing questions, using simple language, and aiming to benefit others.[94] He references Jennifer Doudna's talk as an example of how scientific concepts can be made tangible, explaining the CRISPR genome editing technology through an analogy with a word processor editing DNA. I have previously explored the implications of such approaches, which contribute to an underestimation of DNA's materiality and an excessive emphasis on its code.[95] It is worth noting that these explanations are incomplete and contribute to a belief in and an endorsement of human enhancement. Anderson celebrates the "aha moment" facilitated by such explanations without considering their limitations.

TED talks are designed as motivational tools with the aim of creating change in the world. The global popularity of TED talks suggests that their stories are highly influential, and their values may be adopted by the audience. The TED audience is predominantly young and well-educated, with a higher representation of visitors aged 18–24 and in graduate school compared with the rest of the web.[96] Therefore, it would be valuable to closely examine TED's most popular stories and scrutinize how they can be particularly persuasive. As Kelly's parody demonstrated, persuasion is achieved through formal elements rather than ideas alone. In addition to scientific trust and confidence in a thought leader's persuasive performance, personal confessions strengthen the credibility of TED talks. Speakers often share stories of personal transformation in a confessional tone, recounting experiences of conversion, overcoming personal crises, and acts of resilience. In doing so, TED also promotes a self-help ethic centered on "total self-creation" and "free will."[97]

The confessional style of TED talks aligns with their academic and professional demeanor. Rather than "denying *factuality*,"[98] TED aims to be educational and shares commonalities with the documentary genre. Consequently, the boundaries between science and art become more blurred. TED talks also possess an artful quality, evoking emotions and eliciting feelings. Their genre hybridity serves a dual purpose: it allows science to gain authority by connecting its knowledge with personal experiences and by demonstrating the tangible links between scien-

---

rington, *Cure Within*, p. 58). Thus, it recalls not only the idea of hypnosis, but also telepathy as a form of communication.
94 Anderson, TED's Secret, 00:05:42.
95 Filip, Genetic Enhancement.
96 Cf. Sugimoto et al., Scientists Popularizing Science.
97 Bowdon, *50 Self-Help Classics*, p. 196.
98 Grobe, *Art*, p. 191; emphasis added.

tific findings and everyday human life. Simultaneously, the art of confession gains authority as well. It is not perceived as artificial or as something detached from factuality but is supported by scientific backing. Science and the mystical can coexist in a state of tension rather than negating each other. For example, in Jill Bolte Taylor's talk on "My Stroke of Insight," the understanding that "we are the life-force power of the universe"[99] accompanies the narrative of the right hemisphere as the brain region that facilitates a transcendent experience akin to nirvana.

The confessional style adopted by TED also contributes to the emergence of an "intimate public."[100] TED talks are presented as private moments rather than public displays, creating a sense of safety and authenticity. They presumably provide a space where individuals can express their true selves, allowing for vulnerability, insecurities, and even the disclosure of secrets. The audience transitions from being mere spectators to becoming witnesses and confidants. Speakers may perceive the audience as their "friends"[101] and share intimate details for the first time on camera.[102] Additionally, when speakers discuss their process of writing the talks[103] or their emotions and actions leading up to the talk, it further enhances feelings of sincerity and trust between confidant and confessor. The combination of scientific accuracy and this feeling of intimacy intensifies the persuasive impact of TED talks.

In addition to the intimate confessional moments, TED talks aim to evoke various "honest and contagious emotions" such as "wonder, optimism, anger, and surprise."[104] These emotions serve to increase audience engagement and contribute to the authenticity of the talks. However, they can also be seen as "emodities,"[105] as speakers strategically consider how to elicit emotions from their audience, highlighting the performative aspect of TED talks. Emotional contagion plays a significant role in the persuasive toolbox of TED talks. The prevalence of optimism in TED talks not only reflects an ideology of positive thinking but may also be seen as a manifestation of "cruel optimism."[106] According to Lauren Berlant's concept of "cruel optimism," individuals remain attached to unattainable fantasies of the

---

99 Taylor, My Stroke, 00:16:35.
100 Berlant, *Queen*, p. 4.
101 Gilbert, Your Creative Elusive Genius, 00:05:00.
102 Russell, Looks Aren't Everything, 00:07:55.
103 Ibid., 00:08:20.
104 Rehearsals, *TED*.
105 Illouz, *Emotions*, p. 11.
106 Berlant, *Cruel*, p.1.

"good life" despite evidence that societal structures cannot fulfill promises of upward mobility, job security, equality, and fulfilling relationships.[107]

Consequently, TED talks are aligned with a culture of self-help, evident in their stylistic choices. Rooted in the American tradition of self-improvement, they embody capitalist and psychological perspectives. TED talks incorporate uplifting messages, inspiring quotes, and motivational language. The prevalence of "how-to" conventions[108] and the abundance of playlists offering advice on various topics like shopping, relationships, parenting, sleep, and work-life balance further support this observation. However, the connection to self-help within TED talks is multifaceted. While they promote self-help, they also reshape and reinterpret this tradition from within. Analyzing TED talks provides a unique perspective that complements the study of conventional self-help books, offering new insights and understandings.

The TED talks global archive offers an extensive range of topics to explore, with a staggering 452 categories. These topics encompass various scientific disciplines, industries, scientific concepts, diseases, geographical locations, religions, technology, politics, culture, the natural world, experiences, behaviors, and the web. Notably, there is a strong interest in psychology, as evidenced by the prominence of themes such as mindfulness, memory, consciousness, meditation, and mental health. Additionally, a look through the topics suggests a promotion of capitalist perspectives, with an emphasis on business, marketing, money, shopping, advertising, consumerism, and the figure of the entrepreneur. However, it would be overly simplistic to argue that TED solely supports and advances a capitalist and psychological worldview. Upon closer examination of individual talks, critical perspectives do emerge, including concerns for the working class and a desire to reevaluate capitalism itself.

To gain a deeper understanding of TED's ideas and their connections, it is important to go beyond browsing topics alone or focusing on individual talks with no apparent link. A fruitful approach is to examine playlists, which can provide valuable insights into some of the most significant ideas shared by TED. To begin this analysis, a selection of topics closely related to the culture of self-help was chosen: self, personal growth, psychology, potential, meditation, mental health, mind, mindfulness, motivation, identity, illness/disease, happiness, health, human body, success, failure, fear, finance, decision-making, depression, choice, consciousness, adventure, disability, aging, creativity, death, empathy, life, humanity, love, morali-

---

107 Ibid., 2f.
108 It is worth noting that Benjamin Franklin "launched the tradition of the how-to book" (Benesch, *Romantic Cyborgs*, p. 36).

ty, parenting, personality, simplicity, and vulnerability. By exploring the playlists associated with each of these topics, it becomes possible to identify intersecting themes and connections between them.

Based on my analysis, I have found the following results: The playlist "How to Be a Better You" emerged as the most frequently featured playlist, appearing under seven different topics. Moreover, it held a prominent position at the top of these categories, being among the first four playlists visible without the need for further browsing. These seven topics include vulnerability, failure, success, happiness, potential, personal growth, and self, all of which are central to self-help culture. The second most visible playlist was "Who Are You?" which appeared under five topics: self, psychology, mind, identity, and personality. It also occupied the top position in the identity and personality categories. Another playlist, "Survivor's Wisdom," was present in five sections: illness, disease, health, life, and humanity, and it held a top position in the illness and disease categories. Lastly, the playlist "What Makes You Happy?" was featured in four sections: psychology, happiness, success, and choice, and it remained at the top in all of them. While there is a wide selection of playlists with intriguing titles, it is important to narrow down the focus.[109] The chosen playlists were selected based on their visibility and thematic relevance.[110]

Accordingly, my analysis predominantly focuses on two playlists: "How to Be a Better You" and "What Makes You Happy." I also delve into talks that fall under the "mindfulness" tag or are among the most popular ones.[111] These popular playlists shed light on the elements that resonate the most with the TED audiences, as well as the outstanding figures who feature prominently. Notably, in the "The Most Pop-

---

109 Other interesting playlists include: "In the Mood for Love" (listed under happiness, life, humanity, love), "Talks to Help You Find Your Purpose" (self, mindfulness, motivation, happiness), "How to Overcome Your Fears" (self, motivation, failure, fear), "Motivation for the New Year" (personal growth, mental health, motivation, happiness), "TED Talks for When You're Having an Existential Crisis" (personal growth, happiness, success, life), "Deep Studies of Humanity" (happiness, life, death, humanity), "Personal Tales from the Edge of Life" (personal growth, life, humanity), "What Is Success?" (personal growth, failure, creativity), "Advice to Help You Be a Great Parent" (personal growth, life, parenting), "The Eternal Search to Prolong Life" (aging, life, humanity), "Charming Talks for a Boost on a Bad Day" (psychology, happiness, success), "Overcoming Depression" (depression, mental health, mind), "The Importance of Self-Care" (mental health). Other playlists focus on how to manage stress, build introspective spaces, or form better habits. Others deal with perfectionism, emotional first-aid, or secrets to understanding life.
110 This analysis was done in March 2020, so the order and hierarchies might have changed since then.
111 The most popular talks considered here were featured either in the playlist "The Most Popular Talks of All Time" or "The Most Popular Science Talks."

ular Talks of all Time" playlist, I observed a predominance of American speakers, with a slight overrepresentation of men and limited representation of African American speakers. Both "How to Be a Better You" and "What Makes You Happy?" cater to an audience seeking personal growth and happiness. The other playlists tend to have more specific target audiences and focus, addressing topics such as illness or identity.

My analysis primarily focuses on confessions of happiness, as they have the potential to resonate with a broader audience that may be "generally dissatisfied with life" or seeking to enhance their current level of happiness.[112] However, I acknowledge the significance of other playlists and their intersections with my chosen ones. Notably, three talks featured in my selected playlists also appear in "TED Talks for When You're Having an Existential Crisis."[113] Additionally, five other talks are included in "The Importance of Self-Care,"[114] while two talks resurface in "Talks to Help You Find Your Purpose."[115] These connections highlight the thematic overlaps and provide valuable insights into the diverse range of topics within the TED archive.

Upon a closer examination of the playlist titles, certain intriguing aspects emerge. One notable observation is the underlying assumption that negative emotions and experiences should be overcome. This perspective is evident in playlists such as "How to Overcome Your Fears," which stands alone under the topic of fear. The notion of overcoming is a well-known approach in self-help, but it can reinforce ableism and the survivor narrative.[116] Similarly, in discussions of illness or disease, the playlist titled "Survivor's Wisdom" holds a central position.[117] This reflects the tendency to emphasize overcoming challenges and adopting a survivor mentality within these contexts.

---

112 Parks, I Want to Be Happier. Accacia C. Parks distinguished between depressed, anxious, and dissatisfied readers to make recommendations for self-help books in her article on "I Want to Be Happier! What Should I Read?" (2012). Interestingly enough, Henry David Thoreau has also said at the beginning of *Walden* "that he writes not for the strong and self-reliant souls, if such there be, but for those who find themselves somehow unhappy with their lot" (Cox, Autobiography, p. 265)—so, he also wrote for the "dissatisfied."
113 Gerald, Embrace; Waldinger, What Makes; Hood, Difference Between.
114 Aamodt, Why Dieting; Brown, Power; Puddicombe, All It Takes; Steindl-Rast, Want to Be; McGonigal, How to Make.
115 Smith, Why You Will Fail; Brooks, Should You Live.
116 See also my blog entry on "Self-Help in Times of Corona: Vigilance vs. Positive Thinking?" which discusses this self-help approach toward feelings and considers its effects on contemporary responses to the pandemic.
117 For an in-depth critique of this self-help approach, see also Barbara Ehrenreich's *Bright-Sided*, which considers the effects of the survivor idiom on breast cancer patients.

Interestingly, a similar dynamic is observed in the topic of success. By examining the playlists listed under the topic of failure, it becomes paradoxically clear that success remains integral to the discourse on failure. Four out of eight playlists are shared with the success section, including "Work Smarter," "How to Be a Better You," "Graduation… Now What?," and "The Benefits of Failure." Furthermore, the playlist "What Is Success?" appears under the topic of failure but not in the success category. Additionally, playlists such as "How to Overcome Your Fears" and "How to Learn from Mistakes" highlight positive aspects of failure, suggesting an attempt to redefine failure as a pathway to success.

However, it is worth noting that these playlists present a departure from the traditional self-help narrative found in earlier books. They are not solely firsthand accounts from famous, wealthy, or influential individuals who achieved success. Instead, they are framed within a scientific context, treating success and failure as experimental concepts to be examined and explored. This shift in framing introduces a new perspective and challenges the traditional rags-to-riches format often associated with self-help literature.

By focusing on TED talks, there is a shift away from the spiritual or mystical aspects of self-help and a greater emphasis on its scientific and academic dimension. This perspective explores the interconnectedness between self-help, science, politics, and culture, as well as the authority attributed to expert advice. The incorporation of science in TED talks aims to distance the self from its subjective position. Confessions, for instance, extend beyond mere subjectivity and the first-person perspective of an individual "I." Instead, a split occurs, allowing for a dialogue between the subjective "I" and the "I" which perceives itself through the lens of science. In essence, the audience becomes a witness to this moment of dis/identification, where the self transcends itself by means of scientific insights.

This process has various effects worth further exploration, but one immediate impression is a sense of existential being or nakedness. It suggests that the self detaches from societal expectations and constructs, shedding its known attributes and entering the realm of the unknown. On the other hand, the scientific gaze also has a qualitatively different effect. It may prompt the self to approach certain aspects of itself as a detective would, seeking to control and dissect them. The individual is encouraged to follow the guidance of scientific ideals, implicitly present in moments of self-vigilance and introspection. This self-examination takes on a more analytical and calculated nature, driven by the desire to understand and improve oneself through scientific understanding.

The scientific strand of self-help, exemplified by TED talks, has the potential to create scientific ideals regarding what constitutes a good parent or a good employee. These ideals often prescribe specific behaviors and rules to which individuals are expected to learn and adhere. However, the paradox lies in the fact that while self-help is supposed to empower individuals, the relentless pursuit of these scientific ideals can erode their confidence. The individual begins to doubt themselves, not only because they can never fully meet these ideal standards, but also because they continually seek answers solely within the realm of science. This paradoxical situation leads to a diminishing focus on internal introspection. As individuals immerse themselves in the quest for external scientific answers, they gradually lose touch with their inner selves. The TED playlist titled "Who Are You?" delves deeper into this theme of self-vigilance.

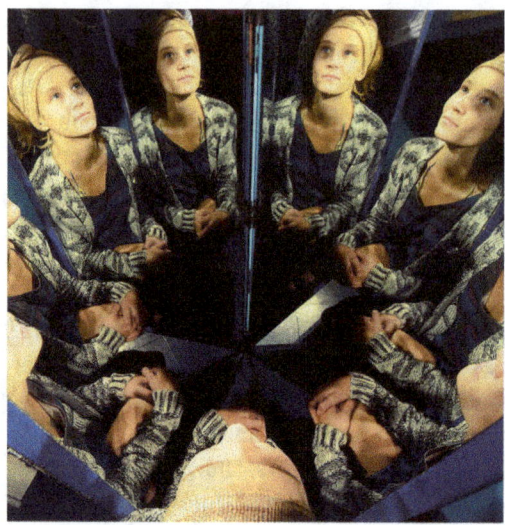

Figure 1: Image for TED's playlist on "Who Are You?" accompanied by the caption: "What makes you, well, you? Get to know yourself a bit better with this collection of thought-provoking talks."

The playlist "Who Are You?" promises to delve into the exploration of self-knowledge and self-understanding by initiating a discussion on the concept of the self. The introductory image accompanying this playlist provides some insights into its underlying assumptions and ideas. It portrays a house of mirrors, where multiple reflections of the same young woman can be seen. This depiction suggests that there is no singular, coherent, and original self. "Knowing thyself" is thus portrayed as a challenging and intricate endeavor, filled with confusion and reminiscent of Sisyphus' eternal struggle. However, the complexity does not stem from the inherent intricacies of the self but rather from its dispersal and fragmentation.

The use of the mirror trope in the image captures a moment of self-observation and visual self-monitoring. However, instead of focusing on the woman's eyes or capturing a moment of introspection, her gaze is directed upward. The framing of self-reflection presents the image as the pursuit of an idealized self. The downward angle of the picture positions the viewer as the embodiment of this ideal, blurring the boundaries between the observer and the observed. Furthermore, the woman's physical attributes, such as fair skin, blonde hair, blue eyes, and youth, already depict an image of a "perfect" self, so she may fail to recognize the ways in which she is already "perfect." The emphasis on the color blue, whether through blue eyes, a blue shirt, or blue frames, may further allude to the transcendental quality of the ordinary self.

Some of these ideas introduced by the image are also echoed by the first speaker in the playlist, reinforcing the thematic threads and perspectives explored in "Who Are You." The first speaker is Julian Baggini, a philosopher and journalist known for his work as the editor of *The Philosophers' Magazine* and author of *The Ego Trick*. In his talk titled "Is There a Real You?" he delves into his concept of "the ego trick"[118] by drawing insights from neuroscience, the Buddhist tradition, and literary analogies. Baggini initiates his talk by questioning the commonly held belief in the existence of a core or essence, a permanent and unchanging self. He suggests that horoscopes and personality types contribute to perpetuating this notion, but he contends that it is a culturally constructed idea that should be challenged.

Baggini aims to encourage a paradigm shift in how we perceive the self. Rather than viewing it as a static entity or a fixed being, he proposes conceiving of the self as a "collection" of all experiences. He emphasizes the notion that "You are a sum of your parts,"[119] echoing the idea of multiple selves depicted in the image associated with the playlist.[120] Baggini employs the analogy of water to support his argument, suggesting that water is essentially composed of hydrogen and oxygen molecules. However, these analogies inadvertently contribute to a sense of division, creating a perceived distance between the self and the body, fostering a process of disidentification. By emphasizing the self as a collection of parts, there is a potential reinforcement of a dichotomous perspective that separates the body from the mind.

---

118 Baggini, Is There, 00:07:25.
119 Ibid., 00:04:06.
120 According to Baggini, the view of the self as a "collection" (00:04:18) has a long lineage: such as Buddhism or the 17th and 18th century philosophy of Locke and Hume. Moreover, he believes this view is reinforced by neuroscience, since scientists such as Paul Broks show that there "is no center in the brain" (00:06:52), no control spot. The way different neural processes relate create the sense of the self, which is what he calls the "ego trick" (00:07:25). However, he tries to distance his view from psychologists Thomas Metzinger, Bruce Hood or Susan Blackmore who claim that the self is an illusion.

In his talk, Baggini explores the significance of physical parts and their relevance in different scenarios. He poses the question of whether a heart transplant or a memory transplant would have a greater impact on one's sense of self. By prioritizing the role of memory over physical organs, he implies that the self is a fragmented entity, capable of being dismantled and reassembled like a puzzle. This portrayal evokes a somewhat Frankenstein-like perspective, suggesting that the self can be reconstructed or manipulated in various ways.

Baggini employs the metaphor of a watch to illustrate his perspective on self-formation, which recalls the analogy of God as a designer. While the watch itself is a mechanical device, its usage in this context adds a mystical dimension. It signifies more than just the passage of time; it implies the existence of a higher order, a design or purpose behind the self. Furthermore, Baggini introduces the metaphor of a waterfall[121] to emphasize the dynamic and ever-changing nature of the self. This depiction highlights that the self is not illusory but rather a fluid process, characterized by its history and structure. This understanding of the self is empowering, as it suggests that individuals have the capacity to influence the direction of their own development.[122] Baggini concludes his talk by quoting Buddha, who stated that "wise people fashion themselves,"[123] emphasizing the transformative potential that lies within individuals to shape their own selves.

Baggini's exploration of identity incorporates the concept of the cyborg, which serves as a representation of a cultural conflict within modern society. This conflict arises from the dichotomy between the rapid advancement of technology and the desire to establish individuals as self-reliant and autonomous beings.[124] The metaphor of the watch aligns with the notion of the "clockwork," symbolizing the ongoing integration of technology into the modern world.[125] On the other hand, the metaphor of the waterfall represents an "organic model" that has never been completely replaced by the symbolism of machines.[126]

These metaphors also find resonance among proponents of human enhancement, who perceive the human self as editable and customizable, akin to the con-

---

121 Finally, the trope of the waterfall also invokes a sense of the sublime and natural power of individuality. Its magnificent beauty captures not only a natural process, but an extraordinary and glorious display or show. It may seem paradoxical to think that one can "channel the direction" (00:10:00) of this flow of water; after all, a waterfall connotes a sense of overflowing and flooding, rather than control.
122 Ibid., 00:09:58.
123 Ibid., 00:11:20.
124 Benesch, *Romantic Cyborgs*, p. 33f.
125 Ibid., 42.
126 Ibid.

cept of the Vitruvian man.¹²⁷ This perspective tends to devalue the "corporeal grounding of human existence" by transforming it into a manipulable or even destructible technological counterpart.¹²⁸ This inclination is reflected in the symbolic representation of the cyborg. Overall, these metaphors and symbolic concepts shed light on the tensions between technology and individual autonomy, as well as the potential consequences and implications of embracing a cyborg-like understanding of the self.

Transhumanists have found a platform in TED talks to promote their philosophy and advocate a future focused on human enhancement.¹²⁹ This group has actively utilized TED talks to spread their ideas and engage in discussions surrounding the ethical implications of human enhancement. The bioethical debates regarding human enhancement primarily involve two opposing perspectives: transhumanists, who argue that enhancement is a moral imperative,¹³⁰ and bioconservatives, who emphasize the unethical nature of enhancement and its potential connections to eugenics.¹³¹

However, these debates often revolve around arguments concerning the desirability of biomedical or technological advancements, without fully considering the interplay between science and culture or the influence of self-help culture on shaping this scientific ideal. TED talks provide a prominent platform that showcases the intersection of science and self-help culture. Through these talks, the convergence of scientific advancements and the aspirations of self-improvement and personal growth within popular culture becomes visible. TED talks offer a unique space for exploring and discussing the multifaceted relationship between science, self-help culture, and the societal implications of human enhancement.

Neuroscientist Jill Bolte Taylor's TED talk, titled "My Stroke of Insight," serves as an illustrative example. This talk holds a prominent place among the most popular science talks and is also featured in "The Most Popular Talks of all Time" play-

---

127 See, for instance, Juan Enriquez' TED talk on "What Will Humans Look Like in 100 Years?" and my analysis of it in "Genetic Enhancement" (2021).
128 Benesch, *Romantic Cyborgs*, p. 33; emphasis added. For a different discussion of the cyborg, check Donna Haraway's Manifesto.
129 Natasha Vita-More and Nick Bostrom are two famous transhumanists who have given TED talks. But other proponents of human enhancement have also gained popularity on this platform. Among the eleven must-see TED talks, the bionic man Hugh Herr features prominently. Juan Enriquez is another famous TED presenter who endorses a belief in a new, better human species. For a more in-depth analysis that considers their TED talks, see also my book chapter on "Vigilance to Wonder: Human Enhancement in TED Talks" (2021).
130 Bostrom, Transhumanist Values; Persson/Savulescu, *Unfit for the Future*.
131 Fukuyama, *Our Posthuman Future*; Sandel, *Case against Perfection.*

list.¹³² In her presentation, Taylor shares personal confessions as a neuroscientist who experiences a stroke, engaging in an act of self-vigilance that is mediated by science. She examines herself through the lens of scientific understanding, observing her own brain from the inside out. Through her talk, Taylor not only imparts knowledge but also shares a deeply emotional personal narrative.

Taylor's performance is notable for several reasons. She brings a replica of a brain on stage, physically showcasing it to the audience. This act symbolizes the ease with which an object can be manipulated, held in one's hands, and examined from various perspectives. Her discourse draws upon metaphors from information sciences to explain the workings of the brain, highlighting how the two hemispheres function as parallel processors similar to computers. She juxtaposes the question "Who are we?" with the vivid imagery of the brain, suggesting that identity resides within the brain and that consciousness is intricately tied to the concept of the self.¹³³

In her talk, Taylor not only delves into the shattering of the self and the fluid boundaries experienced during her stroke but also touches upon profound spiritual aspects. Her narrative resonates with themes of recovery and enlightenment, reminiscent of Dan McAdams' redemptive script. Despite incorporating scientific jargon and emphasizing her credentials as an intellectual and neuroanatomist,¹³⁴ Taylor also invokes a sense of wonder in her description of the stroke. She expresses a deep connection to the universe, referring to herself as the "life-force power" that permeates her form, consisting of the intricate genius of 50 trillion molecular entities.¹³⁵ Through her words, Taylor evokes the mathematical sublime and invites awe and astonishment among her audience at the vastness and complexity of existence.

When viewed in its entirety, Taylor's talk presents a humanist narrative that emphasizes the "power to choose" and the triumph of the rational mind over the brain hemorrhage she experienced. The didactic tone and preaching style, as well as the focus on the interiority of the self and its capacity for mental prowess, align with TED's emphasis on individualism. However, a closer examination of the talk's content, rather than just its interpretation, has the potential to challenge this narrative. Taylor's insight was made possible by the loss of the brain region responsible for the sense of "I am,"¹³⁶ resulting in a story of dis-identification as

---

132 She also has an entire playlist dedicated to her: "Jill Bolte Taylor: Ten Talks on Human Nature."
133 Taylor, My Stroke of Insight, 00:16:35.
134 Ibid., 00:17:23.
135 Ibid., 00:16:58.
136 Ibid., 00:05:58.

she "witnesses" herself "having this experience."[137] Her understanding extends beyond visual perception to encompass all senses, with information exploding into a rich collage of the present moment's sights, smells, tastes, textures, and sounds.[138] This broader perspective challenges the notion that the rational mind alone holds the key to insight and highlights the multifaceted nature of human experience.

The "pounding pain"[139] behind Taylor's left eye serves as both a representation of the internal bleeding she experienced and a metaphorical wound to her vision, which manifests itself further as a headache. Whenever she closes her eyes on stage, it can be seen as a challenge to the predominance of vision, potentially signifying a shift in her way of seeing by directing her focus inward. However, Taylor's interpretation of her experience leans toward a mystical perspective, emphasizing the attainment of nirvana, peacefulness, euphoria, or a beautiful state akin to La La Land. By prioritizing this mystical reading, she overlooks the critical implications of her loss of self, which could be seen through a posthumanist lens. Furthermore, her interpretation reinforces a dichotomy where reason, clarity, and the mind's eye are portrayed as the heroes of the story, overshadowing the vulnerabilities of the body that were overcome.

Taylor's optimistic vision of a future peaceful planet, where individuals choose to activate the inner peace circuitry of their right hemispheres, reflects a utopian perspective.[140] By sharing her personal experience and insights, Taylor aims to foster a sense of community and unity among her audience. This aligns with Giuseppina Scotto di Carlo's observation that TED talks eliminate the traditional "scientist-mediator-audience" triangulation and instead create a shared "knowledge-spreading experience."[141] In this context, TED talks blur the boundaries between the speaker and the audience, emphasizing a collective project that invites active participation and encourages specific attitudes and behaviors for creating tangible changes. The use of confessions in this context aims to promote a sense of inclusiveness and shared responsibility: "'I' and 'you' become 'we', in a common project which invites the audience to take on specific attitudes and behaviours and concretely participate in changes."[142]

The notion of human enhancement, often presented as a potential solution for the survival of the human species, is a recurring theme in science communication within the context of self-help. It represents an extension of the idea of improving

---

[137] Ibid., 00:07:17.
[138] Ibid., 00:04:00.
[139] Ibid., 00:06:20.
[140] Ibid., 00:17:47.
[141] Scotto di Carlo, Patterns of Clusivity, p. 119.
[142] Ibid.; emphasis added.

oneself through scientific or technological means. While it is presented as a scientific solution, it also carries cultural implications, as it reflects a celebration of the power of the human mind. The self-help book *Everything is F*cked: A Book About Hope* by Mark Manson challenges notions of self-control but ultimately presents a similar utopian vision by imagining a future where human enhancement is possible. This illustrates how scientific advancements are reimagined as tools for improving the human self, such as through gene editing.[143] In this context, the future of humanity and the quest for survival are closely intertwined with the pursuit of self-improvement and the belief in the potential of science to enhance human capabilities. It highlights the cultural and social dimensions that underlie discussions of human enhancement, extending beyond the realm of pure scientific inquiry.

In an age dominated by self-help and scientific knowledge production, the role of reading becomes significant. This study seeks to explore the intersection of reading and self-help within a context that promotes the idea of human enhancement, aiming to make individuals "stronger, faster, bolder, and better than ever."[144] Contemporary speculative novels play a crucial role in this discourse, as they not only offer critical commentary on the theme of human enhancement but also propose alternative perspectives on the role of literature in shaping the present and future self. These novels provide insights into the societal implications and consequences of pursuing a path of human enhancement. By examining these dystopian narratives, this study aims to shed light on the complex relationship between reading, self-help culture, scientific progress, and the quest for human improvement. It invites exploration of how literature can offer new understandings and possibilities in the face of these cultural and technological developments.

---

143 The groundbreaking scientific achievement of 2015 was the development of the CRISPR genome editing technique (Travis, Making the Cut, p. 1456 f). This technique holds immense potential for future genetic advancements in what has been dubbed the "century of the gene" (Herbrechter, *Posthumanism*, p. 35). Genetic engineering views DNA as the "code for life" (Perkel, Power and Possibilities, p. 4), shifting the focus away from materiality and highlighting the significance of code and information. The metaphor of code reinforces the notion that humans can be seen as quantifiable machines capable of progressing toward an "ideal" or "more perfect" state (Kozubek, How Gene Editing). For further insights on the topic of genetic enhancement, please refer to my paper titled "Genetic Enhancement."
144 Epstein, Are Athletes Really Getting Faster, 00:14:04.

4 Confessions and Reading: From Self-Writing to Life Writing

> Humanism was a machine for making animals variously able to read and write, and who then found themselves differentiated by whether or not they thought reading and writing important.[1]

The ongoing "crisis of the humanities" is fueled by the influence of "neoliberal expectancies and funding cuts," forcing those engaged with literary studies to once again question, validate, and reevaluate the purpose of literature beyond mere "aesthetic gratification," and to focus on what "literary criticism can contribute to current socio-political discourses."[2] Given that the university remains a central institution for "knowledge production," the increasing dependence of knowledge, or what is deemed as knowledge, upon "economic utility" and monetary value[3] implies that the humanities must justify their value in similar terms—by emphasizing literature as a valuable source of knowledge. In her work, Monja Mohr focuses on speculative literature as a fertile ground for exploring how literature provides access to "*imaginary* other cultures, historical times, classes, genders, religions, and different attitudes."[4] Fiction enables us to delve into alternative worlds, whether they be in the future, past, or even alien realms.

This chapter delves into similar questions, exploring the functions of literature and its significance, particularly through the lens of speculative literature. However, a distinct approach is adopted: instead of reiterating a humanist perspective that portrays literature solely as the pinnacle of human imagination and education, this chapter aims to underscore the relevance of literature extending beyond human concerns.

4.1 From "Critical Vigilance" to "Critical Solace"

Literature conveys the impression that it encompasses virtually every scientific subject: "there is certainly not a single scientific matter which has not at some moment been treated by universal literature: the world of the work is a total world, in

---

1 Yates, Improbable Shepherds, p. 412.
2 Cf. Mohr, When Species Meet, p. 42.
3 Cf. Kloeckner et al., *Knowledge Landscapes*, p. 11.
4 Mohr, When Species Meet, p. 42f.

which all (social, psychological, historical) knowledge takes place."[5] Therefore, literature seems to provide a panoramic perspective, a "view from everywhere." Antje Kley further argues that literature complements the scientific "view from nowhere" by offering the "view from somewhere," which includes practices of questioning, contextualizing, and a general sensitivity to text and discourse.[6] In other words, literary texts not only refer to the external world but also possess a self-referential quality that allows for critical engagement. Rita Felski also regards literary texts as sources of "epistemic insight,"[7] as they recreate the world rather than simply copying it.

In her book *Uses of Literature* (2008), Felski identifies knowledge as a motivation for reading. She critiques the mirror and window metaphors frequently used by scholars to describe the text, as they presume transparency and prioritize an "eye-centered epistemology."[8] Despite the diminishing influence of the claim to transparency, the dominance of the eye-centered epistemology and visual analogies still pervades literary understandings.[9] Even Felski's chapter on "Knowledge" occasionally falls into the same rhetoric as she draws on Paul Ricoeur's concept of "mimesis as metaphor" to reconceptualize literature: no longer as a mere "reflection" but as a "redescription" of the world, where texts become sources of epistemic *insight*.[10] Literature accomplishes this redescription through deep intersubjectivity, which refers to "the intricate *maze of perceptions*, the changing patterns of opacities and transparencies, through which persons perceive and are perceived by others."[11]

Visual metaphors continue to dominate the understanding of reading and its knowledge production within the realm of literary criticism.[12] Emerging approaches such as digital humanities and practices like "distant reading"[13] further

---

5 Barthes, *Rustle of Language*, p. 3.
6 Kley, Literary Knowledge, p. 172.
7 Felski, *Uses of Literature*, p. 84.
8 Ibid., p. 78.
9 Even the other metaphors mentioned by Felski emphasize the significance of vision. Whether the x-ray, cartographic metaphors, the lamp, the metaphor of the symptom, or literature as negative knowledge with its *mise-en-abyme* quality, all these metaphors highlight the centrality of sight and observation.
10 Ibid., p. 84. "Mimesis, then, is an act of creative imitation, not mindless copying, a strenuous shaping, distilling, and reorganizing of texts and experiences" (ibid., p. 85).
11 Ibid., p. 91.
12 However, at the same time, Felski's treatment of ventriloquism also challenges an ocularcentric perspective, since it focuses on "verbal imitation, linguistic echoes, and a panoply of oral and auditory associations" (*Uses of Literature*, p. 94).
13 Moretti, *Distant Reading*.

reinforce this visual focus. Alison Booth, in her essay, demonstrates how digital projects enable the accessibility of data and the *visualization* of trends, patterns, and social networks. She states, "Our graphs visualize networks of collocation and separation of proper names. A parallel-coordinates visualization of cousins displays the somewhat distant relation of Mitfort to Sarah."[14] Franco Moretti, in his approach, draws an analogy between reading a text and observing a painting, emphasizing his focus on "design and layout" rather than "brushstrokes and cathedrals."[15]

Data mining and word clouds have been criticized for potentially encouraging students to bypass the immersive experience of engaging with literary or historical texts.[16] However, they are presented as valuable *"ways of viewing* the cultural record that are as useful as seeing the earth from space when the planet is replaced by a digitally remediated file of features."[17] These computer-assisted readings are often associated with the objectivity of scientific methods, with the notion of distance implying a sense of detachment. The emphasis on graphs, maps, and trees in these approaches can give the impression of a scientific lens applied to literature. Nevertheless, this perspective tends to overlook the sensory dimension of reading, which encompasses more than just cognitive processes, and encompasses affective elements as well.

The "affective turn" within the humanities and social sciences has sparked extensive research on the concept of affect and its political and social implications.[18] However, this study specifically aims to explore the affective dimension of reading, which has been a focal point in recent contemporary discussions on reading and its various emotional moods. Drawing on Linda M.G. Zerilli's perspective, it posits that affect and cognition are not separate systems but intricately intertwined.[19]

---

14 Booth, Mid-Range Reading, p. 623f.; emphasis added.
15 Moretti, Response, p. 686.
16 Drucker, Why Distant Reading Isn't, p. 630.
17 Ibid.; emphasis added.
18 Scholars have delved into various aspects of emotions and their influence, exploring topics such as the politics of fear, hate, or anger (Ahmed, *Cultural Politics*), the pursuit of happiness (Ahmed, *Promise*), the role of melodramatic discourse (Anker, *Orgies of Feeling*), the dynamics of romantic love (Illouz, Romantic Love), and the complexities of ugly feelings (Ngai, *Ugly Feelings*). In their investigations, these scholars aim to reveal the intricate connections between affect and cognition, as well as the significant intersection of affect and politics.
19 Zerilli, Turn to Affect, p. 282. Ruth Leys identifies two distinct vectors within the affective turn: the first is influenced by "Tomkin's psychobiology of affects and bodily drives," while the second follows the "Spinoza/Deleuze/Massumi vector" (La Caze/Lloyd, Philosophy, p. 3). Initially, these two vectors may appear incompatible, as the Deleuze-inspired definition of affect as a nonlinguistic, bodily "intensity" eludes the categories of psychologists (Leys, Turn to Affect, p. 442). However,

Consequently, it suggests a reevaluation of understanding "knowing how" as a mode of knowledge, while also recognizing "knowing that" as an active practice.[20] This leads us to question: What is the prevailing affect within literary studies? It seems that autobiography often elicits a broad sense of suspicion in literary studies,[21] a sentiment that postcritique identifies as prevalent in the field as a whole.

Rita Felski asserts that literary scholars often feel compelled to maintain "analytical detachment," exercise "critical vigilance," and approach texts with "guarded suspicion."[22] This perspective aligns with what Paul Ricoeur calls a hermeneutics of suspicion, characterized by a "paranoid style of critical engagement" that calls for "constant vigilance" and is imbued with negative emotions.[23] Felski expands on this attitude of vigilance in her work *The Limits of Critique*, suggesting that it can limit our ability to fully appreciate the depth and richness of our "aesthetic attachments."[24] Toril Moi agrees, arguing that the "suspicious reader" must constantly maintain self-awareness, be on guard, and exhibit anxiety about being deceived by the text, which can hinder genuine engagement.[25] Instead, Moi, along with scholars embracing the "postcritical turn" in literature, challenges the notion that suspicion is a prerequisite for critical readings. She also sympathizes with Simone de Beauvoir's appreciation for the immersive and absorbed experience of reading.[26]

Scholars advocating for the postcritical turn[27] highlight the loss of excitement, amazement, and passion in critical readings. They argue that critical distance,

---

what unites the new affect theorists and neuroscientists fundamentally is their "shared anti-intentionalism," as they both separate affect from cognition and intention (ibid., p. 443). Linda Zerilli also criticizes this notion of a "layer-cake ontology" (ibid., p. 269) or the belief that affect and cognition are completely distinct systems. She questions whether this perspective relies on a false understanding of the mind-body relationship, one that is "parasitic" on the very dualistic account it seeks to undermine (ibid., p. 281). Consequently, she advocates a more nuanced epistemological stance that avoids drawing stark divisions between cognition and affect, proposing a "feminist ordinary language critique of intellectualism" (ibid., p. 262). Eve Kosofsky Sedgwick, Lauren Berlant, and Sara Ahmed also emphasize the interconnection of thinking and feeling, emotion and judgment, further supporting the entanglement of these aspects.

20 Zerilli, Turn to Affect, p. 282.
21 The "response to autobiography is, in a very broad sense of the term, suspicion" (Abbott, Autobiography, p. 601; emphasis added).
22 Felski, *Uses of Literature*, p. 2. She adds: "Problematizing, interrogating and subverting are the default options."
23 Ibid., p. 3; emphasis added.
24 Felski, *Limits of Critique*, p. 17.
25 Moi, *Revolution of the Ordinary*, p. 220; emphasis added.
26 Ibid., p. 214.
27 Anker/Felski, *Critique and Postcritique*, p. 18.

aimed at removing affective responses from reading, creates a neutral ground that fails to acknowledge the emotional aspects of the reading experience. Postcritique encourages a reconsideration of the emotional "attunements" and "attachments" we develop with texts.[28] Susan Friedman, for example, reflects on Biddy Martin's observations of scientists and their genuine enthusiasm and pleasure in new discoveries: "She was amazed to witness their excitement and pleasure in new discoveries, even at times their *sense of wonder* at the mysteries of life. How, she asked herself, had so many in the humanities lost that enjoyment in discovery?"[29]

Postcritics argue that acknowledging our own affective attachments as readers does not blind us to critical analysis. Felski counters the notion that affective responses are inherently unworthy, "escapist, apolitical, symptoms of bourgeois aestheticism, capitalist manipulation."[30] Her "manifesto for positive aesthetics"[31] calls for a reevaluation of the role of recognition and enchantment in reading, resembling debates in positive psychology that challenge Freudian psychoanalysis, which predominantly focused on negative aspects and the treatment of pathology. However, in *The Limits of Critique*, Felski advocates embracing a range of moods in criticism, not solely focusing on the positive.[32] She suggests expanding our repertoire of critical moods. In this regard, Sianne Ngai exemplifies this approach by examining the aesthetics of "ugly feelings"[33] as well as exploring other affective experiences such as the trivial, the zany, the interesting, and the cute.

Felski presents a perspective that emphasizes a unique intimacy with texts, acknowledging their status as "coactors"[34] rather than treating them as friends or lovers. This perspective recognizes the act of reading as a staged, intimate encounter, resembling a confession. The emphasis on empathy as a significant outcome of reading further reinforces the idea of reading as a confessional space that occurs between texts, authors, and readers.[35] Toril Moi also suggests that reading is a practice of acknowledgment that demands attentive engagement.[36]

---

28 Felski, Response, p. 384, 387.
29 Friedman, Both/And, p. 346; emphasis added.
30 Giusti, Passionate Affinities.
31 Butter, Manifesto for Positive Aesthetics.
32 Felski, *Limits of Critique*, p. 12f. "Some scholars are urging that we make more room for hope, optimism, and positive affect in intellectual life. While I have a qualified sympathy for such arguments, what follows is not a pep talk for the power of positive thinking."
33 Ngai, *Ugly Feelings*. They include animatedness, envy, irritation, anxiety, stuplimity (a paradoxical synthesis of shock and boredom), paranoia, and disgust. These are non-cathartic feelings that emerge in situations where action is suspended, which is why Ngai calls them Bartlebyan.
34 Felski, *Limits of Critique*, p. 12.
35 According to Patrick Hogan, "perhaps the key aspect of readers' affective response is empathy" (Affect Studies, p. 18). Suzanne Keen also addresses narrative empathy in her book (2007). A few

However, this sole focus on "classical humanist values" raises concerns about perpetuating the anthropocentric nature of the humanities.[37] Moi argues that literature facilitates the bridging of gaps between individuals, allowing readers to see through the eyes of others without losing their own identity: "immersed in your text, I can see what you see, but without losing myself, without becoming you."[38] On the other hand, drawing on the ideas of Rosi Braidotti, there is a call for a "posthuman turn" in the humanities to move away from this form of epistemic violence that solely centers on the human experience.[39] In this context, a posthuman turn would encourage a broader perspective that includes nonhuman entities and challenges the exclusive focus on the human. It seeks to dismantle the hierarchical view that places humans at the center and instead embraces a more inclusive and interconnected understanding of knowledge and existence.

The justification of reading often tends to prioritize the role of the reader while neglecting the agency of the text itself. The prevalent view of literature often focuses on writing as a form of self-expression or self-writing. Michel Foucault observed how writing became a "technology of the self" and a means of cultivating self-awareness. The act of taking care of oneself became intertwined with the practice of writing, where the self becomes the subject or object of the writing activity. This tradition predates modernity and can be traced back to ancient Western traditions, as evident in The Confessions of Saint Augustine.[40]

In *The Pathos of Authenticity*, the editors discuss the "theory of sublimation," which suggests that all art, including literature, is to some extent autobiographical. This psychological perspective emphasizes authenticity as "a matter of honesty or emotional intensity."[41] John Dewey further emphasized how artists feel compelled

---

other critics that work with the concept of empathy are Martha Nussbaum and Iris Murdoch, who prefers the term compassion; see also Moi, *Revolution of the Ordinary*, p. 220.

36 Acknowledgment "is not a state of mind, or a particular mental content, but a response, something we do" (Moi, *Revolution of the Ordinary*, p. 207).
37 Braidotti, Posthuman Critical Theory, p. 22.
38 Moi, *Revolution of the Ordinary*, p. 220.
39 "We become painfully aware of being human – in a post-anthropocentric sense – just as the notion of humanity enters into another state of crisis. What the posthuman turn does for critical thought is to manifest a fundamental fracture at the heart of our thinking processes of self-representation" (Braidotti, Posthuman Critical Theory, p. 28).
40 Foucault, Technologies of the Self, p. 27. Foucault adds: "The new concern with self involved a new experience of self. The new form of the experience of the self is to be seen in the first and second century when introspection becomes more and more detailed. A relation developed between *writing and vigilance*. Attention was paid to nuances of life, mood, and reading, and the experience of oneself was intensified and widened by virtue of this act of writing. A whole field of experience opened which earlier was absent" (ibid., p. 28; emphasis added).
41 Haselstein et al, Introduction, p. 28.

to engage in their work as a means of "self-expression."[42] In this context, Felski proposes a similar position for literary critics, inviting them to be honest and authentic about their reading experiences rather than striving for a misplaced sense of neutrality.

The ongoing debates surrounding the role of reading and writing often maintain a humanist perspective in their arguments. Throughout history, literacy has been celebrated as a significant achievement of humanity. The human element remains central in these discussions, and books and texts are often seen as tools that satisfy various human needs.[43] Readings can fulfill our safety needs by providing solace and creating a refuge or a sense of comfort. They can address our social needs by evoking feelings of belonging, empathy, or self-confidence.[44] Aesthetic needs are met when texts exhibit a unique linguistic style or possess qualities of *literariness*. Cognitive needs are stimulated when texts provoke curiosity, build suspense, and lead to moments of discovery. Furthermore, readings can contribute to our self-actualization needs by inspiring us to reach our full potential or facilitating processes of self-formation and self-understanding.[45] Each of these approaches has its merits and contributes to our understanding and experience of literature. However, there is also a sense that something is missing, that none of these perspectives provide a comprehensive answer. While they capture important aspects of the reading experience, they may not fully encompass the breadth and depth of the transformative power of literature.

This book argues that the so-called crisis in the humanities may be perpetuated by the continued focus on human-centered perspectives. It contends that the power of reading extends beyond the impact on readers themselves and instead lies in the blurring of boundaries between the human and the nonhuman. The immersive experience of reading, as described by Felski, involves a "pleasurable self-forgetting" where the distinction between the text and the self becomes indistinct.[46] In this state, our "sense of autonomy and self-control" erodes, and we become absorbed in an unchanging present.[47]

This immersive aspect of reading, often referred to as enchantment, has faced criticism in critical theory due to its perceived lack of reason and vigilance.[48] How-

---

[42] Dewey, *Art as Experience*, p. 9.
[43] Self-help culture approaches reading similarly because it relies on Maslow's theory of motivation, which is the case here as well.
[44] See also Laura Bieger's *Belonging and Narrative* (2018).
[45] See for instance Felski's discussion of recognition.
[46] Butter, Manifesto for Postive Aesthetics.
[47] Ibid.
[48] Ibid.

ever, this blurring of boundaries between reader and text can be seen as a potential pathway to a critical posthumanist understanding of literature. This book seeks to redefine the concept of literary absorption by exploring the role of literary synesthesia in achieving this effect. Rather than inhibiting reader vigilance, this form of textual engagement may foster a different form of vigilance that is less centered on the human and the visual. It is not impersonal or objective, nor is it devoid of affect. It represents a shift away from traditional human-centric and ocularcentric perspectives while still acknowledging the importance of personal engagement and emotional resonance in the reading experience.

To summarize, scholars are beginning to explore alternatives to traditional critical readings, as they find that critique has become stagnant.[49] These debates on reading often center on metaphors of excavation and propose new modes of engagement that go beyond suspicion and hermeneutics, aiming to decouple reading from interpretation[50] and to challenge a humanist approach to literature. Some scholars, like Heather Love, align with Moretti's rejection of the "messy intimacies of traditional forms of humanistic inquiry,"[51] which includes moving away from the richness of texts and practices of close reading. Love advocates a "descriptive turn" that promises "objective accounts of social life," exemplified in her analysis of Toni Morrison's *Beloved*.[52] A "flat reading" of the novel, focusing on documentation and description rather than empathy and witness, suggests the possibility of an "alternative ethics."[53]

> It is this hermeneutics of recognition and empathy – originally sacred and now grounded in an unacknowledged but powerful humanism – that defines literary studies, even in an age of suspicion. In the academic division of labor, literary critics still tend to that part of the world that has been "kept safe from sociology." A turn from interpretation to description might be one way to give up that ghost. But who among us is willing to exchange the fat and the living for the thin and the dead?[54]

However, Love's critique of the powerful humanism still present in literary studies can be seen as incomplete and misplaced. While she appreciates Goffman's thin

---

[49] See also Bruno Latour's "Why Has Critique Run out of Steam?" Scholars have proposed various alternatives to these approaches, including "surface reading" (Best/Marcus), "thin description" (Love), and reparative reading (Sedgwick), among others.
[50] See for instance Matthew Garrett's "you have to read first" or Heather Love's "thin description."
[51] Love, Close but not Deep, p. 374.
[52] Ibid., p. 375.
[53] Ibid.
[54] Ibid., p. 388.

descriptions of "eye behavior," she neglects the significance of interiority, sensation, and affect in her analysis.[55] She fails to acknowledge that the focus on vision, points of view, and acts of zooming in and out are also humanist endeavors that seemingly promise scientific objectivity.[56] Her endorsement of description as a means of achieving objectivity echoes the tenets of literary naturalism but disregards the potential affective charge within Goffman's descriptions.

David James also challenges the prevalent "antipathy towards description" in 20th century criticism and argues against its relegation as a mere "filler" or inferior to narration.[57] He believes that contemporary descriptions in literature exhibit vivacity and possess a consoling power, which he refers to as "critical solace." James emphasizes that description is not meant to heal or provide comfort in a traditional sense but rather acknowledges its intimate connection with loss and grief.[58] In other words, critical solace "does not maintain a cheerful perspective, but it makes grief more prominent, too."[59] By drawing attention to its own "aliveness" and "insurgent tendency to kick against plot,"[60] description has the potential to disrupt the reading process, making the reader more vigilant rather than passive. James illustrates this insurgent tendency in Cormac McCarthy's *The Road*, where the sonorous depiction of the desolate seascape "counterpoints the very desolation" it portrays.[61] In this context, a postcritical reading approach, as advocated by Felski, would be instrumental in identifying the tensions and complexities embedded within literary descriptions.

---

55 Ibid., p. 380. She adds: "Even when he zooms in to address individual agency or zooms out to account for social structure, his account is wholly constituted by minute descriptions of visible, physical acts; no atmosphere of experience or feeling can emerge."
56 Or, as Winfried Fluck writes: "Ideology is thus most successful when it manages to create the illusion of a coherent and internally consistent representation of reality. The literary form that is most effective in achieving this reality effect is realism [...] [and] the form that was formerly considered the potentially most critical of ideology – namely realism – is now the potentially most ideological of all" (Surface Readings, p. 50).
57 James, Critical Solace, p. 485. Here he echoes Love's claim that "[d]escription has had a mostly poor reputation in literary studies, where it has been seen as inferior to narration" (Close but not Deep, p. 381).
58 James, Critical Solace, p. 484. Critical solace "denotes a species of consolation forever aware of its *own intimacy with loss.*"
59 By focusing on temporary memorials, Erika Doss shows a heightened public interest in multiple matters of death and dying. She underscores grief's affective potential, like, for instance, its ability to mobilize public feelings to orchestrate positive change. See "Public Feeling, Public Healing," p. 53.
60 James, Critical Solace, p. 483.
61 Ibid., p. 482.

This book goes beyond previous discussions and proposes description as a potential medium for a text's critical posthumanist aesthetics. Description can be seen as granting agency to the nonhuman elements by providing them with visibility within the text.[62] However, rather than advocating for literary naturalism, this thesis suggests that even in scenes focused on the interiority of characters, description can have a similar effect. Paradoxically, the elements that Love considers too humanistic, such as interiority, sensation, and affect, can emerge strongly in descriptive scenes and facilitate a critical posthumanist perspective. The book focuses on literary synesthesia as an illustrative example, showcasing how this technique can destabilize the ocularcentrism present in traditional epistemic models. Additionally, synesthesia offers a new approach to reading practices by generating a form of absorption that does not compromise vigilance. This book's central argument is that the key issue in debates on reading is not whether critics perceive texts as thick or thin, surface-oriented or deep, but rather the reinforcement of a single model of knowledge formation based solely on vision.

4.2 Literary Synesthesia and the Affect of Aliveness

Since the 1980s, there has been a prevailing sense of "insecurity" regarding the perceived ability of science fiction to serve as "a tool of cognition and imagining."[63] It seems as though the visionary power and spectacular anticipations often associated with science fiction have failed to materialize. John Clute expresses this sentiment, noting that "sf writers had a great deal of catching up to do in order to describe a world which (shamingly) already existed."[64] This perspective on science fiction maintains a humanist view that celebrates the power of imagination, future progress, and the sense of wonder. The connections between science and vision can also be traced back to 19th century literature. Writers like Edgar Allan Poe, Nathaniel Hawthorne, and Charlotte Perkins Gilman played with the power and limitations of vision, simultaneously reinforcing the significance of insight and imagina-

---

[62] Maybe it could even provide a pathway to explore the concept of "alien phenomenology" (Bogost), which merits further investigation. A compelling example can be found in Virginia Woolf's "The Mark on the Wall," where the description of a tree allows the reader to seemingly access its nonhuman perspective and emotions, transcending mere anthropomorphism. This aspect will be explored in greater detail in my postdoc research.
[63] Cf. Clute, Science Fiction, p. 67.
[64] Ibid., p. 68.

tion.[65] These authors acknowledge the "gap between the subject's mind and the object's corporeal reality,"[66] highlighting the unreliability of the senses, as seen in Hawthorne's portrayal of elusive odors in "Rappaccini's Daughter" or Poe's depiction of the haunting sound of a beating heart in "The Tell-Tale Heart."[67]

John Dewey put forth the argument that for many individuals, there exists an "aura" of both awe and unreality surrounding the "spiritual" and the "ideal," while "matter" has been subjected to depreciation, seen as something to be explained away or justified.[68] Michel Foucault also delved into the "twofold evolution" that led to the stigmatization of the flesh as the "root of all evil."[69] However, contemporary dystopias challenge the conventional approach to the senses and redirect the focus toward the material and sensory aspects of reading and writing. In other words, they disrupt readers' expectations of viewing science (fiction) as the product of intellectual power and vision alone. These dystopias go beyond depicting the uncanny, the unknown, or the unfamiliar; they also shine a spotlight on what is already too familiar, but rendered invisible as a result.

Farah Mendlesohn highlights the tendency to criticize science fiction for its perceived deficiency in characterization and emotion.[70] It is often seen as prioritiz-

---

65 In "The Man of the Crowd," the narrator's vision is constantly mediated: by the "smoky panes" of the window, the fog, or the "rays of gas-lamps" that produce "wild effects" (Poe, Man, p. 1564). Poe's detective Dupin also emphasizes the significance of vision, proximity, and the directness or indirectness of vision: "He impaired his vision by holding the object too close [...] To look at a star by glances – to view it in a side-long way, by turning toward it the exterior portions of the retina (more susceptible of feeble impressions of light than the interior), is to behold the star distinctly" (Poe, Murders, p. 326). In "The Yellow Wallpaper," the paper "changes as the light changes" (Gilman, Yellow, p. 834), and the night creates a supernatural atmosphere that facilitates the emergence of new visions (the wanderer) and new patterns (the bars in the wallpaper). Hawthorne, in his preface to *The Scarlet Letter*, also acknowledges the evocative quality of the night and moonlight, which are necessary for igniting the imagination. However, one may question whether this analysis merely reinforces a stereotypical view of Romantic texts and overlooks the more prominent and complex role of the senses, which may require further exploration beyond initial impressions.
66 Scheick, Intrinsic Luminosity, p. 88.
67 "There is something truer and more real, than what we can see with the eyes, and touch with the finger" (Hawthorne, Rappacini, p. 1317). Odors may deceive the senses and "the recollection of a perfume – the bare idea of it – may easily be mistaken for a present reality" (ibid., p. 1327). "The Tell-Tale Heart" is also a story about the hyperacuteness of the senses and how they can overwhelm the self or turn him/her mad.
68 Dewey, *Art as Experience*, p. 6.
69 Foucault, *History of Sexuality*, p. 19.
70 Mendlesohn, Introduction, p. 9.

ing plot and setting over well-developed characters.[71] However, this book takes a different approach by identifying highly affective scenes where emotions are prominently portrayed and easily discernible. These scenes typically occur during pivotal moments of survival, leading to the term "survival scenes" to describe them. They also signify a transition from the perspective of "*I am*" to that of an object or *thing*, making these novels critical posthumanist interventions in a world primarily focused on the human. These shifts are achieved through the utilization of a literary technique that has received inadequate attention from scholars and may even appear contradictory to the pursuit of verisimilitude in science fiction[72]: literary synesthesia.

Synesthesia is gaining increased attention in both scientific and cultural contexts, reflected in a rise in publications on the subject.[73] However, the cognitive study of synesthesia is still in its early stages,[74] resulting in a general lack of knowledge about synesthesia among the scientific community and the general public alike. This lack of understanding leads to misinformation and the perpetuation of stereotypes.[75] Synesthesia is often seen as a condition that needs to be cured or, conversely, as a "super-power" granting access to special insights or hidden mystical truths.[76] This oversimplified view of synesthesia can have negative consequences for synesthetes, who may face social disapproval or feel alienated, as if they are trying to "pass for human" all while feeling like "an extraterrestrial, non-human alien, or, perhaps an animal such as a bat."[77] This misconception also leads to the pressure for institutionalization and harmful testing or the expectation of exceptional abilities. The perception that synesthetes are primarily musicians, composers, creative writers, artists, and scientists further fuels this mystical perspective.[78]

---

[71] As such, stock-like characters like the mad scientist or the damsel in distress are rather common in sci-fi writing.
[72] Stableford, Science Fiction before the Genre, p. 18.
[73] Lovelace, Synesthesia in the Twenty-First Century, p. 413.
[74] Cf. Sagiv, Synesthesia in Perspective, p. 8.
[75] See also Sean Day's "Some Demographic and Socio-Cultural Aspects of Synesthesia."
[76] Sean Day's article provides further insights into these perspectives on synesthesia. While synesthesia shares certain aspects with conditions such as phantom limbs, some forms of autism, epilepsy, and migraines, it is not a disease. Day argues that synesthetes do not require a cure for it and emphasizes the need for synesthesia to be viewed not as an "aberration, but rather as a normal variant of perception" (Some Demographic and Socio-Cultural Aspects, p. 31).
[77] Ibid., p. 18.
[78] In this respect, it becomes the tool of the genius who is able to access "astral seeing" (ibid., p. 28).

Rather than approaching synesthesia solely as a neurological or medical condition, this book aims to explore its literary functions and critical potential. Glenn O'Malley has made a distinction between clinical synesthesia and what he calls "intersense analogy."[79] Surprisingly, despite the significant attention given to affect in scholarly discussions, synesthesia has been overlooked by affect theorists, even though it can be interpreted as a "metaphor of the senses."[80] Within a literary context, this disregard may be attributed to the narrow association of synesthesia with French symbolism[81] or a Romantic sensibility prevalent in the 19th century.[82] As Patricia Lynne Duffy points out:

> In literary portrayals of synesthetes that have appeared over the decades, we find examples of synesthetic perceptions either lifting their hosts to transcendent realms (e.g., extolling the primacy of individual imagination) or plunging them into pathological symptoms of sensory overload, such as headaches, seizures, isolation, or an unwholesome "unraveling" and distorting of the senses.[83]

This binary representation connects synesthesia either with a mystical vision reminiscent of Romanticism or with pathology, reflecting the stereotypical views found in scientific discourse. However, contemporary literature employs literary synesthesia in more complex ways, challenging these simplistic associations where synesthesia is either portrayed as enhancing the mind or causing bodily illness.

Christopher W. Tyler suggests that synesthetic experiences may be more prevalent than commonly recognized, given the "wide range of intersensory links"[84] that exist. Even everyday terms such as "volume" imply a "three-dimensional image space" being filled with sound.[85] Similarly, my analysis of the novels' use of synesthesia does not solely focus on the traditional and commonly observed occurrences, such as colored graphemes, colored time units, and colored musical sounds. Instead, it explores the imagery that exhibits synesthetic qualities through the fusion of multiple senses, transcending the division and hierarchy of sense organs. For instance, examples include the synesthetic experience of sound-synesthetic temperature in *MaddAddam* (describing "a songbird made of ice"), smell-

---

79 O'Malley, Literary Synesthesia, p. 392.
80 Ibid., p. 391.
81 For instance, synesthesia is usually discussed in connection to the poems of Charles Baudelaire or Arthur Rimbaud; it became a marker of decadence, French aestheticism, and modern sensibility.
82 Duffy, Synesthesia in Literature, p. 648.
83 Ibid., p. 653.
84 Tyler, Varieties of Synesthetic Experience, p. 43.
85 Ibid.

synesthetic touch in *Super Sad True Love Story* (referring to "a thing that smells like wet socks"), and vision-synesthetic touch in *Generosity: An Enhancement* (depicting "a sharp blue filament"). It is noteworthy that touch emerges prominently in many instances, and these synesthetic fusions can involve more than two senses.

Synesthesia goes beyond being a mere descriptive tool or a form of metaphorical language; it has the potential to provide fresh insights into human-nonhuman interactions. Firstly, it brings critical attention to the crucial role of bodily sensations and the material self, thus fostering a less anthropocentric understanding of the self. Secondly, it offers a novel approach to engaging with the nonhuman. While anthropomorphism has been criticized for its limited capacity to empower the nonhuman, as it often confines them within human frameworks, synesthesia opens up possibilities for both human and nonhuman entities to flourish. All forms of synesthesia are known for their "idiosyncratic" nature,[86] highlighting the individuality of experience. This emphasis on individuality also carries a "message of diversity," reminding us that our individual perceptions of the world differ from one another.[87] Furthermore, synesthesia, being a "private, subjective experience," presumably cannot be shared directly with an independent observer.[88] This challenges the notion of transparency or "sensation without mediation" discussed in the previous section, emphasizing the inherent subjectivity and mediated nature of perception.

Synesthesia intervenes into the discourse surrounding privacy by questioning the transparency and interpretability of bodily signals. However, synesthetic experiences do not simply reinforce the notion of an opaque and private interiority. Instead, they shift the focus from an autonomous self to the interconnected constellations, contexts, and dynamics in which the self emerges, challenging the panoptic understanding of agency and control and highlighting multiple agencies at play.[89] Building on Cary Wolfe's ideas, Monja Mohr argues that fictions can immerse us not only in the perspective of human protagonists but also in systems operating within larger systems, as conceptualized by Niklas Luhmann.[90] Synesthesia accomplishes something similar by emphasizing the "entanglement of characters and

---

[86] Day, Some Demographic and Socio-Cultural Aspects of Synesthesia, p. 13.
[87] Sagiv, Synesthesia in Perspective, p. 7.
[88] Ibid., p. 5.
[89] Scott Selisker makes a similar argument in his article where he argues that "privacy is less about the self than it is about relationships, and the managing of how information flows within them" (Novel and WikiLeaks, p. 759). Information or media not meant to be shared, like private notes or diaries, show how "the differential distribution of information [...] is frequently a structuring element of novelistic forms" (ibid.).
[90] Mohr, When Species Meet, p. 50.

matter," transcending species and biological forms, including humans, animals, plants, and posthumans.[91]

In alignment with this perspective, synesthesia transcends being a mere indicator of the literary nature of language and its inherent opacity. Paradoxically, it can illuminate aspects that are typically considered inexpressible through language. In other words, it resides on "the edge of unreadability,"[92] even as it facilitates a form of close textual engagement that is immersive, intimate, and empirical. From a postcritical standpoint, synesthesia generates attunement, resonance, and recognition, all while maintaining a sense of critical distance and "cognitive estrangement."[93] It mediates a unique interplay between the reader and the text, enabling a deep engagement that extends beyond traditional modes of interpretation.

The fusion of the senses serves a dual purpose: it defamiliarizes the familiar and familiarizes the unfamiliar, while also heightening embodied awareness. The synesthetic experience can evoke both satisfaction and disgust depending on the degree of sensory "mismatch."[94] It impacts the self on a visceral level, extending beyond the realm of imaginative engagement. Its immersive quality cannot be equated solely with the pleasures of reading; it represents a complex and nuanced state that defies easy categorization. While synesthesia functions as an "intersense analogy" that refines and intensifies sensory experience,[95] it also plays a significant role in the practice of reading by delineating what I refer to as the haptics of reading and its multisensory process.

Gilian Silverman has highlighted the intimate and reciprocal relationship between physical books and readers.[96] Although scholars have previously explored the materiality of books, their focus has often leaned toward reaffirming the primacy of meaning-making over sensory experience.[97] The concept of the haptics of reading extends beyond the materiality of books and encompasses the entire sensory process involved in the act of reading. This perspective challenges attempts to

---

[91] Ibid., p. 52. Monja Mohr also identifies the olfactory element in Margaret Atwood's novel as a mediator of this fusion.
[92] Garrett, You Have to Read First, p. 149.
[93] Science fictional estrangement is tied to the novels' social commentary and cautious plots. Suvin conflated the idea of de-familiarization and Bertolt Brecht's "alienation effect" to describe it. See Istvan Ronay's essay, p. 118.
[94] Sagiv, Synesthesia in Perspective, p. 4.
[95] O'Malley, Literary Synesthesia, p. 393.
[96] Silverman, Reading in the Flesh, p. 452.
[97] Ibid.

separate reading from understanding or judgment,[98] for it highlights the power and relevance of literature as a multi-dimensional experience. Literary synesthesia, as employed in contemporary speculative novels, underscores the significance of sensory engagement, recognizing that sense-making and sensory experience are interdependent. A book is not merely a "vehicle for the transmission of information,"[99] and thus necessitates a focus on the haptics of reading in an era dominated by big data and the quantified self.

Maurice S. Lee identifies the belief that reading is primarily an act of "information management"[100] in 19th century literature, indicating that debates surrounding textual excess are not exclusive to the present. Throughout history, attempts to navigate the abundance of texts and the "accompanying quantitative logic" have recurred.[101] Lee points to an enduring tension in our understanding of reading, characterized by a dialectic between intellectual and emotional realms ("head and heart"), multiplicity and unity, and a "struggle between superabundance and order."[102]

Winfried Fluck delves into this tension and examines it within the realm of American studies. He contends that a central methodological concern in literary and cultural studies is the assumption that a single text can represent a "larger totality."[103] Within the context of American studies, Fluck highlights the distinction between the nation (America as an imagined community) and the state (the United States as a political system). He argues that by dint of critiquing American society, the idea of America as a nation with "superior values" can be reinforced.[104] Consequently, he proposes moving away from the belief in a text's "unifying principle"[105] and reimagining it as a "field of contestation."[106] This book seeks to demonstrate how a careful focus on the senses opens up such a field of contestation. The literary synesthesia employed in these novels is not an attempt to achieve coher-

---

98 Garrett, You Have to Read First; Beckwith, Reading for Our Lives. At the same time, these attempts are also valuable for highlighting the relevance of literature beyond its understanding as a rational, intellectual, or reflective activity.
99 Silverman, Reading in the Flesh, p. 451.
100 Lee, Deserted Islands, p. 209.
101 From Seneca to medieval reference books and 19th century production of dictionaries, encyclopedias, and other print databases. See Lee, Deserted Islands, p. 209.
102 Ibid., p. 227.
103 Fluck, Surface Readings, p. 54. Plurality can also "become the new totality [...] If all texts are part of a totality that is characterized by capitalism, racism or homophobia, then all texts are shaped by these features and can represent them equally well" (ibid.).
104 Ibid., p. 61.
105 Ibid., p. 62.
106 Ibid., p. 64.

ence or resolve the contradictions of mixed modalities. It also goes beyond merely presenting a playful aspect of the text that leads to a "renewed celebration of a postmodern aesthetic."[107] Instead, these novels maintain a textual enchantment that is conflictual, causing irritation and ruptures within the text itself. In this approach, "discontinuous somatic sensations" are no longer subsumed by an artificial unity.[108]

The immersive nature of synesthetic experiences in the text does not conflict with critical vigilance; in fact, it enables it. This is demonstrated through my analysis of how the novels utilize synesthesia and the blending of art and politics. Christopher Grobe has also explored the concept of the "reading's ghostly sensorium."[109] The act of being absorbed in reading has often been associated with a "silent reading" that is isolating, private, and liberating, serving as the source of our individuality.[110] However, there is a simultaneous sense of textual liveliness that enables this immersion in the text. Literature, as a "form of simulation" that is "inseparable from emotion,"[111] has the ability to evoke affective experiences and events. Therefore, it can be assumed that literature has the potential to communicate the experience of feeling alive—an ordinary feeling that has often been overlooked in affect scholarship.[112]

Sianne Ngai's concept of the "affect of animatedness" offers an example of liveliness and exaggerated emotional expressiveness that also carries racial or ethnic connotations.[113] Animatedness is seen as an "ugly feeling" due to its racialized aspect, but it can also serve as a social and political catalyst by producing "disjunctiveness."[114] Building upon Ngai's ideas, this study acknowledges the role of emotion as a mediator between politics and aesthetics. It introduces the concept of the "affect of aliveness" to differentiate it from animatedness, happiness, wonder, or other related affects, and to propose one potential effect of a synesthetic text. The affect of aliveness suggests a shift in how life is approached and understood, which complements the prevailing scientific perspective dominating the public

---

107 Ibid., p. 63.
108 Tell, Rhetoric and Power, p. 111.
109 Grobe, On Book, p. 567.
110 Ibid., p. 568. In this context, Grobe also describes a "conflation of self-forgetting and self-formation" (569).
111 Hogan, Affect Studies, p. 4.
112 Most scholarship on affect focuses on positive (Ahmed) or negative (Ngai) feelings, but no theory touches upon the seemingly trivial notion of feeling alive. By investigating what it means to feel alive, one also intervenes in debates over what animation or artificial intelligence might mean.
113 Ngai, Ugly Feelings, p. 94.
114 Ibid., p. 113.

sphere. The prominence of the biotechnological view of life contributes to the belief that cells are mere "things or instruments to be manipulated by human will," rather than being recognized as independent life forms.[115]

The affect of aliveness manifested in the survival scenes of these novels relies on synesthesia as a narrative device that creates a sense of spatial-temporal openness that is distinct from a cosmic perspective. Klaus Benesch has also explored the capacity of literary texts to capture and establish a "strong sense of place."[116] He discusses a "shift from space-consciousness to place-consciousness," which allows literature to find a new and significant position in a posthuman era.[117] In addition to emphasizing the embodied aspects of tangible locations, synesthesia serves as an "anticathartic device" that expands the perception of time.[118] As a result, these scenes represent moments of "conspicuous inactivity" that remain emotionally charged.[119] In Ngai's analysis, these pauses evoke a Bartlebyan question of suspended agency, offering an alternative form of political engagement that differs from direct activism or the poetics of sympathy.

These synesthetic scenes introduce moments of pause that are essential for choice and transformation, actively mediating agency rather than impeding it. In this sense, these scenes create a state of suspension, as described by Jonathan Crary, where one is so deeply absorbed in "looking or listening" that they are exempt from ordinary temporal conditions, existing in a state that "hovers" outside of time. Suspension, then, also implies a "cancellation" or "interruption" of the ordinary.[120] The body, in particular, becomes an unexpected source of autonomy in these scenes. In a world where embodiment can be dehumanizing,[121] these synes-

---

115 Narkunas, Between Words, p. 8. As the author emphasizes, this perspective reinforces the notion that life itself is a game or puzzle to be conquered by human agency.
116 Benesch, Writing Grounds, p. 436.
117 Ibid. Benesch examines contemporary texts that "foreground the physical, corporeal aspects of concrete public places (including such posthuman 'non-places' as dumping grounds)."
118 Ngai, Ugly Feelings, p. 13.
119 Ibid., p. 14.
120 Crary, Suspensions, p. 10. He further explains: "The roots of the word *attention* in fact resonate with a sense of 'tension,' of being 'stretched,' and also of 'waiting.' It implies the possibility of a fixation, of holding something in wonder or contemplation, in which the attentive subject is both immobile and ungrounded" (ibid.). At the same time, he also wants to indicate "a disturbance, even a negation of perception itself. For throughout the book I am concerned with the idea of a perception that can be both an absorption *and* an absence or deferral" (ibid; emphasis in original).
121 For instance, animatedness becomes a racial marker of the "lively or agitated ethnic subjects" (Ngai, Ugly Feelings, p. 93); whether the hyperexpressive African American or the inexpressive Asian, the focus on the racialized body has a dehumanizing character. Bodies are either disposable, invisible, or when they do become visible, they are just proofs of wild instincts that need to be tamed in a humanist world that celebrates the power of the mind.

thetic moments disrupt conventional ways of perceiving and experiencing the body, offering new possibilities for understanding and engaging with corporeal existence.[122]

In summary, contemporary speculative novels offer a shift in perspective when it comes to understanding life. Rather than solely focusing on quantitative aspects such as age or physical ability, these novels explore the qualitative dimensions of being alive. In this context, I use the term life writing to designate not only a form of writing that is personal and intimate, but also to propose a shift from self-writing to life writing—from an anthropocentric focus on the human self to the notion of life that does not pertain only to the human, but it includes "*zoe*"—"the life of animals and nonhuman entities."[123] It is worth noting that subjective experiences, which are central to life writing, often face skepticism or disregard in medical or scientific contexts.[124] Similarly, literary critics may overlook or downplay the subjective aspects of these novels, focusing primarily on their scientific elements. However, this study aims to emphasize that literature itself can function as a form of life science, offering a space to subjectively explore and test topics related to life, including its diverse manifestations and complexities.

---

[122] Ngai's analysis also underscores the body's elasticity and "plasmaticness," which suggests a spontaneous, liberating automatism that has the potential to subvert. Even if the Taylorized body's learned automatism is susceptible to external manipulation (*Ugly Feelings*, p. 101), in the end, "the very sign of the racialized body's automatization functions as the source of an unsuspected autonomy" (ibid., p. 117).
[123] Braidotti, Posthuman, p. 20.
[124] In general, "subjective experiences tend to be discounted or rejected because they cannot be objectively observed by the physician" (Day, Some Demographic and Socio-Cultural Aspects of Synesthesia, p. 19).

II **Self-Improvement: Finding Success in a Digital Age**

Introduction

In the United States, the pursuit of self-improvement has long been associated with the concept of upward mobility, a historical association that links success to productivity and diligence. Benjamin Franklin's renowned list of virtues, encapsulated by the maxim "Lose no time; be always employ'd in something useful; cut off all unnecessary actions,"[1] reflects a pervasive emphasis on productivity akin to the Protestant work ethic. This *memento mori* ethos persists in contemporary self-help, where the "ideal of individual success and self-invention" embodied by figures like Benjamin Franklin, Andrew Carnegie, and Bill Gates remains closely tied to traditionally masculine characteristics—such as "independence, strength, dominance, invulnerability, and muscular vigor."[2] The enduring myth of the self-made man, often portrayed through rags-to-riches narratives, perpetuates the belief that happiness is synonymous with prosperity. In the nineteenth and early twentieth centuries, success was quantifiable, measured by the accumulation of "wealth, status, or power."[3]

As working conditions evolved, job dynamics grew more stressful, the job market increasingly precarious, and financial crises added further instability to the lives of American citizens. Rather than challenging the prevailing myth of productivity, these changing conditions perpetuated the enduring notion of "no pain, no gain." Toward the end of the 20th century, a shift occurred as "self-fulfillment" emerged to replace the previous benchmarks for defining success. The criteria for success transformed to encompass "emotional well-being, the subjective experience of happiness, and the pursuit of pleasure," marking a departure from the traditional standards.[4] This transition was to give rise to a new work ethic, one that "infuses work discipline with pleasure."[5] Moreover, work became so integral to one's identity that individuals proudly asserted their professions as synonymous with who they are.[6]

---

1 Franklin, *Autobiography*, p. 134.
2 McGee, *Self-Help*, p. 13.
3 Ibid., p. 19.
4 Ibid.
5 Ibid., p. 25.
6 "People with a calling orientation typically love and value what they do in and of itself. [...] it does not matter if people deliver pizza for a living or are highly specialized surgeons, it only matters how they perceive their work" (Biswas-Diener and Dean qtd. in Cabanas/Illouz, *Manufacturing*, p. 99). However, the authors do not consider the ways in which individual perception is also informed by societal values, by the amount of money and respect certain jobs receive.

In a paradoxical twist, the pursuit of improvement necessitates a pre-existing sense of fulfillment. Edgar Cabanas and Eva Illouz critically engage with this new "working ethics" that emphasizes "personal responsibility" and advocates a "progressive transition from external control to self-control."[7] Positive psychologists challenge Maslow's pyramid, asserting that happiness serves as the "precursor" to success, redirecting focus from working conditions to individual attitudes and happiness as guarantors of productivity.[8] Consequently, work undergoes a transformation, evolving from a compensatory deprivation to a means of self-expression, identity, and personal fulfillment.[9] Work began to mean *"work on the self —the quest for a path, the invention of a life, or the search for authenticity— [which] is offered as an antidote to the anxiety-provoking uncertainties of a new economic and social order."*[10]

This phenomenon illuminates the surge in motivational speakers and social media influencers: the contemporary self-made individual capitalizes on sharing life stories online, aligning with an increasingly "visual and media-saturated culture where style is privileged over substance."[11] This chapter delves into TED talks on the subject, examining what I call "the duty to be alive" against the backdrop of an "inward turn."[12] Additionally, it explores a literary example—Gary Shteyngart's *Super Sad True Love Story*—before concluding with an exploration of literature's crucial role in intervening in these social debates.

---

7 Cabanas/Illouz, *Manufacturing Happy Citizens*, p. 89.
8 Ibid., p. 93.
9 Cf. McGee, *Self-Help, Inc.*, p. 42.
10 Ibid., p. 43.
11 Ibid., p. 46.
12 Ibid., p. 47.

5 TED Talks on "How to Be a Better You" and Social Media Influencers

TED Talks serve as a catalyst for confidence-building, fostering self-motivation and independent learning. A participant in a study conducted by Euodia Inge Gavenila, Mega Wulandari, and Willy A. Renandya highlighted this impact, stating, "I become more confident" after engaging with TED Talk videos.[13] Beyond enhancing language skills, the second most cited benefit in this study is a boost in motivation.[14] In the age of the Internet, where knowledge is readily accessible, cultivating confidence online has become a common practice. In the "How to Be a Better You" TED Talks playlist, the exploration of work life unfolds through the perspectives of "calling, path, journey, [and] mission," urging individuals to envision their lives as works of art.[15] With half of the playlist dedicated to the theme of career, the target audience appears to be the public, social self—the individual's reputation, esteem, and confidence in society, akin to the Freudian ego. Yet, how do TED Talks approach success? Despite their diversity, two common threads emerge: the concept of vision, where success mirrors the crowned achievement of scientific genius, and the notion of purpose, encouraging individuals to become part of something greater.[16]

5.1 Digital Culture Meets Self-Help: Building Confidence Online

The visual narrative framing the playlist "How to Be a Better You" is a compelling image featuring a woman ascending the stairs of her own person, symbolizing the

---

[13] Gavenila et al., Using TED Talks, 165b.
[14] Ibid., p. 166.
[15] McGee identifies these masculine models of action (calling, path, journey, mission) in the traditional literature of self-improvement, whereas the books written by and for women focus on imagining life as a work of art. She adds: "the contemporary ideal of life as a work of art is offered to the masses as a route out of meaningless, unsatisfying, and insecure work situations" (*Self-Help*, p. 45).
[16] See also the episode featuring Malcolm Gladwell on the podcast series *The Diary of a CEO* with Steven Bartlett, where he emphasizes the importance of returning to the office, arguing that working from home can lead to a loss of purpose and belonging. *The Diary of a CEO* is worth exploring further with added attention and research. Gladwell is also famous for his TED talk titled "Choice, Happiness, and Spaghetti Sauce" (2014).

ə Open Access. © 2024 the author(s), published by De Gruyter. This work is licensed under the Creative Commons Attribution 4.0 International License. https://doi.org/10.1515/9783111389929-008

Figure 2: Image for the TED playlist "How to Be a Better You" accompanied by the caption: "Ready for a change? These well-researched (and heartfelt) talks offer ideas and inspiration for all aspects of your life, from creativity to vulnerability, from competitive sports to collaborative games."

pursuit of upward mobility. This portrayal, depicting both a personal and progressive journey of self-transcendence, unfolds against a backdrop of blue skies with a subtle allusion to Jacob's ladder. The door high above the woman, emitting light, evokes notions of a spiritual or mystical journey, akin to opening doors to new levels of consciousness. The shadowy blue backdrop behind the woman's hair, coupled with her closed eye resembling a tinier cloud, creates a symbiotic effect, suggesting an intertwining of self and world. The woman's ideal form, prominently showcased as her enlarged portrait at the center, represents a journey inward toward the inner self. The closed eye and the rosy cheek convey an image of inner peace. With the door leading into her own brain or mind, the image subtly implies that the ultimate goal resides within the self—peace, happiness, success, or self-transcendence as an inner state.

This emphasis on internal life resonates with the "inward turn" so characteristic of self-help culture.[17] The distinctive features of long brown hair, tanned skin, and a pink blouse in the playlist's introductory image evoke the stylistic choices of Brittany Packnett, whose talk on "How to Build Your Confidence—and Spark it in Others" is featured in the playlist. Packnett strategically employs self-help rhetoric and the "how-to" logic right in the title, blending the inspirational dimension with the motivational essence typical of both self-help products and TED talks. Her reference to Septima Clark at the talk's outset resonates with the playlist's visual motif: "She sat in perfect profile with her face raised to the sky. She had perfect

---

17 McGee, *Self-Help, Inc.*, p. 47.

salt-and-pepper cornrows plaited down the sides of her head, and pride and wisdom just emanated from her dark skin."[18]

Confidence, synonymous with self-esteem, pride, and certainty, thrives through societal interactions. Since the 1960s, the Black pride movement has stood as a potent response to racism, segregation, and discrimination. Packnett's talk seeks to empower marginalized voices—be they immigrants, low-income individuals, disabled, Black, or Brown voices. She ties injustice not solely to a lack of resources or knowledge but also to a deficiency in confidence. Unlike the individualistic approach prevalent in self-help culture, Packnett emphasizes the communal aspect of building confidence, highlighting the importance of community in her narrative.

Through the narratives of Jamal and Regina, Packnett builds a compelling argument about the differential treatment of confidence in individuals, asserting that "we reward confidence in some people and we punish confidence in others,"[19] a dynamic she acknowledges experiencing herself. Reflecting on an incident with Regina, Packnett admits to a misstep where her attempt to "choose control" inadvertently conveyed that Regina was a distraction, and she watched "the light go out from her eyes."[20] Determined to "crack the code of confidence,"[21] Packnett emphasizes the significance of permission, community, and curiosity, and she illustrates each point with personal anecdotes involving her mother, the Kenya tribe, and her workplace manager.

While Packnett's talk aligns with a self-help framework thematically—centering on confidence, self-empowerment, and envisioning a utopian future—it also manifests within its linguistic choices and rhetoric. This is evident in her adherence to the how-to paradigm, the expressed desire to "crack the code" of confidence, and the formulation of a three-part formula. However, Packnett skillfully redirects the focus from notions of self-reliance and individual power towards the significance of community, social interactions, and collaboration, challenging the ethos of rugged individualism. Illustrating this shift, she emphasizes, "Purity's confidence to chase down lions and catch poachers, it didn't come from her athletic ability or even just her faith. Her confidence was propped up by sisterhood, by community."[22]

Packnett's talk stands out in contrast to the predominant male perspectives on success that characterize the playlist—perspectives emphasizing confidence rooted

---

18 Packnett, How to Build Your Confidence, 00:00:47.
19 Ibid., 00:07:45.
20 Ibid., 00:06:03.
21 Ibid., 00:08:18.
22 Ibid., 00:10:55.

in passion, grit, faith, or patience, traits perceived as intrinsic to the individual. This also applies to psychologist Shawn Achor's TED talk, "The Happy Secret to Better Work" (2012), featured in "The Most Popular TED Talks of All Time" playlist. Achor contends that happiness fuels productivity, a notion resonating strongly with the TED audience. Achor begins with a childhood anecdote, illustrating how he redirected his sister's focus from pain to passion when she broke her leg by telling her she was a unicorn. While this tactic seemingly averted a negative situation, it also implies a strategy of sidelining the "bad" by concentrating on the positive.[23] Achor further presents a graph where positive "outliers" are not disregarded but studied to elevate the "average."

Why some individuals excel in intellectual, athletic, musical ability, creativity, energy levels, and resilience is the question further pursued by Achor in his talk.[24] His response suggests that success is primarily influenced by one's state of mind: "We're finding it's not necessarily the reality that shapes us, but *the lens* through which your brain views the world that shapes your reality. And if we can change the lens, not only can we change your happiness, we can change every single educational and business outcome at the same time."[25] The metaphor of the lens, a scientific and objective way of conveying a concept akin to that in the renowned self-help book *The Secret*, underscores a core idea in American self-help culture —mind-power. However, in Achor's presentation, this concept takes on a scientific twist rather than a purely spiritual one.

TED talks reintroduce the concept of the power of positive thinking as the power of the lens,[26] the power of belief,[27] or the power of intrinsic motivators.[28] However, the fundamental idea remains constant: one's state of mind influences external outcomes.[29] Leadership expert Simon Sinek shares his model of "How Great Leaders Inspire Action" (2010) in a TEDx talk held at Puget Sound. Recognized among the most popular talks of all time, Sinek's presentation begins by probing why Apple excels in innovation, why Martin Luther King led the Civil Rights movement, or why the Wright brothers pioneered controlled flight. Wheth-

---

23 One could also add: ignoring the bad, vulnerable body and focus on the creative, imaginative mind.
24 Achor, Happy Secret, 00:04:57.
25 Ibid., 00:06:07; emphasis added.
26 Ibid.
27 Sinek, How Great Leaders; see the talk's discussion below.
28 Pink, Puzzle of Motivation; see the talk's discussion below.
29 The power of positive thinking "is a resolutely individualistic miracle narrative. Miracles are possible, it tells us; but it is up to us—up to our capacity to believe—whether or not they happen" (Harrington, *Cure Within*, p. 105). In this respect, these speakers reinforce the same ideology of the power of the mind.

er in technological innovation, the pursuit of social justice, or scientific discoveries, the guiding principle is clear: "inspired leaders and the inspired organizations [...] all think, act, and communicate from the inside out."[30]

Sinek's "discovery" or the "golden circle"[31] essentially embodies a self-help virtue: the power of belief. Whether framed as belief, idea, confidence, faith, or conviction, these concepts collectively reinforce the importance of having a vision. According to Sinek, "people don't buy what you do; people buy why you do it."[32] Thus, the shift in doing business, in his view, is not merely targeting needs but emphasizing shared beliefs. In essence, the goal becomes "to do business with people who believe what you believe,"[33] urging a move toward selling ideas rather than simply addressing needs.

The motivational industry has emerged as one of the most successful business sectors, a trend underscored by the success of talks like Sinek's. An ideal self is a "potentially powerful generator of motivation," so exploring future identities is part of this inspirational mechanism where there is a "desire to soothe the feeling of dissatisfaction, guilt, fear, or disappointment."[34] Pinar's study on the impact of TED talks on students reveals the central role of vision: "Vision is a key aspect of future self-guides, and is regarded as 'one of the highest-order motivational forces' [...] and one of the most reliable predictors of students' long-term intended effort."[35] In essence, these talks juxtapose confidence and vision, suggesting that continual efforts to boost confidence are essential for achieving success.

Sinek also delves into biology in a bid to boost his argument, explaining the human brain's division into the neocortex, referred to as the "what level," responsible for rational and analytical thought.[36] Additionally, he highlights the two limbic brains, which govern feelings such as trust and loyalty, along with all human behavior and decision-making, lacking the capacity for language.[37] Sinek illustrates this concept by contrasting Samuel Pierpoint Langley's well-endowed resources with the Wright brothers, who lacked "the recipe for success,"[38] such as funding, education, or fame. The Wright brothers, just like Martin Luther King, thrived on a

---

30 Sinek, How Great Leaders, 00:02:55.
31 Ibid., 00:05:58.
32 Ibid., 00:10:44.
33 Ibid., 00:05:30.
34 Cf. García-Pinar, Influence, p. 234.
35 Ibid., p. 235.
36 Sinek, How Great Leaders, 00:06:05.
37 Ibid., 00:06:14.
38 Ibid., 00:09:14.

shared cause or purpose, underscoring Sinek's overarching theme of belief or vision.

Career analyst Dan Pink's TED talk, "The Puzzle of Motivation," is renowned among the most popular talks and most popular science talks, echoing Simon Sinek's message. Pink aims to present an "evidence-based" case for rethinking business operations,[39] centering on the science of human motivation and the "dynamics of extrinsic and intrinsic motivators."[40] He emphasizes the importance of right-brained creative abilities over "left-brain work,"[41] which can be automated, using the "candle problem"[42] as an illustrative example. Contrary to the common belief in "if-then rewards,"[43] Pink asserts that they do not work. He presents this as a "fact," not as a feeling or a philosophy, and he goes on to list his evidence, including a few studies done on MIT students and the London School of Economics. His case favors intrinsic motivation, driven by "the desire to do things because they matter [...] or [are] part of something important."[44]

Pink introduces a new operating system for businesses based on autonomy, mastery, and purpose, which he identifies as the "building blocks" for a transformative business model.[45] He concludes with examples illustrating the effectiveness of autonomy and self-direction, citing companies like Atlassian and Google, as well as the Results Only Working Environment and the Wikipedia model, highlighting the limitations of the "carrot and stick" approach and the potential transformative power of autonomy, mastery, and purpose.[46]

Sinek and Pink construct a dichotomy in their talks, drawing on the idea of two brain hemispheres. They popularize the notion that ambition, desire, or determination are the sole ingredients for success, downplaying the significance of social factors. Paradoxically, despite advocating for autonomy, both speakers rely on a model where behavior is induced. The carrot and stick metaphor, for instance, reinforces the perception that money merely serves as a tool to influence behavior

---

[39] Pink, Puzzle of Motivation, 00:01:29.
[40] Ibid., 00:04:59.
[41] Ibid., 00:07:17.
[42] Ibid., 00:02:31; 00:08:05.
[43] Ibid., 00:08:12.
[44] Ibid., 00:12:18.
[45] Ibid., 00:12:25. This is how he phrases them: "Autonomy: the urge to direct our own lives. Mastery: the desire to get better and better at something that matters. Purpose: the yearning to do what we do in *the service of something larger than ourselves.*"
[46] Ibid., 00:17:05. This comparison does not consider the many ways in which Wikipedia relies on "carrots" to exist, such as its many calls for donation. Pink adds: "if we get past this *lazy, dangerous, ideology of carrots and sticks*, we can strengthen our businesses, we can solve a lot of those candle problems, and maybe, maybe—we can change the world" (00:18:01; emphasis added).

rather than a force shaping social reality. Their approaches contribute to the creation and perpetuation of a "belabored self," embodying the extensive and ongoing self-labor demanded of individuals in advanced capitalism.[47] In essence, the intense "focus on inventing an autonomous and self-sufficient self"[48] places immense pressure on the individual self's responsibility for achieving success. Confidence becomes framed as a personal trait capable of ensuring success, rather than an outcome of a sense of community.

Richard St. John, a self-described "average guy who found success doing what he loved," epitomizes the self-made man and a success analyst in the field of marketing.[49] In his TED talk, "Success Is a Continuous Journey" (2009), St. John employs the metaphor of a journey to describe success, a metaphor considered rather "masculine" and reminiscent of heroic quests.[50] He seeks to challenge the conventional linear paths leading only upward, advocating for circular directions as his confessions and slides suggest. His talk appears to emphasize the importance of failure as a vital component of success, highlighting his own experience where failure led to an even more successful business—a narrative aligning with the popular self-help belief that every failure presents another opportunity for success. However, St. John maintains a dichotomous view of success and failure, portraying the "downhill" path as a fault of the individual entering the comfort zone and not working hard enough.[51] Success is thus linked to the Protestant work ethic and the continual self-improvement ethos, pushing against notions of being "good enough."[52] Additionally, success is associated with the invention of "good ideas,"[53] introducing a creative dimension to his definition of success.

Throughout his talk, St. John utilizes animations featuring a small stickman, text, and red-colored icons. The stickman serves as a universal representation, implying the applicability of his ideas to all humans. His deliberate use of the color red and clear, simple animations aims to heighten audience awareness and enhance the clarity and persuasiveness of the message. In a slide focused on "ideas" presented in red, St. John offers several suggestions for a successful life: be curious, listen, observe, problem solve, make connections, and ask questions.[54] Accompanied by tiny red bulbs and one large red bulb hovering over the stickman,

---

47 McGee, *Self-Help, Inc.*, p. 16.
48 Ibid.
49 Richard St. John, *TED*.
50 McGee, *Self-Help, Inc.*, p. 44.
51 St. John, Success, 00:00:23.
52 Ibid., 00:00:43.
53 Ibid., 00:00:50.
54 Ibid.

these visuals reinforce the importance of imaginative work, insights, and cognitive efforts. St. John suggests that success hinges on self-discipline and creativity, guided by fundamental principles such as passion, work, focus, push, ideas, improve, serve, and persist—summarized within a broad red circle of success.[55]

Economist Larry Smith's TED talk, "Why You Will Fail to Have a Great Career," centers on the theme of success tied to finding and following one's passion. It appears that traditional masculine metaphors of an individual calling, vocation, journey, or mission are replaced with the concept of passion—an intense feeling often associated with romantic and/or violent contexts. Despite this shift, the sense of devotion and the idea of a predetermined destiny remain prominent in Smith's narrative. In his talk, a "great career" transcends being merely a chosen profession; it becomes a response to an overwhelming feeling that encompasses both desire and suffering. Passion, applied to an emotion that is "deeply stirring or ungovernable,"[56] takes on a nuanced role in Smith's exploration. Notably, the focus on self-control, traditionally associated with signaling rationality and the "capacity to discipline one's passions" for self-interest,[57] seems to undergo a shift. While self-control in the past may have centered on anger management in work culture,[58] Smith's emphasis on passion suggests a different perspective.

According to Smith, the primary reason people fail to achieve great careers is because they invent excuses rooted in laziness or fear, such as attributing success to luck or limiting it to geniuses or those deemed weird and obsessive.[59] However, a paradox arises in Smith's message as he ultimately promotes the figure of the genius, and a "great career" transforms into the measure of an entire life or biography. Smith paints a scenario where, at the end of life, a tombstone initially describing a "distinguished engineer who invented Velcro" should, instead, read "the last Nobel Laureate in Physics, who formulated the Grand Unified Field Theory and demonstrated the practicality of warp drive."[60] The rationale behind considering a career in engineering as less remarkable than being a renowned physicist remains unclear. Moreover, questioning why one's tombstone should exclusively fixate on the career one has chosen raises the broader issue of whether work life should define life more generally.

Smith's approach appears elitist, for it overlooks considerations of a working-class background and broader social issues, such as access to education or social

---

55 Ibid., 00:03:21.
56 Passion, *Merriam-Webster*.
57 Illouz, *Saving*, p. 80.
58 Ibid.
59 Smith, Why You Will Fail, 00:02:10.
60 Ibid., 00:07:55.

discrimination. The struggles of balancing a career with family life are dismissed as insignificant excuses. Notably, Smith fails to provide solutions for discovering passions, instead placing more pressure on individuals and emphasizing their responsibility in the pursuit of success. Aligned with the individualistic worldview of self-help, success is framed as a personal battle, with fear or uncertainty as the sole threats to achievement. Paradoxically, Smith also draws a connection between passion and societal recognition, suggesting that the latter serves as an indication of the former.

Additionally, Smith cynically approaches the topic of "human relationships" and the desire to build a family, incorporating jokes about not liking kids. His blunt and occasionally skeptical manner of presentation serves as a tool to awaken and motivate the audience. In summary, passion, defined as a powerful and intense feeling that can "take over the mind or judgment,"[61] is positioned as the driving force behind a great career. Smith portrays a career not as a rational pursuit but as the outcome of a surge of madness typically associated with geniuses. The talk concludes with Smith placing particular emphasis on the word "unless," creating a sense of continuation in the narrative. This deliberate choice leaves the discussion open for the audience, inspiring them to take action and maintain a sense of hope.[62]

In her widely popular talk, "Grit: The Power of Passion and Perseverance," psychologist Angela Lee Duckworth argues that grit, rather than factors like good looks, physical health, or IQ, serves as a precursor to success. She defines grit as "passion and perseverance for very long-term goals," emphasizing its association with stamina and the commitment to future aspirations over extended periods—living life like a marathon, not a sprint.[63] Duckworth characterizes grit by attributes such as determination, willpower, and mental strength. Both Smith's and Duckworth's talks contemporarily update the concept of passion, portraying it as a catalyst for enhanced confidence and personal devotion. The narrative emphasizes the importance of never giving up and maintaining self-discipline. Duckworth further introduces the "growth mindset," developed by Carol Dweck at Stanford University, which encourages children to embrace the notion that learning is not fixed, and "failure is not a permanent condition."[64] This resonates with St. John's cyclical journey of failure and success, challenging the boundaries between success and failure, a theme further explored in John Wooden's talk.

---

61 Passion, *Thesaurus*.
62 Smith, 00:14:04.
63 Duckworth, Grit, 00:02:54.
64 Ibid., 00:04:50.

In his talk on "The Difference Between Winning and Succeeding," coach John Wooden aims to separate success from winning, accomplishments, or specific goals, associating it instead with an inner state—"peace of mind attained only through self-satisfaction in knowing you made the effort to do the best of which you're capable."[65] Unlike Smith, Wooden does not emphasize success as a "position of power or prestige,"[66] yet his talk contributes to the same trend of internalizing or psychologizing success. While for Smith, success is linked to passion, for Wooden, it revolves more around achieving "peace of mind."[67] Additionally, in alignment with St. John, Wooden suggests that success involves self-discipline, a theme rhetorically reinforced through his set of three rules.[68] These rules include punctuality ("never be late"), immaculate appearance ("neat and clean," "no profanity"), and tolerance ("never criticize a teammate"). His dad had his own set of threes: "Don't whine. Don't complain. Don't make excuses."[69] This echoes Smith's emphasis on avoiding excuses for failure. However, a concern arises that when individuals are no longer allowed to voice complaints, there is a risk of them becoming, in the words of Ghalleb, nothing more than "consenting slaves."[70]

Wooden introduces a pyramid for success, with industriousness and enthusiasm as the cornerstones, emphasizing the importance of working hard and enjoying the process.[71] According to his definition, faith and patience crown success,[72] inviting individuals to wait and see whether their efforts yield successful results. This raises the question of where the boundaries lie between laziness, patience, faith, or procrastination. The increasing popularity of procrastination as a topic in self-help reflects a shifting discourse on productivity and laziness. However, it also highlights how self-help simultaneously produces and maintains a perspective that, despite attempting to "cure" procrastination, inadvertently favors it—an aspect to be further explored in the subsequent subchapter.

---

65 Wooden, Difference, 00:02:59.
66 Ibid., 00:01:56.
67 Ibid., 00:02:59.
68 Ibid., 00:06:32.
69 Ibid., 00:11:48.
70 Ghalleb, *Interdisciplinary Mind*, p. 31. As Ines Ghalleb further argues in her reading of Powers' novel: "[i]f human beings cannot express dissatisfaction, anger or revolt against social, economic, racial, and gender inequalities and injustices [...] then a change of situation [...] would not be feasible" (ibid., p. 30).
71 Wooden, Difference, 00:09:02.
72 The idea of faith as a "wellness technique" emerges here (Harrington, *Cure Within*, p. 136). "Faith moves mountains, faith performs miracles, because faith is blind, because it does not reason, because it *suppresses control* and impresses itself directly upon the imagination, without moderating second thoughts" (Bernheim qtd. in Harrington, *Cure Within*, p. 108; emphasis added).

Whether referencing the pyramid of success,[73] the big red bulb symbolizing ideas,[74] or the allusion to the Nobel Laureate in Physics,[75] TED's concept of success aligns with the image of (scientific) genius. The myth of the self-made person is thus modernized to include not only rags-to-riches narratives or continual self-improvement but also a necessary infusion of creativity and imagination. These talks and presenters not only overlook the notion of privilege, including the privilege of patience, but also cast the journey to success in heroic terms—as the well-deserved outcome of genius. The confidence associated with the self-made individual, however, is a precarious confidence, one that excessively highlights individual efforts while neglecting the comprehensive support network provided by both human and nonhuman agents.[76]

5.2 Self-Surveillance, the Quantified Self, and the "Power of Posing"

Donna Freitas' "happiness effect" describes the social pressures experienced by college students when sharing content on platforms like Facebook or X. Through interviews with students from diverse backgrounds, Freitas uncovers a trend where social media, instead of serving as a confessional space for connection, transforms into a competitive arena. In this digital landscape, individuals strive to portray an idealized, perfect, and happy self—"blissful, enraptured, even inspiring," as some students revealed.[77] Consequently, confidence not only guarantees success, but evolves into a societal obligation on social media, potentially contributing to the resurgence of motivational speakers.

In a review of Freitas's book, Justin Camblin raises questions about the role of the medium itself in fostering the "happiness effect": "What if the media themselves value things that make for a perfect environment for the 'happiness effect' to thrive? [...] Perhaps the medium itself values (and therefore encourages) certain behaviors and mindsets."[78] While Camblin expresses a desire for a more detailed exploration, he does not go into detail either. One potential answer to his question concerns the notion of instant gratification. Actions like receiving likes or endlessly scrolling through news feeds on social media offer users a sense of immediate re-

---

73 Wooden, Difference.
74 St. John, Success.
75 Smith, Why You Will Fail.
76 See also Ken Clark's "Myth of the Genius Solitary Scientist Is Dangerous" (2017).
77 Freitas, *Happiness Effect*, p. 13.
78 Camblin, Book Review.

ward. This instant gratification not only sustains the "happiness effect" but also becomes a primary avenue through which individuals derive confidence online. In essence, it is not solely the act of sharing but the transient, gratifying interactions encountered on social media that contribute to building trust and faith.

Procrastination is often faulted for the tendency to seek instant gratification, a well-explored topic in self-help culture. Procrastination is typically linked to the allure of immediate rewards, contrasting with the "waiting out" approach advocated by John Wooden in his talk. However, the emphasis on faith can paradoxically contribute to procrastination. In self-help narratives, delaying tasks is viewed as counterproductive, signaling a mindset issue in the individual. This perspective tends to overlook external pressures, unrealistic expectations, or decisions beyond the individual's control as contributing factors to procrastination. The discourse on laziness has evolved, shifting focus to procrastination. This change reflects broader uncertainties affecting not only the working class but also the middle class and the privileged. The narrative has transformed from attributing failure to laziness to recognizing procrastination as a prevalent issue. Unlike the negative connotation associated with working-class laziness, procrastination is now sometimes viewed positively, especially in creative professions. It is framed not as a personal weakness but rather as a consequence of the digital age, where constant smartphone use contributes to delaying tasks. In some contexts, procrastination is even hailed as a potential sign of genius.

Motivational speakers, like Jay Shetty, leverage social media in order to discuss the drawbacks of excessive phone use, emphasizing distraction, exhaustion, and procrastination. Shetty suggests strategies for "recharging" the self—through sport, meditation, sleep, and deep and meaningful interactions.[79] While he highlights the negative aspects of phone use, he ironically draws parallels between personal rejuvenation and the ways phones are recharged. In another video, he claims that people spend forty-seven percent of their time on phones procrastinating and suggests finding ways to "increase our attraction" instead.[80] However, he does not consider the ways in which the boundaries between distraction and attraction are looser than they seem: what may look like an act of distraction could be felt like a moment of intense attraction. What appears as distraction could be perceived as a focused, present, and passionate state—a potential state of flow, which he introduces in another video.[81] This concept will be explored further in chapter eleven.

---

79 Shetty, If You're Feeling Drained.
80 Shetty, If You Need to Focus.
81 In this video, Shetty encourages his audience to either increase challenges in their lives (if feeling bored) or to increase skills (if feeling anxious) in order to find flow. See Jay Shetty's "Find Your Flow" (2018).

Self-help content on social media emphasizes the importance of using time wisely and staying productive, often offering solutions to procrastination. Motivational speakers stress the connection between accomplishments and hard work, echoing the Protestant work ethic. Success, they argue, may hinge on delayed gratification, patience, and consistent effort, with no guaranteed quick results. Despite promoting purpose[82] and long-term goals, these messages, paradoxically, might contribute to the popularity of instant gratification. Common productivity practices, such as creating to-do lists and routines, also rely on the instant gratification of ticking off completed tasks.

Self-help content, whether in videos, texts, or posts, is crafted to be impactful and inspirational. Often presented in condensed forms like short videos, these messages utilize simple and effective language, statistics, and emotional appeals to create a strong connection with the audience. Well-known speakers like Dhar Mann, Jay Shetty, or Prince Ea[83] employ confessions not only for moral and pedagogical purposes but also as a tool for catharsis and emotional relief in the audience. These confessions typically follow a narrative arc that leads to success, providing a sense of justice and offering instant gratification, concluding with a call to action for a temporary motivational boost.

Dhar Mann's approach relies heavily on the transformative power of confessions in his inspirational content.[84] Through scripts where oppressors "instantly regret" their actions,[85] he exposes his over-dependence on the notion of instant gratification in his videos. The theme often revolves around individuals realizing the consequences of their behavior by hearing someone else confess to a similar situation. In Mann's videos, compassion takes on a self-centered function, focusing on personal improvement rather than extending to a broader social dimension where one might help others. Despite the emotional impact, the emphasis remains on individual transformation rather than collective well-being. Compassion has

---

[82] Any engagement in self-help is never an end in itself; it always serves a higher purpose. Traditionally, upward mobility has stood out as one of the most renowned objectives, grounded in the conviction that diligent effort is met with financial rewards, success, and happiness. In a notable shift, productivity has now emerged as a standalone goal, particularly in a world where individuals are urged to be cautious about squandering their time.

[83] Prince Ea is the stage name of American rapper, spoken-word artist, and motivational speaker Richard Williams. His videos accumulated over one billion views on Facebook and YouTube. See Richard Williams, on *Forbes*.

[84] According to his website, he is "the highest viewed content creator in the world." Here, he also confesses: "Even if it feels like you're struggling right now, I promise you one day your struggle will become your superpower. Your pain WILL have a purpose" (About Dhar Mann). Mann also ranked #2 on YouTube' official U.S. Top 10 Creators of 2021 list (Degrushe, YouTube).

[85] The oppressors in his videos include a rich man, a spoiled wife, a spoiled son, or a bully.

been scientifically defined as a sentiment that emerges upon witnessing someone else's suffering, accompanied by a subsequent desire to take action.[86] Accordingly, compassion "overwhelms selfish concerns and motivates altruistic behavior."[87] However, in these videos, compassion is mainly used as a tool to improve the self.

Jay Shetty, a purpose coach and former monk, gained fame for his "viral wisdom"[88] and short stories, notably on Facebook with videos amassing millions of views. His podcast, *On Purpose*, features conversations with celebrities like Kobe Bryant and Alicia Keys. In his videos, Shetty often employs a God-like narrative voice, commenting on life scenarios and imparting wisdom.[89] His videos, similar to Prince Ea's "Life Lessons" playlist,[90] frequently involve scripts where individuals "instantly regret" their mistakes,[91] emphasizing transformative moments and life lessons in a dramatic fashion. Both creators leverage impactful storytelling to convey their messages effectively.

As a rule, karma seems to resolve all issues, ensuring that everyone receives what they deserve. The repetitive use of *deus ex machina* in videos by creators like Dhar Mann may inadvertently convey a narrative where external forces solve problems, shifting the responsibility away from the collective fight for social justice. The frequent involvement of a compassionate "stranger" who rescues characters from their predicaments[92] creates a redemptive script. This narrative structure, while aiming to inspire compassion, might unintentionally suggest that justice is served without active engagement. The audience experiences instant gratification as justice is swiftly achieved, reinforcing a desire for quick resolutions and

---

86 Clara Strauss et al. reference this definition of compassion in their essay (via Goetz et al.), which is the working definition of the Greater Good Science Center, too. See also the entry on "What Is Compassion?" in their magazine.
87 Keltner, Compassionate Instinct.
88 See Jay Shetty, About.
89 For instance, his video titled "Poor Mom Teaches a Rich Mom a Lesson" had garnered over 266 million views by January 10, 2023. In August 2021, the view count stood at 261 million views.
90 Prince Ea employs a similar rhetoric in his "Life Lessons" playlist: the janitor "gets the last laugh," a disrespectful son "lives to regret it," or someone imparts a lesson—the professor teaches spoiled students a lesson, a flight attendant teaches a racist passenger a lesson, or an employee teaches the boss a lesson.
91 Like, for instance, "Jealous Girl Instantly Regrets Decision" (2020) or "Jealous Boy Dumps Girlfriend, Instantly Regrets It" (2020).
92 For instance, in Dhar Mann's videos, a stranger saves a poor dad, a homeless mom, and a woman evicted from her home. Poverty and homelessness are solved in a redemptive fashion, obscuring the necessity to actively fight for these social issues. One only needs to wait long enough until salvation comes.

contributing to a sense of pleasure and reward in the viewer's role as a potential savior.

Besides the emphasis on faith and karma, self-help videos also propose self-surveillance and practices of quantification to escape the pitfalls of instant gratification and to remain productive. Mel Robbins' "five-second rule" is a self-management technique that advocates counting down from five in order to interrupt self-rumination and encourage proactive behavior.[93] Used as a technique in anger management, counting down here promises the regaining of control, but also a sense of anticipatory joy—such as on occasions like New Year's Eve. In self-help culture, numerical techniques such as counting down, setting deadlines, and using quantifiable measures align with the pursuit of self-control, but they also promise a sense of fulfillment. By incorporating numbers and measurements, these practices create a structure that fosters predictability and a feeling of completion, presumably aiding individuals in overcoming procrastination and achieving their goals.

Blogger Tim Urban's TED talk, "Inside the Mind of a Master Procrastinator," introduces a fable-like narrative to illustrate the internal struggle between various agents within the self. The "Instant Gratification Monkey," representing the desire for ease and fun in the present, clashes with the "Rational Decision-Maker," embodying the ability to *visualize* the future and consider the "big picture."[94] Additionally, the "guardian angel" or "Panic Monster" takes on the surveillance role, "*looking down*" and "*watching over*" the procrastinator in moments of crisis.[95] As such, this internal battle is depicted visually, as a play of gazes. This focus on vision is reinforced scientifically, too: during his talk, Urban compares the MRI brain scans of his brain with that of a non-procrastinator. The responsibility and accountability imposed by the Panic Monster suggests once more that procrastination is an internal conflict, an inner impulse cured by human reason—an ability that "no other animal" has.

Tim Urban's use of a fable-like narrative with personified characters like the "Instant Gratification Monkey" serves to convey a moral lesson about self-vigilance, primarily focused on taming animalistic impulses. This story aligns with the historical approach of remedying bad habits.[96] Urban's talk reinforces the notion of human superiority and exceptionalism, portraying the rational self as the

---

[93] See Mel Robbins' book with the same name: *The Five Second Rule* (2017).
[94] Urban, Inside the Mind, 00:05:41. It is worth noting that the "Rational Decision-Maker" is gendered as "he," highlighting the connections between the emphasis on vision, humanism, and patriarchy.
[95] Ibid., 00:07:13; emphasis added.
[96] See chapter two in this book and the discussion of "habit" there, including the examples taken from Benjamin Franklin's *Autobiography*.

force that controls the impulsive behaviors of the monkey. The talk emphasizes the detrimental impact of long-term procrastination, where individuals may feel like spectators in their own lives, unable to pursue their dreams. He attributes this problem to a lack of deadlines. The concluding "epiphany" that "we are all procrastinators" acts as a precursor to the *memento mori* theme in his scenario.[97] Urban wraps up with the presentation of a Life Calendar, suggesting that life can be compartmentalized in boxes, while reminding the audience of the constant presence of a *deadline*. Therefore, his talk contributes to a quantification of life and sets the foundation for the notion that the significance lies in age—more years equate to a greater value.

Technologist Matt Cutts further advocates quantification and the setting of deadlines in his talk "Try Something New for 30 Days." His pragmatic approach to combating boredom and stagnation encourages short-term discipline by committing to new activities over a 30-day period. The emphasis on setting a deadline for various endeavors, whether it involves biking to work, hiking on Mt. Kilimanjaro, or writing a novel, underscores the belief that clear numerical goals provide a sense of control and mastery. The talk promotes the idea that making small changes in one's schedule, cultivating habits, and utilizing time wisely lead to a new form of productivity that extends beyond work.[98] The prioritization of quantity over quality, exemplified by achieving a word count goal of 1667 words a day, reinforces the notion that completion is the ultimate objective. Cutts proudly confesses that he can now identify himself as a "novelist" at a TED party.[99]

The quantified approach extends not only to time but also to bodies, exemplified by the Quantified Self movement primarily focused on body measurements for self-awareness. Rooted in self-help culture, this movement employs quantification practices akin to watching the clock or watching the scale. The once subjective aspects of the body become transparent and readable, subjected to analysis and objectification. Ron Gutman delves into a "journey of real science"[100] in his TED talk on "The Hidden Power of Smiling." In this study, he scrutinizes photos of students to "measure their success and well-being" by assessing their smiles.[101] Although the notion of measurement suggests scientific objectivity, the actual quantifiability of such "data" remains uncertain. The researchers not only establish a

---

[97] Urban, Inside the Mind, 00:12:31.
[98] Discussions of career life and success sometimes take a different turn and they become meditations on "life." As such, the boundaries between work and life are blurred, rather than balanced.
[99] Cutts, Try Something New, 00:02:17.
[100] Gutman, Hidden Power, 00:00:30.
[101] Ibid., 00:00:45.

correlation between success and smiley faces but also contend that smiles predict the subjects' well-being.

Gutman cites a study indicating that the smiles of baseball players can predict their longevity. He emphasizes that smiling is a fundamental, biologically uniform expression in all humans, observable even in babies in the womb and members of the Fore tribe in Papua New Guinea.[102] Describing smiling as "evolutionarily contagious,"[103] Gutman notes its role in distinguishing between fake and genuine smiles through mimicking. Charles Darwin's theory is referenced, revealing that the act of smiling itself can make individuals feel better, not merely as a result of already feeling good.[104] Gutman enthusiastically continues by citing sources that equate one smile's impact on the brain to eating 2000 bars of chocolate or receiving £16000 in cash. Additionally, he explores its health benefits, including stress hormone reduction, blood pressure regulation, and enhancement of the self's perceived competence.

Gutman's talk delivers an overwhelmingly optimistic portrayal of the benefits of smiling, linking this human behavior to feelings of wealth, pleasure, health, and social recognition—a kind of magical philosopher's stone. His presentation essentially becomes a heartfelt plea for smiling, encouraging his audience to embrace it as a superpower that contributes to longer, healthier, and happier lives: "whenever you want to tap into a superpower that will help you and everyone around you live a longer, healthier, happier life, smile."[105] This approach resonates with another renowned talk by social psychologist Amy Cuddy on body language, which has amassed over 60 million views as of December 2021.[106]

Cuddy's talk popularized the belief in "power posing," the idea that standing in a posture of confidence, even when one does not feel confident, can enhance feelings of confidence and potentially impact success.[107] Cuddy made the "fake it till you make it" belief popular. Her concept reverses the conventional understanding of bodily gestures as expressive means to display internal feelings. Instead, it suggests that these gestures can be employed in order to induce feelings, emphasizing the shift from "surface acting," which uses the body to "show" feelings, to "deep acting," which uses the body to "inspire" feelings.[108] Thus, Cuddy proposes "deep

---

[102] Ibid., 00:02:09.
[103] Ibid., 00:03:33.
[104] Ibid., 00:04:25.
[105] Ibid., 00:06:47.
[106] As of the last check on 11 January 2023, the talk had amassed more than 67 million views.
[107] Cuddy, Your Body Language.
[108] Hochschild, *Managed Heart*, p. 257. As an illustration, Hochschild adds, "relaxing a grimace or unclenching a fist, we may actually make ourselves feel less angry."

acting," a form of emotional management where bodily performance takes precedence.

The idea that emotions can be controlled with the help of the body reinforces the power of reason. These talks suggest another way of using reason to master the body—through performing and practicing bodily gestures to achieve specific results. In this case, power is contingent on hormonal changes, various brain configurations, and body postures, which differs from Packnett's perspective on confidence introduced at the beginning of this chapter. As Cuddy argues, "this is not about you talking to other people. It's *you talking to yourself.*"[109] In various ways, the predominant view in TED talks revolves around the notion of internal battles or struggles, rather than emphasizing the importance of social networks and interdependency.

Taken together, these talks offer varied perspectives on the concept of success. While they unanimously assert that money is not a prerequisite for success,[110] they diverge on several aspects. Ideas about being "good enough" or the value of working hard are both promoted and criticized. Success is depicted as both the result of setting goals and not setting them; it involves considerations of reputation, power, and prestige, yet simultaneously does not. Faith and passion are acknowledged as components of success. Consequently, success is contingent on numerous factors: habits, self-discipline, and body language—primarily individual choices and behaviors. Self-control in the workplace extends beyond anger management; it has become integrated into every aspect of the self's actions, encompassing time management, habits, and even bodily gestures. This perspective advocates meticulous self-monitoring, where even seemingly insignificant details like hunching one's back can be determinants of success. However, this heightened self-awareness tends to overshadow other social issues, pushing factors such as working conditions, job insecurity, and market oversaturation into the background.

As a result, TED talks and their scientific strand of self-help intensify the focus on the individual self. TED speakers and motivational speakers remain unaware of the ways in which their videos contribute to what they describe as procrastina-

---

109 Cuddy, Your Body Language, 00:13:31; emphasis added.
110 For instance, Wooden challenges the belief that success means "the accumulation of material possessions" (00:01:54). St. John confesses to buying a fast car as a solution to his depression that did not work and he shows a humorous image with himself in it, accompanied by the written text: "Money can't buy happiness" (00:02:02). These claims seem to challenge previous self-help examples, such as Napoleon Hill's *Think and Grow Rich* (1937), where success meant increasing one's income.

tion.[111] They primarily ascribe a lack of productivity to distraction, while their videos promote faith, karma, or a "waiting out" approach. Simultaneously, these videos cultivate a sense of instant gratification, offering a pleasurable experience when social justice is swiftly achieved. Despite challenging the notion of overnight success by reinforcing a Protestant work ethic, they inadvertently contribute to the myth of the self-made man in the Internet age. This myth suggests that any average person can attain online fame by being sufficiently inspiring. They tend to obscure the privilege underlying their success,[112] emphasizing personal narratives framed as missions. Personal struggles serve to illustrate how one can find personal redemption, ostensibly becoming stepping stones to help others. The next section will explore a specific mission embraced by these speakers: the mission of saving humanity.

5.3 The Mission of Saving Humanity and the Duty to Be Alive

On his website, Dhar Mann displays an image of himself wearing a Batman-like suit, featuring the words "Your struggle becomes your superpower."[113] Many TED speakers also frame their work as a mission. Entrepreneur Ron Gutman starts his talk by sharing his childhood dream of being a superhero who saves the world "and makes everyone happy."[114] Health psychologist Kelly McGonigal initiates her talk with a "confession": "I am a health psychologist, and my *mission* is to help people be happier and healthier."[115] Consequently, happiness emerges as a distinct mission for numerous TED presenters, irrespective of their backgrounds. This trend is noteworthy, as it sheds light on why transhumanists have embraced the TED genre to disseminate their ideas. It also reflects what is termed "dangerous altruism" in Powers' novel,[116] a concept explored further in the literary analysis of this book.

However, many times, this personal mission signifies not only a duty to be happy but also a duty to be alive. Prince Ea's performance in "Stop Wasting

---

111 Chapman and Whitlock identify procrastination as a negative affect after using Instagram (Social Media Influencers, 2019).
112 For instance, both Richard Williams and Jay Shetty had completed graduate studies, and achieved partial success before their videos went viral. They were already acquainted with business culture, with Dhar Mann having even ventured into a few other businesses before.
113 Mann, About. https://www.dharmann.com/about/.
114 Gutman, Hidden Power, 00:00:05.
115 McGonigal, How to Make Stress, 00:00:35.
116 Powers, *Generosity*, p. 22.

Your Life" resembles a sermon where he preaches the truth of happiness. It appears to depict a scenario of work versus happiness. His call to "step out of the rat race"[117] which raises zombies, is accompanied by the call to find inner happiness, equating it with vitality and livelihood. The process of growing old is portrayed as a postponing of happiness, prompting his audience to be happy right now and "take control" of the "human console."[118] He flips the notion of work-life balance on its head, suggesting that work life raises zombies and is the opposite of livelihood.

The ticking clock, the progress bar at the video's bottom, and the prominent red "work" button all serve to heighten self-awareness and contribute to the pressure of choosing happiness and waking up. Ea's performance invokes the duty to be happy—thus, happiness is once again considered a "right and a skill that can be developed," rather than a matter of luck, virtue, or divine favor.[119] Therefore, "happiness is now seen as a mindset that can be engineered through willpower,"[120] with sole responsibility lying with the individual self to achieve it. Prince Ea motivates his audience to choose happiness by highlighting its correlation with increased intelligence, productivity, creativity, wealth, and a longer lifespan.[121] His performance takes an interesting turn, presenting happiness not as an end goal but as a means to achieve other goals, notably money and productivity, which are work-related.

He also draws upon the idea of *memento mori* (similar to "time is now" or "live in the moment"), adding to the pressure of "choosing happiness," and it even becomes a matter of life or death, especially given the setting—the hospital and the heart attack with which Ea begins. "Life" in its broad sense is the primary justification behind choosing happiness—so the duty to be happy transforms into a duty to be alive.[122] Even in TED, stress, jobs, and career life become pretexts to discuss "life." Life becomes a central concern, whether there is an interest in longevity or the joy of being alive—life becomes tangential to the main topic of success, as seen in the tombstone reference,[123] the eulogy virtues,[124] Urban's "Life Calendar,"[125] or

---

[117] Prince Ea, Stop Wasting, 00:03:11.
[118] Ibid., 00:03:41.
[119] McMahon, Happiness.
[120] Cabanas/Illouz, *Manufacturing*, p. 3.
[121] Prince Ea, Stop Wasting, 00:04:43.
[122] This analysis is based on the 2020 video version; the 2023 version omits the reference to the "rat race." Additionally, the scientific basis of his video primarily draws from Shawn Achor and his TED talk.
[123] Smith, Why You Will Fail, 00:07:51.
[124] Brooks, Should You Live, 00:00:09.
[125] Urban, Inside the Mind, 00:12:59.

brief promises of living longer and happier.[126] The presence of "life" in these talks does not just imply adopting the metaphor of life as a "work of art"[127] but is linked to a broader interest in humanity and its future survival: life as longevity, the antithesis of death.

Casey Gerald's impactful TED talk relies on the theme of life and death, as his "private revelation" challenges the perception that "queer lives or black lives or poor lives are marginal lives."[128] He contrasts obedience, which he associates with being "a well-liked holy nugget, to be dead,"[129] with embracing one's "raw, strange magic" as a means of being truly alive.[130] Similarly, Brené Brown, in her TED talk, expresses gratitude, stating that "to feel this vulnerable means I'm alive."[131] David Brooks' "Should You Live for Your Résumé… Or Your Eulogy?" is a "short meditative talk"[132] that shifts focus from career virtues to an ethics of life. The eulogy, typically a tribute to someone deceased, prompts the audience to reflect on those values for which they want to be remembered.

Brooks employs a rhetoric reminiscent of Smith's when questioning the audience about headstone inscriptions. While Smith perceived life and career as intertwined, Brooks differentiates between the social self and the authentic self ("who you are"), echoing St. John's distinction between character and reputation. Drawing on the teachings of Rabbi Joseph Soloveitchik, Brooks introduces the dual aspects of human nature—Adam I and Adam II. Adam I seeks to conquer the world, relishes accomplishments, and prioritizes innovation with a motto of "success."[133] Adam II, on the other hand, values humility, honors God, cherishes inner consistency and strength, and aspires to "hear a calling" with a motto of "love, redemption, and return."[134] Brooks argues that society leans toward favoring Adam I and his economic and pragmatic logic. Neglecting Adam II, according to Brooks,

---

[126] Gutman, Hidden Power, 00:06:53.
[127] McGee, *Self-Help, Inc.*, p. 46.
[128] Gerald, Embrace, 00:09:40, 00:11:28.
[129] Ibid., 00:12:30.
[130] Ibid., 00:09:28.
[131] Brown, Power of Vulnerability, 00:19:35. In her famous talk, Brown contends that vulnerability is central to social connection, emphasizing the importance of allowing ourselves "to be seen, really seen" (00:05:20). Rather than numbing vulnerability, she encourages her audience to embrace imperfection and treat themselves with compassion. However, she does not take into account the societal aspects that may punish certain vulnerabilities and render certain individuals invisible.
[132] Brooks, Should You Live.
[133] Ibid., 00:01:25.
[134] Ibid., 00:01:13, 00:01:28.

results in a world governed by a "cold, calculated creature,"[135] hinting at the dehumanizing aspects of society.

Brooks' talk suggests a shift from a pragmatic self-help trend toward a more spiritual one. He advocates the development of a "depth of character" achieved through "fighting your weaknesses."[136] The moments of shame and sin in childhood or the struggles and suffering of the self are seen as pathways toward this depth of character. This concept echoes the redemptive narrative of McAdams or the scientific idea of post-traumatic growth. Brooks concludes with the notion of redemption, quoting Reinhald Neibuhr, who posits that "we must be saved by love, saved by faith, [and] forgiveness."[137] In a stance reminiscent of a "flower power," Brooks' talk reinforces a dichotomous perspective of an inner battle or self-confrontation, depicting a rebellious, binary relationship between two selves governed by different principles. He proposes replacing Adam I with Adam II, suggesting that virtues related to psychology, morality, and spirituality should govern work life. Brooks aims to offer an alternative to the utilitarian promotion of Adam I as the calculated, rational self, advocating for a redemptive approach instead. Viewed from this perspective, Adam II perceives work as a personal mission, akin to the idea of saving humanity.[138]

In "How to Make Stress Your Friend," Kelly McGonigal prompts the audience to acknowledge their stress levels while confessing that she once considered stress an adversary—a perspective she intends to change. Referencing a study, she highlights the influence of belief on stress's physical effects, noting that those who perceived stress as non-harmful had the lowest risk of mortality, even amid high stress levels.[139] She adds:

> When you change your mind about stress, you can change your body's response to stress. [...] And participants who learned to view the stress response as helpful for their performance, well, they were less stressed out, less anxious, more confident, but the most fascinating find-

---

135 Ibid., 00:02:25.
136 Ibid., 00:02:55, 00:03:29.
137 Ibid., 00:04:16.
138 McGee has also shown the ways in which these perspectives offered by Brooks mutually reinforce each other. *Homo economicus*, characterized by instrumental rationality and cost-benefit analysis, is considered a "masculine" worldview, while expressive individualism, rooted in Romanticism, is seen as "soft" or "feminine." The former views humans as calculating and strategic, while the latter emphasizes sensing, feeling, and a connection with others and nature, portraying humans as *Homo ludens*—joyful and playful beings seeking harmony with the natural world. Despite their apparent incompatibility, these perspectives are argued to be complementary within modern capitalism, with the expressive dimension serving as a counterbalance to market-driven instrumental rationality. See *Self-Help Inc.*, p. 29.
139 McGonigal, How to Make, 00:01:45.

ing to me was how their physical stress response changed. The change in their cardiovascular profile showed what happens in moments of joy and courage. Not only did they escape stress, they also turned it into joy.[140]

The presentation further delves into the role of oxytocin, portraying it not only as a neuro-hormone released in joyful moments but also as part of a stress response, compelling individuals to seek help.[141] The juxtaposition of stress and joy, though counterintuitive, aligns with a redemptive approach, suggesting that stress can mediate and even facilitate moments of joy.

At the end of the talk, Chris Anderson reflects on the profound impact of beliefs about stress on life expectancy, pondering the implications for lifestyle choices, such as opting for a stressful job versus a non-stressful one.[142] The notion arises that if stressful jobs carry meaning, they might positively influence the self and contribute to its longevity. This places the responsibility on the individual to either succumb to stress or embrace it as an ally, potentially extending life. A prevalent response to stress is the widespread adoption of mindfulness, a technique and habit explored in many TED talks, becoming the focal point of the next section.[143] For now, delving into a literary example will provide an additional perspective on the themes introduced in this chapter, allowing us to explore the concepts of self-improvement, success, and the duty to be alive from a different angle.

---

[140] Ibid., 00:03:09.
[141] Ibid., 00:10:30. As she notes, "I find this amazing, that your stress response has a built-in mechanism for stress resilience, and that mechanism is *human connection.*"
[142] Ibid., 00:13:27.
[143] McGonigal's talk is also included in TED talks on the idea of mindfulness, even if she does not directly address the concept. Additionally, it holds the distinction of being the most viewed talk on that list and is ranked among the top ten talks on mindfulness in terms of relevance.

6 Gary Shteyngart's *Super Sad True Love Story* and the Privilege of "Merely Existing"

Gary Shteyngart's *Super Sad True Love Story* emerges as a speculative fiction satire[1] and a "modern-day epistolary novel,"[2] interweaving a dystopian perspective with the "life writing" of postcolonial subjects. Through the journal entries of Russian-American Jewish man Lenny Abramov and the thoughts and email correspondence of Korean girl Eunice Park, the novel critically examines the prevailing duty to be alive within self-help culture, revealing it as a disguised duty to work. In a society dominated by social media and credit scoring, a moment of "rupture" unfolds,[3] wherein Shteyngart cleverly puns on Christian apocalyptic "Rapture" depicting a sudden collapse of the United States into irreparable factions as China and Germany rise to global dominance.[4] Beyond its dystopian narrative, the novel becomes a commentary on reading practices, offering a vision that exposes the importance and "impotence of writing and reading in an illiterate age."[5] This chapter delves into how the novel frames self-help culture and introduces alternative perspectives on the duty to be alive.

6.1 Self-Help Culture: "You've Got to Sell to Live"

This is how Lenny introduces himself: "From this day forward, you will travel on the greatest adventure yet undertaken by a nervous, average man sixty-nine inches

---

[1] For instance, scholars have interpreted it as a Menippean Satire that "immerses us, sometimes terrifyingly so, within fear and culture clash, with no 'safe space' available. Not only does the Menippean incursion signify such danger, but the whole of the form enact invasion and vulnerability on every page" (Schmidt, Menippean Satire, p. 2).
[2] Kern, Big Data, p. 87. Or, as Rutledge adds, it is a novel about "digital epistolarity" (Shteyngart's, p. 376).
[3] This moment of Rupture is described as such in the novel: "We are in the process of a profound change, but we urge all members of the Post-Human family *to remain both calm and vigilant*. The expected collapse of the Rubenstein/ARA/Bipartisan regime presents us with great possibilities" (Shteyngart, *Super Sad*, p. 238). The rhetoric of self-help culture permeates it, portraying every crisis as another opportunity for success.
[4] Cf. Schmidt, Menippean Satire, p. 15.
[5] Spahr, Re-Learning, p. 560.

in height, 160 pounds in heft, with a slightly dangerous body mass index of 23.9."[6] Lenny is concerned about his "so-so body in a world where only an incredible one will do. A body at the chronological age of thirty-nine already racked with too much LDL cholesterol, too much ACTH hormone, too much of everything that dooms the heart, sunders the liver, explodes all hope."[7] Lenny's self-perception is governed by data and numbers, illustrating how the Quantified Self [QS] becomes the primary model of human subjectivity. "Self-knowledge and self-understanding have, in part, become about self-measurement and self-quantification, or to invoke the mantra of the QS movement, we achieve 'self-knowledge through numbers.' In this schema, molecular and genetic data form the substrate of human life."[8]

Accordingly, aspects of embodied life are reduced to "data sets that can be quantified, monitored, and compared."[9] The body transforms into a disciplinary space, reminiscent of Foucault's concept that governments exercise control over populations by managing bodies—hence the term biopower. Biopower "is not just about the control of individuals, ensuring their homogenisation and hierarchisation, but, furthermore and centrally, is about dynamics of inclusion and exclusion."[10] As Lenny's summary demonstrates, at least three parameters rank people in society: youth, health, and wealth. They also present a caricaturized perspective of society that perpetuates stereotypical views, such as Koreans appearing young and skinny (as seen with Eunice), Russians having a tendency for being depressed (as seen with Lenny), Jews being rich (Lenny again), Mexicans being poor, and so forth. These stereotypes handicap the postcolonial subjects, teetering on the edge of inclusion or exclusion based on them. The novel simultaneously reproduces and challenges these stereotypes.[11]

---

6 Shteyngart, *Super Sad*, p. 2. At the beginning, Lenny is preoccupied with the idea of being "nullified" (ibid., 1, 2), implying that even death is quantified, highlighting the notion that life is reduced to numbers or digits—the larger the number, the wealthier and more vibrant.
7 Ibid., p. 3.
8 Dolezal, Human Life, p. 3.
9 Ibid., p. 1. Rita Raley terms this regime a "dataveillance" society, "one in which acts of discipline and control occur through the ubiquity of data recording" (cf. Kern, Big Data, p. 82). See also the concept of "algorithmic governmentality" (ibid., p. 90).
10 Dolezal, Human Life, p. 4.
11 For instance, Eunice's sister is also Korean, but she does not conform to the stereotype of being skinny. Additionally, the stereotypes in Shteyngart "appear here in such an exaggerated and reductive form that one can conclude Shteyngart is staging a comedy of multicultural descent, using stereotypes to reveal the absurdity of such essentialism" (Trapp, Super Sad, p. 58)—making them more akin to caricatures.

In this context, life or livelihood is reduced to age as a numerical figure, to health as another numerical value—the body mass index,[12] and to survival as monetary affluence—all represented by numbers. Money, thus, presumably allows people to simply purchase life, or the so-called dechronification treatments that Lenny and his boss sell to "Life Lovers."[13] Business culture and Lenny's working environment adhere to the guidelines and principles of self-help culture: "Little framed humorous hints scattered throughout. 'Just Say No to Starch.' 'Cheer Up! Pessimism Kills.' 'Telomere-Extended Cells Do It Better.' 'NATURE HAS A LOT TO LEARN FROM US'."[14]

> Eunice's development also exemplifies the dangers of self-optimization that Deborah Lupton has described in The Quantified Self: "Illness, emotional distress, lack of happiness or lack of productivity in the workplace come to be represented primarily as failures of self-control or efficiency on the part of individuals, and therefore as requiring greater or more effective individual efforts—including perhaps self-tracking regimens of increased intensity—to produce a 'better self'" (74–75).[15]

Furthermore, aside from Eunice, "Lenny and his co-workers constantly monitor their vital signs and attempt to adjust their lifestyles accordingly."[16] The underlying motivation of the QS movement "largely coincides with the one espoused by Lenny: The self-knowledge that is viewed as emerging from the minutiae of data recording a myriad of aspects of the body is a psychological salve to the fear of bodily degeneration."[17]

In a culture dominated by the "tyranny of positivity,"[18] Lenny attempts to assimilate, yet he appears to figure among the few individuals who resist the pull of this neoliberal ideology. Joshie, Lenny's boss, detects his hesitancy to fully embrace this positive ideology, which he associates with a focus on life rather than death.

---

12 The body mass index was "devised exclusively by and for white Western Europeans" and was the invention of the mathematician Adolphe Quetelet, who aimed to identify the characteristics of the "average man"—a social ideal that later became a scientific justification for eugenics. See also "The Bizarre and Racist History of the BMI."
13 Shteyngart, *Super Sad*, p. 49. *Dechronos* also sounds like an attempt to escape time, as Chronos was the primordial God of time.
14 Ibid., p. 58.
15 Cf. Spahr, Re-Learning, p. 557.
16 Haase, Death by Data, p. 92.
17 Ibid.
18 Cain, *Bittersweet*, p. 118.

However, from another perspective, it is Joshie who fixates on death, while Lenny revels in life.[19] Joshie writes to Eunice:

> You really take care of yourself and it shows in how beautiful and young you look. There's a real overlap between our philosophies on life and staying younger and taking care of oneself, something I think we've both been trying to instill in Lenny, but ultimately I think *Lenny's immune to that*. I've been trying to get him to think about health choices, but he's just really focused on his parents and worried about THEIR death, without really understanding what it means to want to *live life to the fullest*, to the freshest, to the youngest. In some ways, you and I are really from the same generation of people and Lenny is from a different world, a previous world that was *obsessed with death and not life*, and was *consumed with fear and not positivism.*[20]

Joshie articulates himself like a capitalist hippie[21] and self-help guru, extolling the virtues of self-care and optimism. However, from an alternative viewpoint, Eunice is also characterized as rather "pessimistic, feeling the pull of descent and the incomprehensibility of ethnic difference."[22] Her writing also aligns with this perspective, as she shares Lenny's belief (inspired by Freud) in "common unhappiness."[23] Therefore, the novel challenges a clear-cut distinction between optimism and pessimism, portraying them both as unstable and impermanent values.

At the same time, one social role, in particular, takes center stage, even in social interactions that are supposed to form communities: the salesman. Joshie is Lenny's boss[24] and the epitome of the self-made man who became a "posthuman self with no core,"[25] but also the most successful salesman.[26] A member of the

---

19 "With each second I had spent in Rome, lustily minding the architecture, rapturously fucking Fabrizia, drinking and eating enough daily glucose to kill a Cuban sugarcane farmer, I had paved the toll road to my own demise" (Shteyngart, *Super Sad*, p. 75). This scene appears as a plea for hedonism, suggesting that the act of controlling the body is merely replaced with indulgence as its sole alternative. On the other hand, Lenny's sexual vigor also stands in contrast to the standards of American society, where sexual desirability is reduced to the "fuckability" score (ibid., p. 27). Thus, it redirects attention toward the sensuous body rather than the body as data.
20 Ibid., p. 266; emphasis added.
21 The figure of the countercultural hippie has been appropriated to serve as the new model for the successful self in capitalism.
22 Trapp, *Super Sad*, p. 62.
23 Shteyngart, *Super Sad*, p. 295f. In this context, she also adds: "Prof Margaux in Assertiveness Class said, 'You are allowed to be happy, Eunice.' What a stupid American idea."
24 Joshie is like a father figure to Lenny: "As a fellow Jew, he is Lenny's 'second father' (56), his chosen parent of consent who will teach Lenny how to assimilate and transcend his descent" (Trapp, *Super Sad*, p. 68).
25 Trapp, *Super Sad*, p. 68.

"technological elite" and the "creative economy,"[27] Lenny's boss seemingly "didn't give a damn about success. *'Creative thinking*, working with your mind, that's my number-one prescription for longevity. If you stop thinking, if you stop wondering, you die. That simple.' He looked down at his feet, perhaps realizing he sounded more like a salesman than a leader."[28] In this case, Joshie conflates the figure of the salesman with that of the genius, as the salesman becomes a genius in a world where only one form of creative thinking is encouraged and rewarded: that which sells.[29] So, his character also recalls the model of "the artist as an entrepreneur."[30] This idea is reinforced in one of Joshie and Lenny's encounters:

> Those thoughts, these books, they are the problem, Rhesus," he said. "You have to stop thinking and start selling. That's why all those young whizzes in the Eternity Lounge want to shove a carb-filled macaroon up your ass. Yes, I overheard that. I have a new beta eardrum. And who can blame them, Lenny? You remind them of death. You remind them of a different, earlier version of our species. Don't get pissed at me, now. Remember, I started out just like you. Acting. The humanities. It's the Fallacy of Merely Existing. FME. There'll be plenty of time to ponder and write and act out later. Right now you've got to *sell to live*.[31]

Selling and marketing replace all meaning-making jobs, including reading or writing books. Selling ideas[32] becomes the most popular commercial transaction—as Post-Human Services attempt to sell the hope of living forever to mostly rich, white men.[33] Also, people have to sell their own selves to live.[34] The "fallacy of merely existing" mentioned by Joshie is an important key to deciphering the novel's main points of criticism. Initially, it highlights the illusion that society lets peo-

---

26 Joshie "can be seen as a fictional mouthpiece for Ray Kurzweil (credited by Shteyngart in the acknowledgments), a scientist who is well known for his championing of transhumanism" (Haase, Death by Data, p. 93). The same can be said about Kurton in Richard Powers, as discussed in chapter 13.
27 Shteyngart, *Super Sad*, p. 179.
28 Ibid., p. 217.
29 These meanings are collapsed in the äppärät, too. The pebble/stone symbolizes the creative spirit (Rutledge, Shteyngart's, p. 386) which is here juxtaposed with a technological device used mainly for work—the main tool of the salesman.
30 McGee, *Self-Help, Inc.*, p. 22.
31 Shteyngart, *Super Sad*, p. 65; emphasis in original.
32 This shift from writing to selling ideas is a recurrent topic in Atwood and Powers, too. See chapters 8 and 13.
33 Living forever is also an American idea, as Europeans "actually want to die" (Shteyngart, *Super Sad*, p. 67), the reason why Lenny was unsuccessful in Italy. Also, according to him, women are more concerned with taking care of their progeny.
34 "In order to take part in society, Lenny also has to *sell himself*" (Haase, Death by Data, p. 91; emphasis in original).

ple merely exist. Instead, individuals must work to earn the right to live, predominantly through one type of work—"you've got to *sell to live*."³⁵ Consequently, the novel not only comments on the idea of immortality but also exposes how people must work in order to survive. Life and survival are no longer guaranteed. Descartes' cogito argument "I think, therefore I am" is replaced with *I sell, therefore I am*. The entire notion of human rights, including the right to pursue happiness, is thus ridiculed, as there are no rights without the duty to work. The constitutional declaration of life, liberty, and the pursuit of happiness has not only collapsed but has been reduced to the duty to work.

In a postcolonial context, this business approach undermines the immigrant myth or the American dream of the self-made man—where, if one works hard enough, success and assimilation are guaranteed.³⁶ At best, if one sells enough, he or she is allowed to live. Being old, overweight, or poor is a perilous condition—and such individuals are not only excluded from society or subject to discrimination, perpetuating a culture of body shaming, but they are also subjected to violent removal. They are literally at risk of being killed, as the so-called Rupture demonstrates. In various ways, the sheer corporeality of their bodies, and their mortality and vulnerability, become too visible in a society that only accepts the body as data.

Furthermore, and closely related to the previous point, the "fallacy of merely existing" also captures the tacit knowledge that people mostly overlook: merely existing is not a fallacy, but the basis of livelihood. Merely existing should be enough; the problem is that American society does not let its citizens merely exist. Instead, *Super Sad True Love Story* proposes existence or living as a purpose in itself. As a result, the entire rhetoric focused on mission, destiny, journey, and higher purpose is challenged. In short, business culture lets people believe that merely existing is a fallacy, that they should strive for something more, to be part of something bigger, but it does not even let them exist without work or money. As such, to exist becomes a privilege[37] in a world where people can purchase dechronification treat-

---

35 Shteyngart, *Super Sad*, p. 65; emphasis in original.
36 Shteyngart "also undermines its sustaining mythology: the American dream and its meritocratic promise of material rewards that traditionally sped the assimilation of immigrant families" (Trapp, Super Sad, p. 67).
37 Joshie seems to have this privilege: "We were doing brushstrokes with M. Cohen and I couldn't believe the concentration on Joshie's face. The way his lower lip was just hanging there like a little boy's and he was breathing really carefully, like there was nothing more important in the world than brushstrokes. There's something powerful in being able to let go and focus on something that's completely outside yourself. I guess Joshie has had a lot of privilege in his life and he knows what to do with it" (Shteyngart, *Super Sad*, p. 295).

ments to prolong their lives—though, paradoxically, they only do so in order to work even more.

Lenny is a different kind of salesman than Joshie: "Lenny is socially inept and significantly older, fatter, and uglier than Eunice. His one *redeeming* quality is that as a salesman for Post-Human Services, a company promising its clients immortality, he is a high earner with an impressive credit rating."[38] Yet, Lenny also appears to be a distorted reflection of Willy Loman from Arthur Miller's *Death of a Salesman*, where being a salesman has no redeeming qualities, quite the contrary. Even if he is presumably rich, Lenny is actually in debt, so numbers and credit scoring can be deceiving: "I owed Howard Shu 239,000 yuan-pegged dollars. My first stab at dechronification—gone. My hair would continue to gray, and then one day it would fall out entirely, and then, on a day meaninglessly close to the present one, meaninglessly like the present one, I would disappear from the earth."[39]

In this instance, Lenny also hints at the correlation between money and life on which American society rests, which is more explicitly named later on: "Money equals life. By my estimation, even the preliminary beta dechronification treatments, for example, the insertion of SmartBlood to regulate my ridiculous cardiovascular system, would run three million yuan per year."[40] Personal health depends on how much money one has; thus, the novel also implicitly criticizes the American healthcare system, where only the rich can survive. When survival depends on wealth, it reduces everyone else to Miller's protagonist's grim faith.

In a country run by "amoral business interests,"[41] everything else becomes a matter of trade and profit. When everything is reduced to money and business, taking care of one's own health means selling one's own genome to a company; social relationships are reduced to social media spectacle and superficial interactions; creativity is reduced to the "creative economy"[42] or selling ideas; and having a home means owning a property. The idea of building a home is trampled by real estate businesses. Homes are bestowed only upon the rich: "Now they were going to bestow immortality on a bunch of fat, glossy Dubai billionaires who bought a Staatling Property "TRIPLEX Living Unit"?[43] While Lenny's own home is demolish-

---

38 Trapp, Super Sad, p. 57; emphasis added.
39 Shteyngart, *Super Sad*, p. 68.
40 Ibid., p. 75.
41 Trapp, Super Sad, p. 67.
42 Shteyngart, *Super Sad*, p. 10.
43 Ibid., p. 151.

ed, billionaires keep buying properties. So, the world is no longer governed by the idea of building a home or a family, but owning properties.[44]

Not only are working duties omnipresent, but they replace any other loyalties or responsibilities, as they inform each and every social dynamic. For instance, Lenny wishes his parents would stop fighting about his job or education. "Why couldn't they find a better use for their retirement years than *this painful scrutiny* of their only child? Why did they stalk me with their tomatoes and high-school averages and *'Who are you by profession?'* logic?"[45] In other words, people are judged and judge each other only through the prism of their line of work. On the one hand, this is already foregrounded in the practice of credit scoring, which also reduces individuals to "either hyper-specific accumulations of data points (caricature) or broad social types defined by spending habits (stereotype)."[46] At the same time, it shows how American society judges the entire worth of an individual's life by measuring its creditworthiness or success. Not only does success mean accruing wealth and acquiring fame, but it is also the number one criterion for evaluating characters and whether they deserve love. For instance, Lenny believes that "his main genetic defect" is the fact that his "father is a janitor from a poor country."[47] Eunice feels "so undeserving of being with someone like Ben and [...] I just kept picturing him with some beautiful supermodel or some really smart but sexy Mediawhore."[48]

Social media fame is the ideal form of success in the novel, as it allows people to "sell" their lives online—"life writing" is replaced with "life selling." The novel, thus, also comments on the contemporary popularity of social media influencers by exposing the loose boundaries between life and work life. RateMe is one of Lenny's most important job duties—he has to "learn to rate everyone around you [...] An ill-informed salesman is dead in the water these days."[49] Lenny carries his work with him even whenever he meets his friends; not only because people invest even more time at work, but because work duties replace any other form of interaction. In other words, the boundaries between social life or community building and doing one's job are blurred, for they become the two sides of the same coin. This becomes even more apparent in Lenny's interaction with Noah.

---

[44] "My apartment. My home. My investment. I'll be forty in two weeks and I have nothing." I wanted her to say, 'You have me,' but it was not forthcoming" (ibid., p. 311).
[45] Ibid., p. 139; emphasis added.
[46] Bullen, Act Two, p. 247.
[47] Shteyngart, *Super Sad*, p. 58.
[48] Ibid., p. 42.
[49] Ibid., p. 68.

When he meets his friend Noah, they have no intimacy.[50] Noah keeps streaming Lenny's memories of his trip to Italy and even guides his speech, so he does not lose his followers. "I cut short a description of the Pantheon's empty space drenched with early-morning sunlight, as Noah pointed the clumped remains of his frontal hair at me and said: 'All right, here's the situation, Nee-gro. You have to fuck either Mother Teresa or Margaret Thatcher....'"[51] Confessions have to be extraordinary or sensational in order to gain attention, and they have to be crafted that way.[52] In this context, Lenny ponders the carelessness of American society, as "[t]he world they needed was right around them, flickering and bleeping, and it demanded every bit of strength and attention they could spare,"[53] yet they do not do such.

Lenny's editing of his description[54] not only blurs the lines between work and leisure[55] but also reveals the overlooked nuances in this society—elements demanding bodily vulnerability, like the seemingly trivial, ineffable, and short-lived flickers. These nuanced bodily experiences, fundamental to earning one's livelihood, remain ignored in a society where the body only makes sense as data. The body becomes the main currency in social encounters, transforming them into judgmental transactions. Forming a community no longer entails personal interactions but rather adherence to societal standards in a controlled environment.[56] Personal lives and bodies become consumable and marketable, finding

---

50 As Elizabeth Kovach also points out, "Their meeting is constantly interrupted by Noah's addresses to his phone, which records and broadcasts their interaction to a live audience, upon whom Noah is dependent for advertising revenue" (E-Pistolary Novels, p. 268).
51 Shteyngart, *Super Sad*, p. 84.
52 The sensational character of Noah's suggestion does not refer only to the famous characters that he mentions—Mother Theresa or Margaret Thatcher, but also points to the ways in which to "fuck" becomes exceptional in a society that ignores and governs the body.
53 Shteyngart, *Super Sad*, p. 84.
54 A similar kind of cutting is going to be addressed in Powers' novel, too: where the science TV show "cuts" Kurton's mood.
55 Consider Kovach's detailed analysis for further insights into this "confluence of work and leisure," particularly in its connection to Manuel Castells' concept of the "network society." Kovach delves into the significance of the äppärat, exploring how the blurring of traditionally compartmentalized times and spaces, once characteristic of a disciplinary society, now enables life to adopt networked forms. This transition erases the boundaries between alternating roles, spaces, and phases, aligning with Deleuze's notion of a "society of control" (E-Pistolary Novels, p. 268).
56 Deleuze uses the term "society of control" to describe the sociocultural system that has replaced disciplinary society and in which "the man of control is undulatory, in orbit, in a continuous network" (Postscript, p. 6).

meaning only in connection to a larger audience that even dictates the content—in this case, "fuckability."[57]

Sexual desirability is contingent upon fuckability rankings determined by the so-called äppärat and its EmotePad.[58] Lenny's friend Vishnu instructs him on how to "Form a Community" or "FAC": "It's, like, a way to judge people. And let them judge you [...] When you see FAC, you press the EmotePad to your heart [...] The EmotePad picks up any change in your blood pressure. That tells her how much you want to do her."[59] The concept of forming a community is simplified to fuckability, measuring one's attractiveness to a potential partner, thereby reducing love relationships to mere sexual attraction. In this scenario, assessing and being assessed involve looking at a person, allowing the äppärat to interpret bodily signals. This practice exposes bodies to scrutiny, creating an illusion of transparency that penetrates deeper than the act of sharing information online.[60] However, the ultimate determinant of the fuckability score revolves around the triad of youth, health, and wealth—societal ideals seeking to inscribe themselves on the body, though the extent of their impact remains uncertain.

Eunice, being young and attractive, garners a high fuckability score, while Lenny, owing to his older age and less-than-ideal weight, scores lower. His financial status becomes his only "redemptive" factor, elevating his score marginally. Their relationship seems fantastic in this context (or *super*, miraculous, extraordinary), as the äppärat and the practice of rating would have made it impossible. Yet, Eunice's initial attraction to Lenny arises from the financial stability and security he offers her and her family, making their connection quite commonplace in that regard. This financial aspect may contribute to her eventual departure from Lenny in favor of his wealthier boss, who can provide better security post-Rupture. Consequently, the sadness of their love story also reflects the substitution of love with money, illustrating how their relationship is entangled in the "economic totality" of capitalism.[61]

---

57 Shteyngart, *Super Sad*, p. 27.
58 For a more detailed exploration of the äppärat, refer to Rutledge's essay, where he contends that the äppärat "invokes an ancient past that critics ignore" and delves into the word's meanings and etymologies. He highlights that the "Latin *apparatus* is a 'noun of state' that, etymologically, implicates work [...] Apparatus as noun, then, is the 'work of preparing' (obsolete), but also the 'organs or means by which natural processes are carried on'" (Shteyngart's Super Sad, p. 367f).
59 Shteyngart, *Super Sad*, p. 86.
60 The invasion of privacy depicted in the novel extends beyond the practice of sharing information online; it underscores the invasion of the body, involving its data and numbers. The otter, too, intrudes upon the body by inquiring about Lenny's sexual partners.
61 Huehls, Four Theses. This economic totality operates bidirectionally; it not only shapes Eunice's decisions but also underlies Lenny's strategy to woo her. Lenny's plan involves a financial assess-

At the same time, their love story is also *true*; it is not entirely sorrowful or solely governed by financial considerations. Eunice's decisions consistently factor in her family's well-being, reflecting a pursuit of survival rather than profit for its own sake. Despite its initial transactional nature, their relationship evolves into something deeper, revealing both Lenny and Eunice as vulnerable, interdependent, and emotionally connected individuals. The authentic nature of their story is reinforced by its inception in Italy, where Lenny associates Italian behaviors, such as vibrant hand gestures and attention-seeking voices, with the essence of life.[62] While this may perpetuate certain stereotypes about Italians, it also serves as a deliberate counterpoint to the American emphasis on intellectual prowess, Quantified Self principles, and data, redirecting attention to the importance of the body.

6.2 Self-Descriptive Reminiscence: "Dear Diary"

The exploration of societal implications in Shteyngart's novel extends beyond its plot, delving into the intricacies of narrative choices, exemplified by the acts of self-descriptive reminiscence. Rather than adhering to the conventions of traditional biography writing, the novel unfolds as a compilation of confessions meticulously chronicled by Lenny Abramov in his diary and Eunice Park through her online messages. This narrative strategy introduces a unique dimension to the storytelling as Lenny and Eunice occasionally provide contrasting perspectives on shared events (like the first time Lenny meets her parents), fostering dramatic irony and narrative tension. The deliberate choice to present multiple viewpoints enriches the storytelling, offering readers a multifaceted exploration of the characters' inner worlds.

Moreover, the novel diverges from conventional narrative techniques, eschewing both an "external, surveilling point of view" and the intimacy of a "first-person narrator" privy to characters' thoughts and emotions.[63] As scholar Chelsea Kern notes, the narrative avoids a "top-down" or "outside-in" perspective, choosing instead to foreground the online texts themselves without additional mediation. In

---

ment of Eunice's family, as he examines her father's income and observes the declining fortunes of their business, with the "yuan amounts in steady decline" (*Super Sad*, 36). He envisions himself as a potential solution to their economic crisis.

62 Haase also contends that "Had Lenny and Eunice met in America instead of Italy in the beginning of the novel, their love affair would never have happened" (Death by Data, p. 86).

63 Kern, Big Data, p. 87.

this literary landscape, characters almost seem to exist solely as the online texts, the data they generate about themselves.[64]

On the one hand, this narrative choice provides commentary on today's "emergent surveillance society," distinct from the classical Orwellian dystopia or Foucault's panopticon.[65] Simon Willmetts highlights the role of the äppärät as the "main instrument of surveillance" and "ubiquitous mobile computing device resembling a smartphone that collects and projects torrents of personal data."[66] Shteyngart himself notes, "[t]he government doesn't need to spy into your bedroom, [...], because everyone in this society is constantly updating where they are, and what they're doing."[67] It thus offers a broader reflection on contemporary confessional culture and the willingly surrendered erosion of privacy by social media users.[68] Therefore, it suggests "ways in which an Orwellian world of top-down surveillance has now morphed to include a horizontal network of 'voluntary' sharing and competitive status acquisition."[69] Even more, the novel provides a "commentary on the dangers of combining surveillance culture (fascism) with a false sense of individual empowerment."[70]

On the flip side, confessions in the novel are more than just a disciplinary tool; paradoxically, they represent the last opportunity for individuals to seize a semblance of autonomy and agency. The opening confession of the novel introduces Lenny Abramov, contemplating his own existence: "A week ago, before Eunice gave me *reason to live*, you wouldn't have *noticed me, diary.* A week ago, *I did not exist.*"[71] Abramov's coming to life depends on the presence of a woman,[72] but also on the existence of the diary itself. On the one hand, "Lenny's diary en-

---

64 Ibid.
65 Willmetts, Digital Dystopia, p. 268. Surveillance "in both classical dystopian novels (Orwell, Huxley, Zamyatin) and in Michel Foucault's model of the panopticon is remarkably egalitarian, 'massifying' the population and ensuring conformity to a fixed institutional or ideological standard. In *SSTL*, however, the decentralized, modulating, and 'dividuating' nature of surveillance is effective precisely because it is a way to discriminate among populations" (ibid., p. 269).
66 Ibid., p. 272.
67 Ibid.
68 What's more, "with its online omnipresence, the state can turn unsuspecting citizens into spies, which is what happens to Lenny when he communicates with his old family friend [...] When Lenny texts her Noah's location right before the government bombs Noah's ferry, Lenny becomes implicated in Noah's death [...] electronic media disintegrate privacy, providing unprecedented avenues of control and manipulation" (Trapp, Super Sad, p. 65).
69 Schmidt, Menippean Satire, p. 6.
70 Rutledge, Shteyngart's Super Sad, p. 387.
71 Shyteyngart, *Super Sad*, p. 3; emphasis added.
72 In Powers' novel, it is also a woman (Thassa) who instills the protagonist (Russell) with the joy of being alive. See chapter 13.

tries, like Eunice's messages, already constitute a public text oriented toward an *implied reading public* formed through networked devices."[73] This implies that an individual's existence relies on social exchange and community rather than a sense of self-reliance or self-sufficiency.[74] It evokes Sartre's notion that the "I" is generated in the moment of being looked at, though in a moment of mutual recognition rather than shame. On the other hand, the diary itself becomes an interlocutor, a nonhuman agent that transcends its role as a mere recorder or medium, especially since Lenny directly addresses the "diary." The writing process is framed as a space of encounter, transcending mere self-writing or self-expression. Writing becomes a last refuge in a world where social connections often falter, offering a space where they can be salvaged.

Lenny employs the diary as a self-help tool, mirroring, at times, a self-help rhetoric: "I *just* have to be good and I have to believe in myself."[75] The notion that belief and discipline alone should guarantee his success, namely, living forever, is echoed in statements like: "I *just* have to stay off the trans fats and the hooch. I *just* have to drink plenty of green tea and alkalinized water and submit my genome to the right people."[76] Despite adopting these beliefs instilled by American society and his boss, there is an underlying tone of sarcasm in these expressions, emphasized by the repeated use of the adverb "just."

Lenny attempts to align with these cultural norms but does not fully embrace them; he maintains the position of an "intimate outsider"[77] and ultimately rejects them, returning to Italy. His adaptability to the American way is highlighted in a scene where Lenny teaches his father how to write an essay: he advises him to omit details about being "pretty short" and having painful knees because in "America people like to ignore their weak points and stress their incredible accomplishments."[78] Lenny's understanding of American culture allows him to both partici-

---

73 Kern, Big Data, p. 88; emphasis added.
74 Similarly, in Atwood's trilogy, Snowman must assume a reader, no matter how improbable it may seem in his case. Even if Lenny denies it to be true, he has "been accused of writing my passages with the hope of eventual publication" (Kern, Big Data, p. 88).
75 Shteyngart, *Super Sad*, p. 3; emphasis added.
76 Ibid.
77 An "intimate outsider" is a term borrowed from Sutherland and Swan's essay on Atwood, where they highlight how "a member of the society who is in some ways separate from the more powerful elements of the society and not fully convinced of the society's views—tells the tale" (Sutherland/Swan, Margaret Atwood, p. 224). I use it to describe the narrative viewpoints of the characters in the selected novels, such as Lenny. See also my analysis of Jimmy and Toby in Atwood's trilogy or Russell Stone in Powers' novel.
78 Shteyngart, *Super Sad*, p. 136.

pate[79] and critique it from within, to both "play the system" and write "his way out of it."[80]

At the start of the novel, Lenny is in Italy for work, addressing his "dearest diary."[81] Upon his return to America, this shifts to "dear diary," potentially signaling a change in feeling or disposition. His initial objective is to formulate a "strategy for short-term survival,"[82] encompassing tasks such as working diligently for his boss Joshie, securing his protection, loving Eunice, meditating on her freckles, and letting the "potential of her *sweetness* enhance your happiness."[83] Other elements of this strategy involve caring for friends, maintaining niceties with his parents, and appreciating what he possesses, emphasizing the significance of gratitude and social connections. However, these expressions of gratitude take a unique turn when he compares himself with the "poor fat man on the plane," attempting to "feel happy by comparison."[84] This list comes across as an effort to adhere to self-help principles, shedding light on the performative nature of these practices. Lenny strives to cultivate a sense of nostalgia or construct memories even before they unfold, turning these actions into prescriptions rather than genuine feelings. At a certain point, he reflects, "My celebrations were turning *sour*. I took out the list I had written by hand and decided to make immediate use of Point No. 2."[85]

Accordingly, Lenny appropriates the language and rhetoric of American self-help culture, imbuing it with a tension that ruptures it from within. For instance, "It's only page seven and I'm already a liar. Something terrible happened before Fabrizia's party. So terrible I don't want to write about it, because I want you to be a positive diary."[86] This diary is not strictly positive, nor is it a tragedy. It is a "super sad" story that casts a simultaneously happy, humorous, nostalgic, and tragic gaze at American society. Populated with caricatures, both stereotypical and

---

79 "As savvy immigrant children, they [Lenny and Eunice] employ mimicry and adaptation to find success in an alien culture" (Trapp, Super Sad, p. 60). Eunice also wrote: "America might be gone completely soon, but I was never really an American. It was all pretending. I was always a Korean girl from a Korean family with a Korean way of doing things, and I'm proud of what that means. It means that, unlike so many people around me, I know who I am" (Shteyngart, *Super Sad*, p. 295).
80 Spahr, Re-Learning, p. 554.
81 Shteyngart, *Super Sad*, p. 1, 32.
82 Ibid., p. 48.
83 Ibid., p. 49.
84 Ibid.
85 Ibid., p. 59; emphasis added. This emphasis on taste—whether the sweetness of Eunice's freckles or the bitterness of his celebrations anticipate the emergence of the survival scenes, where multi-sensorial apprehension takes central stage.
86 Ibid., p. 5.

nuanced characters, it weaves a tale where Abramov asserts: "And yet Lenny Abramov, your *humble diarist*, your *small nonentity, will live forever.*"[87] The diary, in this context, becomes a tool for a "forever young self-expression."[88] Yet, this is another confession that disrupts its own claim: living forever is not a humble gesture, nor the agenda of a "small nonentity."

In line with the neoliberal spirit, Joshie advocates an inward focus on the individual self. This is underscored by his encouraging the staff to maintain diaries, urging them to "remember who we were, because every moment our brains and synapses are being rebuilt and rewired with maddening disregard for our personalities, so that each year, each month, each day we transform into a different person, an utterly unfaithful iteration of our original selves."[89] Lenny's commitment to journaling both substantiates and challenges Joshie's perspective, as he still perceives himself as a "facsimile of [his] early childhood."[90] In other words, journal writing becomes another tool to combat the mortality of a self in perpetual flux. However, the narrative suggests that Lenny's diary is more than an instance of "self-descriptive reminiscence."[91] It does not solely emphasize the cognitive aspect of memory preservation but rather places significance on how the body and its mortality find refuge within its pages. As Felix Haase aptly notes, "Lenny slowly grasps the impossibility of thinking his identity and his body separate. He is not a floating personality, but an embodied subject."[92]

From a psychological perspective, the act of maintaining a diary seems to serve as a therapeutic tool for dealing with trauma and internal conflicts. Trapp posits that both Lenny and Eunice grapple with psychological damage stemming from the "model minority paradigm."[93] According to Kate Marx, the protagonists "suffer *deep psychological trauma* from trying to survive in the post-animal world," leading them to "self-obsess and find shiny things to distract themselves with, but compulsively refer to each other by the names of other animals."[94] Lenny's double-voiced writing further reinforces the notion of internal conflict. In one confession, a battle unfolds between his various selves: "That's right: I am never going to die, *caro diario*. Never, never, never, never. And you can go to hell for

---

87 Ibid., p. 3; emphasis added.
88 Rutledge, Shteyngart's Super Sad, p. 377.
89 Shteyngart, *Super Sad*, p. 63.
90 Ibid.
91 James, Critical Solace, p. 494.
92 Haase, Death by Data, p. 95.
93 Trapp, Super Sad, p. 60.
94 Marx, Dystopian (Non)Fiction, p. 1; emphasis added.

doubting me."⁹⁵ The "you" Lenny addresses is not merely an implied reading public but his own doubting self—the self that resists and grows weary of the American values adopted by his American persona. Peter Schmidt observes, "Lenny's journal quickly strays from the script Joshie dictated: it is double-voiced, tracing the clash between Lenny's desire to be liberated from human fallibility and mortality and his skepticism about the ethics of such a goal."⁹⁶

Lenny's diary not only expresses skepticism towards ideas of human immortality but also foregrounds the concept of mortality, highlighting the material and sensuous aspects of reading and writing. The "sheer exhilaration of the writing in this book—Lenny's confessional tones, Eunice's teenage slang—is itself a sort of answer to the flattened-out horrors of the world it depicts. It's not that writing of any kind will save us from our follies or our rulers; but *words are a form of life*, and we can't say we haven't been warned."⁹⁷

6.3 Literary Synesthesia: "That Thing Smells like Wet Socks"

In exploring the novel's engagement with body and technology, particularly in Lenny's descriptions of his relationships, Ross Bullen identifies a sense of "mourning" for the body.⁹⁸ This sentiment is evident in Lenny's depictions of his boss Joshie as a "living, breathing gadget" and in his portrayal of Eunice, both described as if they are disembodied.⁹⁹ However, as the narrative progresses, Lenny's return to the "Old World" implies a reconnection with the tangible, corporeal aspects of life that he seemingly abandoned.¹⁰⁰ The novel, while acknowledging a certain nostalgia for the body, goes beyond mere lamentation; it intricately defines and crafts a new space for the body's presence in the digital age. This becomes evident in the novel's uses of literary synesthesia, where the materiality of reading intertwines with the novel's complex understanding of the body and technology.

American society's rejection of the body stems from a fear of its inherent vulnerability, leading to an oversimplified understanding of its functions. The prevailing view reduces the body to a mere source of information, transforming it into a datafied entity that communicates and quantifies life through age and statistics. However, Shteyngart's novel challenges this perspective by presenting an alterna-

---

95 Shteyngart, *Super Sad*, p. 4; emphasis in original.
96 Schmidt, Menippean Satire, p. 10.
97 Wood, Never Say Die; emphasis added.
98 Bullen, Act Two, p. 263.
99 Ibid., p. 242.
100 Ibid., p. 249.

tive view that does not champion youth and slimness as absolute values. The narrative disrupts societal norms by reframing old age and larger bodies as not only acceptable but indicative of a rich and fulfilling life. These qualities are no longer grounds for shame or being labeled as "gross."[101] Even when Lenny's appearance is deemed "gross"[102] by societal standards, Eunice, with a childlike "sense of wonder," appreciates his age.[103] This shift in perception suggests that health is more than just a number on a scale; it encompasses vigor, energy, vitality—an embodiment of feeling alive.

Similarly, fatness in the novel is not merely a sign of an unhealthy life but also an indication of an abundant, plentiful, and flavorful existence. The contrast between Fabrizia's "dying nonelectronic corporeality" and Eunice's "nano-sized" body, which "lacked both breast and scent, who existed as easily on an äppärät screen as on the street before me,"[104] highlights diverse perspectives on body image. Eunice, despite her slimness, perceives herself as having a "fat, fat body."[105] This perception may allude to the societal pressures of an anorexic culture where standards are unattainable, leaving even the slimmest individuals feeling inadequate. Alternatively, Eunice's feeling of fatness might signify a disconnection between her outward appearance and inner experience. Despite appearing disembodied, her perception of fatness suggests a vibrancy and richness in her life. This symbol of fleshiness recurs in two additional instances: the "poor fat man on the plane" and the otter.

At the beginning of the novel, Lenny becomes the subject of investigation by a digital otter named Jeffrey.[106] Jeffrey's intrusion into Lenny's privacy involves inquiries about his sexual partners and, comically, misinterpreting his words. For instance, the otter registers "effeminate life invention" instead of indefinite life extension as Lenny's occupation.[107] This mistake introduces a humorous element akin to autocorrect mistakes in the digital age or the children's game of telephone, underscoring the theme of unreliable information transmission within the narrative of life extension as a fabricated fantasy. Furthermore, it lays bare how life it-

---

101 Shteyngart, *Super Sad*, p. 46.
102 Ibid., p. 72.
103 Ibid., p. 24.
104 Ibid., p. 19.
105 Ibid., p. 72.
106 Ibid., p. 11. Jeffrey is, thus, "a digital cartoon animal that serves as the face for American immigration services" and the "nightmarish visage of Orwell's Big Brother [is] rendered as a cute, furry mammal" (Haase, Death by Data, p. 89).
107 Ibid., p. 7.

self has transformed into a commodity in American society, reduced to just another idea to be marketed and sold.

The otter's symbolism also directs attention to the corporeal sensibility of life. In her essay, Marx cites Steve Barker's assertion that "Western society continues to draw heavily on symbolic ideas involving animals, and that the immediate subject of those ideas is frequently not the animal itself, but rather a human subject drawing on animal imagery to make a statement about human identity."[108] In this context, the otter seems to emerge as a "cute cartoon character, empty of historical meaning and context," with its shape and otter identity appearing as seemingly "arbitrary choices," devoid of "immediately obvious 'otter' characteristics."[109]

However, the otter reappears a few more times in the novel—displayed in a graffiti and vividly portrayed in a dream where its otter characteristics are accentuated: the density of its fur, its whiskers, and the "hot familiar and familial salmon breath."[110] As Lenny's eyes rove across the graffiti, the otter stared back at him: "curved, oddly sexual, *pregnant with life*, the fur smoothed into little charcoal mounds clearly warm and soft to the touch."[111] Otters are renowned for having the thickest fur among animals, aiding them in staying warm. In this context, the otter's characteristics are prominently highlighted, transforming it into a "living animal"[112] and symbolizing the richness of life.

In another instance, Lenny attempts to remember the Italians' "loud, attention-seeking voices and the vibrant Italian hand gestures," equating them with *"the living animal,* and hence with *life itself."*[113] The graffito otter triggers memories of Fabrizia and, implicitly, the "world of the body."[114] The exchange of gazes, where the otter reciprocates Lenny's eye contact, implies a form of agency associated with the nonhuman and its animal gaze. The perception of the otter as a nonhuman agent teeming with life hinges on a multisensory awareness rather than an exercise in empathy or anthropomorphism. The olfactive, tactile, and visual dimensions converge in a single descriptive paragraph, suggesting an abundance of life. The emphasis on texture, warmth, and color transcends a mere visual perspective on the nonhuman otter.

The olfactory experience in the novel serves a similar purpose, challenging the visually oriented American society and emphasizing the quality, rather than the

---

[108] Marx, Dystopian (Non)Fiction, p. 3.
[109] Ibid., p. 4.
[110] Shteyngart, *Super Sad*, p. 247.
[111] Ibid., p. 151; emphasis added.
[112] Marx, p. 4.
[113] Shteyngart, *Super Sad*, p. 22; emphasis added.
[114] Bullen, Act Two, p. 249.

quantity, of life. The symbol of the elephant emerges as a significant motif that explores a distinct form of interaction with the nonhuman—one grounded in a richness of the senses:

> As she did so, I locked eyes with the elephant, and I watched myself being kissed in the prism of the elephant's eye, the giant hazel apparatus surrounded with flecks of coarse gray eyebrow. ... He slowly flicked back one massive ear, like a Galician shopkeeper of a century ago spreading his arms as if to say 'Yes, this is all there is.' And then it occurred to me, lucky me mirrored in the beast's eye, lucky Lenny having his trunk kissed by Eunice Park: The elephant knows. The elephant knows there is nothing after this life and very little in it. The elephant is aware of his eventual extinction and he is hurt by it, reduced by it, made to feel his solitary nature, he who will eventually trample his way through bush and scrub to lie down and die where his mother once trembled at her haunches to give him life. Mother, aloneness, entrapment, extinction. The elephant is essentially an Ashkenazi animal, but a wholly rational one—it too wants to live forever.[115]

As Kate Marx notes, this scene reinforces the "reader's understanding of Lenny's own existential loneliness; he is able to identify more with a captive elephant in a zoo than with any of the people in his life."[116] The exchange of gazes becomes a moment of self-reflection, with Lenny contemplating his own yearning for immortality. Simultaneously, the elephant's eye,[117] surrounded by "flecks of coarse gray eyebrow," echoes the otter's fur, although it conveys a harsher or sharper tactile sensation and is notably less dense. In essence, this scene introduces a haptic dimension to human-nonhuman encounters, typically perceived only as a visual moment of looking or being looked at. The elephant, being large, old, and renowned for its memory, also serves as a commentary on societal standards of youth and weight. Rather than fixating on the brain and its synaptic connections, the elephant imagery redirects attention to the body and its role in memory-keeping.

The elephant's trunk also gains new meaning in the novel's narrative, emphasizing the importance of odors, scents, and flavors. The portrayal of an enlarged nose suggests an enhanced sense of smell, correlating with enhanced memory, and establishes another connection between Lenny and the elephant. There is a moment when Lenny remembers "Eunice's lips on my nose, the *love mixed in with the pain*, the foretaste of almonds and salt. I thought of how *it was all just*

---

115 Shteyngart, *Super Sad*, p. 117; emphasis added.
116 Marx, Dystopian (Non)Fiction, p. 5.
117 Or, as the quote says, the "apparatus," which recalls the äppärat as a device. The juxtaposition of the elephant's eye with the smartphone-like device seems to suggest that both of them propose ways of looking, while blurring the boundaries between nature and technology.

too beautiful to ever let go."[118] This scene recalls the famous contract made by Goethe's Faust with the demon Mephistopheles, particularly the lines:

> If ever to the moment I shall say:
> Beautiful moment, do not pass away!
> Then you may forge your chains to bind me,
> Then I will put my life behind me,
> Then let them hear my death-knell toll,
> Then from your labours you'll be free,
> The clock may stop, the clock-hands fall,
> And time come to an end for me![119]

Paradoxically, the very moment Faust seeks a sense of immortality coincides with the moment he has to die. This is significant because, in this case, immortality does not imply indefinite life extension; quite the opposite. It describes a wonderful moment that is beautiful precisely because it is brief, fleeting, and transient. Time stops, but not in the expected sense of finding eternity; instead, it denotes the feeling of stretched, inflated, or dilated time—a spatio-temporal openness that characterizes the affect of aliveness. Lenny and Eunice's love story is "true" precisely because of its imperfect and ephemeral nature. The "love mixed in with the pain" encapsulates what it means to feel alive—to experience not only wonder but also anticipate its passing, creating an intimacy with loss. Paradoxically, to experience life, one needs to have a sense of death, too. This kind of vulnerability can only be sensed and smelled, rather than rationalized.

In one of his confessions to Grace, Lenny says that "in some ridiculous way I think Eunice will let me live forever."[120] Eunice does just that, though not in the original sense intended by the character and expected by the reader. Stephanie Li emphasized how Lenny seeks "an extension of his life through his newfound love. This reliance on Eunice establishes one of the key tensions of the novel: how Lenny uses her as a surrogate for his own absent children."[121] However, it is in those brief and vulnerable moments that they share, that Lenny finds a sense of immortality. So, even if their love story ends, in a way it remains immortal

---

118 Shteyngart, *Super Sad*, p. 125; emphasis added.
119 Goethe, *Faust*, lines 1699–1706.
120 Shteyngart, *Super Sad*, p. 152.
121 Li, Techno-Orientalism, p. 105. Or, as Peter Schmidt suggests, this perspective points to the novel's "Lolita plot with an Orientalism twist: old insecure guy falls for a Korean American 20-something, convinced she will revive his youth" (7). Thus, it appears as if "[b]oth Lenny and Joshie see in Eunice—not only a young person but youth itself, and something they can co-opt, make their own" (Wood, Never Say Die). Marleen S. Barr has also interpreted Eunice as "the new Jewish male utopian fantasy metashiksa" (America and Books, p. 313).

thanks to those Faustian moments mediated by the body. As such, immortality has nothing to do with having offspring and living on through them or with helping Lenny acquire a higher status and buy his way into treatments that extend his life indefinitely. Rather, it refers to brief moments of embodied awareness: "I thought of how we had kissed in the Sheep Meadow on the day she moved in with me, how I had held her tiny person to me for a hundred slow beats, and how, for that entire time, I had thought death beside the point."[122] Eunice refers to the same kind of tenderness and sensitivity that makes Lenny dangerous when she writes in her journal:

> I wish I were stronger and more secure in myself so that I could really spend my life with a guy like Lenny. Because he has a different kind of strength than Joshie. He has the strength of his sweet tuna arms. He has the strength of *putting his nose in my hair and calling it home*. He has the strength to cry when I go down on him. Who IS Lenny? Who DOES that? Who will ever open up to me like that again? No one. Because it's too dangerous. Lenny is a dangerous man. Joshie is more powerful, but Lenny is much more dangerous.[123]

In her journal entry,[124] Eunice not only captures the sense of intimacy and affection developed in their relationship, but also points to the ways in which they involve vulnerability, making Lenny dangerous and, thus, deadly. She also evokes the image of the nose again, emphasizing the idea of smell and its memorable quality —the quality of Proust's madeleine—which also conveys a sense of belonging and pain.

Smells play a significant role in the novel, even when they are bad odors. For instance, when Sally and Eunice discuss their family situation, which includes their mother being abused by their father, Sally plans on "mak[ing] enough money so that Daddy can retire and not have to worry about *smelly white feet* anymore. And then we'll all feel a little better as a family maybe."[125] Money and success are seen as prerequisites for a happy family, but so is the scented environment in which one works. Lenny, for instance, is surrounded by *"smelly young people* checking their äppäräti [...] The even, nutty aroma of brewing green tea snuck a

---

122 Shteyngart, *Super Sad*, p. 213.
123 Ibid., p. 296; emphasis added.
124 Spahr adds: "Addressed to herself, the entry is a declaration of love for Lenny both thematically and through its adoption of a literary style significantly different from her initial use of internet slang. Through her interaction with Lenny, whose journal entries display the same reflexivity from the outset, Eunice writes her way out of the logic of commodification, achieving at least a rudimentary sense of agency" (Re-Learning, p. 557).
125 Shteyngart, *Super Sad*, p. 47; emphasis added.

morsel of *nostalgia* into my general climate of fear."[126] In this case, nostalgia is not rehearsed but relies on scent and smell. These unpleasant odors also expose another type of vulnerability, raising a sense of alarm and vigilance toward the standards of whiteness and youth imposed by society. Their repulsive and disgusting quality lays bare the decay of American ideals.

This synesthetic aesthetic reappears in the way books are perceived by American citizens: a book is a "thing [that] smells like wet socks."[127] Thus, the olfactory and tactile dimensions are once again intertwined. On the one hand, this imagery captures the aversion toward literature and practices of reading and writing in a postfictional world that primarily focuses on "Images."[128] On the other hand, the book remains the only artifact that manages to evoke embodied awareness in a world that continuously erases the body; the only artifact that elicits a visceral reaction, even if it is negative. Consequently, what is rejected is not only fiction as such but also the intimacy and embodied awareness mediated by them.

Books become the "abject" in a world that disdains the body precisely because of their private and visceral quality, rendering them as dangerous and gross as Lenny. The smell of books is typically enchanting to a reader, evoking associations with "chocolate, coffee, smoke, wood or vanilla. The aroma is so popular, perfumers have tried to capture the essence of a book's smell through candles and even cologne."[129] The foul smell of books also suggests an attempt to sever any connection to history. Books may help "develop a sense of nostalgia for something", as Lenny writes at the beginning of the novel, aiding in figuring out "what's important."[130] The novel depicts nostalgia as a lost value, with characters like Lenny's boss and American society caught in a "rush to the future,"[131] or as "America is so infatuated with the present that history is not only weakened but actively negated."[132] However, Lenny, as a character, highlights the importance of nostalgia as he attempts to summon it up artificially through his to-do list or he encounters it spontaneously, such as when he smells the green tea at work. These two distinct approaches to understanding nostalgia, history, and memory-keeping also suggest that people can only access history through their bodies.

In the novel, family values are linked to the past, while work values are oriented toward the future. For example, Lenny plans to be kind to his parents be-

---

126 Ibid., p. 59; emphasis added.
127 Ibid., p. 35.
128 Ibid., p. 25.
129 Cf. The Science Behind the Smell of Books, Libraries of University of Colorado.
130 Shteyngart, *Super Sad*, p. 21.
131 Trapp, Super Sad, p. 68.
132 Li, Techno-Orientalism, p. 103.

cause "they represent your past and who you are."[133] Both Lenny and Eunice stress family values following the Rupture. Eunice writes to Joshie: "But throughout this whole Rupture thing I guess that's what I found out about myself, that my family matters the most to me and it always will."[134] Similarly, Lenny reflects: "But basically—at the end of the busted rainbow, at the end of the day, at the end of the empire—little more than my parents' son."[135] His old-fashioned demeanor and his fondness for books reminds every one of the past and of death, even if they ultimately prove to be the foundation of life.

Lenny's wealth is not merely monetary; by the end, wealth transcends numerical value and becomes a privilege of mere existence, taking on a new significance. He is likened to a "rhesus monkey,"[136] a term used by Joshie and depicted by Eunice in her drawing. Initially, this analogy might suggest a dehumanizing portrayal, reducing him to an animal state. However, the novel challenges this interpretation by questioning the rhetoric of human exceptionalism that underlies it.[137] A rhesus monkey feeds, rests, and plays all day long—it enjoys the privilege of merely existing. Being gregarious, it lives in social groups and forms cooperative societies. Notably, the rhesus monkey was the first monkey to travel in space and has been a crucial subject for "medical and psychological research."[138] In Shteyngart's novel, this reference to the monkey emphasizes the significance of family, bodily life, and a kinship of posthumanity—a kinship of lives.

At the narrative's conclusion, in a metafictional twist, "the book we have just read is being adapted (for a second time) into a movie, and Lenny (now in Italy) nostalgically meditates on the super sad love story of the *loss* of both Eunice and his American home."[139] Lenny, at this moment "retreats into *silence* and *mourning* for all that has been lost," prompting contemplation on whether this retreat is a "luxury of the privileged" or a "vital check on our delusions."[140] The culmination of his narrative unveils his deepest longing: "silence, black and complete."[141] As he articulates, "I had begun to *grieve*. For all of us."[142]

---

133 Shteyngart, *Super Sad*, p. 49.
134 Ibid., p. 279.
135 Ibid., p. 292.
136 Ibid., p. 48.
137 Also, if the "backgrounding of nature helps to perpetuate the myth of human exceptionalism, the anthropocentric notion that somehow we as humans are apart from our environment, and not reliant on the biosphere, or on other animals, for our survival" (Marx, Dystopian (Non)Fiction, p. 9), in this case, the novel brings the focus back to human-nonhuman interdependency.
138 Britannica, Rhesus Monkey.
139 Trapp, Super Sad, p. 57.
140 Schmidt, Menippean Satire, p. 18.
141 Shteyngart, *Super Sad*, p. 329.

> This story about the demise of U.S.-American democracy and the waning importance of literature within contemporary culture ends in grief and with silence. In its imagination and satirizing of the dangers of living within a networked society of control, the novel points to the need for new methods and modes of literary expression but does not embody such a form itself.[143]

However, the final moment of grieving might be interpreted differently: as a sign that Lenny has left anthropocentrism behind. His grief may extend to humanity ("for all of us"), but it could also imply a departure from egocentrism, hierarchical thinking, and superiority. Clemens Spahr suggests that *SSTL* is a *"tale of loss* that merely declares the need for something other than itself without positively imagining it [...] and the *'failure to imagine a better future'* goes hand in hand with failures to find novel forms of expression that would allow for such imagining to take place."[144] Nevertheless, the novel challenges the terms through which Spahr critiques its perceived shortcomings.

Furthermore, *SSTL* embodies a mode of literary expression that accentuates textual immersion, yet as readers, we often overlook it due to its glaring obviousness, creating a blind spot—an "unknown known." By doing so, the novel calls into question the prevailing expectation of imagining a better future, a notion deeply ingrained in self-help culture and readers of science fiction alike. Consequently, embracing loss in a world that is resistant to losses becomes a beacon of hope; grieving in a world fixated on immortality becomes an act of courage. Far from weaknesses requiring healing, loss, silence, mourning, and grief persist at the core of life—integral to the experience of feeling alive. These manifestations of vulnerability and mortality also carve out a space to "merely exist" alongside other nonhumans, even as mundane as a pair of "old slippers."[145]

---

[142] Ibid.
[143] Kovach, E-Pistolary Novels, p. 273.
[144] Spahr, Re-Learning, p. 273b; emphasis added.
[145] Shteyngart, *Super Sad*, p. 295. "He has these old slippers that are perfectly arranged by his bed just so he can slip right into them first thing in the morning, but they're too big for him." For a comparative analysis of a similar imagery in Tayie Selasi's *Ghana Must Go* and the slippers' significance concerning the themes of home and belonging, please refer to my paper on "Be-Longing in TED Talks on 'What is home?' and Contemporary Postcolonial Fiction."

7 Literature and Scanning: "A Burble of Warm White Spray"

Shteyngart has produced a text that identifies, parodies, and counters narratives that promote digital technology as offering a brave new world of "Post-Human" information analysis ("scanning") that supposedly will be vastly superior to old-school book—and individual-centered reading and interpretation. Shteyngart ironically binds such a commodified future to literary history and its representation of our fallible, non-quantifiable human tragicomedy.[1]

While *Super Sad True Love Story* does contest the notion of "scanning," it also maintains a skeptical stance toward the idea of "individual-centered reading and interpretation."[2] This nuanced dimension is frequently overlooked in critical readings that predominantly highlight the inadequacy of scanning as an alternative. In Shteyngart's narrative, books redirect attention to ordinary yet profound aspects, such as the "fading light [which] is us, and we are, for a moment so brief it can't even register on our äppärät screens, beautiful."[3] Books shift the focus from personal identity to a broader landscape of human-nonhuman interactions. For instance, Joshie urges his employees "to keep a diary because the mechanicals of our brains were constantly changing and over time we were transforming into entirely different people."[4] However, the novel posits a different role for books, asserting that their primary function lies not in shaping individual subjects but in fostering community, whether among humans or nonhumans.

Lenny's Wall of Books ought to serve a comparable purpose in his relationship with Eunice: "what if Eunice and I just said 'no' to all this. To this bar. To this FACing. The two of us. What if we just went home and read books to each other?"[5] Following the Rupture, Lenny endeavors to connect with Eunice through reading. "I wanted us to feel something in common. I wanted this complex language, this surge of intellect, to be processed into love. Isn't that how they used to do it a century ago, people reading poetry to one another?"[6] However, as he whispers into her ear, he returns to an intellectual understanding of reading, rupturing their connection:

---

[1] Schmidt, Menippean Satire, p. 5.
[2] Ibid.
[3] Shteyngart, *Super Sad*, p. 203.
[4] Ibid., p. 191.
[5] Ibid., p. 92.
[6] Ibid., p. 273.

∂ Open Access. © 2024 the author(s), published by De Gruyter. This work is licensed under the Creative Commons Attribution 4.0 International License. https://doi.org/10.1515/9783111389929-010

"*I'm listening*," she half-whispered. "But are you understanding?" I said. "I've never really learned how to read texts," she said. "Just to *scan* them for info." I let out a small, stupid laugh. She started to cry. "Oh, baby," I said. [...] Even I'm having trouble following this. It's not just you. *Reading is difficult.* People just aren't meant to read anymore. We're in a post-literate age. You know, a visual age. How many years after the fall of Rome did it take for a Dante to appear? Many, many years. [...] Go to bed. We don't have to read anymore. We don't have to ever read again. I promise. How can we read when people need our help? It's a luxury. *A stupid luxury.*"[7]

This scene encapsulates both a failure of knowledge and knowledge of failure—a failure of literary knowledge understood as a hermeneutic endeavor to dig deep into the text, and the knowledge of the failure of literature, now deemed a luxury in a world that needs food rather than words. As Rosi Braidotti highlights, "literature and the literary critic nowadays are perceived—by management, policy-makers and a large section of the media—as a luxury, not as a necessity."[8] However, this perception hinges on viewing literature as an intellectual pursuit rather than an integral part of life. Clemens Spahr argues that Lenny and Eunice's turn inward after the Rupture renders their writing and reading inadequate responses to the global socioeconomic crisis, lacking the transformative power to become a form of agency.[9] Yet, this "stupid luxury" serves as another indication of the privilege inherent in mere existence. Reading and writing persist as the only forms of agency available in a world that refuses to grant the characters the simple act of being—the only space where they can truly be.

In this scene, Lenny's demand for "understanding" from Eunice leads to him engaging in "mansplaining."[10] He overlooks that Eunice's act of "listening" is already a profound expression of love. This oversight mirrors a broader theme in the novel: emphasizing the importance of listening and paying attention over hasty conclusions and judgments. The elitist assumption that "reading is difficult" contributes to society's shift toward a post-literate age. This shift is propelled by a rigid adherence to a Western canon centered on white men, neglecting the diverse perspectives of women and other minorities in their approaches to reading. In this context, reading as listening signifies more than just an open and empathetic attention, but it also highlights another sensory dimension of reading: hearing—to be all ears, elephant ears. The elephant, with its large ears, long trunk, and

---

7 Ibid., p. 275; emphasis added.
8 Braidotti, Contested Posthumanities, p. 13.
9 Spahr, Re-Learning, p. 559.
10 Goodwin, Mansplaining.

small eyes, symbolizes a departure from the supremacy of vision, questioning ideas of transparency and readability.

In Eunice's case, her approach transcends the narrow understanding of scanning as merely looking or glancing over a text. Chelsea Oei Kern contends that "[h]ere we see what scanning is not: the slow work of comprehension and interpretation, with attention to detail. Scanning, then, is about speed, 'getting the gist,' and general or aggregate knowledge."[11] However, the novel does not limit the concept of scanning to swift reading. The verb "scan" carries another meaning, originating from the Latin verb "*scandere*," meaning to climb, and can refer to the activity of marking rhythm. In this context, scanning could involve an attention to detail unrelated to the "slow work of comprehension and interpretation" mentioned by Kern. Rather, it could be aligned with listening—observing what is in plain sight by employing more than one sense.

Furthermore, the boundaries between algorithmic scanning and human reading lack clarity. Kern posits "Lenny's literary reading" in contrast to "Eunice's reading habits [that] resemble those of the algorithms and software that collect data rapidly and broadly."[12] However, the novel disrupts this dichotomous perspective, often blurring these categories. For instance, Lenny engages in scanning at work, while Eunice demonstrates attention to detail. Scanning, as portrayed in the narrative, extends beyond speed and is not synonymous with a failure to discern details; on the contrary, when Lenny scans the files of his prospective "Life Lovers," his investigation actually resembles "the slow work of comprehension and interpretation."[13] He meticulously pays attention to "their *charitable* activities, their plans for *humanity*, their concern for our chronically *ill planet*, their *dreams of eternal transcendence* with like-minded yuan billionaires"[14]:

> I *scanned* the good cholesterol and the bad, the estrogen buildups and the financial crack-ups, but mostly I was looking for the equivalent of Joshie's funny limp: An *admission of weakness and insignificance*; an allusion to the broad *unfairness* and cosmic blundering of the universe we inhabit. And an intense *desire to set it right.*[15]

Lenny's scanning, therefore, demands attention to detail and empathy. He attempts to understand the motivations behind men's aspirations for eternal life. His anal-

---

11 Kern, Big Data, p. 92.
12 Ibid.
13 Ibid.
14 Shteyngart, *Super Sad*, p. 121; emphasis added.
15 Ibid.

ysis unveils a "dangerous altruism"[16] linking these men—engaging in humanitarian activities and thoughts, albeit with a highly individualistic approach. While outwardly focused, their actions primarily serve their self-interest. Lenny, exhibiting a form of dangerous altruism himself, plans to care for his friends, show kindness to parents, and love Eunice—all as strategic elements for his own survival. In other words, "Lenny's liberal appeals to empathy, mutual understanding, and respect"[17] might be a façade concealing egotistic feelings and indifference. This could explain his dissatisfaction when friends care for him, for it deviates from his goal of caring for them, rather than evoking gratitude. In this context, scanning and empathy function in ways akin to a house of mirrors, where Lenny perceives and reads himself in other men's pursuit of life.

Eunice emerges as an elusive character, seemingly embodying a shallow, consumerist, and digitally-driven self. Yet, her writing presents a paradox, offering "a welcome relief from Lenny's relentless navel-gazing" and being "more interesting and more alive than anything else I have read from that illiterate period."[18] This vitality stems from "a real interest in the world around her," and notably, "unlike so many Americans at the time of our country's collapse, Eunice Park did not possess the false idea that she was special."[19] As the novel concludes, Lenny emphasizes the significance of letting go of the perception of reading and writing as mere tools for self-expression. Instead, they emerge as activities and spaces that widen the scope of human attention. Eunice plays a pivotal role in this transformation, guiding Lenny away from his previous intellectual perception of the role of books. Despite appearing to embody a superficial self, Eunice possesses a genuine ability to pay attention.

> And when he was talking to me at dinner, usually I *listen* to everything a guy says and try to prepare a response or at least to act a certain way, but with him I just stopped listening after a while and looked at *the way his lips moved, the foam on his lips and on his dorky stubble*, because he was so EARNEST in the way he needed to tell me things. And I thought, wow, you're kind of beautiful, Lenny. You're like what Prof Margaux in Assertiveness Class used to call "a real human being."[20]

---

16 Powers, *Generosity*, p. 22. The phrase "dangerous altruism" is borrowed from Richard Powers' novel *Generosity: An Enhancement* to describe the tension between altruistic behavior and individualistic goals. See also the figure of Crake in Atwood or Kurton in Powers as two other examples where the notion of "dangerous altruism" gains relevance.
17 Trapp, Super Sad, p. 69.
18 Shteyngart, *Super Sad*, p. 325.
19 Ibid., p. 326.
20 Ibid., p. 73; emphasis added.

Eunice pays meticulous attention here, even noticing the foam on Lenny's lips as he speaks. His authenticity and earnestness make him beautiful, transcending any notion of bodily perfection. This same imagery of water merging with the air to create foam reappears in a different context when Lenny observes a seaplane taking flight, forming a fractal-like connection between the human and the nonhuman:

> And all these emotions, all these yearnings, all these data, if that helps to clinch the enormity of what I'm talking about, would be gone. And that's what immortality means to me, Joshie. It means selfishness. A needed distraction. *With a burble of warm white spray behind it*, a northbound seaplane took off so gracefully, so seemingly free of mechanics and despair, that for a moment *I imagined all our lives would just go on forever.*[21]

Rather than looking upward to the skies where the seaplane is headed, Lenny fixates on the "burble of warm white spray" left in its wake—the aftermath of the seaplane's departure.[22] Flight imagery typically evokes wings, transcendental aspirations, and a blend of danger and wonder, as seen in the myth of Icarus. Yet, in this instance, Lenny foregrounds the interaction between different elements: water, air, and the seaplane, emphasizing the dynamics of friction. Thus, the foam on his lips and the foam on the sea act like two fractals on different scales, showcasing similarities between the human and nonhuman realms. Both highlight a sense of beauty and grace found in ordinary, fleeting moments of assemblage— moments that already shelter a feeling of immortality, a Faustian, ephemeral forever: "I imagined all our lives would just go on forever."

Moreover, this imagery brings the body and its mortality to the forefront rather than allowing an escape from it. Eunice directs her attention to Lenny's bodily parts and their communicative nuances, transcending mere reliance on his words. The "burble of warm white spray" encapsulates a multisensory, synesthetic perspective of flight. The murmuring noise of the burble intertwines with the warmth, wetness, and white hue of the foam. In lieu of reinforcing a celestial and disembodied notion of upward mobility, where ascending signifies immortality, the focus shifts toward material sensations. Whiteness is no longer taken for granted; by merging the visual with the tactile and the auditory, whiteness becomes tangible and graspable.

The color white is traditionally associated with a virtuous life, symbolizing light and purity. However, in the United States, it also holds a dual significance

---

21 Ibid., p. 69; emphasis added.
22 This echoes the significance of memory and history examined in the preceding chapter on Literary Synesthesia, which also delved into Lenny's sense of nostalgia.

as the color of power—the White House—and the color of oppression. In short, Shteyngart's imagery illustrates the "artpolitical,"[23] unveiling the intimate relationship between politics and aesthetics. Not only is politics inherently aesthetic, but aesthetic choices also carry potent political resonances. In this instance, Shteyngart's utilization of literary synesthesia contributes to whiteness studies and critical race theory, shedding light on the unknown known of whiteness—the tacit knowledge of white privilege.[24] Accordingly, "the novel establishes a mode of engaged reading that is literary and social at the same time."[25]

Simultaneously, the "burble of warm white spray" brings to the forefront the potency of words and their materiality. In contemplating his eventual departure, Lenny shifts his focus from envisioning an afterlife to pondering the fate of his "words":

> Dear Diary, Today I've made a major decision: I am going to die. Nothing of my personality will remain. The light switch will be turned off. My life, my entirety, will be lost forever. I will be nullified. And what will be left? Floating through the ether, tickling the empty belly of space, alighting over farms outside Cape Town, and crashing into an aurora above Hammerfest, Norway, the northernmost city of this shattered planet—my data, the soupy base of my existence uptexted to a GlobalTeens account. Words, words, words. You, dear diary. This will be my last entry.[26]

Despite the inevitable aging and demise of his physical body, Lenny acknowledges that the "textual version of himself, the only version of himself accessible to either readers of the novel or diegetic readers of his data, is the version that matters."[27] However, the novel also complicates such interpretations that hinge on a Cartesian division between body and mind or body and data. Lenny's existence will not be permanently lost or nullified; it will persist in the form of a book. Books, in this context, become literary spaces that harbor a semblance of immortality—an ephemeral, Faustian notion of "stop moment, you're so beautiful." This conception of immortality does not imply timelessness or an immaterial, disembodied existence; on the contrary, it relies on the presence of time and the corporeal. Lenny, his love story, and his book are already immortal in this nuanced sense:

---

[23] Sartwell, Political Aesthetics, p. 2.
[24] Robert Jensen also underscores how "white" is "not a description of biology but a term that simply means an identifiable group of people [that] are perceived as white by those with power" (Whiteness, p. 23).
[25] Spahr, Re-Learning, p. 551.
[26] Shteyngart, Super Sad, p. 302.
[27] Kern, Big Data, p. 89.

they stand as enduring testimonials to the interplay of affecting and being affected within the intricate network of existence.

When Lenny contemplates words, he is captivated by their evocative capacity: "'Blustery.' Just one word, a word meaning no more than 'a period of time characterized by strong winds,' but it caught me unaware, it reminded me of how language was once used, its precision and simplicity, its capacity for recall. Not cold, not chilly, blustery. A hundred other blustery days appeared before me."[28] In this case, life is not confined to a singular experience; instead, language provides entry to a myriad of other blustery days. The vivid and expressive potency of language extends beyond the visual sense or words merely "floating through the ether"[29] as if they are immaterial. On the contrary, it hinges on a sensory apprehension of what "blustery" feels and sounds like—not only cold or chilly, but also howling and windy.

Words, therefore, are not immaterial. Lenny questions the efficacy of his books when viewed through such a lens: "I felt the weakness of these books, their *immateriality*, how they had failed to change the world, and I didn't want to sully myself with their weakness anymore."[30] However, books persist as the most tangible entities in a world dominated by the visual and the digital, where their existence is consistently denied. Ultimately, it is a book that survives—not due to its immateriality, not because it possesses a visionary idea, but because it resonates on a visceral level.

In the final chapter, it is "revealed that the novel we are reading is an assemblage made two decades after the Rupture by anonymous content-providers [...] Lenny's 'private' diary mysteriously survived, and Eunice's and Lenny's GlobalTeen accounts have been hacked. The resulting textual assemblage has turned into a worldwide bestseller."[31] In this scenario, the act of reading implicates the reader in a breach of privacy and surveillance.[32] The numerous spin-offs and movies inspired by The Diaries of Lenny Abramov suggest that, even if literature survives,[33]

---

28 Shteyngart, *Super Sad*, p. 302.
29 Ibid.
30 Ibid., p. 309; emphasis added.
31 Schmidt, Menippean Satire, p. 15.
32 "First, it dispenses with the notion that surveillance is predominantly visual and instead shows how textual data surveillance increasingly is as an operation of reading [...] Furthermore, by putting the reader in the position of reading these texts, it also positions reading itself as an exercise of surveillance that implicates readers as nodes in the reading/surveillance assemblage" (Kern, Big Data, p. 86, 91).
33 And yet, "[a]s much as Shteyngart (and Franzen) likes to lament the death of reading, this is a false Jeremiad: even in *Super Sad*'s America, literature, as a form of cultural capital, will always be redeemed" (Bullen, Act Two, p. 242).

it can only do so as commodity. *Super Sad True Love Story* itself has a "brand name perfect for marketing."[34] Spahr extends this perspective by asserting that Shteyngart's novel becomes a mere commodity: "The novel's discursive versatility and the marketing campaign that accompanied it perpetually threaten to turn the book into a commodity which surrenders the aesthetic autonomy to which it aspires."[35] Additionally, he contends, the "novel emerges as a commodity traded in a quantified literary world: the audience's standardized, manipulated expectations have been measured and Shteyngart emerges as an author who simply caters to these expectations."[36]

However, an alternative reading is also plausible. Similar to his protagonists, Shteyngart may position himself as an "intimate outsider."[37] He does not claim to be outside the capitalist system but rather tries to challenge it from within, playing with its rules. If the subaltern lacks a voice and the ability to speak,[38] then a disguised authority might emerge. Shteyngart's critique of capitalism takes on a more nuanced, aesthetic form, potentially proving more effective because it is not immediately perceived as critique. This is particularly pertinent in a world where the routine nature of critique has become prevalent. Far from surrendering its aesthetic autonomy, the book, through Shteyngart's use of literary synesthesia, shows how it retains its aesthetic integrity while coupling it with the concept of the political. Shteyngart is not merely an author who "simply caters" to audience expectations[39]; he also challenges those expectations in the process. For instance, one expectation that the novel dismantles is the notion of redemption (and humanity), a concept even critics perpetuate in their readings:

> Shteyngart's novel asserts the self-making functions of literary language and its ability to work through, and perhaps transcend, the logic of optimization and marketability. The entire novel is about the power of literature to at least preserve *a core of humanity* in what it refers to as an 'illiterate period' (327). The narrative of Lenny and Eunice seems to constitute that *redemptive core.*[40]

Even though Spahr interprets the entire novel as an effort to preserve at least a "core of humanity" and sees the narratives of Lenny and Eunice as constituting that "redemptive core," I would argue that the novel takes a different path. It chal-

---

34 Schmidt, Menippean Satire, p. 15.
35 Spahr, Re-Learning, p. 551.
36 Ibid., p. 554.
37 Sutherland/Swan, Margaret Atwood, p. 224.
38 See Gayatri Spivak's famous essay and question—"Can the Subaltern Speak?"
39 Spahr, Re-Learning, p. 554.
40 Ibid., p. 559; emphasis added.

lenges the anthropocentric lenses and rhetoric that Spahr employs here, shifting the focus away from the self and individual stories to the nonhuman world of books and its flows and sprays. *Super Sad True Love Story* demonstrates how textual immersion remains possible even when a text engages with consumerist culture. The stylistic choices and use of literary synesthesia in the novel do not diminish the aesthetic questions it poses; rather, they facilitate the very process of textual immersion.

The last words that Lenny directs toward Eunice may seem irrelevant, but they carry significant meaning: "Words broke out of me. Stupid words. The worst final words I could have chosen, but words nonetheless. 'Silly goose,' I said to Eunice. 'You shouldn't have worn such a warm suit. It's still autumn. Aren't you hot? Aren't you hot, Eunice?'"[41] These words convey an enduring sense of love felt by Lenny—not just as passion but as a form of mutual care, a sentiment he learned from Eunice.[42] Additionally, it suggests that, paradoxically, Lenny has achieved success in his relationship with Eunice. Earlier, he asserted that "[s]uccess would come when neither of us knew where one ended and the other began."[43]

In this case, Lenny's perspective evokes the myth of the androgyne, where humans were supposedly divided into halves, perpetually seeking their other half to regain a sense of wholeness. On the one hand, Lenny aspires to revert to an idealized concept of love, predating its transformation into science or a "universal psychic structure."[44] He aims to capture an ideal of "emotional fusion," "selfless devotion," or "self-sacrifice"—qualities now regarded as symptoms of emotional dysfunction.[45] He addresses a loss of individuality that he seems to discover in their final encounter, especially since Lenny's focus is not on himself or his emotions but has shifted toward Eunice and her nonhuman, warm suit.

The word "hot" briefly encapsulates not only their passionate love story, the anger and pain following their break-up, or the potential shame that Eunice ought to feel, but also embodies their vivid relationship—a liveliness grounded in the body and the sense of touch. The conclusion of their relationship does not signify the end of love but rather portrays an ideal love, emphasizing acceptance,

---

41 Shteyngart, *Super Sad*, p. 320.
42 "But then I started thinking about it from Eunice's point of view. The family was eternal. The bonds of kinship could never be broken. You watched out for others of your kind and they watched out for you. Perhaps it was I who had been remiss, in not caring enough for Eunice, in not correcting her when she ordered garlicky sweet-potato fries" (ibid., p. 165).
43 Ibid., p. 165.
44 Illouz, Romantic Love, p. 24.
45 Ibid.

including the acceptance of its conclusion. According to Brené Brown, "empathy is an other-focused emotion. It draws our attention outward, toward the other person's experience," while "shame is an egocentric, self-involved emotion. It draws our focus inward."[46] Thus, she suggests that these two emotions are incompatible and mutually exclusive.[47] However, this final scene complicates such a perspective, as what appears to be an empathic act—Lenny's concern for how Eunice feels—could also be a means of generating shame in Eunice (and vice versa). Consequently, human relationships are messier and more complicated than a scientific mapping of human connection might imply.

Ultimately, the emphasis lies in recognizing that "words" are not merely ethereal expressions but carry their own "fleshy" baggage, containing multiple meanings and leaving an impact on the body. Asking whether one is "hot" or not can also be a way of generating heat. The love story depicted in the novel extends beyond the narrative of Lenny and Eunice; it is also a story about reading. Reading is portrayed as an act of love because it nurtures care, attention, and, crucially, it heightens embodied awareness—it generates heat, and then it concludes. Reading plays a role in diminishing individuality, even if momentarily, leaving behind nothing but a burble of warm white spray. Amid this intricate exploration of literature, scanning, and sensory engagement, the novel prompts us to reconsider not only how we read but how we listen, feel, and inhabit the words, intertwining the act of scanning with an exploration of the nonhuman.

---

[46] Brown, *Atlas*, p. 141.
[47] Much like Sartre's acts of looking and being looked at.

III Mindfulness and Self-Vigilance in the Anthropocene

Introduction

In the age of the Anthropocene,[1] discussions surrounding humanity and its future survival have gathered momentum. With the looming climate crisis and emerging technological developments promising a future marked by hybridity, scholars are now contemplating *"intended and purposeful consequences"*[2] that may shape our collective destiny. In this context, the discourse on mindfulness has gained traction, not merely for its neoliberal allure as a remedy for the "epidemic of stress"[3] but also for its role in engaging with crucial debates about the survival of the human species. Mindfulness operates not only as a means to alleviate personal stress but also as a tool to reinforce the concept of a shared humanity and advocate transcending the confines of the "human condition." Distinguished from psychoanalysis, mindfulness extends beyond fostering an introspective understanding of the self; it encompasses a broader narrative that implicates all of humanity. This chapter delves into the depiction of mindfulness in various contexts, examining its portrayal in TED talks and literature, notably in Margaret Atwood's *MaddAddam* trilogy.

---

1 The Anthropocene can be perceived "not as a debate about a new geological era but rather as a *way of thinking*—a way of thinking about our identity, and what it will mean to be human in the future" (Potts, Living in the Anthropocene, p. 30; emphasis in original).
2 Potts, Living, p. 30; emphasis in original.
3 Harrington, *Cure Within*, p. 144.

8 TED Talks on Mindfulness and the "Second Sight"

As of February 2022, TED has curated a collection of twenty talks centered around mindfulness, even if some of them seem to tackle the subject only tangentially. While not all talks explicitly focus on mindfulness, their inclusion on this list suggests that it remains a latent topic.[1] Furthermore, TED has organized seven playlists dedicated to mindfulness, encompassing themes such as "Talks to Help You Find Your Purpose," "How to Protect Your Passions from Burnout," "For Those Who Want to Break Out of Their Shell," "TED Talks as the Seven Deadly Sins," "Building Introspective Places," "Talks to Help You Manage Stress," and "Talks to Help Practice Patience."[2] This chapter endeavors to explore the multifaceted approach of TED talks toward mindfulness.

8.1 Mindfulness and Self-Help: Restoring Vigor in the Age of Anxiety

The renowned playlists "Talks to Help You Manage Stress" and "Talks to Help Practice Patience" prominently feature visuals depicting individuals in the iconic yogic posture, both men adorned with glasses, embodying an aura of tranquility. This imagery emphasizes the act of turning inward in order to discover a sense of composure, symbolized by the stillness and closed eyes. The individual in "Talks to Help You Manage Stress" wears rectangular glasses, a fashionable choice that underscores a masculine and intellectually rooted conception of rationality and self-control. Despite the massive, weighty boulder tethered to his hand, the figure remains unburdened, supported by an even larger cloud that not only hovers above his head but also encircles his arms, juxtaposing the constraining weight of earthly

---

[1] For instance, in "Talks to Help You Manage Stress," only Andy Puddicombe's talk on "All It Takes Is Ten Mindful Minutes" deals with the topic explicitly.

[2] An examination of the titles within these playlists reveals the specific contexts in which mindfulness gains relevance: the spheres of work or career life, identity formation, and self-discipline. "Talks to Help Practice Patience" encompasses presentations by Matthieu Ricard, Andy Puddicombe, Judson Brewer, Daniel Levitin, and Pico Iyer—each of whom is thoroughly explored in this chapter. Additionally, the playlist features three more speeches on "The Psychology of Time" by Zimbardo, "The Power of Believing that You Can Improve" by Dweck, and "In Praise of Slowness" by Honoré, providing many insights on mindfulness and its applications.

∂ Open Access. © 2024 the author(s), published by De Gruyter. [CC BY] This work is licensed under the Creative Commons Attribution 4.0 International License. https://doi.org/10.1515/9783111389929-012

Figure 3: Image for TED's playlist on "Talks to Help You Manage Stress".

concerns with the liberating, transcendent expanse of the skies. The ethereal white cloud positioned above the man symbolizes the belief that serenity emanates from above—originating from the mind. The mountainous backdrop and the man's suspended posture above the rock further encapsulates the notion of a transcendental state achieved through the mastery of the mind.

The yogi image has become a stereotypical representation of mindfulness in Western societies, further reinforced and disseminated by American self-help culture. The surge in popularity of mindfulness in America traces its origins back to Transcendentalist ideals of solitude, akin to the philosophy of Henry David Thoreau, and those countercultural movements that fueled the demand for alternative spiritualities.[3] The concept of a serene self firmly rooted in the present moment, detached from one's immediate surroundings, and seeking inner peace—whether through sitting meditations or weekly silence retreats—seems to hold the promise of experiencing solitude within private moments.[4] In contrast to engaging in open

---

[3] See also Shelley Cowden's "Transcendental Meditation: Counter Culture Spirituality to Postmodern Commodity" (2010).

[4] Historically, Western interest in meditative practices experienced surges in the late 19th century, primarily among scholars, and again in the 1960s when it gained widespread popularity in Western society, a trend that has continued to grow. While some scholars attribute this interest to a form of spiritual hunger or the influence of Asians coming to the West, the increasing popularity of meditation also coincides with debates over the erosion of privacy. Interestingly, solitude con-

discussions with a psychoanalyst, mindfulness pledges a path of withdrawal, harmony, and stillness.

Pico Iyer's "The Art of Stillness" is presented by TED as a "counterintuitive and *lyrical meditation* [...] that takes a look at the incredible *insight* that comes with taking time for stillness."[5] Iyer attributes his enhanced perception to stillness, noting that it has enabled him to "develop more attentive and more appreciative *eyes*."[6] While his travels provide him with "amazing *sights*," it is the practice of stillness that "allows [him] to turn those into lasting *insights*."[7] The concept of stillness is thus linked with both the power of imagination and a sense of objectivity or self-detachment, enabling individuals to "begin to see what the canvas means and to catch the larger picture."[8] Iyer's talk reinforces a visionary interpretation of stillness and, implicitly, mindfulness. The predominantly visual understanding of stillness perpetuates a Western approach to and celebration of vision, prioritizing eyesight and imagination over other senses or human abilities.[9]

Furthermore, stillness is conceived not as a privileged position but rather as an individual solution to the challenges posed by the age of acceleration, distraction, and constant movement. The advocacy for slowing down[10] is a well-established theme in discussions on mindfulness, and it is not a novel rhetoric. The 19th-century concern over the "velocity in thought and action" is evident in the Victorian Light Night show organized by the research group Diseases of Modern Life.[11] Anxieties about the consequences of rapid societal changes driven by technology are not new. The apprehension that the rapid and widespread dissemination of infor-

---

stitutes the first stage of privacy—see also Wetzel-Sahm's "Negotiating the Right to Be Let Alone," p. 195.
5 Iyer, Art of Stillness, TED; emphasis added.
6 Ibid., 00:01:39; emphasis added.
7 Ibid., 00:04:02; emphasis added.
8 Ibid., 00:14:37.
9 For a more in-depth analysis of the word "insight," its various connotations, and its linkage to a humanist approach to the self and its visionary powers, check out my blog entry titled "InSight: Making a Case for Self-Vigilance?" available on *Vigilanzkulturen*.
10 Journalist Carl Honoré, in "In Praise of Slowness," has also critiqued the accelerated rhythm of life, noting, "We fill our head with distraction, with busyness, so that we don't have to ask, am I well? Am I happy?" (00:13:33). As such, debates on the role of mindfulness extend into reflections on happiness, as outlined below.
11 Victorian, 00:00:30. The event was organized in collaboration with TORCH (The Oxford Research Centre in the Humanities) and a Projection Studio as part of the Being Human Festival in 2018. The show draws on quotes from the medic James Crichton Browne, who, in 1860, spoke of the "velocity in thought and action." Additionally, it references 19th century newspaper articles, William Morris' first three lines from the "Prologue: The Wanderers," advertisements, and the writings of British radical socialist John Addington Symonds.

mation—whether in the form of "telegrams arriving at all hours"[12] or contemporary emails and social media feeds—may lead to a "mental epidemic"[13] and an "overdriven brain"[14] has persisted throughout the centuries.

The notion that these new technologies contribute to the creation of sleep-deprived, addicted, and overwhelmed selves endures. The Nielsen Total Audience Report on media consumption has just revealed a consistent rise in time spent consuming media, with adults in the United States dedicating over eleven hours a day to watching TV, listening to the radio, surfing the web, or scrolling through the phone.[15] Consequently, the growing volume of new data has given rise to the concept of "information overload," a phenomenon associated with challenges in decision making, a dulling of the senses, consumer distraction, and the retreat into personalized "filter bubble[s]."[16] Herbert Alexander Simon, addressing the "attention economy," emphasizes how "a wealth of information creates a poverty of attention,"[17] underscoring the heightened significance of attention management. Efforts to address information overload extend beyond managing the ever-expanding information supply to include strategies for self-motivation. Paradoxically, responses to data abundance have resulted in the generation of even more content, as motivational speakers and self-help gurus saturate the market with books, videos, podcasts, and various media on the topic. In other words, "the changing configurations of capitalism continually push attention and distraction to new limits and thresholds, with an endless sequence of new products, sources of stimulation, and streams of information, and then respond with new methods of managing and regulating perception."[18]

The Victorian Light Night show illustrates a tension between the fatigued and depressed self and the animated and lively self. The latter part of the projection displays Victorian ads for various consumer products such as electric belts, Parker's tonic, Vigor's horse action saddler, nerve pills, and magnetic corsets[19]—each

---

12 Ibid., 00:01:16. The telegrams were "producing rapid alternations of hope and fear" (00:01:18). And they were "too fast for the truth" (00:01:32).
13 Ibid., 00:01:02.
14 Ibid., 00:01:09.
15 Time Flies, *Nielsen*.
16 Parser, *Filter Bubble*. For further insights into the prominence of distraction in contemporary thinking about the Internet, see also Jesse Ramirez's work on "Contemporary Cultures of Privacy."
17 Simon, Designing Organizations, p. 40.
18 Crary, *Suspensions*, p. 14.
19 Vigor's horse action saddler resembles an early form of a fitness machine, while Parker's tonic and the bitters promise to renew vigor and make life worth living, akin to 21st century anti-depressants.

pledging to restore vigor.[20] Therefore, these products not only claim to remedy stomach disorders or physical ailments but also vow to "invigorate the system" and provide "complete satisfaction."[21] The section begins with the repeated phrase "forget this,"[22] highlighting distraction as an easily accessible escape for the overwhelmed self. Moreover, the proposed remedies are all rooted in economic solutions, suggesting that consumerism is the primary response to the "loss of energy and mental depression caused by excessive brain work."[23] Paradoxically, the proliferation of advertisements promising to restore vigor contributes to the surge of new data, which, in turn, may exacerbate or even cause the fatigue in the first place.

In the 21st century, mindfulness meditation has emerged as a "quick fix" for the overwhelmed self, akin to a method meant to "cultivate repose of mind."[24] The prevailing self-help approach to mindfulness dominates various media, contributing to the dissemination of a stereotypical and oversimplified understanding of mindfulness. It has become synonymous with psychological self-control and the individual mastery of thoughts and emotions. Evolving into a "hot commodity,"[25] mindfulness has captured the attention of Western scientists, notably Jon Kabat-Zinn, who established the Mindfulness-Based Stress Reduction Clinic.[26] Stripped of its spiritual overtones, mindfulness has been now perceived as a therapeutic

---

20 Vigor connotes power, energy, vitality and alertness as opposed to lethargy, apathy, or listlessness. The underlying meanings of liveliness, animation, or spirit suggest a vitalist approach to life. "Today, nobody believes that living beings are inhabited by a soul or by a vital force that opposes the physicochemical forces and is even capable of altering their effects. The death of this kind of vitalism, however, does not remove all vitalistic concepts, nor does it necessarily mean the victory of mechanistic metaphysics" (Federspil and Sicolo 342). Similarly, the concept of a soul seems to have been replaced with an affective, emotional state as the guarantor for being alive—like, for instance, mindfulness.
21 Victorian, 00:03:12, 00:03:22.
22 Ibid., 00:02:43.
23 Ibid., 00:03:29.
24 Ibid., 00:03:50.
25 According to Lee, "[T]eachings from Buddhist traditions have become a hot commodity, generating over $4 billion in sales in 2016. There were 12 million adult coloring books, 100,000 mindfulness books and 700-plus new apps sold to help us eat, walk, commute, and work a little more mindfully" (Has Mindfulness Become the New Kale?).
26 As explained by Mead, "Jon Kabat-Zinn is often credited with being the founder of 'modern day' mindfulness, and the idea and concept of mindfulness that is commonly held across western cultures." His medical center offers a "clinically proven program to help support individuals experiencing a range of conditions including depression, anxiety, insomnia, chronic pain, and cardiovascular problems" (The History and Origin of Meditation).

tool capable of curing the "fundamental dis-ease of humanity"[27] and addressing the anxiety and depression perpetuated by the noise and hectic pace of contemporary life in Western society.

Even within a scientific framework, mindfulness has been marketed and popularized as a pathway to autonomy. Consequently, it has been persistently presented as a remedy for stress and anxiety.[28] In her article "I Want to Be Happier! What Should I Read?" Acacia C. Parks recommends Zinn's *Full Catastrophe Living*, stating, "To my knowledge, nothing works better for most anxiety than mindfulness."[29] The responses to Zinn's *Full Catastrophe Living: Using the Wisdom of Your Body and Mind to Face Stress, Pain, and Illness* prominently feature on the first pages of the book. Provided by both doctors and medical students, these responses also serve as marketing tools, unveiling themes and tropes intended to captivate the reader's interest. The book is positioned as a "true breakthrough in the area of behavioral medicine and *self-control*," with James E. Dalen underscoring the significance of "self-control."[30] Others have highlighted the health benefits of mindfulness, presenting it as a means to "develop an optimal state of mental physical [...] health" or illustrating how *"higher reaches of human consciousness can heal the lower."*[31]

Nevertheless, these concepts have not escaped criticism: "How is it that we are so unhappy with our lots that we will willingly sit cringing in a room with our colleagues while remembering to breathe? Twenty minutes of inhaling in a boardroom is pointless if a lawyer is going back out on the floor to complete a 16-hour day, endlessly interrupted by emails."[32] Emma Barnett highlights systemic flaws in the working environment rather than endorsing the individual attitude change promoted by self-help gurus. Mindfulness, while valuable, does not simply cure the information overload and its resulting fatigue; it is insufficient without concurrent changes in societal values. However, this narrative continues to thrive, primarily due to its promise of clarity and mastery. In a humorous and personal talk on "How I Live with High-Functioning Anxiety" (2017), comedian Jordan Raskopoulos indirectly touches on mindfulness as tacit knowledge underpinning the

---

27 Zinn, *Coming*, p. 112.
28 See also Anne Harrington's chapter on Eastward Journeys as a narrative template that counterpoints the "broken by modern life" lament. Thus, "[e]ven though we live in a harsh, fast-paced, and unnatural world filled with stress," this narrative tells us "that there are ways to heal, to recover balance, to boost immunity, and to increase well-being" (*Cure Within*, p. 174).
29 Parks, I Want to Be Happier.
30 Zinn, *Full Catastrophe*; emphasis added.
31 Ibid. These last comments have been made by Pelletier and Dossey.
32 Barnett, Mindfulness.

power of focusing on one task—such as performing on stage. In other words, mindfulness is associated with a sense of focus and concentration that has the potential to alleviate various forms of distress.

Neuroscientist Daniel Levitin, in his talk "How to Stay Calm When You Know You'll Be Stressed," explores the limitations of rational and logical thinking during moments of stress, emphasizing the need to *"train ourselves to think ahead* to these kinds of situations."[33] Levitin advocates (self-)vigilant behavior as a means of preventing future failures, recounting a personal incident where he accidentally locked himself in his apartment. However, he overlooks the fact that many failures become apparent only in hindsight, and attempting to preemptively avert every potential danger may exacerbate paranoid or anxious feelings. In other words, Levitin neglects the inherent uncertainties of life and suggests yet another rational method to exert control over it, undermining his initial premise. He suggests that the only way to manage stress is to avoid it altogether, a proposition for which mindfulness can provide a solution. As such, he envisions mindfulness as a form of vigilance—not only as a means to cope with stress but also as a proactive tool for preventing it.

Mindfulness expert Andy Puddicombe, the creator of the renowned *Headspace* mobile application, delivered a talk titled "All It Takes Is Ten Mindful Minutes" (2013), echoing a similar argument. Featured among the first six relevant talks on mindfulness,[34] his presentation is recurrent across various playlists, including "Talks to Help You Manage Stress," "Talks to Help You Practice Patience," and the well-known "How to Be a Better You." Puddicombe's engaging performance involves juggling three red balls to illustrate the workings of thoughts in the mind, rendering his explanations tangible, visible, easily comprehensible, and entertaining. At the same time, the act of juggling unintentionally reinforces the myth he seeks to dispel: the notion that the self can control thoughts. By bringing in a sense of "relaxed focus" that helps him detach himself and look at the balls from a distance, the idea that the self can "juggle" with thoughts persists.[35] Mindfulness is presented not merely as a remedy for our busy world, an "aspirin of the mind," but as a preventive measure too—a means to live in the present moment.[36]

---

33 Levitin, How to Stay Calm, 00:11:14.
34 The order of the talks in terms of relevance keeps changing, with Puddicombe's talk being listed as third, fourth, or even sixth in this ranking. As of the last verification on 28 February 2022, it appeared in the sixth position.
35 Puddicombe, All It Takes, 00:05:45.
36 Ibid., 00:02:36.

Puddicombe references a Harvard study revealing that people spend 45% of their time engrossed in thoughts, a trend correlated with unhappiness.[37]

Mindfulness serves not only as a remedy or preventive measure for stress but emerges as the primary tool for cultivating a sense of well-being, too. Matthieu Ricard, a renowned biochemist turned Buddhist monk, delivers a talk that underscores the notion that "we can *train* our minds in habits of well-being, to generate a true sense of serenity and fulfillment."[38] He frames mindfulness as "mind transformation" or mind training, emphasizing the "familiarization with a new way of being, new way of perceiving things, which is more in *adequation with reality*,[39] with interdependence, with the stream and continuous transformation, which our being and our consciousness is."[40] Recognizing the limitations of controlling the outer world, Ricard shifts focus to "inner conditions."[41] He advocates self-control, proudly noting that "some meditators are able, also, to control their emotional response more than it could be thought."[42] Concluding with a humorous reference to "flying monks," Ricard highlights the wonder of self-transcendence and the extraordinary possibilities of the mind.[43] The sense of transcendence has been evoked from the beginning, as Ricard showcases sublime images of the Himalayas.

Over the past two decades, mindfulness meditation has transitioned from a "fringe topic of scientific investigation" to an "occasional replacement for psychotherapy, tool of corporate well-being, [and] widely implemented educational practice."[44] In the contemporary world, mindfulness has become a favorite instrument for achieving self-discipline and self-control, serving as the premise for the pursuit of happiness.

> [In the modern world] psychoanalysis became the privileged site for the expression of the inner self as well as a site that encouraged introspection, a focus on feelings, and most of all, a search for the lost and true self. Less emphasized but no less important is the fact that psychoanalysis is a rational method that enjoins self-knowledge through the use of a detached gaze on oneself in a process of self-examination that ultimately bestows freedom and self-mastery.[45]

---

[37] See also the discussion of mind wandering and rumination introduced later in this chapter.
[38] Ricard, Habits of Happiness; emphasis added.
[39] For a more detailed exploration of "adequation with reality," refer to the section below where I discuss Robert Wright's course on "Buddhism and Modern Psychology."
[40] Ricard, Habits of Happiness, 00:14:38; emphasis added.
[41] Ibid., 00:07:37.
[42] Ibid., 00:18:23.
[43] Ibid., 00:20:33.
[44] Van Dam et al., Mind the Hype, p. 36.
[45] Illouz, *Saving*, p. 50.

Eva Illouz's observations about psychoanalysis now find resonance in the realm of mindfulness. Mindfulness has evolved into a widely embraced "rational method" fostering self-vigilance through a "detached gaze on oneself," leading not only to "self-mastery" but also to happiness. Edgar Cabanas and Eva Illouz attribute the popularity of mindfulness to the individualistic values prevalent in neoliberal societies: "In the last few years, mindfulness has indeed been established as a main theme in public policies, schools, health institutions, prisons, and the military [...] It has also grown as a topic for scholars. [...] mindfulness has itself become a lucrative, global industry raking in more than $1 billion a year."[46] Mindfulness "thrives on the belief that the root of these problems is to be found in individuals themselves, rather than in a socio-economic reality" and it offers "techniques that make them [its followers] *direct their attention to themselves instead of the surrounding world.*"[47] Thus, it both contributes to and is nourished by the "obsessive self-concern and self-scrutiny"[48] that define self-help culture.

Mindfulness, in this context, emerges as another "privileged site"[49] that not only pledges mental healing and self-control but also advocates the pursuit of happiness—restoring the vigor stifled by the age of anxiety. Mindfulness is frequently linked to positive feelings such as gratitude, love, or happiness. Monk David Steindl-Rast presents mindfulness as a method for living gratefully in his talk, "Want to Be Happy? Be Grateful" (2013). Utilizing the first-person plural, he implies a shared experience among all humans, asserting that "we" rush through life and "we" need to pause. Happiness, according to him, is living gratefully "by experiencing, by becoming aware that every moment is a given moment, as we say. It's a gift."[50] He argues for a three-step process of "stop—look—go"[51] to nurture happiness and even "transform the world, make it a happier place."[52] Steindl-Rast suggests gratefulness as a means of transcending self-centerdness and shifting the focus from "I" to "we"—an embodiment of happiness.[53]

His Holiness the Karmapa, a revered figure in Tibetan Buddhism, delivered a talk on "The Technology of the Heart" (2014), where he shared his personal story. Having been separated from his family as a young boy, he lived in a controlled en-

---

46 Cabanas/Illouz, *Manufacturing Happy Citizens*, p. 66.
47 Ibid., p. 67; emphasis added.
48 Ibid.
49 Illouz, *Saving*, p. 50.
50 Steindl-Rast, Want to Be Happy, 00:03:52.
51 Ibid., 00:08:30.
52 Ibid., 00:13:56.
53 This shift away from the individualism of the self in defining happiness constitutes the theme of Part IV, where it will be analyzed in more detail.

vironment with prescribed duties, treated almost like a statue.[54] Despite this, he maintains a strong connection of love to his family, friends, and land. The Karmapa encourages his audience to focus on "inward development and deepening of our heart connections as well as our outward connections"[55]—what he terms the "design of the heart."[56]

> So I think the way forward for the world—one that will bring the path of outer development in harmony with the real root of happiness—is that we allow the information that we have to really make a change in our heart. [...] And I think that sometimes we develop grand concepts of what happiness might look like for us, but that, if we pay attention, we can see that there are little symbols of happiness in every breath that we take.[57]

Paying attention to the "symbols of happiness" is precisely what mindfulness can offer. In other words, mindfulness not only fosters intense self-scrutiny but paradoxically also redirects attention from the individual self toward an understanding of happiness that involves transcending or letting go of the self.

According to these speakers, mindfulness is not only effective in alleviating external stress but also internal stress manifesting as mind wandering. Mindfulness, then, is presented as a solution to the psychological habit of rumination. In "Why We All Need to Practice Emotional First Aid," psychologist Guy Winch describes rumination as the incessant replaying of upsetting scenes in one's head, emphasizing the risks it poses for clinical depression, alcoholism, eating disorders, and cardiovascular disease.[58] He encourages his audience to actively combat negative thinking, visually highlighting the term "negative" in red.[59] He suggests that distraction from negative thoughts is crucial: "Studies tell us that even a two-minute distraction is sufficient to break the urge to ruminate in that moment. And so each time I had a worrying, upsetting, negative thought, I forced myself to concentrate on something else until the urge passed."[60] Remarkably, within a week, his outlook transformed to become "more positive and more hopeful."[61] This narrative not only advocates for countering negative thinking but also emphasizes the replacement of negative thoughts with a positive mindset. In portraying mindfulness as

---

54 The Karmapa, Technology of the Heart, 00:05:25.
55 Ibid., 00:09:44.
56 Ibid., 00:10:05.
57 Ibid., 00:19:25.
58 Winch, Why We All Need, 00:13:36. So, rumination is about being "focused on upsetting and negative thoughts."
59 Ibid., 00:15:32.
60 Ibid., 00:15:10.
61 Ibid., 00:15:26.

a tool of "emotional hygiene,"[62] Winch highlights mindfulness as a disinfectant capable of dispelling negative thoughts and nurturing the positive, despite its neutral characterization.

Neuroscientist Amishi Jha has delved into the study of the "human brain's attention system"[63] and approaches mindfulness from a similar perspective. According to her, attention functions as an amplifier for human perception, and both external stress and internal mind wandering can diminish its power, leaving the self feeling foggy and distracted.[64] Consequently, she asserts that "the opposite of a stressed and wandering mind is a mindful one."[65] Jha also highlights the benefits of mindfulness training for military personnel and shares a testimonial from one such personnel who felt that the mindfulness training program offered a crucial tool in preventing post-traumatic stress disorder "and even allowing it to turn into post-traumatic growth."[66] Once again, mindfulness proves to be more than a stress-management tool; it becomes a catalyst for personal growth.[67]

Scholar Matt Killingsworth's talk on "Want to Be Happier? Stay in the Moment" (2014) delves into mind-wandering as a main topic. He developed "a way to study people's happiness moment to moment as they're going about their daily lives on a massive scale all over the world, something we'd never been able to do before. Called trackyourhappiness.org, it uses iPhone to monitor people's happiness in real time."[68] One of the study's findings reveals a "strong relationship between mind-wandering now and being unhappy a short time later, consistent with the idea that mind-wandering is causing people to be unhappy."[69] Although he does not explicitly mention mindfulness, his talk is included among those on the topic. There are at least two implicit connections to mindfulness: firstly, as an alternative to mind-wandering—a pathway to happiness, echoing the dis-

---

62 Ibid., 00:02:06.
63 Jha, How to Tame, 00:01:14.
64 Ibid., 00:08:43.
65 Ibid., 00:12:04.
66 Ibid., 00:15:43.
67 American psychologist Carol Dweck introduces the concept of a "growth mindset" in her talk on "The Power of Believing that You Can Improve" (2014), which has been frequently referenced by other TED speakers. Dweck advocates for praising children's efforts, focus, and perseverance rather than their inner traits, such as talent or intelligence. This approach aims to cultivate resilience and confidence. Dweck notes, "And we can actually change students' mindsets. In one study, we taught them that every time they push out of their comfort zone to learn something new and difficult, the neurons in their brain can form new, stronger connections, and over time, they can get smarter" (00:05:31).
68 Killingsworth, Want to Be Happier, 00:02:14.
69 Ibid., 00:08:00.

infectant rhetoric of Guy Winch. Secondly, as a newfound awareness facilitated by technology: "by tracking people's moment-to-moment happiness and their experiences in daily life, we'll be able to uncover a lot of important causes of happiness, and then in the end, a scientific understanding of happiness will help us create a future that's not only richer and healthier, but happier as well."[70] In this case, mindfulness remains associated with happiness, yet also intersects with technology—a theme further explored by Ariel Garten.[71]

The discourse on mindfulness within TED talks often intertwines with discussions about the impact of technology, feeding off each other.[72] Design thinker Tristan Harris, known for his study of the ethics of manipulating thoughts at Google, explores the "race for our attention"[73] in his talk on "How a Handful of Tech Companies Control Billions of Minds Every Day" (2017), delving into the persuasive techniques taught at the Persuasive Technology Lab. Harris highlights how technology often directs attention, as seen in Facebook's preference for an "outrage feed" over a "calm newsfeed."[74] However, he proposes an alternative interaction with technology, envisioning a paradigm shift in human self-perception:

> I think we need to see ourselves fundamentally in a new way. It's almost like a new period of human history, like the Enlightenment, but almost *a kind of self-aware Enlightenment*, that we can be persuaded, and there might be something we want to protect. [...] So imagine we're running, like, a find and replace on all of the timelines that are currently steering us towards more and more screen time persuasively and replacing all of those timelines with what do we want in our lives. [...] Instead of handicapping our attention, imagine if we used all of this data and all of this power and this new view of human nature to give us *a superhuman ability to focus* and *a superhuman ability to put our attention* to what we cared about and *a superhuman ability* to have the conversations that we need to have for democracy.[75]

Although mindfulness is not explicitly mentioned, Harris's talk is classified among the first five relevant talks on the topic. His proposal of a new "self-aware Enlightenment" and repeated emphasis on a "superhuman ability to focus" indirectly re-

---

70 Ibid., 00:09:37.
71 See below in 8.2. for more detailed content on this topic.
72 Usually, technology has been perceived as the culprit behind the stress of modern life, and many cultural products depict a stereotypical image of business individuals in tech companies attempting to alleviate the stress of their work life through mindfulness retreats. However, in TED, technology also emerges as a mediator of mindfulness, aligning with the principles of the Quantified Self movement.
73 Harris, How a Handful, 00:02:54.
74 Ibid., 00:05:15.
75 Ibid., 00:07:05; emphasis added.

fers to mindfulness.⁷⁶ In this context, mindfulness is depicted as a method for intentional actions, offering a means to exert agency over the persuasive tactics targeting the "lizard brain."⁷⁷

In a concluding dialogue with Chris Anderson, Harris adds, "I think right now it's as if all of our technology is basically only asking our lizard brain what's the best way to just impulsively get you to do the next tiniest thing with your time."⁷⁸ His depiction of these covert strategies to capture attention implies that "the only way to get more is to go lower on the brain stem, to go lower into outrage, to go lower into emotion, to go lower into the lizard brain."⁷⁹ This rhetoric takes a notably humanist tone, reinforcing a dichotomous and hierarchical perspective where emotions and the "lizard brain" are positioned lower than the "superhuman" ability of the mind to reason. Simultaneously, it situates his narrative within a logic of survival, as the reference to the "lizard brain" invokes evolutionary ideas and addresses a limbic system responsible for fight or flight. Consequently, this narrative reinforces the belief that bodies are and need to be manipulated, with mindfulness emerging as a potential aid in this endeavor.

8.2 The "Inner Scientist" Is Noticing the Body

Mindfulness emerges as a powerful tool in combating suffering, earning its place among various practices known to enhance happiness. In the sixth episode of the *Greater Good* podcast,⁸⁰ host Dacher Keltner and guest Krista Tippett delve into a mindfulness exercise: the body scan meditation. Tippett openly shares her spiritual journey, revealing a focus on "inhabiting [her] body."⁸¹ She explains the purpose of the exercise, stating:

> I think it's about *connecting ourselves up*. I think, like, you know, you move through the day like propelled by your brain and by whatever you're thinking. And the things you're thinking that you don't even intend to be thinking. And *not noticing your body*. And it's about kind of *settling in your body*, and connecting your mind, and your breathing, and your heart. And really the rhythm of yourself with your feet on the ground, and the fact that you're breathing in air.

---

76 Ibid., 00:07:11, 00:10:28.
77 Ibid., 00:14:58.
78 Ibid., 00:14:55.
79 Ibid., 00:16:36.
80 Chapter eleven will introduce and discuss the *Greater Good* podcast in more detail.
81 Keltner, Krista Tippett, 00:02:55.

8.2 The "Inner Scientist" Is Noticing the Body — 157

> And there's a little bit of that feeling with the body scan of like, *I'm sinking. I am now resting on the earth*, right? Like where I always needed to be anyway, *rather than floating*, flitting above it. I think we're going to learn more and more that if we can get in touch with how feelings, memories, experiences, problems are lodging in *our physical selves* and we can address our physical selves. You know, we may be able to do so much healing through our bodies.[82]

Tippett challenges the notion of self-transcendence, emphasizing the importance of the physical self. However, even when addressing the body, such examples are often framed as advocating self-control, treating physical sensations merely as data requiring processing. The episode concludes with science expert Wendy Hasenkamp reflecting on the "training of attention to both remain on a spot, and also to move it [attention] around as you would like."[83] The exploration of alpha waves and their role in brain function aims to illustrate how the brain processes information.

> So wherever alpha waves are low, that's where your kind of *lens of attention* is. So it's a way of kind of selecting information that you can pay attention to or that you are aware of. [...] So it suggests that this type of meditation practice or mindfulness training can really help us *learn to shift our attention flexibly*. [...] You know, just *having a sense that you can control your attention*.[84]

Consequently, mindfulness is predominantly promoted as a tool for self-control and attention management, serving personal benefits such as stress reduction, alleviating suffering, and enhancing happiness. Despite Tippett's acknowledgment of "inhabiting the body," the ultimate focus of the episode centers on the idea of "control[ing] your attention."[85]

TED talks on mindfulness contribute to reinforcing the notion of mind-power as a means of self-control, a prevailing theme in self-help culture. Challenges to this conventional understanding of mindfulness are often overshadowed by the allure of the popular concepts of self-mastery and discipline. In Andy Puddicombe's TED talk, links to his published book and mobile application further underscore this perspective. The audience is encouraged to "Sign up for a free mindfulness program with Headspace" under "Take Action."[86] The initial free online session, titled Basics 1, is marketed as a self-improvement opportunity: "Live happier and health-

---

[82] Ibid., 00:04:44; emphasis added.
[83] Ibid., 00:12:36.
[84] Ibid., 00:14:20, 00:15:10, 00:16:11.
[85] Ibid., 00:16:12.
[86] Puddicombe, All It Takes.

ier by learning the fundamentals of meditation and mindfulness."[87] A brief video illustrating the basics features an animation depicting a woman in a classic yogic posture—sitting on a couch, eyes closed, hands on her lap, breathing deeply. The painting on the wall, evoking a tranquil mountain landscape and sunny weather, reinforces the idea of peace of mind and self-transcendence, reminiscent of Matthieu Riccard's talk.

Figure 4: Word cloud generated by MonkeyLearn after the guidelines of Basics Session 1, Headspace.

However, a word cloud analysis of the guidelines presented in the first session reveals a noteworthy aspect: the word "body" emerged as the most frequently used term, occurring sixteen times, and consequently, it holds the top position in terms of relevance in the generated cloud. Additionally, the session incorporates a body scan exercise. This disparity between the predominant focus on mind-power in the interpretations of mindfulness and the underlying significance of the body and its physical sensations in the practice guidelines is evident. Whenever attention is directed toward the body, it tends to serve either as a supporting argument for the promotion of self-control or as a spotlight on the body's perceived bad habits that mindfulness aims to remedy. These habits are often framed as outcomes of the evolutionary journey, positioning natural selection as a seemingly "negative" agent.[88]

---

87 Basics: Session 1, *Headspace*.
88 This rhetoric consequently strengthens a dichotomy between the bad instincts inscribed in the body (attributed to natural selection) and the good reason that not only redeems it but also facilitates enlightenment and spiritual elevation (through mindfulness). Advocates of human enhance-

Ranked among the most popular science talks and considered either the first or second most relevant talk on mindfulness, psychiatrist Judson Brewer's "How to Break a Bad Habit" sheds light on the connections between mindfulness and addiction. Brewer proposes mindfulness as a simple yet effective strategy to combat undesirable habits, including smoking, stress eating, and addictive behaviors like texting while driving. Rather than attempting to eliminate cravings, Brewer suggests paying close attention to them.

Similarly, neuroscientist Sandra Aamodt advocates for "mindful eating" over dieting or relying solely on willpower in a bid to control eating habits. Mindful eating involves "learning to understand your *body*'s signals so that you eat when you're hungry and stop when you're full."[89] Brewer illustrates the concept with a woman's revelation of "mindful smoking", describing it as something that "*smells like stinky cheese and tastes like chemicals, YUCK!*"[90] Furthermore, he elucidates how relying on cognition to control behavior, "the first part of our brain that goes offline when we get stressed out," is counterproductive.[91] In contrast, the woman transitioned from intellectually understanding that smoking was harmful to knowing it at a visceral level—"in her bones"—ultimately breaking the spell of smoking.[92]

Thus, both speakers emphasize the corporeal dimension of mindfulness, a point reiterated by Brewer in another statement: "And this is what mindfulness is all about: *Seeing* really clearly what we get when we get caught up in our behaviors, becoming disenchanted on a *visceral* level and from this disenchanted stance, naturally letting go."[93] However, he falls short of delving deeper into the physicality of mindfulness and concludes with a shift in focus toward staying curious. His assertion that "we [can] become *this inner scientist* where we're eagerly expecting the next data point"[94] reinforces a self-vigilant behavior that requires cognition, seemingly contradicting his earlier statement about cognition diminishing in stressful moments.

In summary, although Brewer initially challenges the concept of mindfulness as a means of rational control over bodily temptations, his subsequent emphasis on curiosity and the "inner scientist" implies a different perspective. Concurrently,

---

ment similarly rely on this dichotomy, exemplified in their promotion of concepts like evolution by design. For further exploration, see also John Harris' *Enhancing Evolution* (2007).
89 Aamodt, Why Dieting, 00:09:20; emphasis added.
90 Brewer, How to Break, 00:03:55; emphasis added.
91 Ibid., 00:04:57.
92 Ibid., 00:04:23.
93 Ibid., 00:05:38; emphasis added.
94 Ibid., 00:07:04; emphasis added.

these emphases might serve as rhetorical devices shaped by the TED format and its individualistic aesthetics. Although presented as an alternative to willpower, mindfulness is still framed as another form of self-discipline and positioned as the primary tool of the inner scientist. Self-monitoring emerges as the primary objective of mindfulness. However, unlike in psychotherapy, where the self engages in a dialogue with an analyst, mindfulness transforms into a solitary endeavor. Assuming the role of a spectator to one's own existence, the self transitions from being merely a patient to becoming the scientist who observes and interprets their own thoughts and emotions, thus assuming sole responsibility for their own being. This self adopts the role of the "citizen scientist," a figure reminiscent of the genius. Traditionally, the genius has been associated with exceptional male scientists, influencing the act of self-observation: the genius' creative prowess remains the implicit expectation underlying self-monitoring, thereby framing it as a predominantly male and visual practice.

In *Coming to Our Senses: Healing Ourselves and the World Through Mindfulness*, Jon Kabat Zinn draws analogies between Buddha and figures like Darwin or Einstein, thus emphasizing the qualities of scientific genius rather than a religious figure: "Their efforts at self-observation led to remarkable discoveries [...] aspects of the mind that can be examined by everybody anywhere."[95] Zinn's book delves into the ways in which "senses overlap and blend together"[96], acknowledging the dominance of vision in language and metaphor. However, he continues to underscore the visual aspects of meditation, presenting it as a practice capable of enhancing our seeing, offering "fresh" lenses,[97] or encouraging us to look and to see.

The persistent emphasis on vision also fosters a belief in the attainability of complete transparency. Entrepreneur and CEO of InteraXon, Ariel Garten, delivered a talk proposing a new approach to "Know[ing] Thyself with a Brain Scanner" (2012). She critiques the escapism often associated with mindfulness retreats and suggests an alternative method in order to achieve the same "heightened sense of self-awareness" through "thought-controlled computing."[98] Garten showcases a video featuring an undulating blue line reminiscent of the rhythmic movement of a heartbeat. She explains, "[t]hat blue line there is my brain's wave. It's the direct signal being recorded from my head, rendered in real time. The green and red bars show that same signal displayed by frequency, with lower frequencies here

---

95 Zinn, *Coming*, p. 25.
96 Ibid., p. 190.
97 In this context, Zinn paraphrases Marcel Proust's famous words: "The true journey of discovery consists in not seeking new landscapes but in having fresh eyes" (ibid., p. 196).
98 Garten, Know Thyself, 00:03:02, 00:03:31.

and higher frequencies up here. You're actually *looking inside my head* as I speak."⁹⁹ In doing so, she alludes to fantasies of telepathic information transmission, enticing the audience with the promise of accessing her innermost thoughts, akin to a vision of total transparency. Throughout her talk, Garten revisits this notion frequently, commenting: "By the way, feel free to check in on my head at any time."¹⁰⁰

Ariel Garten offers a vision of mindfulness that does not require a "secluded retreat,"¹⁰¹ but instead manifests itself as a new awareness facilitated by technology. She justifies this intrusion into privacy by highlighting the unreliability of feelings. "We're trying to create technology that uses the *insights* to make our work more efficient, our breaks more relaxing and our connections deeper and more fulfilling than ever."¹⁰² Garten proceeds to illustrate examples of "humanized technology,"¹⁰³ such as thought-controlled home appliances or the CN tower's interactive display at the Olympics: "Over 17 days at the Olympics, 7,000 visitors from all over the world actually got to individually control the light from the CN Tower, parliament and Niagara in real time with their minds from across the country, 3,000 km away. So controlling stuff with your mind is pretty cool."¹⁰⁴ Additionally, she highlights the Zen Bound game as another instance where technology aids in self-awareness: "you control the wooden form that's on the screen there with your mind. As you focus on the wooden form, it rotates. The more you focus, the faster the rotation."¹⁰⁵ Garten believes that such applications could assist children with ADD in improving their symptoms by rewarding "focused brain states."¹⁰⁶

> We can *peer inside our heads* and interact with what was once locked away from us, what once mystified and separated us. Brainwave technology can understand us, anticipate our emotions and find the best solutions for our needs. Imagine *this collected awareness* of the individual computed and reflected across an entire lifespan. Imagine *the insights* that you can gain from this kind of *second sight*. It would be like plugging into your own personal Google.¹⁰⁷

---

99 Ibid., 00:03:52; emphasis added.
100 Ibid., 00:05:39.
101 Ibid., 00:01:55.
102 Ibid., 00:05:22.
103 Ibid., 00:12:00.
104 Ibid., 00:06:40.
105 Ibid., 00:08:24.
106 Ibid., 00:10:05.
107 Ibid., 00:10:38; emphasis added.

Throughout her discourse, Garten consistently underscores the insights that technology can provide, and her conception of self-knowledge is predominantly shaped by the visual sense. However, it remains unclear how a moving line on a screen could yield insightful knowledge, and she overlooks the potential for such visual representations to obscure rather than illuminate. Garten neglects to address the crucial hermeneutic question: who is responsible for interpreting this data?

Despite commencing her talk by acknowledging how technology has "cluttered" our lives,[108] Garten ultimately proposes an even greater reliance on technology: individuals are urged to depend on devices to "rank on a scale of overall happiness which people in your life made you the happiest, or what activities brought you joy."[109] This suggests that people should prioritize their daily choices based solely on what brings them joy, disregarding the multifaceted spectrum of emotions. Garten concludes with a personal anecdote about observing her mother paint:

> As I sat easel-side, watching her transform canvas after canvas, I learned that you could create your own world. I learned that our own inner worlds—our ideas, emotions and imaginations—were, in fact, not bound by our brains and bodies. If you could think it, if you could discover it, you could bring it to life.[110]

Creativity and human imagination form the core of Garten's understanding of self-awareness, once again portraying mindfulness as a trait of the genius. She perpetuates the stereotypical view of mind control as a means to attain it. Thus, even though her talk revolves around games and computing, it is categorized under the mindfulness rubric.

This choice likely stems from TED's perception of mindfulness as a tool for training the mind to pay attention. Consequently, Mehdi Ordikhani-Seyedlar's talk, although lacking explicit mention of mindfulness, is listed as the first or second most relevant discussion on the topic.[111] Seyedlar, a machine learning engineer, addresses the human brain's attention system in his TED talk. Much like Garten, he focuses on "bringing together the brain and the computer."[112] He posits that "covert attention [is] an interesting model for computers" because "we can shift

---

[108] Ibid., 00:01:50.
[109] Ibid., 00:12:26.
[110] Ibid., 00:13:57.
[111] Ordikhani-Seyedlar's talk appears after Judson Brewer's talk, which is the first one. While reloading, this order might change—once it has even been listed as the first relevant talk. So, its position is maintained at the top. As of 28 February 2022, it has been featured as the first most relevant talk.
[112] Seyedlar, What Happens in Your Brain, 00:01:15.

our attention not only by our eyes but also by thinking."[113] Here, attention is predominantly viewed as a visual and cognitive achievement. The brain filters relevant information, a task challenging for individuals with ADHD. Seyedlar speculates on the potential for individuals to "play a specific computer game with his brain connected to the computer, and then *train his own brain* to inhibit these distractors."[114] His concluding remarks contemplate a future where thoughts can be accessed transparently with the aid of a computer, echoing Ariel Garten's vision:

> Imagine if we can find brainwave patterns when people think about images or even letters, like the letter A generates a different brainwave pattern than the letter B, and so on. Could a computer one day communicate for people who can't speak? What if a computer can help us understand the thoughts of a person in a coma? We are not there yet, but pay close attention. We will be there soon.[115]

Seyedlar does not consider the potential privacy implications of such advancements, as his proposition is grounded in a fantasy of telepathic communication —a vision also introduced by Chris Anderson as his ideal for TED.[116] This scenario is critiqued in Dave Eggers' novel *The Circle*, where the body remains the final barrier against complete transparency.[117] Thus, Garten and Seyedlar rely on the notion that bodies can be seen-through (and, implicitly, manipulated) in order to promote their vision of mindfulness. At the same time, mindfulness is depicted as a means of transcending the body and heralding a new future for humanity.

8.3 Mindfulness and the Survival of the Species

Robert Wright launched an online course entitled "Buddhism and Modern Psychology" on Coursera, drawing over half a million participants.[118] From the outset,

---

113 Ibid., 00:01:55.
114 Ibid., 00:04:45; emphasis added.
115 Ibid., 00:05:44.
116 See chapter two and Anderson's talk on "TED's Secret to Great Public Speaking."
117 At the end of the novel, Amy escapes the total transparency of society by entering a coma and even then, the proponents of *The Circle* want to gain access to her thoughts, though it remains impossible for the moment. The body remains the last defense against the dystopian transparency of American society. For a more in-depth analysis, check my article published with *COPAS:* "The Future of the Enhanced Self and Contemporary Science Fiction: TED Talks and Dave Eggers' *The Circle.*"
118 Nayak, Over Half a Million. Besides being a visiting lecturer at Princeton University and one of the top 100 global thinkers, Robert Wright has been a bestseller author of *The Evolution of God*, *The Moral Animal: Evolutionary Psychology and Everyday Life*, which was nominated as one of the ten

Wright distinguishes between religious Buddhism and its secular or Western counterpart. He favors the term "naturalistic" Buddhism,[119] as it aligns well with scientific inquiry. Despite this initial departure from traditional religious elements and beliefs in supernatural deities or reincarnation, Wright argues that Western Buddhism does not have to be secular. Embracing William James' definition of religion as a "belief in an unseen order" necessitating human adjustment, he endeavors to identify a "religion that is compatible with modern science," like Buddhism.[120]

The "unseen order" does not have to entail a cosmic plan; within Buddhism, it seems to refer to the "hidden truths about our reality."[121] In other words, mindfulness is presented as a response to Plato's allegory of the cave—the philosopher perceives the shadows as distortions of reality, so mindfulness emerges as the best tool to combat the mind and its deceptive tendencies. Wright draws upon arguments from evolutionary psychology to illustrate the inherent distortions in the human brain that give rise to suffering.[122] As such, mindfulness can presumably offer a pathway to liberation—it can alleviate suffering and facilitate enlightenment.[123] Nirvana, rather than being solely a spiritual state, is depicted as an awakening to "reality." Thus, the mindfulness narrative effectively preserves and safeguards the concept of reality in a world governed by epistemological skepticism.

Mental healing has long held allure in America, a trend exemplified by the widespread reception of Freud's ideas as well.[124] However, the focus of healing shifts within the mindfulness narrative: the endeavor to heal past traumas is supplanted by an emphasis on training or disciplining the mind in the present moment. Mindfulness depersonalizes and strips away the self's biographical context, replacing past traumas with innate predispositions or habits of the mind instilled by natural selection. Although the past still looms as a threat to the present self, it is viewed through a scientific lens rather than personal history. Additionally, mindfulness redirects attention away from the family, traditionally seen as the cradle of identity formation, and toward science. It substitutes the "salvation narrative" in-

---

best books of 1994, as well as *Nonzero*, which was recommended to White House staff members by Bill Clinton.
119 Wright, *Why Buddhism Is True*, p. 262.
120 Ibid.
121 Wright, Buddhism.
122 Ibid.
123 In *The Moral Animal*, Wright wrote: "we're all puppets, and our best hope for even partial liberation is to try to decipher the logic of the puppeteer [...] noting here that the puppeteer seems to have exactly zero regard for the happiness of the puppets" (p. 27).
124 See Eva Illouz, *Saving the Modern Soul*.

herent in psychoanalysis, as described by Illouz,[125] with salvation reimagined as a scientific pursuit—namely, the survival of the species.

The "focus on everyday life" initiated by Freud[126] persists within the mindfulness narrative, albeit with a distinct purpose. While Freudian focus revolved around the construction of the self through everyday experiences, mindfulness directs attention toward the deconstruction of the self. Whereas the hermeneutic approach sought to integrate and interpret all life experiences into the self's narrative, mindfulness advocates detachment and aligns with emerging scientific perspectives that challenge the notion of a fixed self. Mindfulness advocates shedding individual experiences and practicing dis-identification. Jon Kabat Zinn introduces the concept of "non-doing" as a method of self-transformation.[127] By disentangling the self from its thoughts, feelings, and impulses, mindfulness promises self-mastery through detachment rather than self-analysis. In other words, feelings are no longer probed for hidden, unconscious meanings; instead, they are viewed as distinct entities separated from the self.

Robert Wright illustrates how mindfulness goes as far as to refute the existence of a self, elucidating the concept of "not-self" in light of recent findings in evolutionary psychology, which introduce a modular view of the self.[128] According to this perspective, the self is no longer in crisis—it simply does not exist. These notions echo themes within postmodernism, which frequently underscore the death of the subject.[129] However, it is noteworthy that the very elements with the potential to challenge essentialisms are often repurposed in order to construct another form of it. In the realm of self-help, the concept of the "not-self" is leveraged to propagate the idea of transcendence—a notion of boundless potential through the power of the mind. Paradoxically, this narrative fosters the image of

---

[125] Illouz, *Saving*, p. 40.
[126] Ibid., p. 43.
[127] In the chapter on "Doing Non-Doing" from *Wherever You Go There You Are*, Zinn describes non-doing as an "effortless activity" that "happens at moments in dance and in sports at the highest levels of performance" (44), which recalls the concept of "peak performance" introduced by Maslow and the "flow state" described by Mihaly Csikszentmihalyi. Zinn even adds: "Some people speak of this as flow, one moment flowing seamlessly, effortlessly into the next, cradled in the streambed of mindfulness" (46). Since this was published in 1994, it came only four years after Mihaly Csikszentmihaly published his self-help book entitled *Flow: The Psychology of Optimal Experience*.
[128] Wright, Buddhism. Evolutionary psychology conceptualizes cognitive processes as adaptations within the human brain. The "modular view" of the mind, as proposed by Kenrick et al., challenges the notion of a unified self, suggesting instead the existence of modular "subselves" (Renovating the Pyramid of Needs, p. 22–23).
[129] They also recall Julian Baggini's TED talk on "Who Are You?"—see also chapter two.

an exceptional, enlightened self, one that transcends the confines of human existence. The mindfulness narrative thus shifts the focus away from individual biographical details toward the broader concept of shared humanity.

Anthropologist Kathryn Bouskill's talk does not explicitly mention mindfulness, but she delves into the importance of "slow time" within our "fast-paced world" (2018). She highlights the discrepancy between the pace of modern culture and our "prehistoric brains," leading to a growing misalignment between our biology and lifestyles.[130]

> When we have to make fast decisions, *autopilot* brain kicks in, and we rely on our learned behaviors, our reflexes, our cognitive biases, to help us perceive and respond quickly. Sometimes that saves our lives, right? *Fight or flight.* But sometimes, it leads us astray in the long run. [...]
>
> They're failures that happen when we made decisions too quickly on autopilot. We didn't do the *creative or critical thinking* required to connect the dots or weed out false information or make sense of complexity. That kind of thinking can't be done fast. That's slow thinking.[131]

Implicitly, Bouskill connects slow thinking with mindfulness, describing it as the capacity for "critical and sustained" thought essential for allowing our "Stone Age brains" to calm impulses and let thoughts flow freely.[132] Like Tristan Harris, who referenced the "lizard brain,"[133] Bouskill anchors her discussion in the survival narrative. Slow thinking, she argues, entails taking the time "to reflect, to percolate at your own pace; time to listen, to empathize, to rest your mind, to linger at the dinner table."[134] It serves as a counterbalance to the automatic responses of the "autopilot brain,"[135] advocating for the incorporation of mindfulness practices into our decision-making processes.

Mindfulness transcends being a tactic to combat survival instincts; it emerges as the next evolutionary leap for humanity. In other words, not only is mindfulness popularized as another form of mind-power, but is positioned at the core of survival itself. Mindfulness is portrayed not merely as a diversion or a temporary respite from stress but as an urgent and vital choice—a matter of life or death. If the primal instinct of fight or flight once ensured human survival, now it is mindfulness

---

[130] Bouskill, Unforeseen Consequences, 00:02:39, 00:03:04.
[131] Ibid., 00:05:12, 00:05:40.
[132] Ibid., 00:06:40.
[133] Harris, How a Handful, 00:14:58.
[134] Bouskill, Unforeseen Consequences, 00:08:46.
[135] Ibid., 00:05:14.

that holds the power to sustain life. In Garten's talk, the blue line served as a lifeline symbol as well, albeit with the motif of the heart replaced by the brain.

The significance of mindfulness for survival is further underscored in Guillaume Néry's talk. Despite not explicitly mentioning mindfulness, the French freediving champion's presentation on "The Exhilarating Peace of Freediving" (2015) is consistently ranked among the top five most relevant talks on the topic, usually occupying third position. Even though he shares his deep diving experience without directly invoking mindfulness, his description of a "journey between two breaths" seems to capture its essence and establishes it as fundamental for survival.[136] Néry's speech brims with wonder as he describes not only his physiological reactions during diving, but also his "inner journey."[137] He vividly portrays the sensation of "flying underwater" during the free-fall phase, evoking an extraordinary feeling of freedom.[138] Moreover, he challenges the instinct to fight when confronted with obstacles. Underwater, such a reaction could prove dangerous, necessitating *a mental effort* to accept the power of nature. Néry recounts his experience of surrendering to the water's pressure: "And so I let the water crush me. I accept the pressure and go with it. At this point, my body receives this information, and my lungs start relaxing. I relinquish all control, and relax completely."[139]

The sensation of humility, inspired by the awe of nature's grandeur, is further evoked by Néry who feels "like a tiny dot, a little drop of water, floating in the middle of the ocean."[140] This feeling is akin to the perspective of observing planet Earth from a distance, where "our home [becomes] that small dot over there, floating in the middle of nothing."[141] Similarly, Néry expresses feeling like "a small dot, a speck of dust, stardust, floating in the middle of the cosmos, in the middle of nothing, in the immensity of space. It's a fascinating sensation, because when I look up, down, left, right, in front, behind, I see the same thing: the *infinite deep blue*."[142] This profound sensation culminates in an awareness of non-self rather than self-awareness. Néry repeats, "I'm nothing, I'm a little speck of nothingness lost in all of time and space,"[143] suggesting a dissolution of the boundaries of his ego.

---

136 Néry, Exhilarating Peace, 00:02:33.
137 Ibid., 00:02:52.
138 Ibid., 00:05:44.
139 Ibid., 00:07:34.
140 Ibid., 00:10:14.
141 Ibid., 00:10:37.
142 Ibid., 00:10:46.
143 Ibid., 00:11:28.

In his narrative, Néry enters a new phase characterized by nitrogen narcosis, signifying a shift or alteration in consciousness. This state induces a merging of the conscious and unconscious mind, where a whirlwind of thoughts swirls through one's head. Attempting to control these thoughts proves futile, and surrender becomes imperative: "You can't control them, and you shouldn't try to—you have to let it happen. The more you try to control it, the harder it is to manage."[144] This is the second time he mentions the importance of relinquishing control, which also resonates with mindfulness practices.

Furthermore, Néry highlights the importance of anchoring oneself in the present moment: "Never look up to the surface—not with your eyes, or your mind. You should never picture yourself up there. You have to stay in the present."[145] His ascent to the surface, symbolizing a literal journey of enlightenment, is described in vividly sensorial terms: "I go from complete darkness to the light of day, from the near-silence of the depths to the commotion up top. In terms of touch, I go from the soft, velvety feeling of the water, to air rubbing across my face. In terms of smell, there is air rushing into my lungs."[146] This experience echoes Jon Kabat-Zinn's idea of "coming to our senses" and Sister True Dedication's notion of "opening-up" the senses.[147]

> Today, in the 21st century, we're under so much pressure. Our minds are overworked, we think at a million miles an hour, we're always stressed. Being able to free dive lets you, just for a moment, *relax your mind.* Holding your breath underwater means giving yourself the chance to experience weightlessness. It means being underwater, *floating,* with your body completely relaxed, letting go of all your tensions. This is our plight in the 21st century: our backs hurt, our necks hurt, everything hurts, because we're stressed and tense all the time. But when you're in the water, you let yourself float, as if you were in space. *You let yourself go completely.*[148]

In conclusion, Néry's account of deep diving correlates with the principles of mindfulness, including aspects such as the inner journey, imagery of floating or flying, surrendering control, the concept of non-self, altered consciousness, a focus on the present moment, and heightened sensory awareness—all of which have been associated with a mindful state. These elements are then leveraged to suggest the importance of mind-control. Néry's talk both challenges and contributes to this view. While he acknowledges the concept of non-self, his assertion that the experience is

---

144 Ibid., 00:12:17.
145 Ibid., 00:13:06.
146 Ibid., 00:14:51.
147 Sister True Dedication's talk is tackled below and ends this subchapter.
148 Ibid., 00:16:52; emphasis added.

about "connecting with yourself"[149] may seem contradictory. Yet, he further elucidates that this connection involves tapping into the "body's memory" and "marine origins,"[150] thus emphasizing the neglected role of the body in mindfulness discussions. Finally, Néry's journey underscores the survival aspect of mindfulness. Rather than triggering the instinctual fight or flight response, mindfulness facilitates clarity of mind, offering a form of second sight that can be life-saving in critical situations. In essence, his narrative reinforces the idea that mindfulness is not just a practice for stress relief but a vital tool for survival in the face of modern challenges.

In her talk on resilience, Zen Buddhist nun Sister True Dedication emphasizes the absence of "insight" in today's technologically dominated world and espouses being "fully present, grounded and alert, fearless and free."[151] She advocates mindful walking as a visionary practice:

> Mindful walking can help. We really *feel the contact between our feet and the ground.* And we enjoy the harmony between our breathing and our steps. With each step, *we arrive into our body*, into *the present moment.* [...] And we open up *our senses* to the sky, to the trees, to the people around us, or simply to the hum of life in the city. And we have a chance to *wake up* to what is going on, in us and around us.[152]

Her concept of "insight" challenges the Western approach governed by visual perception and imagination. Instead of promoting the stereotypical "floating" imagery associated with mindfulness, Sister True Dedication emphasizes the "contact between our feet and the ground," redirecting attention to the Earth rather than the sky.[153] Furthermore, the idea of arriving into the body suggests a shift away from prioritizing the power of the brain or mind, a notion reinforced by the emphasis on "opening-up" the senses. Consequently, the form of awakening she describes underscores the significance of sensory perception and fosters a different kind of awareness compared with the rational models epitomized by Plato's philosophical truth, Robert Wright's "unseen order," or Daniel Levitin's "thinking ahead."

---

149 Ibid., 00:18:34.
150 Ibid., 00:18:38.
151 Sister True Dedication, Three Questions, 00:02:44.
152 Ibid., 00:03:04; emphasis added.
153 Ibid., 00:03:07. She also resonates with Krista Tippett and her notion of inhabiting the body. Interestingly, it seems predominantly women tend to stress the nuanced significance of the body, challenging the stereotypical narrative of mind-control. This trend mirrors the intersection of new materialism and feminism. Hence, this section on mindfulness concludes with the speculative writing of a woman.

> In this very moment, we are all made of Earth, sun and stars. Mountains and rivers, savannahs and rainforests. It is impossible for us to be without all these elements. And realizing this is to *see with the insight of interbeing*. This isn't just intellectual knowledge. But the *living insight* that you and I, we are much more than we think. And this is an immense source of love and strength as we take action in the here and now. [...]
>
> *Training our body and mind to be fully present in the here and now is essential to our survival and to the future we are creating.* It is in the present and only in the present that we can truly nourish our happiness and handle and take care of our pain and our suffering.[154]

Sister True Dedication's discourse on "the insight of interbeing" further accentuates the theme of vitality, distinguishing it from mere intellectual knowledge. In the end, her talk works with the same premises: mindfulness is about being present in the moment,[155] which is "essential to our survival" and to "our happiness." Yet, she also distances herself from the power of the mind narratives that prevail in TED talks. Interestingly, her talk is notably ranked as the least relevant among discussions of mindfulness, indicating divergence from those mainstream narratives. Her notion of an "insight of interbeing" serves as a lens through which to examine Margaret Atwood's *MaddAddam* trilogy, providing a vital counterpoint to the popular TED perspectives.

---

154 Ibid., 00:06:26, 00:08:21; emphasis added.

155 This focus on the present moment is sometimes more nuanced than a mere attention to the present. For instance, American psychologist Philip Zimbardo discusses the importance of time perception in his talk listed under "Talks to Help You Practice Patience." He advocates for a specific formula conducive to individual well-being: "And it resonated for me. I grew up as a poor kid in the South Bronx ghetto, a Sicilian family—everyone lived in the past and present. I'm here as a *future-oriented* person who went over the top, who did all these sacrifices because teachers intervened, and made me future oriented. Told me don't eat that marshmallow, because if you wait you're going to get two of them, until I learned to balance out. I've added *present-hedonism*, I've added a focus on the *past-positive*, so, at 76 years old, I am more energetic than ever, more productive, and I'm happier than I have ever been" (The Psychology of Time, 00:05:06; emphasis added). His understanding of the right mixture of tenses recalls Edmund Husserl's phenomenology of temporality, which includes retention of the past and protention of the future. The science of happiness further underscores the value of reminiscence, savoring in the present, and anticipation. Furthermore, self-help rhetoric consistently returns to the significance of gratitude (*past-positive*), future awareness, and the importance of delayed gratification.

9 Margaret Atwood's *MaddAddam* Trilogy and the "Insight of Interbeing"

Margaret Atwood's *MaddAddam* trilogy delves into various themes central to the discourse on mindfulness. It not only critiques the humanist assumptions inherent in this discourse but also presents an alternative perspective to the Western-centric view of mindfulness. Mindfulness extends beyond the survival of the human species, which can sometimes be used to justify exploitation of the nonhuman; it encompasses the survival of all species. The individual self is no longer seeking detachment from its surroundings in a bid to find inner peace and solitude, but it is intricately connected with its environment, engaging in a dynamic interaction between the human and nonhuman realms. As such, the self emerges not merely as an "inner scientist" observing the body, but as a character deeply immersed in a rich sensory world, evoking a profound sense of aliveness.

The "insight of interbeing" proposed by Atwood introduces the human within nonhuman assemblages, with the body serving as a primary mediator. Despite the widespread reception of her novels,[1] scholarly discussions have not focused on the theme of mindfulness. This may be attributed to the fact that her novels do not overtly address the subject. However, this theme does remain a latent and crucial dimension of her writing, underpinning central themes such as the importance of the present moment (now-here), altered consciousness, and mystical insight—all vital for future survival.

Atwood reworks the notion of vision in her novels, moving away from associating insightful knowledge with mind-power and redirecting attention to the body and its multiple senses—an aspect largely overlooked in TED talks and other mainstream media. This becomes possible through the medium of literary fiction, which allows the author to emphasize the sensory experience. Consequently, her novels also assert a broader claim about the value of fiction in a posthuman world. What role does literature play in a world where humanity is no longer perceived as an advanced or superior species? How does literature function when it no longer defends the humanist beliefs in the primacy of imagination, as seen in mindfulness narratives? Atwood sees literature's relevance precisely in its critical posthumanist potential, offering a fictional space for human-nonhuman interaction. Books,

---

[1] Many responses have focused on the first novel and its characters Jimmy, Oryx, and Crake. As such, "most of the literary criticism surrounding the trilogy has focused only on the first two novels; this leaves us with an incomplete understanding of how by the end of *MaddAddam*, the trilogy is far more invested in a posthumanist perspective than is apparent in *Oryx and Crake* and *The Year of the Flood*" (Jennings, Anthropocene, p. 19).

∂ Open Access. © 2024 the author(s), published by De Gruyter. This work is licensed under the Creative Commons Attribution 4.0 International License. https://doi.org/10.1515/9783111389929-013

words, texts, characters, narrators, authors, and readers are all woven into the same web of life, reflecting the interdependence and interconnectedness of all beings.

9.1 Self-Help Culture: "What People Want Is Perfection"

The *MaddAddam* trilogy unfolds in a near-future, apocalyptic, dystopian world where a mad scientist named Crake triggers the extinction of humanity by selling a deadly pill promising eternal bliss. A handful of survivors emerge, including Snowman (also known as Jimmy), once Crake's closest friend, whose perspective drives the narrative of the first novel—*Oryx and Crake*. Another woman survivor is Toby, a former member of the Gardeners, an environmentally conscious community introduced in the second novel—*The Year of the Flood*.[2] Alongside other ecotopian Adams and Eves (which is how the Gardeners call themselves), there are also the violent criminals and former convicts known as the Painballers. Additionally, the novel features the Crakers, a genetically modified species engineered by Crake, intended to represent a perfected version of humanity.

Atwood's fiction draws on many literary genres: the castaway narrative, detective and action-thriller novel, romance story, Gothic tale, and Bildungsroman or coming-of-age novel.[3] While many critical readings tend to focus on its dystopian elements, there is a preference among critics to classify it as "speculative fiction,"[4] a term also favored by Atwood herself as she seeks to distinguish her writing from traditional science fiction.[5] Regardless of the label, critics tend to emphasize the

---

2 It may be tempting to argue that the Gardeners reinforce the mindfulness narrative in Atwood's trilogy, especially since they "interweave an Evangelical environmentalism with a New Age ecoconsciousness and contemporary ecological and evolutionary knowledge" (Keck, Paradise Retold, p. 32). Additionally, they "advocate human earth care alongside survival training and political resistance against a corporate take-over" (ibid., p. 33). However, as this chapter aims to show, Atwood's argument is more nuanced.
3 Cf. Bosco, Apocalyptic Imagination, p. 141, 158; See also Wisker, Imagining beyond Extinctathon.
4 See Arias, Life after Man; Mohr, Where Species Meet; Storey/Storey, History and Allegory, Vials, Margaret Atwood's Dystopic Fiction.
5 The famous distinction Atwood makes between science fiction and speculative fiction primarily concerns the focus on human society (see Wrobel, Negotiating Dataveillance). "Speculative fiction, in other words, relies on imagination and projection, but unlike science fiction proper, its plots and settings hue much more closely to empirically observable, social and technological trends. It is arguably closer to the project of literary realism" (Vials, Margaret Atwood's Dystopic Fiction, p. 239). Monja Mohr has also interpreted the genre along similar lines: "Many of these often post-apocalyptic novels connect the discontent with current *social (in)justice* with ecocriticism, animal/human or human/posthuman relations and explore new relationalities, 'messmates', entangle-

cautionary aspect of her fiction. For instance, Françoise Storey and Jeff Storey claim that the use of "the speculative mode in both novels serves the same purpose as real History should do in an ideal world: *warning* the reader of potential dangers."[6] This vigilant aspect is continuously underscored in critical analyses, explaining the focus on the dystopian qualities of the novels and their potential to serve as warnings on multiple levels.[7]

Atwood's narrative serves as a dystopia that sends "danger signals,"[8] a "skeptical anti-utopia,"[9] and a "millennial dystopia,"[10] among other interpretations. A common thread across these readings is Atwood's critique of utopian ideals—Crake's project does not just warn us of the dangers of science but of utopian approaches to science.[11] Even if her novels alert us to the dangers of ecological damage, Atwood also questions "utopian environmentalism."[12] Moreover, while her trilogy carries a strong critical posthumanist message, questioning what it means to be human, Atwood remains skeptical of utopian visions of the posthuman. As such, her writing blurs the lines between dystopia and utopia, giving rise to the term "ustopia,"[13] and remains vigilant toward idealized depictions of existence—be it bliss, paradise, or the Garden of Eden.

---

ments, and take first steps toward a multispecies justice" (When Species Meet, p. 50; emphasis added).
6 Storey/Storey, History and Allegory; emphasis added.
7 Throughout her essay, Rosario Arias emphasizes the vigilant aspect of Atwood's writing. Atwood, according to Aris, is *"warning* us of the fatal consequences of newly acquired scientific knowledge," her novels *"warn* us of the damage we are causing to nature," and they are also *"warning* us of the danger of creating a posthuman world" (Life after Man, p. 379, 383, 394; emphasis added). *The Year of the Flood* might even be interpreted as a "meta-narrative, a cautionary tale about our cautionary tales" (Jennings, Anthropocene, p. 11).
8 Bone, Environmental Dystopias, p. 628.
9 Stein, Problematic Paradise, p. 153.
10 Sutherland/Swan, Margaret Atwood, p. 223. According to them, millennial dystopia is a contradictory dystopia: "it is the increasing intertwining of the Orwellian Big Brother with the economics of the Brave New World that marks *Oryx and Crake* as a millennial dystopia" (ibid.).
11 Stein, Problematic Paradise, p. 153.
12 Dunlap, Eco-Dystopia, p. 3.
13 She coined the word "ustopia" to illustrate "the dialectic relationship between utopia ('the imagined perfect society') and dystopia ('Great Bad Places' characterized by 'suffering, tyranny and oppression of all kinds') because 'each contains a latent version of the other' following a 'yin and yang pattern': 'within each utopia, a concealed dystopia; within each dystopia, a hidden utopia'" (Wrobel, Negotiating Dataveillance, par. 3). Therefore, ustopias "emphasize the best and worst elements of humans" (Narkunas, Between Words, p. 5).

Atwood's novels critique self-help culture[14] by highlighting how its humanist values contribute to the downfall of humanity. She does not solely blame science but rather society and its norms and cultural values; so, the novel is "not anti-science, for science, in her view, is a neutral tool."[15] In other words, "it is not technics or technology or biotechnology that is dangerous; it is the uses human beings put these things to. The end of the human is a human problem, not a technical one."[16] In her narrative, self-help culture fosters a society governed by indifference and carelessness. Atwood depicts a world where "conspicuous consumers" pursue pleasure and comfort as "remedies for feelings of inadequacy or existential alienation."[17] However, this pursuit of comfort ultimately dulls the conscience and leads to a lack of vigilance.[18]

Chris Vials argues that the novels in *MaddAddam* trilogy challenge neoliberalism as a political philosophy, yet this aspect has not been thoroughly explored. He posited that the novels depict a consumer capitalism that undermines liberal freedoms "through a social order which authorises pleasure at every turn, and yet, like any fascist regime, inevitably relies on violence precisely because it cannot deliver the well-being it promises."[19] Self-help culture plays a significant role in authorizing pleasure while perpetuating "willful blindness" and "political paralysis."[20]

---

[14] J. Bouson has also picked up on the self-help rhetoric that governs Snowman's thoughts: he "often resorts to the borrowed phrases and clichéd speech that clutter his mind—especially self-help discourse—when thinking of his plight. "Get a life," Snowman tells himself (p. 12); 'Routines are good,' he says to himself at another point, only to think that his 'entire head is becoming one big stash of obsolete fridge magnets' (p. 148); 'Each one of us must tread the path laid out before him, or her,' says a man's voice in his head in a style Snowman identifies as 'bogus guru' [...] he hears various women's voices offering encouragement: 'Oh honey, . . . Cheer up! Look on the bright side! You've got to think positive!' (p. 169); 'Oh honey, don't beat yourself up!' (p. 42); 'Oh sweetie. . . . You're doing really well' (p. 238); 'Oh Jimmy, this is so positive. It makes me happy when you grasp this. Paradice is lost, but you have a Paradice within you, happier far' (p. 308)" ("It's Game Over," p. 152).

[15] Stein, Problematic Paradice, p. 146.

[16] Cooke, Technics, par. 7.

[17] Bosco, Apocalyptic Imagination, p. 161.

[18] Ibid., p. 162. The notion of millennial dystopia points precisely to this tension between "totalitarian power abuses" and "the free and open market," as "corporate America happily manipulates the world marketplace to sell cures to diseases they themselves have created, and the workers (many of whom appear to be complicit in the corporation's darker activities) *blissfully enjoy the pleasures of life* within the heavily patrolled walls of their Compounds" (Sutherland/Swan, Margaret Atwood, p. 223; emphasis added).

[19] Vials, Margaret Atwood's Dystopic Fiction, p. 238.

[20] Harland, Ecological Grief, p. 593. He further explains: "A slightly different version of numbing oneself to the truth is to assume a false happiness, an attitude promoted by the HelthWyzer West corporation which sees itself as 'one big happy family': 'All staff were expected to be unremittingly

Thus, individuals within the social hierarchy, such as those in the Compound, may sense their lack of autonomy but "consent to their own subjugation" due to their "privileged position."[21] For instance, Jimmy's father relinquishes his rights gradually in exchange for "access to material wealth and consumer pleasures."[22] The influence of this ideology extends beyond individuals and their pleasures, shaping social structures and impacting lives and biographies in numerous ways.

The pervasive influence of self-help culture extends into every corner of society, industry, and even scientific practice within Atwood's dystopian world. Jimmy's academic background includes a dissertation on 20th century self-help books, which ironically leads him to a job in the advertising industry. Here, he must cater to society's desire for perfection and self-improvement. His interviewers emphasize the need for presenting steps to perfection in a "simple," encouraging, and "positive" manner,[23] reflecting the commodification of feelings in this society. In this consumer culture, where the arts and humanities are deprived of their importance, Jimmy must offer "visions" of "hope and fear," "desire and revulsion."[24] This creates the societal conditions that enable the pandemic, as individuals eagerly purchase pills promising bliss without second thoughts.[25] The AnooYoo compound epitomizes this phenomenon by offering a plethora of self-help and self-improvement products, promising a "new you" through "superficial treatments" such as herbal elixirs and dermal mood lifts rather than radical gene therapy.[26] Ultimately, the spa capitalizes on "selling hope," perpetuating the cycle of consumerism and self-improvement.[27]

Crake's pursuit of perfection extends to his creation of the Crakers. Various readings have scrutinized different facets of Crake: as a capitalist scientist and a

---

cheerful, to meet their assigned goals diligently, and—as in real families—not to ask too much about what was really going on' (232). Chris Hedges has analyzed the pernicious positive psychology cult of contemporary corporations: 'Here, in the land of happy thoughts, there are no gross injustices, no abuses of authority, no economic and political systems to challenge, and no reason to complain' (139). Not to put too fine a point on the matter, he claims, 'Positive psychology is to the corporate state what eugenics was to the Nazis' (117)" (ibid.).

21 Vials, Margaret Atwood's Dystopic Fiction, p. 247.
22 Ibid., p. 248.
23 Atwood, *Oryx and Crake*, p. 246.
24 Ibid., p. 248.
25 Thus, Atwood envisions the end of literature (and the end of the world) in a similar vein to Shteyngart, who has also emphasized the ways in which writing has been reduced to marketing and selling. Richard Powers also addresses the commodification of feelings that self-help culture relies on in his novel *Generosity* (see chapter twelve).
26 Atwood, *Year of the Flood*, p. 153. See also Cooke, Technics, par. 27.
27 Atwood, *Year of the Flood*, p. 155.

"dreamer, a creator, a utopian."[28] He is depicted as both "misanthropic and altruistic,"[29] with a seemingly "rationalistic" and "affectless" demeanor,[30] yet also infused with a "utopian spirit."[31] While his actions are seemingly motivated by his desire "to make Oryx happy" by eliminating chaos and hurtful people,[32] others perceive him as "power-crazed."[33] What remains evident is his ambition to "impose his own version of *the greater good* on the world: the 'Paradice Project'."[34] This form of "dangerous altruism"[35] resurfaces in the other novels by Gary Shteyngart and Richard Powers, illustrating how acts of kindness and generosity may conceal selfishness and egoism.[36] This characterization applies to Crake, whose pursuit of the greater good is tainted by pride, overconfidence, and a belief in the superiority of his vision.[37] He presumes to possess the truth, insisting that his vision is the right one and expecting everyone else to embrace it. As such, "he is not to be read as an ecotopian but as a satire of neoliberal environmentalism."[38]

The creation of the Crakers can be interpreted as an "act of artistic creativity."[39] Koziol delves into Crake's artistic ambitions, suggesting that they are governed by the belief that "art could contribute to the creation of a better world,"[40] and his art takes the form of living beings.[41] Despite his artistic inclina-

---

[28] Dunlap, Eco-Dystopia, p. 4.
[29] Bouson, "Joke-Filled," p. 350.
[30] Bouson, "It's Game Over," p. 146.
[31] Marks, Pleeblands, p. 223.
[32] Atwood, *Oryx and Crake*, p. 12.
[33] Bone, Environmental Dystopias, p. 629.
[34] Sutherland/Swan, Margaret Atwood, p. 233; emphasis added. Interestingly enough, the "Greater Good" is also the name of University of California Berkeley's magazine and podcast on the science of happiness, a topic that will be explored further in chapter eleven.
[35] Powers, *Generosity*, p. 22.
[36] Harland also writes: "The altruistic need to protect often cannot be distinguished from being infantry. The justice of civilization cannot be separated from the barbarism inherent in its execution. The only hope for humankind, Atwood suggests, is to recognize the complexity of human nature for what it is, and to act on it" (Ecological Grief, p. 591).
[37] Koziol even points to the eugenic aspect of Crake's agenda: "the means employed by Nazi eugenicists could be put alongside Crake's killer plague" (Crake's Aesthetic, p. 498).
[38] Desbiens, Environmental Discourses, p. 146.
[39] Koziol, Crake's Aesthetic, p. 493.
[40] Ibid., p. 496.
[41] Foucault's critique of the separation between art and other aspects of life is evident in his statement: "But couldn't everyone's life become a work of art? Why should the lamp or the house be an art object, but not our life?" (Genealogy, p. 350). Koziol elaborates on this, noting that while Foucault discusses the care of the self, he also refers to "the art of oneself," and how his concept of the "aesthetics of the self" stems from the idea of the "government of the self," which itself emerged from his research on governmentality and bio-power. In art history, there have been movements

tions, Crake derides the notion of art as merely a means to fulfill personal desires, dismissing it as an "empty drainpipe," an "amplifier" or a "stab at getting laid."[42] Atwood's novels also contemplate the role of literature and the humanities in a society marked by "dysphoria"—a "crisis of faith in literary studies."[43] Rather than embracing a utopian perspective on art or subscribing to postmodern aesthetics,[44] Atwood endeavors to carve out a space for literature beyond human subjectivity.

Atwood questions the reader's expectation of well-rounded characters, as noted by Michael Spiegel, who points out that critics of the novel often share the same criticism: "the novel's eponymous characters Oryx and Crake both lack psychological depth and plausibility."[45] Another critic describes Oryx and Crake as "eerie characters, since they resemble automata."[46] Additionally, they appear to be "devoid of personality, as if their symbolic value superseded their importance as characters."[47] However, Spiegel offers a more nuanced interpretation of this narrative choice, drawing on Jameson's concept of "the waning of affect" to explain how both characters become commodities: "Like Oryx, Crake is a commodity, but a commodified mind rather than body. His value lies in the potential of his mind to be translated into money value. [...] That Crake can both collude with the system and conspire against it demonstrates [...] the necessity of *affective detachment*."[48]

---

advocating for the alignment of art with power to create new people, and these artists "could be seen as Crake's predecessors" (Crake's Aesthetic, p. 496).
42 Atwood, Oryx and Crake, p. 168.
43 Brydon, Atwood's Global Ethic, p. 449.
44 As Debrah Raschke argues, the trilogy "dramatizes the postmodern condition gone amuck. The once subversive alternative narratives have given way to an implosion of meaning and inefficacy of agency that has produced a kind of cultural paralysis. Co-opted and corporatized, postmodernism's multiplicity of narrative has become a means to distract and beguile the public" (Postmodernism, p. 23). Another example from the novel concerns the wet T-shirt contests at Martha Graham Academy, which show a "conflation of high culture and popular culture and pastiche [which] renders this cultural fragmentation post-modern" while at the same time "in their irony, [they succeed] in divesting theatre, aesthetics, and literary masterpieces of their cultural relevance as they become integrated into the global market economy" (Spiegel, Character, p. 124). As such, even if her own writing has been read using postmodern lenses—for instance, Michaela Keck argued that Atwood "employs a self-reflexivity regarding myths that is characteristic of postmodern pastiche" (Paradise Retold, p. 23)—Atwood remains critical toward these literary developments.
45 Spiegel, Character, p. 119. Spiegel reads this as a "subversive narrative strategy" meant to "subvert the realist novel and challenge its claim to fully represent an increasingly post-national world" (ibid., p. 120, 121).
46 Northover, Strangers, p. 125.
47 Storey/Storey, History and Allegory.
48 Spiegel, Character, p. 128; emphasis added.

In the end, Spiegel elucidates how this narrative strategy might impact the reading experience:

> Snowman and the novel's detractors share the same expectations of psychological plausibility because they share a common preconception of human subjectivity [...] But if the narrative fails to make Crake and Oryx comprehensible or plausible, it does succeed in revealing Snowman's emotional depth and psychological complexity, as well as that of the reader who identifies with him. Perhaps this explains why the modern novel persists despite its inability to represent a changing reality: like violence, it offers the illusion of fixed and charged identities. To reject it is to acknowledge our own dwindling depth and complexity, our own flatness. In other words, perceiving Oryx and Crake as "cardboardy creation[s]" beats the alternative: recognizing that we are becoming "cardboardy creation[s]" ourselves, excised of our third dimension by a late capitalist world trending towards the post-national.[49]

However, Atwood's novels present an even more nuanced argument, inviting readers to contemplate intersubjectivity rather than human subjectivity; to shift the focus from human "fixed and charged identities" to a new realm of human-nonhuman interaction. Therefore, the alternative is not to become "cardboardy creation[s]," but to imagine alternative modes of existence that are less anthropocentric. The lack of psychological depth in *Oryx and Crake* may signify not only their dehumanization but also a challenge to the (readerly) expectation of solely delving into characters' inner lives. In other words, the text encourages a shift in perspective: from the inner workings of the human psyche to the outer environment and the intricate network of relationships; from a form of mindfulness characterized as "affective detachment"[50] to mindfulness as an "insight of interbeing."

As a result, even when the novels delve into inner lives, they highlight the notion of interbeing rather than solely focusing on psychological growth. This emphasis is further reinforced by the presence of multiple voices within the narrative: "The narrative web of stories reflects this biological entanglement, as Jimmy's narration (OC) and Ren's and Toby's voices (YF) merge with Blackbeard's, the post-humanimal's 'postscript' (MA)."[51] Bosco highlights the "journey motif" which "signifies Jimmy-Snowman's *inner transformation* as he confronts his post-catastrophe world and remembers his pre-catastrophe past."[52] While many critics have indeed concentrated on the character of Jimmy due to his generosity as a character, Atwood subtly inserts her critique even within this aspect of the narrative.

---

49 Ibid., p. 131, 133.
50 Ibid., p. 128.
51 Mohr, When Species Meet, p. 57.
52 Bosco, Apocalyptic Imagination, p. 158; emphasis added.

Oryx and Crake is not merely a Bildungsroman: Jimmy is neither hero, nor antihero, but rather exists as another entity within a complex network of human and nonhuman actors.[53] Furthermore, Toby emerges as another central character, with *MaddAddam* thought to encapsulate "the essence of Toby's *emancipated selfhood*, which is reflected in her keen observation powers, her effective storytelling, her teaching of a Cracker child and her keeping a daily diary to record the post-pandemic world."[54] However, this chapter aims to examine their characters in a slightly unconventional manner compared with prevalent readings. Rather than adopting a purely psychological perspective, the focus lies on how Atwood utilizes Jimmy and Toby to introduce nature and the nonhuman, going beyond mere exploration of their individual selves and personal development.

Instead of merely delving into the characters' inner thoughts, the novel adopts "a typically dystopic viewpoint on its narrative. *An intimate outsider*—a member of the society who is in some ways separate from the more powerful elements of the society and not fully convinced of the society's views—tells the tale."[55] Both Jimmy and Toby find themselves occupying this position of an "intimate outsider." Toby serves as a focalizer in both *The Year of the Flood* and *MaddAddam*, described as "a reluctant convert, wary of these 'friendly though bizarre people, with their wacky religion.'"[56] The perspectives of Jimmy and Toby are simultaneously involved and detached, biased and open-minded; they are both witnesses and participants. So, they serve as mindful focalizers, both reporting and experiencing their stories, and both capable and incapable of influencing them.

---

53 Raschke presents another interesting interpretation of the novel as a Bildungsroman, proposing to view the entire trilogy as a Bildungsroman for the Crakers, whom she identifies as the narrators. According to her analysis, *"The Year of the Flood* and *MaddAddam* (excluding 'BOOK') have been compiled by the Crakers, with some added narrative flourish, and *Oryx and Crake* (and the section 'BOOK' from *MaddAddam*) are written by them" (Postmodernism, p. 24). This perspective sheds new light on the issue of "cardboardiness" raised in Spiegel's paper. She argues that given a Craker narration, the perceived "cardboardiness" becomes "perfectly explicable, in that Crake is beyond their imaginative repertoire" (ibid., p. 26).
54 Ringo/Sharma, Reading, p. 112; emphasis added.
55 Sutherland/Swan, Margaret Atwood, p. 224; emphasis added. The same principle applies to the entire trilogy, as demonstrated by the sequel novels: "Instead of an omniscient narrator, the stories are intercut with journal entries from Toby and others, which allow for first-person accounts. The stories themselves, primarily told by Toby, explicitly do not belong to the person narrating" (Gretzky, After the Fall, p. 43). Similarly, even though the first novel's title is *Oryx and Crake*, the story does not belong to them but to Jimmy. According to Garrard, the "narrator's intimacy and complicity with the protagonist is near-total, often sliding in and out of free indirect discourse almost imperceptibly. This narrator—whom one can only characterize as masculine—is frank, wryly observant, mordantly funny, and unillusioned" (Reading as an Animal, p. 239).
56 Defalco, Maddaddam, p. 447.

9.2 Self-Descriptive Reminiscence: Jimmy's Autobiography

Jimmy has been traditionally read as an "alienated and troubled boy and a disassociated man" who "offers *his autobiography* as a testament to the catastrophic events that have occurred. In a traditional sense, Jimmy delivers up an ostensible *story of survival*, a Robinson Crusoe epic."[57] However, Atwood juxtaposes these two different registers: Jimmy's testimony functions as a means to stay alive, too. So, his survival does not only depend on staying safe from danger, but also on recovering his story and on making it last.[58] Moreover, Jimmy's act of storytelling "becomes a means not only for his personal *survival* but a *revival* of a human narrative in the Craker community."[59] He seems to assume the role of the "last man standing," particularly as a representative of the humanities: "As a writer, Jimmy is a lover of words, a natural storyteller, but he is also a product of a society that has devalued the humanities and elevated the sciences, a society in which words have lost their meaning."[60]

By means of his character, Atwood's fiction invites psychological approaches to her text, as evidenced by the plethora of such responses to her novel. Nathalie Foy addresses Snowman's "coming into consciousness" or awakening.[61] He presumably overcomes trauma through mythmaking, showcasing emotional growth as he struggles psychologically with his circumstances.[62] Critics note Snowman's "emotional sensitivity" and the "streaks of tenderness, sensitivity, and empathy in him" as feminine traits,[63] which all serve to humanize him. Empathy emerges as a key trait highlighted by other critics as well: "At the same time that Snowman's *empathetic* nature is emerging as a result of his *therapeutic journey*, he is also, in effect, beginning a period of linguistic deprogramming."[64] According to Wolter, "Jimmy, with his 'old' internalized system of moral values and his ability to feel responsibility, compassion, and love, represents the only possibility to save the new race of Crakers."[65]

---

57 Appleton, Myths of Distinction, p. 9; emphasis added.
58 Paul W. Harland also identifies the value of fiction along the same lines, in Atwood's "poetics of survival": "The greatest value of fiction, as Atwood's own poetics and evolutionary biology confirm, is in aiding survival, touching the heart in such a way as to forestall disaster and allow escape" (Ecological Grief, p. 584).
59 Bosco, Apocalyptic Imagination, p. 170; emphasis in original.
60 Osborne, Mythmaking, p. 26.
61 Foy, Representation, p. 410.
62 Osborne, Mythmaking, p. 42.
63 Banerjee, Towards 'Feminist Mothering,' p. 242.
64 Osborne, Mythmaking, p. 38; emphasis added.
65 Wolter, Science as Deconstruction, p. 125.

However, other critics present less favorable readings of Jimmy. Shannon Hengen, for instance, challenges the idea of an "'old' internalized system of moral values,"[66] arguing that this system has been replaced with the individualist values of capitalist, self-help culture:

> Jimmy has *no access to the traditions of deep meaning* encoded in religious belief. Instead, he has been led by his culture to mistake consumerism for peace of mind, sexual vigour for wellness, denial of aging for intuition of the immortal human spirit, and the genetic editing-out of human failings for the work of redemption [...] Growing up in a soulless, materialistic world that is cut off from the spiritual wisdom of the past, Jimmy, like the rest of his generation, is left with the body and its demands. Thus as a young man, Jimmy insists that he wants only *"to be himself, alone ... self-created and self-sufficient"* with ties to no one (176).[67]

As such, Atwood challenges the famous Emersonian notion of self-reliance. What's more, rather than being empathetic, Jimmy is depicted as using empathy to attract women with his story of the absent mother, and only Oryx refuses to empathize with it.[68] Thus, empathy is not depicted as an absolute good; sometimes, a refusal to empathize translates into a rejection of manipulation. Additionally, it appears as if "Snowman's *mea culpa* is not really a confession but, rather a denial, and he still rejects his share of the responsibility for the outcome of the BlyssPluss plague."[69]

The ideal of autonomy, independence, self-government, and sovereignty is further challenged on a narrative level. While a "third-person omniscient narrator records the voice of the protagonist, Snowman, through whose consciousness the narrative is focalized. [...]," there are also various "slippages" between these perspectives.[70] Furthermore, "the creation of a gap between Snowman and Jimmy" creates a distance that may facilitate "self-realization and understanding in Snowman" while also highlighting "his failure to achieve completely this understanding of the past."[71] Nathalie Foy has also addressed the "multiplicity of focalizing identities" that create an "unstable narrative voice," constantly prompting "the reader's suspicion" and leading them beyond the limitations of Jimmy's/Snowman's perspective: "The instability of the narrative voice makes it possible to question Jimmy's perspective of his absent mother and find a redemptive side to her desertion."[72] I would further argue that these narrative slippages challenge the

---

66 Ibid.
67 Hengen, Moral/Environmental Debt, p. 130, 138; emphasis added.
68 Cf. Foy, Representation, p. 415f.
69 Ibid., p. 411.
70 Banerjee, Toward 'Feminist Mothering,' p. 239.
71 Ibid., p. 240.
72 Foy, Representation, p. 417.

distinctions between the extradiegetic and intradiegetic worlds, offering an "insight of interbeing" between characters, readers, and narrators rather than solely focusing on individual selves and their quest for redemption.

Critics often search for signs of redemption in Atwood's writing, questioning whether Jimmy, his mother, or humanity as a whole can be redeemed. Yet, this pursuit of redemption operates within a human-centric perspective, a perspective that Atwood actively challenges. Her argument is more nuanced than simply offering a path to redemption or overcoming traumas and painful pasts. For instance, Hilde Staels suggests that Jimmy grapples with a "trauma of emotional and physical deprivation" stemming from his mother's absence, which he is unable to overcome.[73] Staels notes Jimmy's "repetitive sense of failure and guilt, sorrow and pain, and with a sentimental longing for an imaginary happy mother who loves him unconditionally."[74] Moreover, Jimmy is attached to the concept of "home," an archaic notion in Crake's dystopian world. "The ocean is the closest he can get to the archaic mother; it fills him with a death wish, a subconscious desire to return to the oceanic primordial state inside the womb, in which the self disintegrates."[75]

However, Atwood's novels present a challenge to the conventional notion that death must be overcome, and they offer a different perspective on the disintegration of the self. This disintegration is not portrayed as something to be feared or avoided but rather as an alternative to the idea of actively creating or fashioning the self, a theme echoed in mindfulness narratives. The "death drive" identified by Staels[76] could be interpreted as a "life wish," a concept with which the text both begins and ends. Staels suggests that the mirroring of the novel's beginning and end implies a "mythical 'hero's' cyclical journey back 'home'"[77]:

> On the eastern horizon there's a greyish haze, lit now with a rozy, deadly glow. Strange how that colour still seems tender. [...]

---

[73] Staels, Oryx and Crake, p. 438.
[74] Ibid. She also adds: "As a result of his upbringing in the absolutely safe compounds, [...] the protagonist is trapped in a fantasy, believing that unambiguous feelings such as true love or true happiness can be achieved in real life, and that such feelings can be provided by an ideal mother. Thus, his wounded, sentimental self proves to be in search of pure, uncontaminated feelings and singularity of meaning. In this way, he is also the Doppelgänger of Crake, whose ideal of absolute perfection and stability, which is the opposite of the 'monstrous' abject, appears to be achieved in his children" (p. 441).
[75] Ibid., p. 438.
[76] Ibid., p. 445.
[77] Ibid., p. 443.

On the eastern horizon there's a greyish haze, lit now with a rozy, deadly glow. Strange how that colour still seems tender. He gazes at it with rapture; there's no other word for it. *Rapture.*[78]

These passages describing the "greyish haze" on the eastern horizon are primarily seen through Jimmy's perspective. Staels highlights Jimmy's sense of "tenderness" toward his new home, "the remnants of Mother Earth," akin to "Frankenstein's monster" finding solace in nature.[79] Jimmy's feeling of rapture, though seemingly obsolete, temporarily counterbalances his "unspeakable suffering"[80] and echoes his sentimentalization of extinct words.

> Savouring the musicality, the pure materiality of these beautiful words similarly causes a release of unconscious affects, for it provides an aesthetic pleasure and a *consolation* that temporarily fills an emotional void. Beauty is indeed the other world of the depressed, when melancholia resulting from a traumatic experience of loss is temporarily overcome.[81]

The consolation Staels discusses here recalls David James' notion of "critical solace."[82] While Staels suggests a narrative of overcoming trauma or loss, critical solace, as proposed by James and echoed in Atwood's work, focuses on acknowledging the omnipresence of loss without necessarily seeking to overcome it. Atwood's novels imply that finding solace in beauty and nature does not necessitate overcoming loss but rather entails an intimate coexistence with it. Loss and plenitude coexist paradoxically, reflecting the intertwined nature of life and death. Therefore, intimacy with loss is what allows Jimmy to feel beauty and to feel alive in the midst of despair.[83]

Readers of this passage tend to focus on how Jimmy (or the human) is "enraptured by the beauty of the world," finding relief in nature.[84] However, this description goes beyond suggesting a return to nature à la Romanticism. It portrays an affect of aliveness—or, what it means to feel alive—which involves both beauty and pain. The glow is simultaneously "tender" and "deadly"; describing light or

---

78 Atwood, *Oryx and Crake*, p. 3, 371.
79 Staels, Oryx and Crake, p. 444.
80 Ibid.
81 Ibid.; emphasis added.
82 James, Critical Solace, p. 484. Narkunas is less positive about Jimmy's solace: "Rather than celebrating Jimmy as an antidote to instrumentalization, Atwood depicts him, however, as paralyzed with self-pity and resentment, seeking solace in manufactured nostalgia or fantasy" (Between Words, p. 11).
83 See also my discussion of Kweku in Selasi's *Ghana Must Go* and the affect of aliveness depicted there (Be-Longing, p. 291).
84 Harland, Ecological Grief, p. 586.

color as "tender" blurs the lines between sensory impressions, thereby blurring boundaries between the self and its environment. This paves the way for a synesthetic perception of the world and human-nonhuman interactions.

Atwood's description of nature at the outset of *Oryx and Crake* employs a less common form of synesthesia: time-space synesthesia, wherein "contiguous time units such as months are spatially linked forming idiosyncratically shaped patterns such as ovals, oblongs or circles."[85] In other words, units of time are experienced as physical realities with specific sizes, locations, or colors. The opening of *Oryx and Crake* captures a similar imagery as it introduces the thoughts of the lonely Snowman after the apocalypse.

> "Now I'm alone," he says out loud. "All, all alone. Alone on a *wide, wide sea.*" One more scrap from the burning scrapbook in his head. [...] He scans the horizon, using his one *sunglassed eye:* nothing. The sea is *hot metal*, the sky a *bleached blue*, except for the *hole burnt in it by the sun.* Everything is so empty. Water, sand, sky, trees, fragments of past time. Nobody to hear him. "Crake! He yells. [...] He listens. The salt water is running down his face again. [...] Senseless panic. "You did this!" He screams at the ocean. No answer, which isn't surprising. Only the waves, wish-wash, wish-wash."[86]

The reference to Samuel Coleridge's "The Rime of the Ancient Mariner" may not be coincidental, nor out of context. The novel updates Romantic approaches to nature with a view to describe a new form of interaction with the environment that is less exploitative. In the above passage, the ocean, the horizon, and the sky depict the vastness of a cosmic landscape. According to Damien Broderick, science fiction's "best imaginative stories are told in the full blinking awareness of the true open dimensionality of space and time, by contrast with the provisional and largely contingent character of our own locality."[87] By "open dimensionality," he refers to the entire cosmos, which stretches infinitely and evokes a sense of awe and wonder. However, for Snowman, such vastness brings about a sense of panic and emptiness, highlighting the importance of "our own locality" instead. The fusion of time-space is presented in various ways: first, the "fragments of past time" are envisioned as a place listed among other places. Second, synesthetic imagery where the sense of sight is coupled with the sense of touch—where the blue color of the sky and the burning sensation of the sun are fused—also functions as a reminder

---

[85] Smilek et al., Ovals of Time, p. 507. Mikhail Bakhtin describes the literary chronotope in a similar manner: "time thickens, takes on flesh" and "spatial and temporal indicators are fused" (*The Dialogic Imagination*, p. 84). As such, this "fusion of indicators" echoes a synesthetic perception that encapsulates a fusion of the senses.
[86] Atwood, *Oryx and Crake*, p. 10–12.
[87] Broderick, *X, Y, Z, T*, p. 11.

of the interconnectedness of space and time, as the sun—which is Snowman's only marker of time—pierces the sky, the vast fabric of space.

Snowman's filtered vision sees nothing, thus challenging the correlation of vision with insight. And yet, his vision is also very lively, despite the described emptiness. The connections he makes seem all wrong: associating the sea with hot metal. Hot metal evokes not only high temperatures but also incandescent hues of red and orange, which are properties shared by the sun rather than the sea. The fluidity of the hot metal intensifies the sensorial imagery, as color, touch, and dimension merge together in a single passage. Snowman's vision captures a multisensory perception, rather than focusing solely on the eye. His vision of the cosmic landscape does not reach optimistically into the future; instead, it captures a NowHere that is at the same time a NoWhere.[88]

The boundaries between the self and his environment seem to vanish, as the reader witnesses a form of human-nonhuman interaction where the inner void is translated into outer emptiness and vice versa. The repetitive sound of the waves as they "wish-wash"[89] also seems to literally wash away Snowman's wish, desire, or will-to-live. At the same time, "[t]he sound of nature commingling with culture is then compared to a symbol of both—the heartbeat—an image associated both with a biological organ and with cultural constructions of love and vitality."[90] Paradoxically, the novel introduces a hopeless world, yet full of life, due to the lively descriptions—a paradox inherent in the word "rapture" too.[91] Rapture may not only refer to Jimmy's ecstatic feeling but also to the eschatological event when both the living and the dead meet.

Snowman stands in for the human self robbed of his anthropocentric worldview: an "apelike man or manlike ape."[92] His survival is not synonymous with the "heroic, punctual overcoming of obstacles, that once accomplished, allows life to go on by itself."[93] Snowman ends this passage with the words: "Get a life!"[94]—which entails that even though he survived, his life does not merely continue. Neither did his survival have anything to do with a struggle because he did not fight to stay alive. He just happened to be at the right place at the right time. The disintegration

---

88 "Utopia is both a 'good place' and 'no place', but also a 'u-chronia;' a no time, a place where time has stopped, a place of stagnation" (Stein, Problematic Paradice, p. 152).
89 Atwood, *Orxy and Crake*, p. 12.
90 Dunlap, Eco-Dystopia, p. 4.
91 Or, to use David James' words, it stages "a competition between content and form" (Critical Solace, p. 483).
92 Atwood, *Oryx and Crake*, p. 8.
93 Ginsburg, Narratives of Survival, p. 410.
94 Atwood, *Oryx and Crake*, p. 12.

of Jimmy's self and emergence of Snowman also offers a critical posthumanist perspective on subjectivity, rather than being a sign of mental illness. Throughout her novels, Atwood blurs the "fine line between humanity and monstrosity"[95] and she does so with Snowman, too: "Snowman's becoming-ghost, becoming-animal, and becoming-monster (in contrast to the Crakers) actually disrupt the hierarchy implicit in the anthropocentric *homo faber.*"[96]

But there is a more subtle way in which anthropocentrism is challenged on an extradiegetic level, too. Storey and Storey argued that "Snowman's redeeming feature, in a sense, is that he is fully human, aware of some (but certainly not all) of his own inner contradictions, and this may be one of the novel's greatest messages."[97] And yet, the novel challenges precisely this humanist logic of redemption, which is just another anthropocentric preference or expectation that focuses on Jimmy while ignoring the environment in which he moves. Naama Harel, for instance, showed how "[t]he rejection of nonhuman animals as a subject of literary exploration is a result of nothing but anthropocentric preferences."[98] Similarly, the focus on Jimmy in secondary readings may show a similar bias toward human matters while it ignores the rich environment in which he finds himself.

However, by making use of literary synesthesia, Atwood pushes nature and human-nonhuman interactions forth. Literary synesthesia foreshadows the notion of interbeing, as human and nonhuman merge together in a rich imagery where the self and outer nature connect. This deep and intricate conjunction presents an insight of interbeing and interdependency. In other words, literary synesthesia is not used to suggest a superior form of mental power in the human self, nor is it used to merely anthropomorphize the nonhuman. Rather, it depicts the human and the nonhuman on a continuum, placing them on the same nonhierarchical level without denying human features, nor ignoring the nonhuman. Literary synesthesia appears as a form of human experience while also giving life to and making tangible the nonhuman.

Thus, Atwood's use of literary synesthesia illustrates the intersection of art and politics. Atwood "posits a politics of the posthuman that is associated with feminist new materialist thinkers, who argue for more ecological frameworks that engage with the multiple ways in which all lifeform, organic and inorganic,

---

95 Ku, Of Monster and Man, p. 109.
96 Ibid., p. 129.
97 Storey/Storey, History and Allegory.
98 Harel, Constructing the Nonhuman, p. 905.

human or otherwise, exist in a network of entangled relations and agencies."[99] The development of a posthuman ethics is an urgent matter precisely because colonialism, racism, and humanism are intertwined discourses, and much of the social injustices in the world are undergirded by a humanist rhetoric.[100] Synesthesia becomes an important aesthetic tool because it gestures toward a politics of the posthuman.

Yet, Atwood also distances herself from an empathic approach that necessitates an identification with the nonhuman: "to identify oneself with an animal one can rely only on the power of empathy."[101] Empathy is often invoked in order to suggest a less anthropocentric approach to the nonhuman. According to Harel, "[t]he few non-anthropomorphic representations of nonhuman animals are usually achieved by empathic observation and not by scientific knowledge."[102] She adds: "Empathic observation enables us not only to avoid anthropomorphism in representing nonhuman animals (both in science and literature) but also to reconstruct their viewpoint behind anthropomorphized representation."[103] However, this is yet another utopian gesture that Atwood negates. Empathy also perpetuates a hierarchical view of the power relationships between the human and the nonhuman: as it is in the power of the human to empathize with the nonhuman, whereas the nonhuman remains in a position of victimhood.[104]

---

[99] Jennings, Anthropocene, p. 17. More specifically, those thinkers include Karen Barad, Donna Haraway or Rosi Braidotti who "have been re-conceptualizing a nature-human continuum that foregrounds the autonomy and agency of (living) matter" (Keck, Paradise Retold, p. 25).
[100] For instance, Atwood criticizes "how Anthropocene discourses often reiterate imperialist ideologies" (Jennings, "Anthropocene" 24). She also demonstrates "the importance of critiques of anthropocentrism and speciesism; however, she shows how they seemingly lack a concept of power except as anthropocentrism" (Narkunas 4).
[101] Ferrando qtd. in Koziol, From Sausages, p. 289.
[102] Harel, Constructing the Nonhuman, p. 904.
[103] Ibid., p. 911.
[104] It is precisely this perpetuation of victimhood that Atwood may seek to challenge. Monja Mohr writes: "Where British literature (e.g. Potter, Kipling) anthropomorphizes animals conversing in perfect English and represents class-conscious or colonial 'social relations' (74), and American literature's 'imperialist mindset' equates animals with nature as the other that must be hunted, conquered, and killed (e.g. Melville, Faulkner, Hemingway), Canadian animal 'failure stories' (74) sympathetically focus on the (narratively impersonated) animal's point of view, 'as felt emotionally from inside the fur and feathers' (74). For Atwood, the 'Canadian animal stories present animals as victims' and a 'trait in our national psyche' (75), positioning the US in the role of the conquering nation/human and Canada as animal/victim. *MaddAddam* then rewrites the Canadian animal story for the 21st century on a planetary scale, where the 'threatened and nearly extinct' (79) 'Canadian (non-human) animal' triumphantly resurfaces" (55).

Atwood's use of literary synesthesia effectively acknowledges the nonhuman without necessitating identification with it or the reconstruction of its viewpoint.[105] Synesthesia allows for a mutual exchange that acknowledges, responds, and listens to the nonhuman: "not (directly) representing but *acknowledging* other lifeforms' views, avoiding the ventriloquist's pitfall, is in fact an honest and post-anthropocentric narratological stance."[106] In other words, "multispecies justice does not entail identifying how humans and nonhumans resemble one another; rather, it involves establishing modes for responding to and honoring differences."[107] Listening, being responsive, or practicing "response-ability"[108] is what matters. For instance, Toby's "evolving relationships with the Crakers, Pigoons, and the bees are possible because of her openness to listening and *responding* to their differing needs and viewpoints without assuming a position of superiority."[109]

Jacques Derrida has also rejected "approaches that promote sympathy for animals on the basis of some positive similarity and argues, instead, that what is of significance is *a profound lack* that we share with animals: our *suffering, vulnerability and mortality*."[110] However, Atwood's novels go even further in claiming mortality not as a "profound lack" that only inspires "the fear of being eaten,"[111] but as the basis of feeling alive, too. The insight of interbeing allows humans to "re-enter the great circle of life"[112] that includes the nonhuman.

Jimmy's rapture is also a form of rupture from the redemptive script that imprisoned him. He seems to acknowledge the fact that there is something bigger or larger than his own egotistic self—something that Crake was unable to do: "Victor Frankenstein's heir, the gifted young scientist Crake stands for human beings who are no longer able to imagine that we are part of something larger than ourselves, as we used to be."[113] This acknowledgement requires an exercise in mindfulness that is mediated mainly by the body and its rich sensory life, a topic that will be further explored in the next section, which will focuses on Toby's character. In short, "Toby and Ren, provide a different way of seeing and relating to 'other-

---

105 So, humans can never truly know, nor should they attempt to know, in the words of Thomas Nagel, "what is it like to be a bat" (1974). However, it is necessary to acknowledge the bat.
106 Mohr, When Species Meet, p. 58; emphasis added.
107 Jennings, Anthropocene, p. 28.
108 Ibid., p. 29.
109 Ibid., p. 28; emphasis added. This form of "listening" also echoes that of Eunice when she reads the book with Lenny. There, she listens.
110 Northover, p. 132f; emphasis added.
111 Koziol, From Sausages, p. 273.
112 Ibid., p. 274.
113 Wolter, Science as Deconstruction, p. 266.

ness'," adopting a "posthuman ethics that refutes the disposability of human and nonhuman life alike,"[114] and they do so by relying on a synesthetic perception of the world.

9.3 Literary Synesthesia: "A Songbird Made of Ice"

Even if the body plays a central role in Atwood's novels, few critics have extensively focused on this topic. Those who do engage with it usually center their critique on its commodification, particularly the commodification of the female body, as seen in the experiences of Oryx, Ren, or Toby, who resorts to selling her hair and ovaries.[115] In various ways, "Atwood's trilogy stages the desire to transcend humanity by transcending the materiality of the body."[116] Giuseppina Botta also delves into the effects of an "unscrupulous use of *zoe* which turns out to suggest a dehumanized and too mechanized vision of the human body."[117] She adds:

> Science gives a different and wider perspective of "what a body can do," but at the cost of changing the meaning of "what a body is"; [...] In my view, it is not only the female body that is dehumanized but the body in general, owing to an excessive focus on its smallest parts and fragments. The continuous act of depriving the body of all its meanings recalls Deleuze and Guattari's concept of the "Body without Organs"—"what remains when you take everything away [...]".[118]

The "mechanized perception" of the human body identified by Botta is also contested in the novels. While the trilogy does indeed depict a mechanical and abused body, evident in the portrayal of violent games and pornographic scenes, it also presents examples of "what a body is." This encompasses what nature and literature offer, restoring the "body" that has been taken away by science.

Hilde Staels claims that "Atwood's satire warns against the techno-scientific preoccupation with the abolition of all human imperfection,"[119] which primarily targets the human body. She suggests that Crake "expels the human feelings, de-

---

114 Jennings, Anthropocene, p. 26.
115 Cf. Northover, Strangers, p. 128. This trope also emerges in Richard Powers' novel, where Thassadit Amzwar is another female character who ends up selling her ovaries.
116 Narkunas, Between Words, p. 17. "Whereas Crake believed in biology as stable ontology for social engineering to remake the human thing, Adam One and God's Gardeners believe in a transcendent soul connected to nature as a way to transcend thingness" (ibid., p. 18).
117 Botta, Faustian Dreams, p. 244.
118 Ibid., p. 252.
119 Staels, Oryx and Crake, p. 433.

sires and bodily drives" from his children, reflecting his desire to extinguish these traits in himself, and which he "sees grotesquely reflected in Jimmy, his repressed dark shadow."[120] This expulsion includes the "maternal body," which serves as a reminder of "his own mortality and corporeality."[121] Additionally, Atwood's critique extends to sensorial approaches to the human body, moving beyond psychology to address the impact of the senses.

Atwood's dystopia is governed by the sense of sight, with surveillance understood as a perpetual state of being looked at.[122] Paula Lopez Rua draws parallels between the compounds and Bentham's panopticon, which is "a disciplinary building whose major effect is to induce a state of conscient and permanent *visibility* that ensures the automatic functioning of power."[123] This form of discipline appears successful, as Snowman internalizes "the feeling of being monitored," believing he is constantly watched even in the post-apocalyptic world.[124]

However, the exercise of power goes beyond mere monitoring; it also involves visually imprisoning citizens. The on-going conflicts and violence depicted online serve to "divert people's attention from their actual problems," creating "a sense of grateful well-being which results from comparing their situation with what is happening somewhere else."[125] In other words, when not being watched, people feel compelled to keep watching. This becomes evident in their engagement with violent computer games and pornography, which "turn mass destruction into an enjoyable spectacle."[126] As long as individuals are reduced to the sense of sight, power remains entrenched and perpetuated, whether it is through Jimmy and Crake's "voyeuristic male gaze" on Oryx,[127] or Jimmy's prying on the nonhuman, naked Crakers, who appear to lack any sense of privacy.

---

[120] Ibid., p. 437.
[121] Ibid.
[122] Claire Wrobel does a more in-depth analysis of the ways in which surveillance and dataveillance operate in Atwood's novels. She also shows how God's Gardeners resist surveillant technologies by blocking them (for instance, avoiding technology such as smartphones), by masking themselves (when Toby acquires a new identity and changes her appearance), or by practicing countersurveillance.
[123] Rua, Manipulative Power, p. 154; emphasis added.
[124] Marks, Pleeblands, p. 219.
[125] Rua, Manipulative Power, p. 156.
[126] Bouson, "It's Game Over", p. 143.
[127] "Even so, Oryx openly challenges the spectators'—Jimmy and Crake's—voyeuristic male gaze by looking 'right into the eyes of the viewer,' as if to say, '*I see you watching. I know you, I know what you want*' (104). Her gaze simultaneously underlines and defies her exploitation and commodification. While her look into the webcam confirms its presence, it at the same time elicits feelings of guilt, shame, and desire in Jimmy, forcing him—and by implication other (male) customers—to

While many dystopias focus on the act of monitoring and the Orwellian concept of Big Brother, Atwood takes her argument further. The Paradice dome created by Crake appears to epitomize visual scrutiny, as he seeks to maintain a God-like "all-seeing eye" on his Adam and Eve.[128] However, the ideal of omniscience and transparency ultimately fails: the dome is likened to a "blind eyeball,"[129] in stark contrast to Emerson's concept of the "transparent eye-ball."[130] Sharon R. Wilson has also tackled the role of distorted vision and blindness in *Oryx and Crake*, highlighting how Crake and Jimmy are both monsters "in their contrasting ways of seeing without seeing."[131]

Besides the focus on vision (or lack thereof), Atwood hints at the introduction of other senses through her spelling of *"Paradice."*[132] According to Brydon, the ironically spelled "Paradice" might be paying homage to Coleridge's "Kubla-Khan," in which the poet rhymes Paradise with ice; moreover, this "conflation of two concepts through a deviant spelling links utopian desire to cold (as in Shelley's *Frankenstein*) while also suggesting Jimmy's frigid emotional state and the frozen North."[133] Additionally, if fire symbolizes hell, then ice would define paradise. This juxtaposition also evokes a binary relationship between the hotness of passion or the untamable body and the coldness of the mind or rational control.[134]

Thus, Crake's paradise depicts the scientist's dream of rational control. If "ice" defines Crake's dome, the "blind eyeball" also gathers additional meaning: it could

---

recognize her as a human subject rather than a virtual sex object (252)" (Keck, Paradise Retold, p. 34; emphasis in original).

128 Marks, Pleeblands, p. 219. Paul Hamann interprets the dome as a "central spatial metaphor for the trilogy's exploration of genetic privacy" (Under Surveillance, p. 68).

129 Atwood, *Oryx and Crake*, p. 297.

130 "Standing on the bare ground,—my head bathed by the blithe air, and uplifted into infinite space, all mean egotism vanishes. I become a transparent eye-ball. I am nothing. I see all. The currents of the Universal Being circulate through me; I am part or particle of God" (Emerson, Nature, p. 1109).

131 Wilson, Frankenstein's Gaze, p. 403.

132 Atwood, *Oryx and Crake*, p. 151; emphasis in original.

133 Brydon, Atwood's Global Ethic, p. 450. The spelling of "Paradice" has been interpreted by scholars in various ways: Paul Hamann highlights the "ironic reference to the elimination of chance in creation—'dice'—through genetic engineering" (Under Surveillance, p. 69). Michaela Keck focuses on how it "resonates with the onomatopoeia of 'splicing' and, thus, points to the implementation of genetic engineering and scientific management" (Paradise Retold, p. 11). My focus lies on "ice" and its sensorial connotations and implications.

134 In Dante's *Inferno*, the worst sinners are frozen into the ice of the ninth circle, rendering them unable to move or speak. Atwood's conflation of ice and paradise also invokes a rich history, offering another layer to the concept of "ustopia"—wherein every utopia conceals a dystopia; within every perfect society, lies suffering and pain.

hint at the materiality of vision or its inextricable connection to the other senses, like the sense of touch. Ice can be both transparent and opaque, due to air and impurities, but its imagery mostly evokes low temperature and coldness. Atwood adds a haptic and tangible feeling to the description of an ineffable and transcendent realm. Her novel suggests that things become accessible only if the body is allowed to function on a multisensory level. A snowman, which is how Jimmy comes to be known, is also an anthropomorphic structure, moist and compact, always on the brink of melting, morphing, and disappearing. Yet, besides connoting transition, ephemerality, and the idea of being abandoned, a snowman is also sensorially rich—white, wet, and cold.

As long as the Crakers are confined to the visual realm only, power relationships are maintained, and they also remain obscure, ambiguous, out of reach to humans. These perfect beings "look like retouched fashion photos, or ads for a high-priced workout program."[135] Yet, later on in the trilogy, Toby begins to challenge this one-dimensional view of the Crakers. Paradoxically, according to Bone, they "show extreme empathy," but also, "it is in their lack of emotion that the Crakers most resemble machines and morph into automatons."[136] However, this reading is also challenged in Atwood's novel, as Blackbeard begins to cry "as if his heart will break" when he encounters the "smelly bones" of Oryx and Crake.[137]

At first sight, the Crakers appear to be humanized by granting them an affective life. The Crakers "initially appear monstrous to readers to the extent that they lack the creative vitality of humanistic thought" and they "*become human*—sympathetic, compassionate, understandable—when they begin to tell stories, and use those stories to understand their experiences and find meaning in their world."[138] However, the novel also complicates the narrow association of feelings with humans only—not only do some humans have no feelings at all (Painballers), but feelings belong to other species, too (such as the pigoons or the Crakers).

Accordingly, it is through the body and an affective life that the human and the nonhuman are able to communicate—mediating the insight of interbeing. When Toby looks into a Craker child's eye, she "sees that they seem backlit,"[139] hinting at a rich inner life. Additionally, when she meets Blackbeard, she notices the smells of orange and "citrus air freshener."[140] Moreover, Crakers "have the ability to purr

---

135 Bouson, "It's Game Over," p. 149.
136 Bone, Environmental Dystopias, p. 632, 635.
137 Atwood, *MaddAddam*, p. 356.
138 Gretzky, After the Fall, p. 46 f; emphasis added.
139 Bone, Environmental Dystopias, p. 631.
140 Atwood, *MaddAddam*, p. 113.

and the purring is a healing aspect of their touch."[141] These images not only blur the boundaries between different species and animals but also add to their sensorial richness. The Crakers are no longer mere photos; they smell, purr, and sing. Therefore, it is not empathy as a cognitive mode of observation, but rather sensorial and affective perception that mediates the insight of interbeing, which extends beyond humans. In other words, the Crakers do not merely "become human"[142] because they tell stories; they become more accessible to humans once they are grasped on a multisensory level.

This idea culminates in one of *MaddAddam*'s survival scenes, where Atwood employs literary synesthesia to challenge the humanist belief in mind-power and to shift attention to the insight of interbeing. In this scene, Toby, Zen, and Blackbeard visit Pilar's grave and have a seemingly dangerous encounter with a giant pig. Paradoxically, Toby seeks answers to questions concerning life by visiting a burial site; she seeks Pilar's guidance regarding the newly developed pregnancies of female characters. On one hand, this suggests that life continues even after human life ends, especially since Pilar seems to communicate through the nonhuman—through a pig. Yet, rather than sustaining a belief in reincarnation, this scene points to the myriad ways in which life persists. Additionally, this scene explicitly references "Meditation" or is framed as a mindfulness scene mediated by a mushroom:[143]

> Toby can feel the full strength of the *Enhanced Meditation formula* kicking in. [...] A morphosplice butterfly floats down the path, luminescent. Of course, she remembers, it's luminescent anyway, but now it's *blue-hot*, like a gasfire. [...]
>
> Nettles arc from the sides of the walkway, the *stinging hairs on their leaves gauzy with light*. All around there are sounds, noises, almost-voices: hums and clicks, tappings, whispered syllables.
>
> And there is the elderberry bush, where they planted it on Pilar's grave so long ago. It's much larger now. *White bloom cascades* from it, *sweetness* fills the air. A *vibration* surrounds it: honeybees, bumblebees, butterflies large and small. [...]

---

141 Bone, Environmental Dystopias, p. 632.
142 Gretzky, After the Fall, p. 47.
143 Even the mushroom as a nonhuman is an interesting topic. "Pilar and Toby's superior knowledge of the Amanitas as either invigorating tonic, consciousness-enhancing drug, or deadly poison, becomes a powerful tool in an oppressive phallogocentric society" (Keck, Paradise Retold, p. 35). Additionally, new research suggests that mushrooms are "more closely related to humans than to plants" (see Staughton, How Are Mushrooms), so they have their own life story that tends to be neglected or confused with a "mere" vegetable state.

> "Watch it," says the voice of Zeb. "Stay still. Look slowly. To the left."
>
> Toby turns her head. Crossing the path, within stone-throw, there's one of the giant pigs. [...]
>
> "*Wait*," Toby says. *Such enormous power.* A bullet would never stop the sow, a spraygun burst would hardly make a dent. She could run them down like a tank. Life, life, life, life, life. Full to bursting, this minute. Second. Millisecond. Millennium. Eon.
>
> The sow does not move. [...] The piglets freeze in place, their eyes red-purple berries. Elderberry eyes.
>
> Now there's a sound. Where is it coming from? It's like the wind in branches, like the sound hawks make when flying, no, like a *songbird made of ice*, no, like a ... Shit, thinks Toby. *I am so stoned.*
>
> It's Blackbeard, singing. His thin boy's voice. His Craker voice, not human.[144]

The scene depicts a survival scenario that typically involves a fight or flight response, rooted in antagonism and fear as a form of vigilance. Zeb, guided by his visual sense, issues cautious remarks like "watch it" or "look slowly," preparing for a potential battle. Toby disrupts this anticipation by advising him to "wait," introducing a third response—"freezing"—into the mix. However, this does not entail shutting down interaction; rather, Toby creates a space where humans and nonhumans can engage on a multisensorial level beyond vision. She acknowledges their shared mortality, realizing that both sides face "imminent death."[145] As such, her actions are not driven by compassion or empathy in the traditional sense; rather, Toby recognizes the sow's potential to kill her, acknowledging their shared vulnerability in the face of her "enormous power."[146]

In contrast to Zeb, Toby is not solely governed by the visual sense; she is overwhelmed on a sensorial level. Not only does she see the butterfly, but she also notices the stinging hairs on a leaf, described as "gauzy with light."[147] As such, this creates a vivid, luminescent scene, but it is not vivid solely because of visual observation. The floating butterfly is described as "blue-hot,"[148] which is not only oxymoronic but also illustrates literary synesthesia by coupling color with touch. It

---

[144] Atwood, *MaddAddam*, p. 222 f; emphasis added.
[145] Rowland, Speculative Solutions, p. 60.
[146] Atwood, *MaddAddam*, p. 223. Rowland adds: "Here Atwood uses Toby's voice both to establish a heterarchical worldview, one that recognizes the 'enormous power' of the non-human being (*MaddAddam* 223), and to drive forward an anti-Romantic consideration of the surrounding non-human 'natural' environment" (Speculative Solutions, p. 60).
[147] Atwood, *MaddAddam*, p. 222.
[148] Ibid.

is an unusual pairing, as blue typically connotes coldness and red, hotness.[149] This burning blue suggests that luminescence is not only visible but tangible. By transcending the visual, Toby does not respond solely out of fear; she recognizes the beauty of the nonhuman and their "elderberry eyes,"[150] experiencing the destabilizing "gaze of an individual animal."[151]

Blackbeard's response concludes this scene in an almost anticlimactic way, as no battle ensues. Yet, it offers a highly meaningful resolution. Blackbeard is singing —words that sound very similar to a blackbird singing. His intervention eludes the notion of survival as struggle yet again; the scene stops being a play of gazes or a struggle for power. His song comforts both the human and the nonhuman.[152] And it does so because it reminds everyone of life and its simple beauty. A "songbird made of ice"[153] couples sound and touch in its imagery. The chirping of birds and their cheery birdsong are typically associated with the warmth of summer days.

However, here, the "songbird made of ice" does not only couple the senses but implodes them. It also brings to mind the "ice" in "Paradice," though here it appears to evoke the angelic singing echoing throughout the Garden of Eden.[154] Yet, the focus also lies on the nonhuman birds rather than on supernatural, spiritual angels. The icy quality of the bird's song cuts like a knife: it is so cold it burns,

---

149 The same kind of odd pairing occurred in Jimmy's description of the sun and the sea, too. And it echoes the spelling of Paradice, too.
150 Atwood, MaddAddam, p. 223.
151 Northover, Strangers, p. 134. Above Pilar's burial site or body, an elderberry bush is planted to attract the bees. Thus, the symbol of the elderberry creates a strong connection between the human and the nonhuman, between Pilar and the sow. Northover makes a similar claim, focusing on the connection between the female and the animal, aligning with the essay's aim to demonstrate Atwood's "critique of animal exploitation [which is] closely related to the exploitation of women" (ibid., p. 129). So, "[t]he fact that the pigoon is female with farrow makes the connection between females and animals in the dominant text of meat clearer. The sow's fecundity also reassures Toby that the pregnant humans—especially Amanda—need not fear bringing their pregnancies to term" (ibid., p. 134).
152 Monja Mohr has also highlighted the significance of singing as a means of fostering community: "Singing in fact seems to connect humans, Crakers, pigoons, and other animals, and is one trait Crake cannot eliminate, "[w]e're hard-wired for singing" (OC, 352). The Crakers communicate with the pigoons and other animals by singing [...] Both God's Gardeners and the Crakers close their gatherings with singing to create a calming community spirit (and both *The Year of the Flood* and *MaddAddam* end with singing)" (When Species Meet, p. 61). Additionally, as my analysis aims to show, this imagery not only serves as a mythical reference but also foregrounds the interplay of the senses and the notion of feeling alive.
153 Atwood, MaddAddam, p. 223.
154 Cf. Keck, Paraside Retold, p. 31.

suggesting a crystal-clear sound. This scene's brightness extends into auditory perception, introducing notions of lucidity and simplicity—mindfulness understood not as cognition but as multisensory perception. At the same time, it foregrounds the necessary entanglement of beauty and pain, both stemming from vulnerability.[155]

The above scene presents Toby's visionary moment without relying solely on the visual and imaginative power of the mind to describe it.[156] It challenges the notion of mystical insight because it does not focus on the act of knowing the unknown. It also diverges from Jill Bolte Taylor's description of insight as a brainy feat bred in the right hemisphere. The scene functions like a "light bulb" moment, for it enacts an explosion of brightness and introduces the idea of insight, yet in a different, counter-intuitive fashion. Rather than suggesting a "moment of insight into yourself"[157] or moving inward to find inspiration, Toby shifts her attention to the outer environment. This is not just an example of empathy either, or empathy narrowly understood as an ability to understand and share feelings.[158] Instead, it depicts a moment of recognition that can only occur on a multisensory level.

To sum up, this scene hints at visions mediated by mindfulness or drug-induced states similar to those once sought by hippies aiming to open the door to new levels of consciousness.[159] Yet, it also challenges these notions by shifting the focus from mind-power to human-nonhuman interactions mediated by multi-

---

[155] This imagery also adds a new layer of meaning to the cheerful end debated by other critics: the end is not merely cheerful, as they suggest, nor is it entirely dystopian.

[156] In Virginia Woolf's novel *To the Lighthouse*, Lily, the artist figure, declares, "I have had my vision" (209). According to Debrah Raschke, "Toby echoes these words at Pilar's grave, morphing them into an over-the-top mushroom-inspired epiphany in which she is communing with feral pigs. In *Oryx and Crake*, Woolf's novel becomes an echo without context" ("Postmodernism" 37). Yet, Woolf's novel is not just an "echo without context," as the synesthetic aesthetic of Woolf's writing is an overlooked element that reemerges in Atwood's novels as well.

[157] Vincenty, Oprah Explains.

[158] Jennings explains: "Although Toby resists the Gardeners' romanticized notions of 'interspecies empathy' and solidarity, she does so with a skepticism that allows her to intra-act with nonhuman others (*Year* 311). Her skepticism—which rests in doubt, ambiguity, and appropriate responses to the limitations of human knowledge—facilitates a relationship defined by respectful proximity, ongoing negotiation, and mutual exchange" (Anthropocene, p. 28).

[159] Toby also challenges the belief that this is just an altered state of consciousness mediated by psychoactive substances or some form of "neurological manipulation": "I was communicating with my inner Pilar [...] And just because a sensory impression may be said to be 'caused' by an ingested mix of psychoactive substances does not mean it is an illusion" (*MaddAddam*, p. 227). Quite the contrary, it appears to make her more aware of her environment—so, her "inner Pilar" is to be found in the spirit of feeling alive that she recognizes everywhere, in the plethora of nonhumans that surround her.

sensory experience and various sensory fusions. Alan Northover suggests that in such states of altered consciousness, perceptions are "defamiliarized," and the world "takes on an otherworldly aspect."[160] However, it could also imply the opposite: not only does the world take on an otherworldly aspect, but it also reveals the hitherto unnoticed, making the "unknown known" visible by slowing down. This shift does not uncover something esoteric or out-of-this-world; rather, it brings to light the mundane aspects of our surroundings that often go unnoticed. Thus, the narrator zooms in and out—revealing details such as the walkway, nettles, leaves, or even a glint of light on a tooth. Time slows down, capturing the split-second when decisions are made, hinting at a spatio-temporal openness that is not cosmic. Survival becomes a space of human-nonhuman encounter that is not entirely antagonistic, as in a fight or flight scenario. It illustrates how life is interwoven with both beauty and pain, showing their interdependence rather than presenting them as opposites.

In *The Year of the Flood*, Atwood employs sensorial imagery to portray yet another survival scene wherein Toby and Ren attempt to rescue their friend Amanda from the Painballers. This scene challenges traditional depictions of fight and flight once more, as Toby chooses to fight despite their slim odds against three ruthless and powerful men trained in survival tactics; and they emerge victorious despite these impossible odds:

> Left foot, right foot, *quietly* along. The *faint sounds* of her feet on the fallen leaves hit her ears like shouts. How visible, how audible I am, she thinks. *Everything in the forest is watching.* They're waiting for blood, they can *smell* it, they can *hear* it running through my veins, katoush. Above her head, clustering in the treetops, the crows are treacherous: Hawhawhaw! They want her *eyes*, those crows.
>
> Yet each flower, each twig, each pebble, *shines as though illuminated from within*, as once before, on her *first day in the Garden*. It's the stress, it's the adrenalin, it's a chemical effect: she knows this well enough. But why is it built in? she thinks. Why are we designed to see the world as *supremely beautiful* just as we're about to be snuffed?
>
> [...]
>
> This is very fast, but at the same time *slowed down*. The voices are coming from far away; the sun's so bright it hurts me; the light crackles on our faces; we glare and sparkle, as if electricity's running all over us like water. I can almost *see into the bodies* – everyone's bodies. The veins, the tendons, the blood flowing. I can hear their hearts, like thunder coming nearer.[161]

---

160 Northover, Strangers, p. 133.
161 Atwood, *Year of the Flood*, p. 242, 244; emphasis added.

Despite the ostensibly silent nature of the scene (Toby moves "quietly" alone and hears "faint sounds"), it is profoundly sonorous. Toby's footsteps "*hit* her ears like shouts," underscoring their palpable audibility as sound and touch intertwine in her perception. Her heightened state of fear or vigilance seems to enhance her embodied awareness; she not only feels watched but also heard. Even her own blood is making too much noise, recalling Edgar Alan Poe's use of hyper-sensory awareness in stories like "The Tell-Tale Heart," where the heartbeat becomes painfully audible.

Toby's sense of being highly visible and exposed finds validation in Ren's account of their battle. Ren's assertion that she can "almost *see into the bodies*" may seem improbable, given the opacity of the human body, but it serves as another expression of an enhanced bodily awareness that transcends mere visual perception.[162] Ren concludes the passage in a similar vein, by noting how she can "hear their hearts, like thunder coming nearer," emphasizing that internal bodily processes are not only perceptible but overwhelmingly audible and conspicuous. This auditory perception could also be Ren's own heartbeat, blurring the boundaries between selves. Thus, this scene underscores the significance of the "material embodiment of human and nonhuman encounters."[163]

Despite the pervasive sense of fear, anguish, or anxiety, this scene is also imbued with aesthetic qualities. However, it does not merely romanticize stress; rather, it illustrates how the body serves as the locus of both stress and joy, often in paradoxical ways.[164] This portrayal suggests a departure from the prevailing biotechnological narrative that reduces life to molecular biological data and views the aging body as a countdown clock toward death. Atwood's novels propose a qualitative approach to life: what does it mean to feel alive? Life, in this context, transcends considerations of age or physical ability; it becomes about the capacity to experience aliveness, a quality shared with nonhuman entities as well. This perspective echoes Rosi Braidotti's advocacy for a *zoe*-centered understanding of life that encompasses not only human life but also that of animals and nonhuman entities.

Toby experiences a similar sense of joy, relief, and gratitude during her first day in the Garden, where everything appeared "supremely beautiful":

---

[162] As such, it also implicitly challenges the visions of total transparency on which Ariel Garten and Mehdi Seyedlar relied in their TED talks.

[163] Jennings, Anthropocene, p. 29.

[164] And that these characters are so "disembodied," that they are reminded of joy only in moments of heightened stress, because that is the only time they return to their bodies. Stress is the only way they know how to inhabit their bodies.

> The Garden wasn't at all what Toby had expected from hearsay. It wasn't a baked mudflat strewn with rotting vegetable waste—quite the reverse. She *gazed around it in wonder:* it was so *beautiful,* with plants and flowers of many kinds she'd never seen before. There were vivid butterflies; from nearby came the vibration of bees. *Each petal and leaf was fully alive, shining with awareness of her.* Even the air of the Garden was different.[165]

The wonder evoked in this description is not directed toward the universe or the discovery of some unknown landscape; it does not depict a sense of amazement at technological achievements. Instead, Atwood employs wonder in a Romantic or Transcendentalist sense, shifting the gaze back to nature. At the same time, she also updates this Romantic imagery to highlight the idea of an "ordinary miracle" found in one's immediate environment, which serves as the source of feeling alive. Feeling alive entails becoming aware of the human, the nonhuman, and their entanglement. The petals, the leaves, and Toby all engage in a play of mutual gazes, asserting their respective vitality. Feeling alive can only emerge in the presence of the nonhuman and through acts of mutual recognition.

This scene evokes the myth of the Garden of Eden as a mythical space and time where the relationship between the self and its environment was not solely governed by vigilance. The development of self-consciousness, alluded to by Adam One during his sermons, is understood as the original fall into sin. When Ren leaves the Garden and returns to the pleeblands, she becomes more self-aware as she looks into the mirror and smells her own earthly scent. In other words, recognition is what matters in these exchanges—a sense of being heard, listened to, and seen, without being obliterated or consumed. Posthuman agency proposes a shift from self-control to "response-ability":

> Toby enacts this kind of 'response-ability' toward the bees, as well as the Pigoons and Crakers, by respecting that they must work together through a process of becoming that makes possible not merely survival but a world of expanded opportunities for community (and communing) that goes beyond the limitations of humans (or humanist binaries).[166]

Atwood underscores the power of literature and reading along similar lines: as nonhuman spaces that foster mutual recognition and "response-ability." She endeavors to carve out a literary space that is less humanist or anthropocentric by redirecting focus to the body through her use of literary synesthesia.

---

165 Atwood, *Year of the Flood*, p. 32; emphasis added.
166 Jennings, Anthropocene, p. 29.

10 Literature and Storytelling: "These Stories Are Real as Kitchens"

Margaret Atwood's uses of literary synesthesia appeal to multiple sensations and her combinations go beyond ordinary language. Touch, dimension, color, sound, smell—these elements intertwine in a manner that blurs the lines between them, and it becomes difficult to identify sources and targets, which is the case in synesthetic transfers that "tend to move upward, that is, from the lower senses to the higher senses."[1] Her metaphors transcend "the divisions of sense organs"[2] and even disrupt the senses with oxymoronic additions. This artistic approach gains political relevance as Atwood's synesthetic metaphors engage readers and raise awareness. On an extradiegetic level, readers can be "brought to life" by these multisensory perceptions, compelling them to pause in their reading—a crucial moment where choices and changes become possible.

Following Ernst Cassirer, Michaela Keck observes how the "different symbolic forms of language, myth, or science [...] share their transcending of a merely sensual, associative or affective view of the world and place humans in a reflective relationship with their environment."[3] Yet, Atwood's fiction challenges such approaches by emphasizing the importance of the affective, which cannot be separated from the reflective. Her use of literary synesthesia shows how language provides a sensuous view of the world, a perspective often overlooked or underestimated.

Literature provides the greatest clarity not by eliminating ambiguities and complexities, but by rendering them tangible and felt through embodied awareness, rather than merely seen. Therefore, the role of literature extends beyond storytelling, imagination, and speculation, despite these being the terms through which Atwood's own fiction is often understood. Atwood seeks to carve out a space for literature that transcends reliance solely on the power of words or linguistic representation. For instance, Amanda's "Vulture Sculptures" have been interpreted as a form of cyborg art.[4] According to Valeria Mosca, Amanda's Living Word functions like Derrida's *animot*, merging "verbal and corporeal constituents of reality."[5] This juxtaposition reveals their "conflicting natures, their lopsided co-

---

1 Yu, Synesthetic Metaphor, p. 22.
2 Ibid., p. 28.
3 Keck, Paradise Retold, p. 28.
4 Lacombe, Resistance in Futility, p. 431.
5 Mosca, Crossing Human Boundaries, p. 48.

evolution and the way in which they ultimately consume one another."[6] Thus, the function of words in literature surpasses mere linguistic representation.[7]

In Atwood's trilogy, the power of rhetoric emerges as a central theme, with its influence and limitations explored extensively. Both corporations and religious groups such as the God's Gardeners rely heavily on verbal manipulation to achieve their goals.[8] This theme is also reflected in the narrative style, as shifts in writing techniques highlight different aspects of the story: for instance, "the spliced words reflect the world of the compounds and biotechnology" and the "semi-religious prayer-like ritual words are reminiscent of the time of Adam One and the Gardeners."[9] Paula Lopez Rua similarly delves into the linguistic aspects, illustrating how language is used by privileged groups, such as scientists, to shape reality and maintain the status quo.[10] For instance, they make "youth, health, beauty, sexual pleasure, birth control and scientific and technological advances appear as highly desirable."[11] The choice of specific vocabulary such as "happy, new, youth, health, bliss, paradise," serves to foster positive perceptions of the group in power.[12] Ultimately, this group employs language to control behavior by "narrowing thought," achieved through simplification of vocabulary, and contributing to "mental restraint."[13]

In essence, whenever language is taken for granted, individuals become more susceptible to control, particularly in a society that undervalues the humanities and treats words solely as tools for manipulation.[14] Snowman's struggle with language is evident "not only through his exasperated attempt at communicating with the Crakers, but also through his nostalgic approach to the language of the past."[15] Language itself is elusive, resisting fixed and predictable meanings. Snowman was also "trained to sell items that might well be seen as abominations if described ac-

---

6 Ibid.
7 Mosca questions whether Atwood is "trying to posit a bleak future for any possibility of linguistic representation" and whether she may seek to "explore new representational territories" (Crossing Human Boundaries, p. 49 f). John Moss contemplates a similar question, offering a more optimistic outlook, suggesting that "language in Atwood's jurisdiction may incarcerate the reader and still set us free" (Haunting Ourselves, p. 3). However, Atwood may also endeavor to transcend the logic of representation altogether.
8 Cf. Mosca, Crossing Human Boundaries, p. 47.
9 Bone, Environmental Dystopias, p. 636.
10 Rua, Manipulative Power, p. 150.
11 Ibid., p. 152.
12 Ibid., p. 161.
13 Ibid., p. 162.
14 In short, "[a]rt is reduced to marketing, in the service of science and numbers, which has allowed the CorpSeCorps to take power with little resistance" (Gretzky, After the Fall, p. 52). This trend is echoed in the novels of Shteyngart and Powers, too.
15 Storey/Storey, History and Allegory.

curately; he learns to *massage words*, and this skill is precisely what makes him valuable to Crake who needs someone he can trust to market his Blyss-Pluss pills."[16] Thus, it is not just the pills themselves that precipitate the apocalypse, but also the stories people embrace—the promise of bliss. Jimmy's skill in manipulating words, also understood as a "massage" of words or form of polishing,[17] is just as responsible for the world's demise as Crake's scientific pursuits.

Many scholars argue that Atwood's trilogy concludes with the message that "if humanity does not survive, something essential to humanity—the act of *storytelling*—will somehow be kept alive."[18] Atwood presumably reveals that "the essence of humanity is not DNA, but our capacity for stories and art."[19] Michaela Keck also suggests that the novels pinpoint "storytelling as the distinguishing characteristic of humankind" and Toby "seeks to contain her dread of death with storytelling."[20] However, the trilogy also challenges the idea of an inherent "essence of humanity," including the concept of storytelling, because stories and art connect the human with the nonhuman world rather than being uniquely human traits. Storytelling not only helps Toby confront her fear of death but also helps her navigate what it means to feel alive, ultimately leading her to embrace death rather than flee from it. At the same time, Atwood "disrupts language as an exclusively human affair."[21] She demonstrates that storytelling is not solely a human pursuit, as evidenced by Crakers learning it from humans and their successful communication with pigoons through singing. Even Blackbeard yearns to have his own journal.

However, journal-keeping transcends mere self-expression or creating a space for individual privacy—a turn toward inner life. It becomes part of a ritual aimed at enhancing Crakers' awareness of the world beyond themselves, fostering embodied and embedded awareness. In his essay, Paul Hamann explores "how closely entangled notions of privacy and private correspondence are with traditional forms of enacting this privacy in reading and writing," highlighting how, by the trilogy's end, "reading and writing are again emphasized as crucial forms of giving shape to experiences of the private."[22] Specifically, he considers Toby's diary-keep-

---

16 Sutherland/Swan, Margaret Atwood, p. 28 f; emphasis added.
17 The concept of "polishing" to describe the process of editing and writing is introduced in Richard Powers' novel and is elaborated on in chapter twelve.
18 Bouson, "Joke-Filled," p. 352.
19 Gretzky, After the Fall, p. 53.
20 Keck, Paradise Retold, p. 37.
21 Jennings, Anthropocene, p. 30.
22 Hamann, Under Surveillance, p. 73. In this context, he also references Spacks, who frames the birth of the novel as inextricably linked to notions of privacy: "the developing novel of the eighteenth century helped to consolidate as well as to explore the notion of an inner life," adding that a

ing and how she passes "the concept of human individuality" to Blackbeard by introducing him to the "private practices of reading and writing."[23] However, an alternative interpretation is also possible, for reading and writing are not solely understood as "private practices." Blackbeard highlights other aspects that humans often overlook in their preoccupation with individuality.

> Now I have added to the words, and have set down those things that happened after Toby stopped *making* any of the Writing and putting it into the Book. And I have done this so we will all know of her, and of how we came to be. And these new Words I have *made* are called the Story of Toby.[24]

The words "made" by Blackbeard are titled the "Story of Toby." Even in this brief description, it becomes uncertain which words belong to whom—thus, drawing attention to the notion of interbeing, remembering Toby, and understanding their origin, but also their interpenetration—as the "I" is as much the story of someone else.[25]

Most significantly, this passage highlights an overlooked element: materiality. Writing is made, and Blackbeard makes words—the verb "make" appears twice in this context, reinforcing the act of construction, building, and assembling using materials. Words are then likened to bricks, gold, clothes, furniture, or a cake—not just symbolic, immaterial signs, but actual substances. This materiality is emphasized in this passage, too:

> Now this is the book that Toby made when she lived among us. See, I am showing you. She made these words on a page, and a page is made of paper. She made the words with writing, that she marked down with a stick called a pen, with black fluid called ink, and she made the pages join together at one side, and that is called a book.[26]

While quoting this passage, Rano Ringo and Jasmine Sharma emphasize the "cognitive labor" described by Blackbeard, stating: "The book typifies Toby's cognitive

---

belief "in that inner life's reality and importance necessarily led to its cultivation; hence, to a perceived need for privacy" (ibid., p. 65).
23 Ibid., p. 74.
24 Atwood, *MaddAddam*, p. 387; emphasis added.
25 "The book charts Toby's words uttered through Blackbeard, merging the two voices into one. Blackbeard's voice embellishes the genre of writing by fusing itself with Toby's narrative. Ultimately, he inserts Toby into the story of his own, one that he undertakes to complete after Toby's death. *MaddAddam* begins with the voice of Toby and ends with the voice of Blackbeard, integrating feminine and masculine, human, and posthuman entities into a unique dialogue. 'This is the end of the story of Toby.'" (Ringo/Sharma, Reading, p. 122)
26 Atwood, *MaddAddam*, p. 385.

labor that Blackbeard yearns to imitate. It not only presents the first written account of posthuman reality but also describes the meta-fictionality of the novel itself. It is writing about writing, how writing came into existence."[27] Yet, the paragraph teems with another visible meaning right on the surface, so obvious that it does not require hermeneutical labor, though it is easily overlooked due to its simplicity: Blackbeard does not describe "cognitive labor" as much as he emphasizes the materiality of the book. The paper, pen, ink, and other physical elements, although familiar to humans, often go unnoticed and thus remain unknown. They exist in the background, overshadowed by the focus on intellectual pursuits.. Yet, Toby had to scavenge for writing supplies before she could even start writing her journal. In the process, she does not merely "realize her subjectivity"[28] but her writing also forms the basis of community belonging, thus inextricably linking the two.

In this context, the Crakers appear childlike not because of their innocence or gullibility, but due to the powerful ways in which they shed light on the "unknown known," practicing a different form of mindfulness that does not aim to transcend things.[29] According to J. Paul Narkunas, "Atwood describes the human as creative force and material limit embedded in reality that no technological and financial innovation can *transcend* due the *materiality* of the body and the *limits* of human intelligence or mind."[30] In the same vein, the primary function of reading is not predicting or imagining extraordinary worlds, as the discourse on science fiction implies, but making the materiality of the body and the limits of knowledge visible. Atwood, therefore, "employs the aesthetic as a critical technique of world making and materiality to challenge technocapitalism [...] nature, God, and bodies become tools for understanding complex processes that exceed the limits of human knowledge."[31]

---

27 Ringo/Sharma, Reading, p. 122.
28 Ibid., p. 118.
29 Transcending "thingness" becomes a staple of the human, regardless of the agenda. What connects everything in the novel, from techno-capitalism to the ecocritics, is "an unrecognized faith in the human ability to correct life's imperfections through scientific rationalism and/or directed will —human, divine, natural, or otherwise. In short, there is an ironic residual Enlightenment humanism amid all the posthuman technological innovation, transhumanist futurist discourse, and non-anthropocentric thinking" (Narkunas, Between Words, p. 2). It appears as if Atwood produces two versions of paradise: "Crake's techno pagan and Adam One's eco-millennialist paradise. Seemingly opposed to each other, both are patriarchal versions of human dominance refracted through evolutionary science and ecology" (Keck, Paradise Retold, p. 25 f).
30 Narkunas, p. 5, emphasis added.
31 Ibid., p. 6.

Reading and writing are not just tools for the dissemination of knowledge, nor mere instruments that provide the "potential for amelioration."[32] The bedtime stories for the Crakers suggest that knowledge "becomes diffused among the two species through constant cross-questioning and seeking of innovative responses,"[33] but they also become part of a familiar routine that connects them all. Toby's journal looks like an example of *écriture feminine* that expresses a "bisexual writing style that is fluid and flexible."[34] Additionally, it also highlights the closeness developed between the human and the nonhuman.

Atwood positions literature's value within a critical posthumanist context where the written text is considered "one of many ways of communicating rather than essential," precisely because "[b]eing named, having words, reading and writing are the traditional differentiators between human and not human."[35] Similarly, Atwood's novels imply that literature's value does not lie in crowning humanity or showcasing the power of imagination. Instead, literature serves as a space akin to nature,[36] allowing the human to step down rather than up, to acknowledge species horizontally rather than vertically, and to reconnect with the body and practice recognition. It is not about "saving" humanity, but rather about repositioning it within its environment; not about focusing on inner life or constructing a private space or individual voice, but rather about embracing a concert of voices.

Consequently, the role of literature transcends mere storytelling; its role is seen to reside in its ability to raise embodied awareness. John Moss claimed that Atwood's brief description—"These stories are real as kitchens"—refuses to "settle into meaning [and] excites the mind on a visceral plane."[37] It is precisely this "visceral plane" that tends to be ignored not only in readings of Atwood, but in debates over the role of literature more generally. There is an anthropocentric bias at the core of these debates, as they overlook the ways in which texts function as nonhuman actors that pull the readers outside of themselves, rather than solely illuminating their innermost lives.

Atwood's use of literary synesthesia urges readers to reconnect with a body that is intertwined with a rich environment, rather than solely delving into human thoughts and feelings. It prompts acknowledgment of the notion of inter-being, where the novel and the reader engage in an intimate dance, intertwining

---

32 Ringo/Sharma, Reading, p. 112.
33 Ibid., p. 118
34 Ibid., p. 121.
35 Bone, Environmental Dystopias, p. 634.
36 Atwood develops a "satirical homology in which whatever happens to nature happens to language and vice versa" (Garrard, Reading as an Animal, p. 238).
37 Moss, Haunting Ourselves, p. 4.

with one another. While Francesca Ferrando argues that "the epistemological recognition of the encaged animal as an agent of knowledge can only be experienced by humans on an *empathic* level, underlying the limits of current interspecies communication,"[38] Atwood updates this perspective: literature can mediate a form of interspecies recognition, not necessarily through empathic means, but by redirecting attention back to the body and its complex interactions with the world. "From a critical posthumanist perspective, human corporeality makes us irrevocably dependent and interdependent, embedded within ecological and technological systems, rather than independent of them."[39]

It is precisely this interdependence and affectivity that literature can rescue in a world dominated by a "paucity of sensation."[40] This "lack of affect" disconnects individuals from their embodied experiences and fuels a craving for sensorial stimulation, as evidenced by the populace's eagerness to buy the BlyssPluss pill.[41] While "biotechnology focuses exclusively on the technological body, to the detriment of affective life, relational identity, and care," literature seems to counter this trend by introducing not only "vulnerable, dependent, and affective subjects,"[42] but also vulnerable, dependent and affective nonhumans. In other words, Atwood is cautious not to make affective life a staple of the human only.

Gina Wisker suggests that the trilogy underscores the importance of preserving "arts, compassion, creativity, passion, imagination, humanity, and diversity," warning that without these elements, "humankind, nature, and the reason for all life are under threat of extinction."[43] However, from all these concepts, it is only "humankind" which is endangered. For instance, "[t]he pigs indulge in human rituals, know about weapons and can communicate through the Crakers, and they feel grief and are cunning. They are able to make a treaty and form an alliance with the remaining humans."[44] Many qualities that humans consider exclusive to their species are actually present in other species as well. Hence, instead of seeking something unique to distinguish "us" from "them," Atwood advocates mutual recognition and "response-ability." Harland's assertion that the greatest value of fiction lies in aiding "survival, touching the heart in such a way as to fore-

---

[38] Ferrando qtd. in Bone, Environmenta Dystopias, p. 635; emphasis added.
[39] Defalco, Maddaddam, p. 437.
[40] Ibid.
[41] "What Atwood's novel continues to endorse is not humanity's capacity for collective action toward social change but, rather, its inextinguishable individualism, not its capacity for reason but its susceptibility to emotion" (Brydon, Atwood's Global Ethic, p. 455)
[42] Defalco, Maddaddam, p. 442, 443.
[43] Wisker, Imagining, p. 421.
[44] Bone, Environmental Dystopias, p. 633.

stall disaster and allow escape," interprets Atwood's work as a "therapeutic corrective."[45] However, the novels aim to transcend this therapeutic viewpoint.

Literature is not merely therapeutic but also a communal space that compels us to be responsible. "Atwood provokes her readers to think the unthinkable by seeming to find a remedy to humanity's ills not only in interspecies cooperation but also in interspecies breeding."[46] Yet, this "interspecies breeding" appears to already manifest in the act of reading itself; or, it is perhaps more broadly understood not only as giving birth to human offspring, but also to nonhuman ones—such as books. Calina Ciobanu suggests that "at the end of the world, Atwood reserves another possibility—a mode of reproducing the world beyond reproduction—for 'woman' as well. This she leaves to Toby, who gives birth not to a baby but to a book."[47] Books become such spaces of "interbeing" that ensure future survival, not by elevating the status of the human, but by illustrating what it means to feel alive. Feeling alive is not just some minor affect that is taken for granted, but rather the catalyst for "response-ability." Thus, literature cultivates mindfulness—not just towards ourselves and our inner thoughts, but also towards the nonhuman world.[48]

"These stories are real as kitchens"[49] is brimming with meaning. It summons the image of a familiar setting, evoking a sense of intimacy and sustenance, where food is prepared and consumed—a tangible space within a home dedicated to nourishment and survival; a physical shelter permeated with smells, tastes, and sounds.[50] Similarly, stories are crafted and consumed, essential for survival and providing solace. They also evoke multisensory experiences that break the boundaries of words, leaking into the outer world, where they illuminate the "unknown known" of life. This includes a "pervasive sadness" or "awareness of loss"[51] intertwined with the pleasure of feeling alive. The affect of aliveness encompasses not only joy but also a sense of mourning for what has already passed:

---

45 Harland, Ecological Grief, p. 584.
46 Bouson, "Joke-Filled," p. 343 f.
47 Ciobanu, Rewriting the Human, p. 161.
48 In the end, human writing serves as "the archival remnant and basis for a new media archaeology," while "nonhuman forms of 'writing' come into their own"; thus, "the novels accomplish this task by staging the extinction of a genre, the novel itself fading into still another order of yet-to-be-named textuality" (Yates, Improbable Shepherds, p. 414).
49 Moss, Haunting Ourselves, p. 3.
50 Interestingly enough, in my analysis of Richard Powers' novel *Generosity: An Enhancement*, I will also delve into a breakfast scene set in a kitchen.
51 Harland, Ecological Grief, p. 585.

These images are hard to face, but they keep her present to her own situation and the need to be on guard. As she wakens, she recalls Adam One warning against the Pillar of Salt and his instruction, "Don't look back" (25). These are the images that keep her focused on survival. Maintaining routines, staying fed and watered, she recalls, stave off the negative influences of the imagination, such as the "voices that tried to get into her head, as such voices do when you're solitary. . . . It was like a trance, or sleep-walking. Give yourself up. Give up. Blend with the universe" (137).[52]

Paul Harland's analysis draws attention to Toby's struggle to maintain her sense of self amidst solitude. He also underscores the demanding nature of storytelling, reminding us that the vocation of a storyteller is a "'hard thing,' not meant for personal pleasure or mere self-expression."[53] Rather, literature becomes a way of fostering vigilance, survival, and community. Solitude is depicted as a trance-like state or sleep-walking, rather than mindfulness.

In the end, Toby gives in to those voices urging her to blend with the universe, leaving the reader with a sense of grief or sorrow despite the seemingly happy conclusion.[54] However, viewed from another angle, the trilogy's final message could also be interpreted similarly: as an invitation to confront loss rather than seeking redemption or utopian ideals. Literature confronts readers with taboo subjects and uncomfortable topics they prefer to avoid, such as death. In this context, Toby's act of blending with the universe takes on a courageous significance in a world focused on moving forward with life.

The trilogy concludes with existential questions framed within a posthuman context: is Toby's final suicidal act a sign of hopelessness, despair, and meaninglessness, or is it another way of experiencing life beyond the human? While the novels leave these questions unanswered, certain insights can still be gleaned. For instance, the trilogy lacks a "salvific balm that heals all wounds—no magical fish [...] There is no restoring the world to its former splendor."[55] So, Atwood is weary of the optimistic outlook prevalent in many contemporary apocalyptic narratives, which often portray survival as a feasible outcome. Instead, perhaps a

---

52 Ibid., p. 596.
53 Ibid., p. 598.
54 The "too chirpy" life described in the final pages of the trilogy and the impressive number of children who are born suggest a specific perspective from which the ending should be viewed: as Raschke points out, in the French tradition, the equivalent formula for "they lived happily ever after" is *"ils eurent beaucoup d'enfants"*—they had many children ("Postmodernism" 26, 29). Thus, "the ending should be seen in the category of a fairy tale and not as something that ought to be taken seriously: not all's well that ends well" (Koziol, From Sausages to Hoplites, p. 284).
55 Raschke, No Magical Fish, p. 91.

"more productive view would be to take care of the world we have."[56] Despite this somber outlook, Atwood's portrayal of survival scenes retains a sense of beauty, joy, and vitality, as evidenced by her use of literary synesthesia. This depiction reflects her concept of "ustopia," where the life and death wishes are paradoxically conjoined.

---

[56] Ibid. What both Jimmy and Toby do with their writing is caring. For instance, Yates interprets "Jimmy's mundane epiphany" as a "peripheral citation of pastoral" and he demonstrates how his shepherding is "less of the Crakers as 'sheep' than the possibility of their relation to a future without him. No distributive violence here. Only the care and an awful lot of waiting, waiting around to see what the Crakers need and when they need it" (Yates, Improbable Shepherds, p. 420).

IV Self-Transcendence in the Age of Empathy

Introduction

In the United States, the founding creed revolves around the "pursuit of happiness," suggesting political relevance[1] and tacit knowledge embedded within the term. This "pursuit" implies the belief in the "perfectability of one's own life," as evidenced by the proliferation of American self-help books.[2] Happiness, therefore, becomes a yardstick for "measuring and qualifying lives,"[3] distinguishing between normalcy and deviance. Additionally, it encompasses "the social-Darwinist notion of competition" and is central to the "myth of expressive individualism."[4] The question arises: does science uphold or challenge this myth, and how does it approach the concept of happiness?

---

[1] Happiness economists like Sir Richard Layard were convinced that the main and most legitimate goal of politics should be to "maximize the sum of happiness in society," which they saw as primarily a matter of maximizing pleasure (Cabanas/Illouz, *Manufacturing*, p. 31). This philosophy harkens back to utilitarianism, with Jeremy Bentham being one of its foundational figures.
[2] Paul, Tacit Knowledge, p. 210.
[3] Ibid.
[4] Ibid.

11 TED Talks on "What Makes You Happy?" and the Science of Happiness

The playlist "What Makes You Happy?" features fourteen talks exploring various aspects of happiness. These talks delve into the relationships between happiness and choice,[6] happiness and science,[7] happiness and gratitude,[8] happiness and material possessions,[9] and happiness and the body.[10] Dan Gilbert's and Robert Waldinger's talks are also listed among the most popular talks of all time, and Gilbert's talk is additionally featured among the most popular science talks. This section will mostly deal with the talks on the relationship between happiness and science, as some of the other talks have already been tackled elsewhere,[11] but also because it aims to trace the discourse on happiness in science.

11.1 Science Meets Self-Help: "Where Do You Go to Find Happiness?"

The image of the playlist "What Makes You Happy?" evokes associations of happiness with the innocence, playfulness, and liberating joy of childhood, depicted through a young girl swinging and smiling. The bottom-up angle of the picture, capturing the moment the girl reaches the peak of her swinging movement, suggests an upward gaze toward the clear blue sky. This movement toward the sky conveys feelings of calmness, peace, and serenity, along with a sense of self-transcendence. Simultaneously, the image portrays an everyday activity—a simple, commonplace pastime—emphasizing its ordinariness. The fact that the young girl wears pink house slippers reinforces this sense of the ordinary, evoking a feeling of homecoming. Consequently, the image embodies a tension between notions of greatness and simplicity, juxtaposed within this playful game where the girl's feet seemingly leave white traces across the sky. Thus, notions of higher purpose, meaning or destiny emerge

---

6 Gladwell, Choice, Happiness, and Spaghetti Sauce; Schwartz, Paradox of Choice.
7 Gilbert, Surprising Science; Waldinger, What Makes a Good Life?; Csikszentmihalyi, Flow; Etcoff, Happiness and its Surprises; Kahneman, Riddle of Experience vs. Memory.
8 Steindl-Rast, Want to Be Happy?; Trice, Remember to Say Thank You.
9 Norton, How to Buy Happiness; Hill, Less Stuff, More Happiness.
10 Gutman, Hidden Power of Smiling; Ensler, Happiness in Body and Soul.
11 See, for instance, Steindl-Rast in 8.1. Mindfulness and Self-Help, and Gutman in 5.2. Self-Surveillance.

∂ Open Access. © 2024 the author(s), published by De Gruyter. [CC BY] This work is licensed under the Creative Commons Attribution 4.0 International License. https://doi.org/10.1515/9783111389929-016

Figure 5: Image for the playlist "What Makes You Happy?" accompanied by the caption: "Everyone wants to be happy. But how, exactly, does one go about it? Here, psychologists, journalists, Buddhist monks and more gives (*sic*) answers that may surprise."

within fleeting and transitory moments. As a snapshot of a larger movement, happiness itself appears ineffable yet far-reaching in its transient occurrence.

Throughout the 21st century, capitalism has fostered "a huge and powerful economy of happiness."[12] The science of happiness not only encourages individuals to seek out happiness but also places blame on them if they fail to achieve "successful and fulfilling lives."[13] Happiness, in this context, is more than just an emotion; it is a commodified concept, representing a "specific and normative model of selfhood" primarily defined in "psychological and emotional terms," strongly influenced by market dynamics.[14] Cultivating happiness as a habit involves adopting science-based techniques that facilitate self-control.

The necessity for managing emotions or self-regulation is fundamental for achieving happiness, a trend exemplified by mobile applications like Happify, as noted by Cabanas and Illouz. They argue that the popularity of these self-tracking apps reflects both the growing expectation for individuals to take charge of their health and well-being and their willingness to engage in daily self-monitoring and

---

[12] Cabanas/Illouz, *Manufacturing*, p. 115.
[13] Ibid., p. 10.
[14] Ibid., p. 116.

management.[15] Moreover, individuals are shaping their identities based on societal assumptions and expectations regarding thoughts, actions, and emotions.[16] But what defines the mindset, behavior, and actions of a "happy citizen"? Examining the techniques promoted by science is insightful for several reasons, particularly because it appears to shift the focus away from individualistic self-help approaches toward promoting prosocial behaviors indicative of an "Age of Empathy":

> The 20th century was the Age of Introspection, when self-help and therapy culture encouraged us to believe that the best way to understand who we are and how to live was to look inside ourselves. But it left us gazing at our own navels. The 21st century should become the Age of Empathy, when we discover ourselves not simply through self-reflection, but by becoming interested in the lives of others. We need empathy to create a new kind of revolution. Not an old-fashioned revolution built on new laws, institutions, or policies, but a radical revolution in human relationships.[17]

Roman Krznaric makes a case for the "Age of Empathy" in his article "Six Habits of Highly Empathic People," featured in the *Greater Good* magazine. However, the notion that empathy can be cultivated as a habit to "improve the quality of our own lives"[18] still aligns with the ethos of self-help culture.

The Greater Good Science Center, located at the University of California, Berkeley, serves as an authority on the science of happiness.[19] It disseminates its knowledge through various channels, including the *Greater Good* magazine, which provides insights into well-being. Moreover, the Center offers the first MOOC (Massive Open Online Course) on positive psychology, titled "The Science of Happiness." Hosted on the edX platform, an American online course provider established by Harvard and MIT, this self-paced program aims to provide "practical, research-backed tips on living a happy and meaningful life."[20] Additionally, the Greater Good Science Center extends its outreach through a podcast, among other resources.

The podcast explores the science of happiness and has garnered recognition as an editor's pick and one of the top ten science podcasts on iTunes. Hosted by award-winning professor of psychology, Dacher Keltner, each episode introduces a "happiness guinea pig" who explores various practices aimed at enhancing hap-

---

15 Ibid., p. 125f.
16 Ibid., p. 127.
17 Krznaric, Six Habits.
18 Ibid.
19 It is worth noting that during the Covid-19 pandemic, the *Greater Good* was also featured in Facebook's Covid-19 Info Center, so it is the main authority in questions of psychological health, including in (and especially in) times of crisis.
20 Gregoire, Free Online Course.

piness and who shares their personal experiences. The episodes conclude with a reflective segment featuring a scientific expert who discusses the practice and highlights important research studies or findings related to the topic. In its first episode, Keltner poses the question: "where do you go to find happiness, to pursue happiness? You know, the new-age gurus and the books, the self-help books in the bookstores certainly have lots of answers, or at least, they think they do. But science has taken a crack."[21] However, it is worth noting that the podcast itself also contributes to the self-help culture by addressing this question and suggesting ways "to find more joy" through scientific insights.

Among the main learning objectives of the online course, the instructors emphasize understanding the connection between happiness, human connection, and prosocial qualities like "compassion, altruism, and gratitude," as well as applying lessons to enhance "self-understanding."[22] The course features ten ungraded happiness practices, each linked to particular podcast episodes, including activities such as three good things, active listening, random acts of kindness, forgiveness, mindfulness, self-compassionate letter, best possible self, gratitude letter, gratitude journal, and awe walk. Many of these practices involve confessional work, such as writing down or recording feelings, thoughts, or impressions related to positive experiences. While these practices may help with "hedonic adaptation"[23] and boosting happy feelings, there is a risk that the focus on positivity could lead to self-censorship. The boundaries between positivity and the "tyranny of positivity"[24] are not always clear, especially since these techniques prioritize happiness to the exclusion of other emotions.

The uses of confession in the podcast are multifaceted: guests not only confess to Keltner during their interviews but also share parts of their written or recorded confessions. Thus, confessions serve not only as a stylistic device but also as objects of scientific study and facilitators of happiness. Similarly, in "The Surprising Sci-

---

21 Keltner, Three Good Things, 00:01:03.
22 Keltner/Thomas, Course Syllabus, p. 5.
23 In the episode on "Three Good Things," Sonja Lyubomirsky—a renowned positive psychology professor at UC Riverside—defined hedonic adaptation as the tendency to take familiar things for granted: "when things are familiar, then we don't tend to notice them or pay attention to them very very much" (00:10:16).
24 Cain, *Bittersweet*, p. 118. In an interview for Forbes, Susan Cain defines the tyranny of positivity as: "the cultural message that all of us are sent that no matter what is happening, we should be putting on a happy face, that we should be soldiering through it and whistling cheerfully. I call it the tyranny of positivity and some people call it toxic positivity. What it really is, is a cultural directive that says, *Whatever you do, don't tell the truth of what it's like to be alive.* That said, it's still important to have boundaries. You don't have to divulge everything" (Cording, In New Book; emphasis added).

ence of Happiness," Harvard psychologist Dan Gilbert employs confessions alongside statistical research to present his findings on the notion of "synthetic happiness" and to illustrate how individuals adapt to "major life traumas."[25] In other words, confessions possess the same authoritative weight as scientific research. They provide further validation and support for Gilbert's theory, with their authenticity and reliability taken for granted.

The TED speaker references three confessions published in *The New York Times*. Initially, Gilbert keeps the identity of those confessing anonymous, setting the stage for potentially shocking revelations. One confession, "I'm better off physically, financially, mentally...," was made by disgraced congressman Jim Wright, who lost everything after a book deal.[26] Another statement, "I don't have a minute's regret. It was a glorious experience," was uttered by Moreese Bickham, a seventy-eight-year-old man who had spent thirty-seven years in prison despite being innocent.[27] Lastly, the confession "I believe it turned out for the best" came from Harry S. Langerman, who missed the opportunity to buy the McDonald's franchise in 1949.[28]

Gilbert utilizes these confessions in order to illustrate how happiness can be synthesized, even when individuals do not satisfy their desires. He suggests an alternative understanding of happiness, one that is not tied to traditional markers like wealth, power, prestige, or freedom; rather, it emerges paradoxically when needs remain unfulfilled. However, Gilbert fails to acknowledge the potential pressure these men may have felt to present only positive perspectives. This is especially relevant considering their statements were published in *The New York Times*, a renowned American newspaper known for its extensive coverage that reaches "beyond news and politics."[29] Esteemed as a reliable source of information on subjects that "touch our readers' daily lives,"[30] this publication even includes "guides" on their website, such as "How to Find a Hobby," "How to Dress Up," "Make the World a Better Place," or "How to Be Happy."[31] Consequently, *The New York Times* employs self-help rhetoric and seeks to inspire its audience.

---

25 Gilbert, Surprising Science, 00:08:15, 00:03:53.
26 Ibid., 00:05:20.
27 Ibid., 00:05:25.
28 Ibid., 00:05:27.
29 Journalism, *New York Times Company*.
30 Ibid.
31 The guide on how to be happy offers advice such as "conquer negative thinking," "controlled breathing," "rewriting your story," "get moving," "practice optimism," "choosing a happy community," "spending time in nature," "declutter," "spend time with happy people," "money doesn't buy happiness," "buying time promotes happiness," "be generous," "volunteer," "give yourself a break" (Pope, How to Be Happy).

Confessions also presumably serve as a form of catharsis, providing a sense of satisfaction and fulfillment. This notion reinforces the prevalent belief in contemporary US-American culture that "happiness is sharing," which may contribute to the resurgence of confessional culture. The popular dictum "happiness is only real when shared," popularized by the movie *Into the Wild*, similarly replaces the Thoreauvian ideal of solitude with an emphasis on human connection. Likewise, the science of happiness appears to shift the narrative of happiness from individual pursuits to prioritizing human connection. In the first week of the online course, the instructors address the cultural interpretation of happiness, advocating a departure from the European-American model and instead emphasizing social connections, compassion, kindness, cooperation, and reconciliation—all of which have a "relationship orientation."

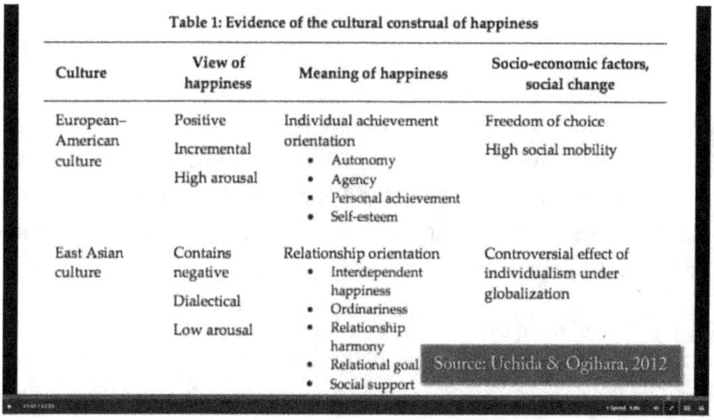
Table 1: Evidence of the cultural construal of happiness

Culture	View of happiness	Meaning of happiness	Socio-economic factors, social change
European–American culture	Positive Incremental High arousal	Individual achievement orientation • Autonomy • Agency • Personal achievement • Self-esteem	Freedom of choice High social mobility
East Asian culture	Contains negative Dialectical Low arousal	Relationship orientation • Interdependent happiness • Ordinariness • Relationship harmony • Relational goal • Social support	Controversial effect of individualism under globalization

Figure 6: "Evidence of the Cultural Construal of Happiness." From: Uchida & Ogihara, 2012, featured in *The Science of Happiness* online course.

Throughout the episodes of the podcast, there is a consistent emphasis on social behavior. For example, the concept of "self-esteem" is challenged and replaced with self-compassion.[32] However, paradoxically, self-compassion is justified using similar rhetoric, suggesting it can enhance personal motivation and drive for self-improvement. Similarly, Michael Norton argues that spending money on others increases happiness, urging the audience to engage in more "pro-social" behav-

32 Keltner, Quieting.

ior: "People who spent money on others got happier; people who spent it on themselves, nothing happened."[33]

In this discourse, the goals remain the same, with only a shift in language and proposed solutions. These scientific techniques still operate within the realm of self-help. Rather than critically confronting self-help culture, the science of happiness expands its scope, lending it further legitimacy. The promotion of "prosocial behavior" could be seen as a way to disguise the same individualistic values.[34] Ultimately, the rationale behind these techniques highlights their primary benefit to the self—"you spend on other people in order to make yourself happy."[35]

Director of the Harvard Study of Adult Development, Robert Waldinger, is a psychiatrist and psychoanalyst known for his talk on "What Makes a Good Life? Lessons from the Longest Study on Happiness" (2015). At the outset, he seeks to dispel myths linking happiness with wealth or fame. Before delving into his research findings, Waldinger poses thought-provoking questions: "But what if we could *watch* entire *lives* as they unfold through time? What if we could study people from the time that they were teenagers all the way into old age to see what really keeps people happy and healthy?"[36] He then reveals that the Harvard study has accomplished just that—for seventy-five years, "we've *tracked* the *lives* of 724 men,[37] year after year, asking about their work, their home lives, their health."[38] The choice of words, such as "watched" and "tracked," suggests that life is treated as a commodity subject to scientific scrutiny. However, the question remains: What constitutes the data used to define lives?

> To get the clearest picture of these lives, we don't just send them questionnaires. We interview them in their living rooms. We get their medical records from their doctors. We

---

33 Norton, How to Buy Happiness, 00:04:00.
34 The emphasis on compassion, kindness, altruism, and generosity highlights prosocial behaviors that recent studies link to happiness. For example, Delia Fuhrmann's "Being Kind Makes Kids Happy," Alex Dixon's "Kindness Makes You Happy... and Happiness Makes You Kind," and Elizabeth W. Dunn and Michael I. Norton's "How to Make Giving Feel Good" are essays published in the *Greater Good* magazine. These readings are offered in the online course during the third week, which focuses on compassion and kindness. However, even a single examination of the titles suggests the individualistic approach underlying these practices.
35 Norton, How to Buy Happiness, 00:06:15.
36 Waldinger, What Makes a Good Life?, 00:01:30; emphasis added.
37 The focus on men shows the patriarchal focus of the study. However, at one point, Waldinger mentions: "And when, about a decade ago, we finally asked the wives if they would join us as members of the study, many of the women said, 'You know, it's about time'" (00:05:34).
38 Ibid., 00:01:58; emphasis added.

draw their blood, we scan their brains, we talk to their children. We videotape them talking with their wives about their deepest concerns.[39]

As such, besides these men's confessions, researchers have access to a wealth of private and intimate details, including health data and family dynamics. This invasion into privacy is justified under the premise of studying "lives" rather than individual selves.

The study's conclusion underscore the toxicity of loneliness and challenges the notion that happiness stems from wealth, fame, or hard work. Instead, it emphasizes the significance of "good relationships."[40] This underscores a shift toward prioritizing social interactions over individualistic pursuits, suggesting a paradigm shift toward a communal perspective—or what could be termed a "getting out of the self" perspective. However, despite these implications, Waldinger ultimately circles back to an individualistic worldview, which may align with TED's aesthetic. He reinforces an egocentric viewpoint by suggesting that these findings could protect one's health and brain function, including memory. In other words, he suggests that close relationships matter because they benefit the self, rather than being inherently valuable in their own right.

This is what could be termed *the self-help pitfall:* when feelings like empathy or compassion become skills or techniques to be learned, they become individual pursuits rather than genuine exercises in human connection. Often, these pursuits are justified by invoking longevity or health benefits, transforming them into something else: for instance, they may no longer be about fostering a sense of community, but about prolonging life. So, they might conceal a form of "dangerous altruism"[41] that calls for prosocial behavior while still encouraging a focus on the self. This discrepancy again becomes evident in how scientists approach the topic of self-compassion.

Even though self-compassion embodies qualities such as kindness, tenderness, and empathy toward oneself, it is frequently used to promote introspection, an inner scientist mindset, and self-analysis. Likewise, contemporary calls to "save humanity" often appeal to universality to mask the underlying focus on individual

---

39 Ibid., 00:05:13.
40 Ibid., 00:06:43, 00:06:09.
41 As previously discussed in Margaret Atwood's chapter, the term "dangerous altruism" is borrowed from Richard Powers' novel *Generosity: An Enhancement*, and it is employed throughout this book to describe the critique presented by the novels under examination.

self-improvement.[42] Such assertions of universality overlook geographical, cultural, and historical contexts, perpetuating a humanist approach that prioritizes individual self-improvement under the guise of benefiting the human species.

11.2 Self-Compassion and "Looking at it Outside of Yourself"

In "The Varieties of Self-Transcendent Experience," psychologists explore various forms of *self-loss* accompanied by feelings of *connectedness:* mindfulness, flow, peak experiences, mystical-type experiences, and positive emotions such as love or awe. The authors suggest that these experiences can lead to "positive outcomes, such as well-being and prosocial behavior."[43] Contemporary self-help culture has also seemingly embraced this "reduction of self-centeredness and selfish motivations"[44] by emphasizing self-transcendence. The main critique against self-help—the focus on individualism—appears to be addressed and neutralized in this approach. Self-transcendence is also sometimes interpreted as a "*value* emphasizing universalism and benevolence," contrasting with "self-enhancement values focused on personal power-seeking."[45] However, the boundaries between self-transcendence and self-enhancement are not necessarily clear. In other words, claims of human universality could conceal the same focus on self-improvement that still permeates self-help culture, as the emphasis remains on improving oneself for the benefit of the human species.[46]

These two trends are evident within contemporary self-help culture as well. Firstly, there is a shift from self-focus to self-loss, which is here referred to as the annihilational component: "Self-loss should thus be considered an *alteration of consciousness* with potentially pathological or positive consequences."[47] Secondly, there is the "relational component,"[48] which emphasizes closeness, intimacy, and social connection. These two components complement each other, suggesting

---

42 Under the Enlightenment's assertion of universality lies a Eurocentric, colonialist, and racialized discourse, a point emphasized by the postcolonial critique of scholars like Edward Said or Gayatri Spivak.
43 Yaden et al., Varieties, p. 2.
44 Ibid.
45 Ibid., p. 3; emphasis in original.
46 Contemporary science novels (Atwood; Powers; Shteyngart) critique this assertion of universality as a manifestation of "dangerous altruism," an aspect I delve into further in my forthcoming paper in the *Miranda* journal.
47 Yaden et al., Varieties, p. 7; emphasis added.
48 Ibid., p. 8.

a transition from an individualistic society to an interconnected world that is perceived as *home:*

> For example, William James observed that one outcome from mystical experiences can be the feeling of *being at home in the universe* (as cited in Sagan & Druyan, 2011, p. 333). Similarly, Einstein remarked that one of the most important questions that one can ask is whether the universe is a "friendly place" (Goldman, 2002). STEs may provide both a temporary, yet emphatic "yes!" in answer to Einstein's question and turn, for a while, a threatening universe *into a warmer and more inviting home.*[49]

The notion of the universe as a new home for the self is a theme often explored in science fiction narratives dealing with space colonization.[50] In these stories, it typically represents humanity's last hope for survival, implying that leaving Earth behind is necessary for continued existence. However, self-transcendent experiences do not require physical movement through space; instead, they involve an "alteration of consciousness."[51]

Self-transcendence thus combines personal fulfillment with the broader imperative of preserving humanity. It posits that self-improvement benefits not only the individual but also plays a crucial role in securing the future of humanity. The narrative of human enhancement relies on this same premise to spread its ideas, too. This evolving discourse within self-help, emphasizing humanity's redemption, underscores self-improvement as an even more urgent and relevant endeavor. The science of happiness contributes to shaping and solidifying this narrative shift, albeit at the expense of potentially overshadowing other social concerns and individual struggles.

The *Greater Good* podcast has popularized the concept of self-transcendence or "getting outside of the self." Self-compassion, for instance, extends beyond a personal attitude or feeling; it involves "being connected to the larger humanity."[52] Furthermore, this connection entails a loss of self, as Keltner confesses:

> But the other reason that I think it's effective has a lot to do with how when you sort of step away from first person perspective you take sort of a *third person perspective*, you're dampening down the emotionality of the experience. All the negative affect that you could feel, you're able to literally *distance yourself,* have a *calmer* and more balanced perspective. So

---

[49] Ibid., p. 10; emphasis added.
[50] For an exploration of the theme of home, homelessness, and what it means to belong, see also my essay on "Be-Longing in TED Talks on 'What is home?' and Contemporary Postcolonial Fiction" (2022).
[51] Yaden et al., Varieties, p. 7.
[52] Keltner, Quieting, 00:06:49.

> I think it helps in that cognitive emotional way as well to look at the situation from somebody else's perspective, pretend *you're looking at it outside of yourself*.[53]

Interestingly, self-compassion is portrayed here in detached terms rather than warm ones, despite its intended purpose of adopting a friend's voice to self-talk. The lack of emotional engagement and the calm, distancing viewpoint evoke a rational perspective, rather than empathy.[54]

Alternatively, empathy is primarily understood in rational terms and is mainly used as a label to describe the same principle of scientific objectivity. Self-transcendence thus becomes synonymous with the supremacy of reason. The objectivity inherent in the third person perspective further reinforces the rhetoric of the rational self. It manifests itself as a different form of self-mastery, strengthening the self rather than losing it. Self-monitoring evolves into a scientific pursuit, as the methods of scientific inquiry are applied to dissect the self—the self becomes a citizen scientist of its own life. Although self-compassion should presumably quieten the self-critic in one's head,[55] the scientization of inner life also perpetuates an analytical and investigative attitude toward the self.

In "A Better Way to Talk to Yourself," Keltner also shares a personal experience to further illustrate the concept of getting outside of the self:

> So the basic idea of the gaining perspective on negative events practice is you kind of *get outside of your own immersed point of view and you look at yourself.* My first experience of this was kind of comical. My parents told me they were getting divorced. I was 16 and it was traumatic. And I remember that night I had this chance to go bounce on a trampoline with friends, and I literally was getting perspective on my life by like *floating in the air.* [...] research suggests that start to *see ourselves through the eyes of an outside observer,* and that helps us deal with our negative feelings in a more constructive way. [...] What we think is happening with these *distant self talk instructions* [...] that can be sometimes really useful for helping people *think more constructively and objectively* about really painful life experiences.[56]

Once again, Keltner emphasizes the objectivity of this exercise, suggesting that self-compassion paradoxically presupposes neutrality, impartiality, and detachment. It appears to define a similar attitude to that described in mindfulness.[57]

---

53 Ibid., 00:13:40; emphasis added.
54 Similarly, anger management in the workplace and the "advice literature on successful management incessantly requires that one examine oneself as if through someone else's eyes, thus suggesting that one adopt another's point of view to increase one's chances at success" (Illouz, *Saving*, p. 90).
55 Cf. Keltner, What to Do.
56 Keltner, A Better Way, 00:06:54; emphasis added.
57 See the previous chapter on mindfulness and self-vigilance in this book.

The parallels to mindfulness become even more evident in the meditative practice of gratitude. Mindfulness, gratitude, and self-compassion—they all contribute to quieting down the incessant stream of thoughts that often trap the self in its own mind. In response to Samuel Getachew's confession of practicing self-compassion after receiving a lower grade, Keltner remarks: "The science shows, you know, you practice a little self-compassion like you did, Samuel, and you feel calmer or a little bit of oxytocin flowed through your blood. But really, interestingly, and most connected to what you're saying is you *ruminate* less."[58] In this case, self-transcendence is equated with halting or mitigating anxious and negative thoughts, echoing the discourse surrounding mindfulness.

Besides compassion, awe is another "self-transcendent positive emotion."[59] Awe walks are another technique that could potentially induce a loss of self. For instance, Pete Docter confesses: "I generally, I come in with a lot of anxiety and things that I'm chewing on and somehow, again just being out, and *not so self-focused* I think, for one, you're kind of aware of all these other things it kind of *takes you out of your own head.*"[60] In this case, self-transcendence relies less on rational distancing and more on sensory experiences:

> It's been kind of a stressful day. A lot of changes going on and… I smell… spaghetti. That's kind of good. There's sounds everywhere and you think of just traffic but just heard someone whistle, sound of leaves, kind of comforting that sound. Actually a lot of smells. Beyond the spaghetti now, I'm getting candles. Maybe a little bit of, some sort of like, lavender. There's a fork. Somebody dropped a fork. Where did that come from?
>
> The more I start to notice, I want to slow down investigate things. I've always liked walking because it's kind of therapeutic. I feel like it relaxes me. Instead of focusing on outward stuff, I usually go inward, but I find then I can get home and realize I didn't actually see anything. I was just in my head the whole time.[61]

Keltner interprets Docter's experience in terms of savoring. "Studies show that by taking time to stop and smell the roses or what researchers call *savoring* it can enhance happiness and boost feelings of appreciation and gratitude just by paying attention to the sights smells and sounds that we often neglect."[62] Craig Anderson, a guest in the same episode, also defines savoring as "paying attention to and really appreciating positive things," and Keltner adds that it is "sort of being absorbed in

---

58 Keltner, How to Be, 00:13:25; emphasis added.
59 Yaden et al., Varieties, p. 5.
60 Keltner, Walk Outside, 00:06:25; emphasis added.
61 Ibid., 00:07:03; emphasis in original.
62 Ibid., 00:13:28; emphasis added.

or taking in what's good around you or what's beautiful"[63] (00:14:28). Tchiki Davis defines savoring as an "attempt to fully feel, enjoy, and extend our positive experiences [...] a good way to develop a long-lasting stream of positive thoughts and emotions."[64] In various ways, these authors describe savoring as another form of positive thinking, akin to an exercise in mindfulness that focuses on the positive. Daniela Ramirez-Duran further elucidates this aspect in her work on "Savoring in Positive Psychology":

> Bryant and Veroff (2007) define savoring as attending, appreciating, and *enhancing* positive experiences that occur in one's life. [...] Although intimately related to pleasure, savoring is more about *becoming aware of* the experience of pleasure and appreciating the positive emotions derived from that experience. To savor an experience, one must possess and apply a certain degree of *mindfulness and meta-awareness* (Bryant & Veroff, 2007).[65]

The focus on the sensorial and visceral aspects of the awe walk described by Docter takes a backseat compared to savoring, which is mostly defined in terms of mental effort and intentional attention to the positive. This stands in contrast to Keltner's emphasis on "being absorbed,"[66] which implies a complete engagement of attention away from the self. Savoring, thus, becomes another form of self-transcendence, even though Ramirez-Duran's distinction between savoring and meditation suggests that "savoring does not attempt to transcend the self, but to focus on pleasant feelings."[67]

Flow presumably differs from savoring because it requires "much less conscious attention to the experience."[68] The excessive focus on the reflective aspects of savoring turns it into a deliberate, rational or calculated experience. This implies that individuals have control over it and can choose to savor an experience. Whether it is reminiscence, savoring the present moment, or anticipation—savoring underpins practices such as three good things, the awe walk, or the best possible self. In other words, rationalizing these feelings and experiences is necessary for these techniques to be effective.

Despite their distinctions, mindfulness, savoring, and flow function as affective cousins or closely related concepts. They all form part of a scientific narrative on happiness that ostensibly aims at self-transcendence while tacitly reinforcing self-reflection. Flow, for example, is presented as another solution to self-rumination.

---

63 Ibid., 00:14:20, 00:14:28.
64 Davis, What Is Savoring?
65 Ramirez-Duran, Savoring in Positive Psychology; emphasis added.
66 Keltner, Walk Outside, 00:14:28.
67 Ramirez-Duran, Savoring.
68 Ibid.

Coined by Mihaly Csikszentmihalyi in his study on the psychology of optimal experience, flow has been heralded as "the secret to happiness" in his TED talk (2014). Self-help proponents also embrace the concept of flow. Musician Jason Silva, for instance, discusses his experience of flow in an Impact Theory video.[69] During his conversation with Tom Bilyeu, he explains the mental processes behind his creative work, describing them as "free associations" or "stream of consciousness":

> I try to put myself in an *altered state* before I do it and you talk about flow [...] flow is characterized by *getting outside of your self* and by outside of yourself I mean beyond the *monkey mind*, beyond the inner chatter, *beyond the inner critic* and the questioning mind, this excessive rumination and self-consciousness, deliberating whether you should ever get out and do something, you know just overthinking and too much scenario planning, too much *neocortical hardware* [...].[70]

Silva's description of flow touches on several important concepts. Firstly, the notion of an "altered state" harkens back to the countercultural movements of the sixties and the exploration of consciousness through drug-induced states, emblematic of the hippie culture's rebellious attitude and spiritual dimensions, which often sought to transcend conventional modes of perception. Secondly, the reference to the "monkey mind" possibly draws on Buddhist philosophy, suggesting an effort to quieten and "tame" the restless nature of the mind through disciplined practice: "the random, uncontrollable movements of the monkey symbolise the waywardness of the native human mind before it achieves a composure which only Buddhist discipline can effect."[71] Finally, the mention of "neocortical hardware" invokes the software-hardware analogy from information sciences, reinforcing a dualistic perspective on the mind and body. In various ways, these metaphors contribute to the belief in achieving a higher state of consciousness and propagate ideas of mind-over-matter, often sidelining the significance of the body.

11.3 Flow and Out-of-Body Experiences

Mihaly Csikszentmihalyi's original work on flow highlights the same "loss of self-consciousness [that] can lead to self-transcendence, to a feeling that the boundaries of our being have been pushed forward."[72] He presents flow as a challenging

---

[69] Impact Theory is a weekly interview show that explores the "mindsets of the world's highest achievers to learn their secrets to success" (*Impact Theory*).
[70] Bilyeu, Jason Silva, 00:14:14; emphasis mine.
[71] Carr, Mind-Monkey, p. 166.
[72] Csikszentmihalyi, *Flow*, p. 5.

activity that demands skill, blending action and awareness into an optimal experience that fosters "a sense of mastery."[73] Csikszentmihalyi describes flow as an exercise in concentration, control, and discipline, stating:

> One of the most universal and distinctive features of optimal experience is the people become so involved in what they are doing that the activity *becomes spontaneous*, almost automatic; they stop being aware of themselves as separate from the actions they are performing. It often requires *strenuous physical exertion*, or *highly disciplined mental activity* to enter a continuous flow.[74]

Csikszentmihalyi captures a tension between the spontaneity of flow—its automatic and instinctive qualities—and the intentional character that demands discipline and skill training. This tension appears to be resolved by suggesting that flow functions like a habit,[75] where the constant and intentional repetition of an activity leads to a sense of mastery that transcends mere control, evoking a feeling of surrender. Paradoxically, relinquishing control is not seen as the opposite of self-control but rather as its natural outcome. Csikszentmihalyi's concept of flow thus contributes to the idea of mind-power: "A person *can make himself happy*, or miserable, regardless of what is actually happening 'outside', just by *changing the contents of consciousness*,"[76] suggesting that individuals have the ability to manipulate their feelings and thoughts, including happiness.

Csikszentmihalyi presented his theory of "flow" in a TED talk, referring to it as "the secret to happiness" (2004). Flow is a concept that explores the idea of self-transcendence—getting outside of the self. In his quest to understand happiness, Csikszentmihalyi turned to the study of creative individuals like artists and scientists. In this case, he posits a correlation between creativity and happiness, assuming that the more creative a person is, the happier they tend to be. According to this perspective, the genius would thus epitomize the happiest individual, representing the pinnacle of the actualized self. Happiness, therefore, is achieved not through fame or fortune but through experiencing flow. Csikszentmihalyi illustrates the concept of flow by sharing the confessions of the various artists interviewed, showcasing instances of flow in music composition, poetry writing, and figure skating. The first confession, offered by an American composer, depicts flow as an ecstatic state:

---

73 Ibid., p. 2.
74 Ibid., p. 4; emphasis added.
75 See also, the brief analysis of habit and the denigration of the body in chapter two.
76 Ibid., p. 2; emphasis added.

> You are in an *ecstatic* state to such a point that you feel as though *you almost don't exist*. I have experienced this time and again. *My hand seems devoid of myself*, and I have nothing to do with what is happening. *I just sit there watching it in a state of awe and wonderment*. And [the music] just flows out of itself.[77]

This confession delves into the concept of self-loss by describing an ecstatic state where the individual feels detached from their own being. Despite this feeling, the self remains present as a passive observer, watching its own hand as if it has a life of its own, as if a split occurs between the individual's body and its self-awareness. Csikszentmihalyi offers his interpretation of this confession during the talk:

> Well, when you are really involved in this completely engaging process of creating something new, as this man is, *he doesn't have enough attention left over to monitor how his body feels*, or his problems at home. He can't feel even that he's hungry or tired. *His body disappears*, his identity disappears from his consciousness, because *he doesn't have enough attention*, like none of us do, to really do well something that requires a lot of concentration, and at the same time to feel that he exists. *So existence is temporarily suspended.*[78]

Csikszentmihalyi repeatedly emphasizes the idea of the vanishing body as a means of transcending the self and suspending existence, akin to an out-of-body experience. He suggests that during the flow state, basic biological needs are overlooked, although it is unclear how he arrives at this conclusion bearing in mind that the quoted confession does not mention hunger or tiredness. Csikszentmihalyi's assertion that the body cannot be monitored or disappears seems contradictory given the focus on the hand in the confession. It could be argued that the composer's attention is actually directed toward the body or a specific bodily part, such as the hand, especially considering the sense of awe and wonder it evokes. Similarly, Csikszentmihalyi emphasizes the lack of attention, but the opposite could also be argued: that the composer experiences heightened awareness. Therefore, Csikszentmihalyi's interpretation may reflect his own assumptions and expectations rather than the composer's actual experience, just like any reading. The speaker presents the confession of a poet in order to further illustrate the effortless and spontaneous qualities of flow:

> It's like *opening a door* that's floating in the middle of nowhere and all you have to do is go and turn the handle and open it and *let yourself sink into it*. You can't particularly force yourself through it. You just have *to float*. If there's any gravitational pull, it's from the outside world trying to keep you back from the door.[79]

---

77 Csikszentmihalyi, Flow, 00:05:20; emphasis added.
78 Ibid., 00:08:38; emphasis added.
79 Ibid., 00:11:04; emphasis added.

The metaphor of the door invokes imagery similar to Jacob's ladder or Aldous Huxley's *The Doors of Perception*, which suggests mystical insight often associated with psychedelic experiences. The imagery of floating and sinking evokes self-absorption, facilitating self-loss and mindfulness. Csikszentmihalyi suggests that Einstein used a similar description when contemplating the forces of relativity, reinforcing the idea of flow as a genius experience, perhaps inspired by the poet's mention of "gravitational pull." The third confession portrays the same automatism of flow:

> It was just one of those programs that *clicked*. I mean everything went right, everything felt good... it's just such *a rush* like you could feel it could go on and on and on, like *you don't want it to stop* because it's going so well. It's almost as though you don't have to think, it's like everything goes *automatically without thinking*... it's like you're *on automatic pilot*, so you don't have any thoughts. You hear the music but you're not aware that you're hearing it, because it's a part of it all.[80]

The perfect alignment of forces facilitating the flow experience suggests a serendipitous moment, akin to living out one's destiny. This echoes Goethe's famous phrase in Faust—"Linger, you are so fair." Being on "automatic pilot" is depicted positively, for the self merges with the environment. This blurring of boundaries between self and surroundings recalls Wright's definition of an "extended version of the not-self."[81] In other words, the self disappears—the pilot who usually controls everything through its thoughts. Self-vigilance and control are replaced with an instinctive manner of engaging with the world. However, Csikszentmihalyi does not elaborate on this example and these effects in more detail.

His talk takes a different turn as he connects flow to the ways in which CEOs describe success. The CEO, being the chief executive officer responsible for an entire company, embodies notions of control. The examples he references resemble traditional self-help advice, such as Anita Roddick encouraging individuals to pursue their passion or Ibuka Masaru discussing "the joy of technological innovation."[82] The speaker argues that these examples illustrate how flow can manifest itself in the workplace. However, these statements do not follow the same logic or structure as found in the previous examples. The connections seem arbitrary at best, yet Csikszentmihalyi continues to frame flow using a career-oriented language.

Csikszentmihalyi's interpretation of flow is intertwined with work life, linking happiness to one's career and blurring the boundaries between life and work life

---

80 Ibid., 00:12:05; emphasis added.
81 Wright, Buddhism.
82 Csikszentmihalyi, Flow, 00:13:34.

—personal and professional spheres.[83] Flow becomes emblematic of "intrinsic motivation,"[84] echoing Dan Pink's analysis of intrinsic incentives—an idea aimed at fostering self-direction and autonomy in the workplace culture. The feelings of ecstasy and serenity associated with flow suggest a transcendent quality to the experience, where the focus on the self paradoxically coexists with an emphasis on its escape. And yet, Csikszentmihalyi's notion of "getting out of the self" is also depicted as "growing beyond the boundaries of the ego,"[85] implying more of an expansion and enhancement of the self rather than its dissolution.

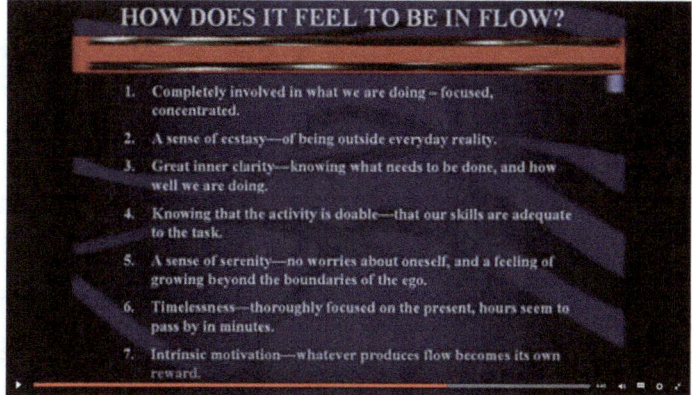

Figure 7: Mihalyi Csikszentmihalyi's answer to the question "How does it feel to be in flow?" in "Flow: The Secret to Happiness," TED talk (00:13:48).

An additional slide introduces flow by using a business model that emphasizes challenges and skills as the two main vectors:

Upon closer examination, this chart reveals an intriguing dimension: flow implies possessing an even higher degree of control—it represents what comes after mastery or control. This notion is reiterated throughout by emphasizing that flow requires extensive training. Csikszentmihalyi's concept of flow does not challenge self-control or the individualism inherent in the business model. Quite the contrary, it positions flow as the natural progression beyond mastery. By juxtaposing images of the businessman and the genius, it suggests that successful work operates similarly to the imaginative insights of a genius. The idea of "getting out of the self"

---

83 See also the discussion of success in the second section of this book.
84 Csikszentmihalyi, Flow, 00:13:48.
85 Ibid.

during moments of flow is used to imply notions of self-transcendence, presenting flow as a higher form of consciousness.

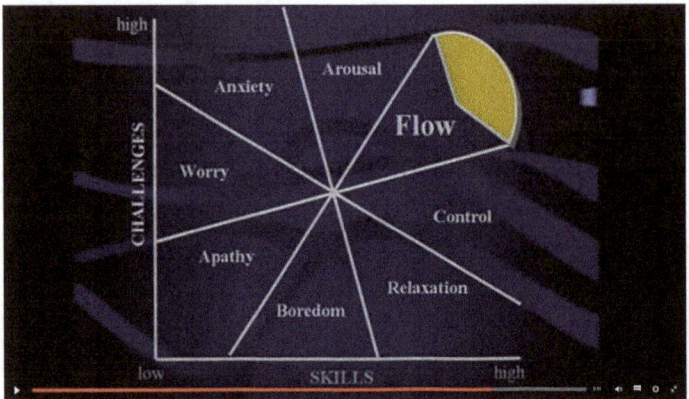

Figure 8: Mihalyi Csikszentmihalyi's chart for flow in "Flow: The Secret to Happiness," TED talk (00:15:30).

Cognitive researcher Nancy Etcoff approaches happiness from an evolutionary perspective in her talk on "Happiness and Its Surprises," where she also discusses flow, albeit in a different context. She begins by highlighting the shortcomings of traditional routes to happiness, such as self-help books, antidepressants, and illegal drugs, noting that despite their prevalence, rates of depression and anxiety continue to rise. Etcoff suggests that the science of happiness could serve as the missing link in psychotherapy, especially since Freudian psychoanalysis largely focused on the concept of "ordinary misery."[86] She further explores the "human emotion system,"[87] emphasizing its dual nature encompassing both positive and negative emotions, with the negative often exerting more significant impact. Etcoff examines this predisposition from an evolutionary perspective:

> If we were only governed by pleasure we would not survive. We really have *two command posts*. Emotions are short-lived intense responses to challenge and to opportunity. And each one of them allows us to *click into alternate selves* that *tune in, turn on, drop out* thoughts, perceptions, feelings and memories. We tend to think of emotions as just feelings.

---

86 Etcoff, Happiness, 00:02:35. Etcoff's reference to Freud's "ordinary misery" is echoed in Shteyngart's novel, where Eunice and Lenny subscribe to a similar notion of "common unhappiness" (*Super Sad*, p. 295f).
87 Ibid., 00:02:45.

> But in fact, emotions are an *all-systems alert* that change what we remember, what kind of decisions we make, and how we perceive things.[88]

Etcoff's explanation of emotions is interesting for several reasons. Firstly, she employs the military terminology of "command posts," suggesting that emotions exert control over and in organizing behaviors and actions. Secondly, she recalls the famous phrase "turn on, tune in, drop out" popularized by Timothy Leary, implying that emotions can provide access to higher levels of self-awareness. In this case, emotions function similarly to phsychedelic drugs, capable of opening doors to new levels of consciousness.

Finally, the notion that emotions are "an all-systems alert" points to their vigilant aspect: they steer the attention of the self and inform its worldview. She explains this vigilance of emotions by arguing that "the body can both look for opportunity and also protect itself from danger, at the same time. And they're sort of two reciprocal and dynamically interacting systems."[89] The awareness raised by happiness has been neglected, even if humans are born "pleasure-seekers."[90] Etcoff mentions a few examples of innate or ancient pleasures that influence happiness, such as: biophilia (or the profound response to the natural world), sociability, and cooperation.

> One problem that psychology has had is instead of looking at this *intersubjectivity*—or the importance of the social brain to humans who come into the world helpless and need each other tremendously—is that they focus instead on the self and self-esteem, and not *self-other*. It's sort of "me," not "we." And I think this has been a really tremendous problem that goes against our biology and nature, and hasn't made us any happier at all.
>
> Because when you think about it, people are happiest when in *flow*, when they're absorbed in something out in the world, when they're with other people, when they're active, engaged in sports, focusing on a loved one, learning, having sex, whatever. *They're not sitting in front of the mirror trying to figure themselves out, or thinking about themselves.* These are not the periods when you feel happiest.[91]

Etcoff's emphasis on the profound need to belong echoes Waldinger's assertion that loneliness is toxic and happiness can be found in social relationships. She builds a strong case for intersubjectivity and advocates a shift from a focus on the self (and self-vigilance) to intersubjectivity; a transition from "I" to "we," which she also illus-

---

88 Ibid., 00:03:55; emphasis added.
89 Ibid., 00:05:16.
90 Ibid., 00:06:00.
91 Ibid., 00:09:25; emphasis added.

trates by referencing the concept of flow. Flow is used here to critique individualistic values, as well as the introspective act of self-monitoring. Instead of mediating the extraordinary visions of a genius, flow is present in ordinary activities.

Etcoff concludes by advocating a shift away from materialist values, which she argues cause people to overlook the "basic pleasures of life,"[92] to post-materialism. However, her reliance on Maslow's pyramid of needs contradicts her previous critique of self-esteem and her focus on "self-other."

> Maslow had this idea back in the 1950s that as people rise above their biological needs, as the world becomes safer and we don't have to worry about basic needs being met—our biological system, whatever motivates us, is being satisfied—we can rise above them, *to think beyond ourselves toward self-actualization or transcendence*, and rise above the materialist.[93]

Her reliance on Maslow's humanistic psychology to bolster her notion of "getting out of the self," "to think beyond ourselves," seems self-defeating, especially since she mentions self-actualization. In this case, her understanding of post-materialism implies a shift away from biological needs toward a higher state of consciousness that transcends the physical—a notion akin to an out-of-body experience. Despite her previous challenges to this focus on the self, she inadvertently reinforces it. Her final quotations further underscore this focus: "And Rilke, 'If your daily life seems poor, do not blame it; blame yourself. Tell yourself that you are not poet enough to call forth its riches.' 'First, say to yourself what you would be. Then do what you have to do.'"[94]

The "getting out of the self" paradigm presented in this playlist serves as a pretext to discuss humanity, yet it ultimately reinforces another individualist worldview. Under the premise of creating a better world and shared humanity lies an implicit invitation to embrace a belief in individual superiority—in the capacity for transcendence and continuous self-improvement. The opportunity to move beyond anthropocentrism and critically examine humanist visions is limited by the TED format and its aesthetic constraints. In other words, even talks that appear to divert attention away from the self or challenge it end up refocusing on self-awareness and the importance of self-vigilance.[95] In this case, self-vigilance also entails a duty to be happy and alive. While the concept of the "happiness duty" has been extensively discussed and theorized, *the duty to be alive* is another powerful rhet-

---

92 Ibid., 00:12:29.
93 Ibid., 00:12:44; emphasis added.
94 Ibid., 00:13:48.
95 Etcoff, Waldinger or Néry (and their talks) are just a few examples that end with a focus on the self, and they may be influenced by TED's aesthetics of individualism.

oric often intertwined with the onus to be happy. This duty typically translates into an obligation to transcend biological confines, thereby reinforcing a dichotomous view of body and mind.

Daniel Kahneman, a Nobel laureate and founder of behavioral economics, is regarded as the "world's most influential living psychologist" in the TED world. His talk on "The Riddle of Experience vs. Memory" (2010) is featured in both the "What Makes You Happy" and "Who Are You?" playlists. Kahneman presents a dichotomous view of the self: on the one hand, the experiencing self, which resides in the present moment, and on the other hand, the remembering self, which constructs the narrative of one's life and makes decisions. His talk suggests that memories are the most important deciding factor when it comes to achieving happiness. This concept harkens back to medieval notions wherein memory was considered "*the interior sense*," serving as the integrative force that "transforms *the rich but disordered experience of the external senses*" into "the stuff of selfhood, giving to that experience the shape and pattern of the interior sense itself."[96]

As a result, according to this perspective, bodily senses need to be sifted, explained, and transformed into data. Even the visual sense is predominantly valued for its physiological data. Many episodes of *The Greater Good* podcast repeatedly underscore the power of *eye contact* in fostering human connection and happiness. This point is reiterated across various contexts, including discussions on active listening,[97] random acts of kindness,[98] forgiving,[99] or gratitude.[100] Dacher Keltner keeps reminding the audience that "one of the really potent triggers of oxytocin in the sense of connectivity and trust and collaboration is eye contact."[101] Physiological responses are utilized to validate and reinforce the narrative of happiness, such as the release of oxytocin. Moreover, forgiveness, which is also construed as involving close, "face-to-face, eye-to-eye contact,"[102] offers additional physiological benefits by calming the fight or flight response.

Subjective experiences and feelings are often translated into physiological data and vice versa. Intimate moments, once rich with context and complexity, are oversimplified as mere responses to eye contact or other bodily stimuli. They are stripped of their social context and turned into individual, yet universal

---

96 Olney, Memory, p. 871; emphasis added.
97 Keltner, Listen.
98 Keltner, Making Kindness.
99 Keltner, How to Forgive.
100 Keltner, How Gratitude.
101 Ibid., 00:08:09.
102 Keltner, How to Forgive, 00:16:50.

and quantifiable responses.[103] This reductionism echoes the sentiments expressed by Ron Gutman in his talk on smiling or Amy Cuddy's discussion of "power posing." It suggests that happiness can be achieved through meticulous control of the body's smallest actions, while flow requires transcending biological confines. In "Happiness in Body and Soul," Eve Ensler reflects on her own relationship with her body, admitting, "I live in my body a lot, and I don't live in my head very much anymore. And this is a very heady place."[104] However, her assertion that we need to attach "our bodies to our heads"[105] perpetuates a dualistic understanding of mind and body. Ensler introduces the concept of "vagina warriors" as a new species that "can hold the violence in their bodies,"[106] complicating the discourse surrounding bodily autonomy and agency.

Counterintuitively, the playlist on happiness concludes with a story about violence. However, it is also a narrative of transformation: using grief as a pathway to joy, reminiscent of the "redemptive" perspective often found in American biographies.[107] According to Ensler, stories serve as vessels to "transmit information, where it goes into our bodies,"[108] thus affecting us at a visceral level. Stories and literature are envisioned as redemptive tools, echoing the ancient concept of catharsis—the purging of emotions through art. In contrast, contemporary literature challenges conventional notions of the body found in TED, embracing the raw and unfiltered experiences of the senses,[109] which become the basis of one's livelihood, rather than something to be controlled. Reading these texts does not necessarily offer comfort or resolution; grief remains palpable, pain unresolved, and synesthesia employed to evoke a profound emotional complexity—one that produces a lingering irritation.

---

103 Similarly, homes presuppose "life editing," such as moving from "3000 to 2000, from 1500 to 1000" square feet (Hill, Less Stuff, 00:04:40).
104 Ensler, Happiness, 00:12:23.
105 Ibid., 00:12:45.
106 Ibid., 00:13:02, 00:11:59. The label "vagina warriors" also challenges the universality of the discourse on humanity by highlighting the variety within a "species."
107 Cf. McAdams, Redemptive Self.
108 Ensler, Happiness, 00:12:14.
109 Or, the "disordered experience of the external senses," as Olney calls it (Memory, p. 871).

12 Richard Powers' *Generosity: An Enhancement* and the "Small Shared Joy" of Reading

Richard Powers' novel of ideas, *Generosity: An Enhancement*, critically engages with the scientific discourse on genetic enhancement and the culture of self-help that sustains it. Described as an "interdisciplinary novel,"[1] Powers' text intricately weaves together science and culture, offering not only a philosophical exploration of life, survival, and happiness but also a commentary on the power and relevance of literature in a "postfictional age."[2] The story centers around Thassa, an Algerian refugee and student in Russell Stone's class on creative nonfiction. Geneticist Thomas Kurton believes that Thassa's overwhelming happiness, or "hyperthymia," can be genetically isolated in order to find the happiness gene and enhance the entire population.[3] However, Thassa's life takes a drastic turn after agreeing to be studied and appearing on a television show called Oona—she becomes a "renegade" for selling her eggs.[4] Attempting to flee to Canada, Thassa finds herself pursued by the police, her flight ironically labeled by the media as "The Pursuit of Happiness,"[5] despite being anything but happy.

12.1 Self-Help Culture: "Dangerous Altruism"

The "pursuit of happiness" permeates every aspect of society, including written texts, making it "the single motivator and central motor of the text."[6] This suggests that even Powers' novel is not immune to its influence. In other words, it appears

---

1 Ghalleb, *Interdisciplinary Mind*.
2 Ickstadt, 'Asynchronous Messaging,' p. 37.
3 For further exploration of the cultural shifts catalyzed by the Human Genome Project and the metaphorical treatment of DNA as code, see my article on "Genetic Enhancement, TED Talks and the Sense of Wonder" and Alexander Scherr's essay on "The Emergence of 'Genomic Life Writing' and 'Genomic Fiction' as Indicators of Cultural Change." In this context, this chapter also aims to demonstrate how Powers' emphasis on the materiality of words, language, and literature offers a counterpoint to a discourse that often overlooks the materiality of DNA.
4 This scene also exposes the hypocrisy and double standards inherent in capitalist culture, which facilitates and even encourages such financial transactions while simultaneously condemning them as immoral. Additionally, it highlights the commodification of the female body, echoing themes present in Margaret Atwood's *MaddAddam* trilogy. Furthermore, Thassa's actions reveal not only a pursuit of profit but a naïve belief that she can and should please everyone.
5 Powers, *Generosity*, pp. 312.
6 Höpker, Happiness in Distress, p. 289.

to be both complicit with the culture of self-help and critical toward it.[7] From the outset, advertisements urge everyone to "Make your life just a little *perfecter*."[8] This grammatical mistake exposes the illusory nature of the pursuit, as the adjective "perfect" does not have a comparative form. Yet, in a society where constant improvement is expected, the notion of perfection remains elusive and unattainable.

Russell Stone is deeply entrenched in the culture of self-help, evidenced by his habit of reading self-help books and his role as an editor for the magazine *Becoming You*. One of the articles he edited focused on "how to fight depression by feeding squirrels."[9] Russell's brother takes a serotonin reuptake inhibitor, which presumably enhances his generosity, although his interactions with Russell suggest a self-absorbed demeanor. He makes assumptions without truly listening to his brother which leads Russell to lament the scarcity of genuine engagement "You never have anyone's full attention anymore."[10] Candace Weld, another character, works as a psychologist dedicated to helping individuals improve themselves, further illustrating the pervasive influence of self-help culture in the novel.[11] Even the narrator seems complicit in this culture, engaging in the same act of "polishing" as Stone, structuring the text along the lines of a tragedy in five acts, and incorporating recurring sentences resembling leitmotifs.[12] The narrator even hints at the possibility of an alternative ending, suggesting a desire for continuous improvement and revision.

---

[7] This complicity is marked and highlighted rather than concealed; there is a self-aware acknowledgment of its presence. It serves as a reminder of the ways in which the author, the novel, and the reader cannot simply position themselves outside the system but are intricately entwined within it.
[8] Powers, *Generosity*, p. 4; emphasis added.
[9] Ibid., p. 20. It is also interesting to note the presence of nature and the nonhuman in this context, serving as another avenue for self-healing or improvement, as commodified tools and objects to aid the human.
[10] Ibid., p. 42.
[11] At one point, Candace employs an analogy with two graphs to illustrate humanity's inclination toward narratives of progress: she suggests that people invariably favor the diagonal line over the straight one due to its promise of evolution. It shelters the potential for growth, akin to the plot of a novel that unfolds toward a climax and resolution. Through this analogy, Candance demonstrates how individuals are inherently complicit with a self-help perspective from which they cannot extricate themselves, but can only become aware of.
[12] Alexander Scherr has also highlighted the connections that Powers draws between "the genomic agenda of making the future predictable and the role of the Oracle in ancient tragedies" (Emergence, p. 129). Accordingly, this sensitivity to ancient Greece may not be an endeavor to polish his writing, but rather a method of underscoring the potency and significance of history, and how knowledge is predominantly derived from the past or viewed retrospectively.

At the same time, these invitations to continual improvement also imply that personal feelings are a matter of choice, something to be actively worked on—and it is the individual's responsibility to cultivate happiness. The commodification of feelings, as depicted in mass media, is humorously exposed in the novel. In Oona's show, reminiscent of *The Oprah Winfrey Show*,[13] the audience's reactions are orchestrated with the assistance of a trainer. Similarly, the public love and hatred for Thassa are virtually constructed through the narratives circulating in mass media. Thus, happiness becomes "one fungible commodity that the future will trade in," and Thassa herself is portrayed as a "publicly traded commodity" in an insecure "market" of feelings: "When we tire of happiness, someone will make a market in useful despair."[14] The public sphere becomes a playground of stories that shape both facts and feelings, blurring the lines between them: "feelings are the new facts" and "facts were never private."[15]

The "pursuit of happiness" infiltrates scientific endeavors as well, exemplified by ambitious scientists like Thomas Kurton who aim to genetically enhance humans. The phrase "Make your life a little perfecter" is interpreted literally, as scientists manipulate the "building blocks of life." The metaphor of carbon atoms and other molecules as these "building blocks" has become commonplace in scientific discourse. However, it also perpetuates notions of design, creativity, and the potential for manipulation—constructing life just like building houses, piece by piece. Similarly, in the novel, genetic enhancement entails discovering the "happiness gene" to liberate "the subjugated populace."[16] Kurton frames his mission as a battle against nature's in-built predispositions: "stress kept us alive. Natural selection shaped us for productive discontent, with glimmers of heavenly mirage to keep us going," and he argues that "depression had its uses once, when mankind was on the run."[17]

Kurton's rhetoric not only promises individual redemption but also suggests the salvation of the entire species. He envisions the possibility of an "upgraded version"[18] for future generations through artificial chromosomes, employing the language of information sciences to describe the future transformation of humanity. This discourse inherently compares humans with computers, assuming a dualistic view of mind and body while emphasizing the supremacy of the mind. Despite acknowledging that happiness is only chemical, Kurton suggests that the manipula-

---

13 See also Hamner, Predisposed Agency, p. 428; and Schäfer, Pursuit of Happiness, p. 274.
14 Powers, *Generosity*, p. 192, 220, 267.
15 Ibid., p. 217.
16 Ibid., p. 43.
17 Ibid.
18 Ibid., p. 106.

tion of the genome is achievable through the creative endeavors of scientific genius.[19]

The novel exposes the loose boundaries between science and science fiction in the public sphere, where science communication relies on spectacle and visual shows not only to inform the public but also to speculate on future breakthroughs. Kurton articulates his vision of enhancement in a science TV show titled "Over the Limit," stating, "Why shouldn't we make ourselves better than we are now? We're incomplete. Why leave something as fabulous as life up to chance?"[20] Scientists, by taking "life" into their own hands, believe they can effect change. Computer-generated images are employed to create a spectacle of "self-replicating information,"[21] using zoom effects and close-ups alongside voice-overs. The screen is filled with a "cavalcade of talking heads,"[22] further reinforcing the perception of genius. One scene in particular emphasizes Kurton's philosophy: "Superdrugs, smart drugs. Healthier people. Stronger people. Smarter people,"[23] followed by his transformation into a watercolor. Amidst this visual extravaganza, one brief comment appears to be overshadowed: "He's driven by a massively *dangerous altruism*."[24]

The film contains criticism as well, despite likely being included in the show as a form of praise.[25] The reference to Kurton's "dangerous altruism" seems to present his agenda as generous, kind, and benevolent. However, the "danger" lies in the inherent selfishness at its core, disguised as generosity. What was once viewed as hubris is now marketed as a humanitarian endeavor.[26] Generosity has been

---

[19] The novel introduces Kurton as a mad scientific genius pursuing immortality; he wears a "red medical-alert bracelet [that] instructs the finders of his dead body to act quickly, administer calcium blockers and blood thinner, pack his corpse in ice water, balance its pH, and call the 800 number of a firm that will helicopter in paramedics to begin cryonic suspension" (ibid., p. 24). This portrayal bears resemblance to the character of Joshie from Shteyngart's novel, and it is possible that the persona of Ray Kurzweil inspired both of these characters.
[20] Ibid., p. 21.
[21] Ibid., p. 23.
[22] Ibid., p. 21.
[23] Ibid., p. 22.
[24] Ibid.; emphasis added.
[25] Ines Ghalleb has also analyzed this scene, noting that "[e]ven though Anne Harter bashes his [Kurton's] intentions, the rest of the guest speakers disagree with her" (*Interdisciplinary Mind*, p. 39). It could be argued that, in this context, Harter's criticism might even be mistakenly interpreted as another form of praise, especially if the emphasis is placed on "altruism."
[26] Hamner has also commented on this discrepancy: "genomicist Kurton knows how to appear the very embodiment of scientific eminence but also a humble man who only wants to serve the public good. We see enough behind the scenes, though, to sense that Kurton suffers from as great an obsession with public attention as his narcissistic counterpart in Crichton's novel" (Predisposed Agency, p. 428).

commodified, used to adorn self-help culture. Happiness, once associated with individualism and competition, now emphasizes empathy and concern for others. The novel also critiques this shift, warning that an exclusive focus on empathy may be perilous. This is not only because it could conceal a selfish agenda, as seen in Kurton's case, but also because it could be mistaken for naïveté.

For instance, even when she is in danger of being raped, Thassa feels empathetic toward her attacker: she is more concerned about what John might do to himself than about her own safety. It seems as though this compassionate attitude also serves to protect her, as the "young man collapses in self-hatred."[27] In this case, Thassa appears to survive not by fighting or fleeing, but rather by displaying empathy. On the one hand, her altruism is beneficially dangerous, for it compels John to confront himself, to look at himself in the mirror, and release his grip on power. In other words, it shatters his illusion of control. In this respect, Thassa embodies the ideal of the emerging scientific trend of self-help: the generous, forgiving, and gratitude-filled self. On the other hand, her altruism is dangerous in a different sense: it exposes her vulnerability and sets her on a path to future "doom."

Alexander Scherr connects the rape scene with an attempt to control Thassa's life, viewing it as a "metaphorical representation of an individual life's subjection under external pressures of (narrative) control."[28] Furthermore, Karsten Piep suggests that this scene perpetuates a power dynamic and criticizes the "Orientalist promise of true happiness she is imagined to embody."[29] He adds:

> [N]either he nor the narrator (who may be one and the same) pause to consider that Thassa's repeated victimization might be enabled by the very notion of excessive happiness they continue to project onto her eroticized body (Powers 105). Equally unsettling is that Thassa appears to remain utterly oblivious of the larger implications of the sexual assault. Having refused to press charges against Thornell, Thassa, selfless to a fault, not only absolves her assailant, but allays Russell's feelings of guilt: "In the sparkle of her glance, she reassures him: John couldn't help himself, you know. The problem was inside him. The man just couldn't help himself."[30]

Therefore, this scene serves as a crucial juncture for grasping the novel's overarching argument. Thassa's remark is not solely a means of allaying Russell's guilt; it also underscores John's lack of bodily autonomy, though it does not excuse his abusive actions. On the contrary, it reveals not just a desire to manipulate lives, but to

---

27 Hamner, Predisposed Agency, p. 431.
28 Scherr, Emergence, p. 134.
29 Piep, 'You're Going to Make Us,' p. 51.
30 Ibid., p. 52; emphasis added.

exert control over bodies. This scene, therefore, signals the most dangerous attitude in society: the urge to dominate the body, which often leads to violence precisely because it resists control. It also offers a parallel to the genomic agenda, illustrating how attempts to genetically engineer the body underscore the limited extent of control. Consequently, the rape scene is significant not only for its metaphorical implications but also because it directly depicts the violence inflicted upon the body, highlighting the paramount issue of bodily abuse in contemporary society.[31]

Piep illuminates the novel's engagement with the "hippie Orientalism" of the sixties, a phenomenon it both challenges and perpetuates.[32] Thassa's remarkable ability to "convert bad feelings, which Ahmed associates with 'unhappy racism,' into 'good feelings,' which Ahmed connects to 'happy multiculturalism'"[33] is a central concern. Essentially, Thassa adheres to the "migrant's 'happiness duty' by taking pains not to relate her life story 'from or out of unhappiness.'"[34] Her autobiographical narratives consistently adopt a redemptive perspective,[35] exposing the prevalence of "neoconfessional"[36] discourse in American society. Thassa's influence on Russell and her peers mirrors the impact of self-help literature, as a "chronic, viral euphoria" seems to infect everyone and they are "all addicted to the woman's elation."[37] In the end, the disappearance of her journal[38] raises doubts about the authenticity of her happiness. Everett Hamner further suggests that much of Thassa's apparent cheerfulness may be fabricated,[39] complicating the novel's portrayal of happiness and authenticity.

Ultimately, Russell also ponders, "Maybe she has faked a good half of her bliss."[40] However, such interpretations arise in the context of Thassa becoming a "renegade,"[41] her sense of "coming apart,"[42] and her evident misery, suggesting

---

[31] Thassa's act of selling her eggs is another example of how bodies can be abused, which is correlated with her growing unhappiness, too.
[32] Piep, 'You're Going to Make Us,' p. 53.
[33] Ibid., p. 52.
[34] Ibid., p. 53.
[35] "The stories she shares with Russell and her classmates are set before the backdrop of civil war, genocide, expulsion, and personal tragedy, yet always begin and end on decidedly hopeful notes that put her audience at ease" (Piep 53).
[36] Gilmore, American Neoconfessional.
[37] Powers, *Generosity*, p. 35.
[38] Searching through her bag, Russell finds "no journal" there (Powers, *Generosity*, p. 315).
[39] Hamner, Predisposed Agency, p. 432.
[40] Powers, *Generosity*, p. 308.
[41] Ibid., p. 292.
[42] Ibid., p. 304.

a binary view where one feeling negates the other. Yet, the text does not necessarily support the notion that her happiness was counterfeit. Rather, it suggests that feelings, including joy, are interconnected and cannot be owned or manipulated. It is possible that a sense of unease always lurked beneath Thassa's apparent happiness, overshadowed by its radiant façade. Thus, the novel might argue that feelings cannot be artificially constructed and remain in a state of flux. This perspective helps explain why Thassa's happiness wanes over time and why Russell experiences moments of contentment despite his underlying melancholy. Additionally, their emotional states are influenced by their perception of generosity and selfishness.

The novel delves into the intricate relationship between egotism and empathy, revealing how such feelings can coexist rather than standing in opposition to each other. Throughout the narrative, Stone finds himself identifying with Thassa, even during her most distressing moments. Karin Höpker emphasizes his "boundless egotism," noting that he paradoxically treasures Thassa's presence more amid her suffering.[43] At the same time, this could also signify an empathic grasp of the emotional turmoil Thassa endures, as he himself has experienced similar feelings of despair and fragmentation, such as the "death wish"[44] or the sensation of "coming apart."[45] This nuanced portrayal suggests that sadness is not solely an individual experience but is intertwined with "mourning, empathy, and compassion."[46] Additionally, Stone's empathy is evident in his genuine concern for Thassa's well-being, as he reflects on the impact of constant demands for "magic mood bullets"[47] on her mental state.

As the novel progresses, Stone and Thassa seem to evolve in opposite directions. Thassa's alienation from her friends results in a move toward egotism, moodiness, and edginess. Conversely, Stone appears to exhibit an upsurge in empathy. However, these changes also highlight the limitations of empathy. It becomes a privilege that is challenging to exercise while enduring social exclusion, and it can only be practiced within the confines of personal experience. Paradoxically, Thassa remains an outcast regardless of her emotional state—whether happy or sad.

Across American society, any deviation from perceived "normalcy" is often pathologized. Heike Paul highlights how happiness has been used as a tool to conform to societal norms, frequently tied to the institution of the family. Yet, in Powers' novel, Thassa's happiness defies this conventional narrative, causing concern

---

43 Höpker, Happiness in Distress, p. 299.
44 Powers, *Generosity*, p. 36.
45 Ibid., p. 304.
46 Ghalleb, *Interdisciplinary Mind*, p. 31.
47 Powers, *Generosity*, p. 128.

for Russell. In her case, happiness takes on a dangerous aspect: in a society characterized by indifference and skepticism, happiness deviates from the norm. Happiness becomes a disease in a culture where narcissism prevails. This challenges the notion that happiness is solely an individual trait, suggesting instead that it arises from social connections and a sense of community beyond familial bonds. Thassa's happiness, particularly in the absence of her family, contradicts expectations based on her tragic past. Russell anticipates bitterness or trauma, rather than the "exuberant cheerfulness, empathy, and generosity of spirit"[48] Thassa displays. This discrepancy leads him to investigate her condition, framing her happiness as a form of sickness, termed hyperthymia by Candace Weld.

The pathologization of happiness is further reinforced by the belief that it behaves like a virus: a disease that "is more contagious than genetic."[49] The narrative suggests that "life is the disease,"[50] with Stone also experiencing its symptoms. This perspective challenges Kurton's belief that happiness is merely chemical and rejects determinism, as a virus exhibits its own autonomy. It is irreducible to nature or nurture alone, despite being influenced by both.[51] The novel grants agency to this feeling, echoing Elizabeth Gilbert's perspective on creative genius. In her talk, Gilbert introduces the concept of "daemons" and the idea of a creative spirit, a "genius":

> [T]he Romans did not actually think that a genius was a particularly clever individual. They believed that a genius was this, sort of magical divine entity, who was believed to literally live in the walls of an artist's studio, kind of like Dobby the house elf, and who would come out and sort of invisibly assist the artist with their work.[52]

---

48 Schäfer, Pursuit of Happiness, p. 265.
49 Powers, *Generosity*, p. 221. Happiness may be "one of those bugs that sits for a long time, so we don't even know we are infected. A virus can even change your genes, can't it?" (ibid., 239).
50 Ibid., p. 122.
51 The nature-nurture debate in Powers has been explored by other critics as well. Hamner, for instance, argues: "for Powers, human beings are neither the meaningless products of biological or authorial determinism nor all-transcending entities who can self-help their way out of anything. Instead, they are possessed, for a time, of a hybrid status, a predisposed agency. Their genes are not predictors of an absolute fate but prerequisites for multiple futures, each of which remains free to unwind in its own unforeseeable manner" (Predisposed Agency, p. 438). Heike Schäfer also identifies the ways in which the novel depicts the "feedback loops between genes and environment—which makes formulas like nature *through* nature or *Nature Via Nurture* [...] a lot more plausible than the old-fashioned nature *versus* nurture dichotomy" (Pursuit of Happiness, p. 268; italics in original).
52 Gilbert, Elusive Creative Genius, 00:06:47.

Gilbert's analysis sets out to challenge rational humanism and individualist notions of creativity. She does not merely reinforce the image of the genius as a "vessel" either, as she points to the laborious process of writing, too: "I'm not the pipeline! I'm a mule, and the way that I have to work is I have to get up at the same time every day, and sweat and labor and barrel through it really awkwardly."[53] Rather, she sees the creative process as a collaboration or an exchange with other nonhuman agents, much like the joy that behaves like a virus in Powers' novel. Feelings do not become part of identity; they cannot be possessed, nurtured, or manipulated. They behave like a nonhuman other that the individual self encounters in a generous exchange. Hence, generosity in the novel carries other connotations too: it does not merely define a sense of selflessness but also bountiful encounters with the nonhuman, offering an alternative way of being to the enhanced self-vigilance of American society.

12.2 Self-Descriptive Reminiscence: Russell Stone's "Creative Nonfiction"

Generosity: An Enhancement portrays the contemporary individual as self-conscious, scrutinized, fearful, and lacking in confidence. The narrator zooms in on Russell Stone, highlighting his insecurities, such as his tendency to "borrow" life philosophies and his shame and fear as a teacher whenever he tries to conceal *his shaking hands*[54] during his first encounter with the students. Stone's lack of confidence extends to his identity as a writer; he wants to take his pad out and write but hesitates, being "afraid of getting arrested for suspicious activity."[55] In a world dominated by visual and digital media, the act of writing becomes dubious, mirroring the obsolescence of reading depicted in Shteyngart's novel. Stone's self-doubt is further exemplified in another scene where he feels ill-prepared and lacks confidence in his choice of Graham P. Harmon's *Make Your Writing Come Alive.* This reliance on Harmon's book underscores the pedagogical aspect of writing and emphasizes its craft.

Self-help culture infiltrates even creative and innovative endeavors, such as writing, suggesting that even writers seek guidance on their craft. Paradoxically, while self-help ostensibly celebrates the power of imagination and self-confidence, it can also stifle them with its multitude of rules and guides. Moreover, the novel

---

53 Ibid., 00:11:50.
54 The metaphor of the shaking hands will be discussed in more detail in the following subchapter.
55 Powers, *Generosity*, p. 6.

throws into question the idea of self-confidence and the American tradition of self-reliance: Russell's lack of confidence is diagnosed by self-help culture as an imperfection to be fixed. However, viewed from a different angle, Russell's attitude may be seen as displaying a healthy dose of uncertainty and vulnerability rather than something to be healed.

Across American society, an enhanced sense of self-vigilance prevails, fueled by ocularcentrism. Whether through mass media or television, the dominance of the visual sense can evoke not only acute self-consciousness but also a diminishing capacity for affect, transforming simple joy into pathology.[56] Stone's "life philosophy" encapsulates this ethos: "When you're sure of what you're *looking* at, *look harder.*"[57] This belief reflects a sense of caution and skepticism, necessary to maintain a healthy distance from the unwavering certainty and confidence exemplified by figures like Kurton. Moreover, it symbolizes a visually-dominated world, where the act of looking and being looked at become pervasive even at the narrative level. The novel employs a third-person perspective, with the narrator observing a man and commenting on his appearance and behavior, while also delving into the man's innermost feelings and motivations—"he's dressed for being overlooked."[58] Ironically, in this instance, he is scrutinized by the narrator.

The narrator's descriptions are filled with comments such as "I picture him," "I know," "look again," "I watch him," "I force my eyes," "I stare at," or changes of feeling—"no, *look harder.*"[59] Most of these narrative tasks imply a visual activity of looking. Initially, the narrator struggles to see Stone's students in detail, as they hide behind the "shiny performance of youth,"[60] suggesting not only a lack of self-confidence but also a blockage of vision, where knowledge is not only limited but also obscured by the brightness of what is in plain sight. It is only later in the book, after Thassa has been introduced, that Stone's "details are coming to me now."[61]

This narrative comment challenges visions of authorial control, as the narrator appears to figure things out spontaneously rather than shape them deliberately. It suggests a different form of interaction between the narrator and the characters: not only is there no possibility of omniscience, but also vision alone does not

---

[56] See also the chapter on Margaret Atwood's *MaddAddam* in this book, which also tackles the "paucity of sensation" as a contributing factor to the apocalyptic scenario (Defalco, Maddaddam, p. 437).
[57] Powers, *Generosity*, p. 8; emphasis added.
[58] Ibid., p. 3.
[59] Ibid., p. 3f, 8.
[60] Ibid., p. 8.
[61] Ibid., p. 55.

suffice. Sole reliance on looking stages a play of gazes where everyone is caught in a house of mirrors, rather than paying attention to one another. This form of self-vigilance develops right from the opening pages, as the narrator keeps watching.

The detailed description of the man's spine, shoulders, and chin enhances the voyeuristic nature of the scene, instilling a sense of watchfulness and self-monitoring as the boundaries between the narrator and the man blur at times. Russell is not merely a character in the story; after Thassa's death, "art at last overtakes him, and he writes."[62] Various critics have also noted the ambiguity surrounding the narrator, who may potentially be revealed as Stone. For instance, the "likeness between Russell and Thassa" could be explained if "Russell is drawing on his memory to conclude his narrative."[63] However, there is more than just likeness between them; at times, the narrator adopts Thassa's words as if they were his own: "The time for deciding how much you like it is after you're dead,"[64] or when he attempts "to decide no more than God."[65] This borrowing of Thassa's life philosophies blurs the lines of narration, making it uncertain to whom those words originally belonged. Through this form of borrowing, Thassa herself becomes the narrator, too. In a different context, the narrator empathizes with Russell, borrowing his life philosophy: "It's his own fault, for thinking that Thassa's joy must mean something [...] I know exactly how he feels."[66]

The blurred boundaries between the narrator and the characters serve as a powerful means of giving voice to the characters, not just to one protagonist. It appears as if empathy operates on a narrative level as well, becoming the primary way characters gain agency. Scriptedness emerges as an important theme in the novel.[67] For instance, Stone grapples with "fighting the sense of being scripted."[68]

---

62 Ibid., p. 314.
63 Schäfer, Pursuit of Happiness, p. 282.
64 Powers, *Generosity*, p. 75.
65 Ibid., p. 320.
66 Ibid., p. 94.
67 Throughout the novel, characters appear to be "doomed" to certain outcomes: Kurton was destined to study genomics, Stone was "doomed to end up here, in her bed" (Powers, *Generosity*, p. 207), Candace's character "had her chained" (ibid., p. 245) when she violated her professional ethics, and even Thassa was compelled to become a public interest. However, despite Thassa seeming imprisoned by both her nature and environment, she manages to escape from both: her happiness gene does not prevent her from changing and experiencing a nihilistic episode, just as her traumatic experiences did not stop her from being a happy person. The "interpenetrating loops of inheritance and upbringing" (ibid., p. 249) are difficult to untangle, and one wonders if they tell the whole story. Thassa's final act of suicide can be interpreted as succumbing to the overwhelming pressures of her surroundings, but also as an escape from its labels: she demonstrates she is not Jen, and she offers a commentary on the fatality of the pursuit exemplified in the happiness pills.

However, if he is also the narrator, then these limitations are also self-imposed. The novel thus highlights the tension between being a victim of outer forces and scripts versus being the architect of one's own destiny, suggesting that the answer is more complicated. Numerous forces and agents are at play, making it impossible to be governed just by one.

Rather than implying an even greater imprisonment of the self, the multitude of agents—whether genetic data, social environment, free will, or other human-nonhuman interactions—with which the self interacts serves to highlight the unlikelihood that just one agent can dictate the entire narrative. Similarly, the self cannot simply fashion itself into what it desires, as there are too many actors at play. Free will alone is not enough, yet personal agency is possible. As Scherr argues, the story of Thassa's personality does not solely belong to her, Russell, or the narrator—it emerges as an "interwoven story" that arises "as an accomplishment of various actors."[69] Consequently, the novel shifts the focus to the flow of ideas and the network of actors, rather than solely emphasizing individual character development.

The preference for the third-person perspective of an "intimate outsider"[70] may also stem from this conviction. The boundaries between the third-person and the first-person perspective are not always clear, as they often seem to emanate from the same person. For instance, after describing the crowded train car, the narrator confesses: "Just brushing against them in memory makes me panic."[71] These connections become visible only in hindsight, upon re-reading the novel, aligning with what Scherr refers to as "the logic of recursion" or the principle of "anticipation of retrospection."[72] Thus, reading the novel requires a similar kind of confessional engagement that was involved in its writing, akin to what James termed "self-descriptive reminiscence."[73] This highlights the importance of memory and historicity in the novel, although not for the purpose of constructing a grand narrative or autobiography. The narrative does not pessimistically suggest that the past inevitably shapes the future,[74] nor does it promote the idea

---

68 Ibid., p. 81.
69 Scherr, Emergence, p. 133.
70 Borrowed from Sutherland and Swan's essay, the phrase "intimate outsider" (224) has been used to describe this new form of confessional writing that is neither too personal, nor completely detached—one that I have also used to describe the perspectives of Lenny in *SSTL* or those of Jimmy and Toby in *MaddAddam*.
71 Powers, *Generosity*, p. 4.
72 Scherr, Emergence, p. 138.
73 James, Critical Solace, p. 494.
74 Critics often emphasize the bleak and pessimistic worldviews evident in Powers' work (see Scherr, Emergence, p. 131), though that may not always be the case.

12.2 Self-Descriptive Reminiscence: Russell Stone's "Creative Nonfiction" — 249

that the future can be entirely shaped by individual will—rejecting both notions of scriptedness and total control.

The narrative of the "intimate outsider" serves as a new form of confessional expression that challenges traditional biographies, focusing instead on what the novel introduces as "creative nonfiction."[75] In other words, the novel adopts a cautious approach toward life writing, evidenced by the revelation that the narrator, presumably Russell, has been recounting his own experiences in the third person: this "self-distancing effect" underscores Russell's reluctance to prematurely impose narrative interpretations on human lives, even his own.[76] Furthermore, this approach transforms the entire novel "into a record of its own composition—rather like the human genome."[77]

The third-person perspective creates a chasm between the narrator and Russell, leading to various implications. For instance, self-surveillance becomes the primary intrapersonal relationship, the default mode through which the self relates to itself. However, this form of interaction is also subject to challenge, as demonstrated in the novel's opening pages:

> A man rides backward in a packed subway car. [...] *I picture him* [...] *I watch* until he solidifies. [...] Every few minutes, a voice calls over the speakers: If you observe any suspicious behavior or unattended packages... [...] *I force my eyes* back down over the scribbler's left shoulder, *spying* on his notes. The secret of all imagination: theft. *I stare* at his yellow legal pages [...] *I know* this man. [...] I know this story, like I wrote it myself. [...] His pen freezes in midair; *he looks up. I glance away, caught spying.* But his hand just hovers. *When I look back, he's the one who's spying on someone else. He's watching a dark-haired boy* across the aisle, a boy with *a secret quickening in his hand.* The boy quiets the bird. *The boy sees him looking*, and he hurries the bird back into a bamboo cylinder. *My spy* flushes crimson and returns to his notes. *I watch him* shuffle pages.[78]

The novel's opening pages set forth an interesting play of gazes, with an atmosphere permeated by heightened vigilance and suspicion. Notably, surveillance occurs in multiple directions, with spies themselves becoming subjects of observation. Even the narrator is caught spying, which challenges conventional notions of authorial control, as characters can stare back—Russell "looks up"[79] and the narrator "glance[s] away"—thus challenging the point of view from above by forc-

---

75 Powers, *Generosity*, p. 5.
76 Cf. Scherr, Emergence, p. 138.
77 Ibid.
78 Powers, *Generosity*, pp. 3–5; emphasis added.
79 The act of looking up could have several meanings: it might signify looking up to an omniscient narrator that hovers above, or alternatively, looking up to an idealized, future self.

ing it to shift its direction. The scene involving the boy and his bird further complicates matters, for each act of spying is met with a reciprocal gaze. This dynamic evokes Sartre's concept of shame and its role in cultivating self-consciousness, highlighting the nuanced interplay between observation and introspection in the narrative.

Furthermore, the boy may symbolize a younger version of Russell, just as Russell represents a younger iteration of the narrator, particularly given the anonymous character's reappearance at the novel's conclusion. This play of gazes not only depicts a moment of surveillance but also evokes a house of mirrors, suggesting that every act of looking is also an instance of self-reflection. Moreover, Gérard Genette's categorizations of homodiegetic, heterodiegetic, and autodiegetic narrators become blurred, as the heterodiegetic narrator emerges as the story's protagonist, especially given that these are his confessions. Additionally, the novel challenges the distinction between narrators and characters, seeing how the narrator frequently borrows the characters' words, and vice versa.

This dissolution of boundaries serves as a broader commentary on the significance and role of literature, reading, and writing, especially since the act of spying pertains to Russell's notes. The narrator's admission, "I know this story, like I wrote it myself,"[80] may sound paradoxical, given that these words belong to the narrator, the story's author. However, it also suggests a note of doubt or skepticism, hinting at the idea that multiple writers contribute to the narrative, and the story emerges from various selves and ideas, with characters who may have broken free from scripted lines.

From a psychological perspective, the chasm between the narrator and the character may also be interpreted as indicative of hidden trauma, particularly given Russell's strong aversion to self-monitoring, which echoes the concept of a psychological double or split-personality. Yet, this fracture does not necessarily represent a moment of crisis; on the contrary, it seems to aid the self in confronting its fears and anxieties. The chasm resembles the role of the double in psychodrama, where an auxiliary ego articulates "the presumed inner thoughts of the protagonist."[81] This therapeutic technique allows individuals to gain new "insight[s] about themselves and others,"[82] offering a reflective alternative to first-person testimony that necessitates identification with inner thoughts and feelings.

---

80 Powers, *Generosity*, p. 5.
81 Double, *APA Dictionary of Psychology*.
82 Ibid.

For instance, "Stone hasn't kept a journal for years. [...] Self-examination leaves him seasick. [...] He could no longer read anything even vaguely confessional. Intimate revelations or domestic disclosures creeped him out."[83] Russell's aversion to the first-person perspective may explain his choice to use a third-person narrative in the novel, thereby detaching himself from the intimacy of confessional writing. However, this does not imply avoidance of self-examination; rather, it remains a central theme throughout the novel.

Therefore, the rupture between Russell and the narrator can be explained in various ways. On the one hand, it highlights the estrangement that unfolds over time, as recollective memory does not function as a cohesive technique that shapes the autobiographical self. Instead, it emphasizes its fictive and alienating effects, portraying the past self as just another character in a story replete with other characters, rather than simply depicting an earlier version of the same self. Thus, the traditional memoir is supplanted by "creative nonfiction," which is no longer solely a personal, historically linear account of a single individual, but rather a narrative encompassing many selves and their interactions. In other words, the blurring of lines between fiction and nonfiction, introduced in the novel as "creative nonfiction," captures not only the fluid boundaries between fiction and reality but also between the self and its other selves. It also draws attention to the interdependence of selves, rather than their independence, as they continue to influence each other.

12.3 Literary Synesthesia: "A Sharp Blue Filament of Need"

Powers' novel exemplifies "creative nonfiction," a genre with a "paradoxical orientation towards both fact and fiction," making it "an ideal vehicle to complicate the binary logic that governs and limits our understanding of the interactive loops between the given and the possible, the inherited and the enhanced."[84] This genre challenges additional binaries, such as the inner self and outer world, body and mind, or literature and science. In the novel, these binaries are also questioned through the use of literary synesthesia. Thassa's creative work moreover embraces a synesthetic aesthetic. For instance, in her video "compositing,"[85] she presents

---

[83] Powers, *Generosity*, p. 13.
[84] Schäfer, Pursuit of Happiness, p. 276.
[85] Powers, *Generosity*, p. 54.

brief impressions of places and shots of individual confessions, all colliding in a single film, described as a "living watercolor."[86]

The "watercolor" effect draws a parallel to the science TV show featuring Thomas Kurton, where the impression of "watercolor" is also mentioned.[87] However, Thassa's filming differs from the editing done by the science crew. For example, the voice behind the camera, belonging to Thassa, responds to her characters by replying "I know," resonating with their words rather than hiding behind the camera, just as the narrator writes the novel. Furthermore, the watercolor she paints is not merely a visual picture; it relies on multisensory richness, encompassing both color and the liquid, fluid feeling of water.

Thassa's compositing stands apart from other visual shows depicted in the novel—such as Over the Limit and Oona's show—where the cult of individualism prevails. These shows focus on one man (Thomas Kurton in conversation with Tonia) or one woman (Thassa in conversation with Oona) in an attempt to capture their greatness. In contrast, Thassa's video celebrates the limits of vision by including only brief shots, providing access to partial knowledge. The audience is left with impressions, focusing on the body and the shaking hand. For instance, a man from Italy sitting by a fountain is overheard on camera as he proclaims: "But you know what would be great? If all this water just—if it all just kept flowing... Venice!"[88] Following his confession, "[w]ith the sweep of his illustrating hand, the water spills over the fountain rim and streams its way up Congress."[89]

The narrator describes the visual impression as a "living watercolor," implying that art grants the man's wish, as Thassa edits the video footage in such a way as to keep the water flowing. Also, it is "his hand" which brings the water into being. Similarly, the words of other men come alive as the film conjures the "tube of tunnel stone" or "Music falling out of the sky! He has only to speak it, and a third-story paradise of visible melody springs up all around him."[90] Art, then, functions like a genie, and Thassa does not need to make her writing come alive—it already is. Even though she relies on a visual medium, the "visible melody" hints at a synesthetic implosion of the senses that transcends the limits of the visible, describing another form of interaction not governed by ocularcentrism.

Thassa's writing exhibits a similar effect; it possesses "the open confidence of a child who might still become an astronaut when she grows up. All her sounds ring, all colors shine. [...] she's swept along by the stream, marveling. Her words

---

86 Ibid.
87 Ibid., p. 22.
88 Ibid., p. 53.
89 Ibid.
90 Ibid.

are naked. Her clauses sprout whatever comes just before wings."[91] The novel correlates the concept of happiness with writing and reading, primarily through Thassa's written confessions, which are particularly inspiring and bring joy to the classroom. While they continue to debate Harmon's book *Make Your Writing Come Alive*, it is Thassa's writing that exemplifies what lively writing truly means: "she reads her words like she's just discovered them. Her voice brings Algiers—dry, white, and merciless—into the fluorescent classroom."[92] She and her classmates even spend time together afterward, "laughing and strolling, tuned to one another."[93]

This scene evokes memories for Stone of another night with his "literary gang," during which they dreamed of revolutionizing the act of writing, breaking free from "the tyranny of convention," and rekindling the enthusiasm of "the tired reading public with a runaway playfulness that not even the dead could resist."[94] However, their vision was short-lived, overshadowed by the demands of "realism" as each member eventually succumbed to office jobs.[95] Nonetheless, the novel keeps alive the possibility of viewing art and fiction as the sprouting of liveliness, the purpose of living, echoing the famous words of Mr. Keating from DEAD POETS SOCIETY: "We read and write poetry because we are members of the human race. And the human race is filled with passion. And medicine, law, business, engineering, these are noble pursuits and necessary to sustain life. But poetry, beauty, romance, love, these are what we stay alive for."[96] Mr. Keating, based on Walt Whitman's persona, is an inspiring teacher who briefly ignites his students' desires to pursue their dreams and passions. In contrast, Russell Stone appears to be a disillusioned version of Mr. Keating. By focusing on "creative nonfiction," the novel does not wholly endorse either Russell's cynical skepticism or Mr. Keating's idealistic creativity; instead, it juxtaposes and explores the tension between them.

The novel also explores a tension between confessions as a source of joyful sharing and a potentially narcissistic form of personal branding. Stone, in particular, prefers to "dose himself with popular science and commodity histories,"[97] favoring nonfiction over creative pursuits. However, the novel illustrates that this preference is illusory, as the boundaries between "creative" and "nonfiction" blur and intertwine, much like the Möbius strips that weave through its para-

---

91 Ibid., p. 32.
92 Ibid., p. 34.
93 Ibid., p. 35.
94 Ibid.
95 Ibid., p. 36.
96 Quotes (DEAD POETS SOCIETY). *IMDb*.
97 Powers, *Generosity*, p. 17.

graphs.[98] Consequently, many conventional associations linked with this dichotomy are also deconstructed: journalism, realism, documentary, science versus journal, postmodernism, fiction, and the humanities. For instance, the science show featuring Thomas Kurton titles his episode "The Genie and the Genome."[99] This portrayal suggests that a documentary is never just a documentary. It depicts Kurton as a genius or a genie with the ability to manipulate the genome to ensure universal happiness. In this context, the genie figure serves to bolster notions of human exceptionalism and genius, rather than symbolizing a nonhuman entity.

Powers' novel delves into the parallels and distinctions between enhancing life through genetic engineering or doing so through fiction. Hence, the title takes on new significance: it not only addresses enhancement as a scientific pursuit but also suggests that the novel itself is a form of enhancement. Heike Schäfer has highlighted the ways in which the book's subtitle serves as a self-referential commentary on its capacity to enhance the tradition of the novel. By replacing the conventional marker "a novel" with "an enhancement," Schäfer argues that it seeks to "advance genre and alter our concept of narrative fiction."[100] Echoing Schäfer's interpretation, Alexander Scherr also contends that the subtitle serves as a "self-conscious proclamation of literary change."[101] However, these interpretations reinforce the narrative of progress and improvement that the novel also seeks to subvert.

An alternative interpretation may highlight the ways in which the subtitle could be a commentary on the novel's inherent quality. Instead of positioning the novel as enhancing the literary tradition, it proposes the novel itself as an enhancement. In this context, literary culture does not necessarily need to enhance or reinvent itself in order to remain relevant in the age of social media. Literature has always been and will continue to be relevant due to its inherently abundant nature. Indeed, it is literature's very sense of generosity that serves as an enhancement to life, though not necessarily in a way that makes life objectively better. This interpretation does not advocate a top-down approach but rather emphasizes a horizontal generosity, one that brings together and collides various perspectives: not polishing, but compositing.

---

[98] Hamner also pointed out the "infinite feedback loop" created by "the Möbius strip": "A character writes a novel in which he has an experience enabling him to write a novel in which he has an experience ... ad infinitum." (Predisposed Agency, p. 437). But they are also figure-eight knots that join the past and the future, the creative and the nonfiction.
[99] Powers, Generosity, p. 20.
[100] Schäfer, Pursuit of Happiness, p. 264.
[101] Scherr, Emergence, p. 135.

In this context, generosity extends beyond Thassa's kindness or Kurton's rhetoric of altruism to encompass the abundant quality of books themselves. Generosity becomes the sought-after enhancement for everything. It challenges the fundamental notion of making something greater, inviting instead appreciation for what already exists, rather than striving for an imagined improvement. In doing so, it renders the entire project of enhancement a Sisyphean task. The novel draws on Albert Camus' myth of Sisyphus in a bid to frame its critique of the pursuit of happiness, portraying this venture as absurd, impossible, and burdensome. The myth perpetuates the idea that happiness can only be attained through hard work and is solely the responsibility of individual—hence, the recurring image of Atlas bearing the weight of the heavens on his shoulders throughout the novel. Visually, both Sisyphus and Atlas carry heavy burdens, juxtaposing these two myths. The absurd quest for meaning echoes Camus' assertion that the "struggle itself toward the heights is enough to feel man's heart. One must imagine Sisyphus happy."[102]

In her review, Helen Brown concluded that the novel's message is that "all the stuff we have doesn't make us happy."[103] However, the novel also posits the opposite belief: that everything (and nothing) could make us happy. Thassa's secret knowledge is not esoteric but a simple statement that blinds everyone with its obviousness: "We don't need to get better. We're already us."[104] Candace similarly claims that "most people are already pretty happy."[105] Merely being alive should be sufficient reason to be happy, echoing Alan Watts' famous words: "The meaning of life is just to be alive. It is so plain and so obvious and so simple. And yet, everybody rushes around in a great panic as if it were necessary to achieve something beyond themselves."[106] Powers updates this view by placing it in a scientific context, challenging Kurton's ego-centric claim of a higher purpose than what nature and survival provide for everyone, not just humans: to live. Simply feeling alive is

---

102 Camus, *Myth of Sisyphus*, p. 123.
103 Brown, Generosity.
104 Powers, *Generosity*, p. 241. This recalls the old philosophical debate: is there a best possible world or not? The novel seems to be ambiguous in its responses: first, its focus on the act of "rewriting" and the infinite marks that separate the fragments seem to imply the possibility of a better world in an "infinite continuum of worlds" (Murray n.p.). At the same time, through Thassa's figure, the novel also suggests a Leibnizian answer: the actual world is already the best possible world—which, paradoxically, in the end turns out to be the worst possible world for her, too. Accordingly, it recalls Atwood's notion of "ustopia."
105 Ibid., p. 136.
106 Colagrossi, Allan Watts Quotes.

already the greatest feeling, akin to the privilege of "merely existing" identified in Shteyngart's novel as well.[107]

The novel's critique is also connected to its more substantial commentary on visual culture and the ideal of transparency. What is visible is so convoluted and rich and opaque that it runs the risk of becoming a blind spot, much like life itself. Even if one tries to look harder, some things remain in the shadow. For instance, even though Thassa's happiness is continuously invoked and probably the most visible theme, the reader is never granted direct access to it. It is narrated but never described. The narrator describes the effects Thassa's stories have on her teacher and fellow students, so her confessions are not only mediated and retold but also remain out of reach, replaced with the narrator's confessions. On the one hand, the novel seems to imply that content is less important than form, suggesting that what matters is the way Thassa reads her story, her present performance, rather than its subject matter. Especially since she seems to describe a boring and tedious activity, a Sisyphean mounting: an ordinary climbing of stairs.

On the other hand, this inaccessibility points to the qualities of writing and reading, which do not rely solely on vision but on a multisensory apprehension.

> Her voice is one of those mountain flutes, somehow able to weave a second melody around the one it plays. *Russell misses the gist of the words, he's so wrapped up in the cadence of the sentences.* It's something out of the dawn of myth, set in a Chicago all but animist. One thing worth telling a total stranger, and the thing is: an ancient woman, hoisting her aluminum walker up the Grand Staircase of the Cultural Center at the rate of one step a minute. *The ascent* is glacial, the staircase infinite, the climber a Wednesday-afternoon *Sisyphus mounting* toward the world's largest Tiffany dome. The worn marble steps droop like cloth under the feet of a century of ghosts. *But every word of Thassa's description, lifts the climber toward the light.* By the third step, Russell realizes *he's never looked hard at anyone*. By the top of the stairs, a *sharp blue filament* of need *makes him want to see what will happen to the species,* long after he's dead.[108]

In a manner reminiscent of Margaret Atwood's exploration of vision, Powers also delves into its significance. Thassa's writing inspires Russell in a way that deters him from looking hard only at himself, prompting him to contemplate "what

---

[107] Thassa's character redefines happiness as the feeling of being alive. If Anselm's ontological argument tried to prove the existence of God by defining God as "something than which nothing greater can be thought" (*Anselm of Canterbury*, p. 87), the novel rewrites this argument: and God, happiness, or life is something than which nothing greater can be felt: "Happiness *is* the virtue" (Powers, *Generosity*, p. 321; emphasis in original). It appears as if there is no distinction between what one feels and the actual reality: "He feels vaguely criminal. He *is* vaguely criminal" (ibid., p. 57; emphasis in original).
[108] Ibid., p. 27f; emphasis added.

will happen to the species." Rather than focusing on the future of humanity, as Kurton does, Russell's vision is turned toward the "species." At first, the reader may be tempted to add the term "human" before "species," but the text omits it. "Species" is a biological term that refers to "groups of organisms that evolve in a unified way. Outside of biology, the concept of species plays a role in debates over environmental law and ecological preservation. Our conception of species even affects our understanding of human nature."[109]

As such, the text shifts attention from the human to the "group of organisms" that the word "species" references. Moreover, the biological focus is enlarged so as to include not only an ecocritical perspective but also an animistic view—Thassa's words give life to all human or nonhuman things. Not only does the "ancient woman" gather meaning, but also the "worn marble steps" that "droop like cloth," which are apprehended not only on a visual level. Their description includes a tactile dimension, one that adds a smooth touch to the rigidity of marble. It seems to make the ascent less difficult and more generous or acceptable, as if the stairs are laid out before the woman in a ceremonial way, much like a red carpet in front of a celebrity. If Jacob's ladder reaches up to heaven and makes the self look up, Thassa's story turns the attention back to the stairs and the journey itself, rather than the destination, which is the dome.[110]

This scene also captures the vastness of space and slowed-down time[111]—but in a different light than the science fiction genre. Perception of spacetime is necessarily linked to other sensory perceptions, so they are not just psychological constructs, but they also behave like physical entities. The universe is apprehended as a snapshot instance, "an infinite staircase" in a local space (Chicago's Cultural Center) and as a story of balance and coordination, but also synesthetic awareness. The "sharp blue filament of need" that Russell experiences at the end of the paragraph couples the sense of touch with vision in a salient way: the blue color with a stinging sensation, as if blueness has a structure that cuts like a knife. It reimagines insight not as a lightbulb moment of intense vision, hovering somewhere in the mind, but as a corporeal and highly embodied awareness. A filament refers not only to yarn or material thread, but also to the cosmos with its galaxy filaments,

---

[109] Ereshefsky, Species.

[110] The rounded roof of the dome evokes the architecture of cathedrals, and on a metaphorical level, it might also invoke visions of heaven and paradise. See also the dome in Margaret Atwood's *MaddAddam*.

[111] "Reports of slowed-down time are closer to what some call 'flow' or 'the zone,' characterized by deep concentration, highly efficient performance, emotional buoyancy, a heightened sense of mastery, a lack of self-consciousness, and even self-transcendence" (Csikszentmihalyi qtd. in Broderick, Brain).

the protein filaments found in hair or muscle, or even the electrical filaments found in light bulbs. As such, it seems to shape a Whitmanesque sense of interconnectedness that also relies on an implosion of the senses.

Literary synesthesia is then used to enact a more substantial critique on the supremacy of vision, imagination, and scientific genius. But it also makes accessible all the omissions, shadows, and blind spots that a sole focus on vision creates. If, in the former passage, the reader does not have access to Thassa's happiness, the novel includes a different scene where Russell's happiness is described in detail:

> It stuns Russell the next morning to discover: her disease is still contagious. Life-threatening but not serious. He wakes up ravenous. He can't remember the last time that breakfast seemed such a brilliant plot twist. The winter air through the wall cracks braces him, and the table spreads itself. The boiling teapot sings like a boy soprano. The raisin muffin crisping in the toaster smells like muscatel. He's on a houseboat, moored on one of those mythical rivers that Information has not yet reached. That's how surely this mood has come on. [...] He takes the coffee beans from the freezer, spoons them in the grinder, and churns. No evolutionary psychology will ever account for the pull of that smell. He actually sits to eat, like it's some holiday. It is: Spontaneous Healing Day. He closes his eyes and holds a winter strawberry to the tip of his tongue. The fruit is spongy and sublime.[112]

Even if this scene describes a seemingly ordinary and trivial activity—having breakfast—it is one of the most generous passages in the novel. First, it comments on the infectious quality of happiness, which paradoxically is "[l]ife-threatening but not serious." Danger and starvation are usually the most basic needs that raise the vigilance of the self and compels one to fight for survival. And yet, in this context, vigilance is not limited to caution and being on the lookout, but is endowed with an alertness and watchfulness that escape the limits of the visual; with a form of awakening that embeds the self in its immediate environment, rather than placing it in a fight-or-flight situation.

Russell's savoring of the present moment is not just a mental effort to focus on positive experiences.[113] This "mood" comes to him spontaneously, so it appears as if he has no choice. And yet, decisions are still made on the spot: "He actually sits to eat, like it's some holiday. It is: Spontaneous Healing Day"—so, his decisions are just as sudden and spontaneous as the moment he lives. The scene maintains a high-level of meta-awareness: as the breakfast is a "brilliant plot-twist," and to-

---

112 Powers, *Generosity*, p. 122 f.
113 See also the discussion of savoring in chapter eleven on the dangerous altruism of self-help culture.

ward the end, Russell closes his eyes to taste the strawberry. So, he deliberately pays attention to sights, smells, and tastes that are often neglected.

However, the overflow of sensorial impressions—sound, taste, smell, texture, warmth, or proprioception—acquires an additional meaning. It does not merely describe a pleasurable experience, but also a peculiar form of selflessness and selfless interaction, recalling the notion of self-transcendence introduced in chapter eleven. However, this scene does not merely depict a feeling of awe; it shapes a different notion of generosity: as the "winter air through the wall cracks braces him." The self is enveloped by the vastness of the winter air that leaks through the cracks in the wall. Becoming part of nature or the environment is a generous and vulnerable process. It is the realization of human-nonhuman coexistence and codependence, rather than an attempt to improve on the human. Generosity as selflessness takes the form of human-nonhuman interaction. And it is mostly writing and art that can give access to such generosity.

In a different context, the narrator keeps searching for Russell, or Russell keeps searching for himself: "I search for Russell Stone all over. I read the almanac for that year. I read his class textbook, of course. [...] I even loot those hall-of-mirrors avant-garde novels whose characters try to escape their authors, the kind he once loved, the kind he thought he'd write one day, before he gave up fiction"[114] and which, in the end, the narrator seems to be writing. In this relentless pursuit, Russell comes to a realization: "He's nowhere, except in his work. [...] What pleasure does he get from his *selfless editing?*"[115] Thus, the novel replaces the search for the self with the idea of "selfless editing"—paradoxically, one can only find oneself by relinquishing the act of creation or self-fashioning, rejecting these individualist methods. It also explains the uses of the third perspective anew—as a method of "selfless editing," recalling Thassa's empathic stance.

The process of writing takes on the semblance of self-renunciation, a predilection which has a long history and tradition, but which in this case means to stop focusing on the self and give place to the nonhuman. Writing and reading foster care by diverting attention from a house of mirrors, embedding the self within the rich environment of the nonhuman. Rather than shaping the image of a unique and authentic self, Powers' "creative nonfiction" focuses on a process of unbecoming, shedding personal details so as to focus on human-nonhuman interactions. Russell's aversion to "books with teacher protagonists"[116] or school settings, despite being a protagonist in such a tale, is ironic. This statement frames the narra-

---

114 Powers, *Generosity*, p. 40.
115 Ibid., p. 41; emphasis added.
116 Ibid., p. 13.

tive as an exercise in self-denial or estrangement. And yet, it could also be a comment on the book's different focus—not on character growth or coming of age, although Russell does undergo changes, with his peak achievement being the writing of the novel itself. Instead, the narrative directs attention to porous boundaries between the self and others, challenging the notion of a single protagonist. Thassa, for instance, emerges as another central character whose journey and evolution defy conventional notions of progress or human-centric protagonism.

13 Literature and Compositing: "The Secret Quickening in the Hands"

Russell Stone once kept "florid diaries," as "he couldn't see, hear, smell, or taste anything without *polishing* it into a perfect paragraph."[1] Similarly, the narrator of *Generosity* also engages in a process of refinement, whose effect is the hindrance of an empathic response from readers. Some critics find it challenging to empathize with the text and its "flimsy characters."[2] Christopher Tayler critiques the author's "limited character-making skills."[3] These reactions seem to stem from the text's "metafictional noodling" and sparse depictions of "sentiment or romance."[4] The narrator's continual acknowledgment of the characters' fabrication, despite the simultaneous urging for readers to "care about them,"[5] appears to disrupt the suspension of disbelief and subsequent identification. Interestingly, this literary strategy also positions the reader as an intimate outsider.

Thus, this self-awareness is also deemed "brilliantly relevant."[6] As noted by Heike Schäfer, "the text does not merely use metafiction to comment on its narrative procedures and its production of knowledge."[7] Powers reimagines this postmodern strategy, utilizing it to "complicate the distinction between fact and fiction, creative and nonfiction, documentation and invention."[8] The novel itself embodies this duality: it oscillates between fact and fiction, as the narrator remains caught "between allegory and realism, fact and fable, creative and nonfiction."[9] In doing so, Powers exposes the "polishing" typical of the realist tradition, where "sentiment" and "romance" are carefully constructed within the narrative. Furthermore, the text may aim to transcend mere identification with the characters—moving beyond empathy derived from such readings—and instead advocate a different kind of generosity: one where readers, authors, and characters engage in "selfless editing."[10]

---

1 Powers, *Generosity*, p. 13; emphasis added.
2 Brown, Generosity by Richard Powers.
3 Tayler, Generosity by Richard Powers.
4 McInerney, Why Is She Smiling?
5 Brown, Generosity by Richard Powers.
6 Charles, Book World.
7 Schäfer, Pursuit of Happiness, p. 274.
8 Ibid., p. 277.
9 Powers, *Generosity*, p. 129.
10 Ibid., p. 41.

Open Access. © 2024 the author(s), published by De Gruyter. This work is licensed under the Creative Commons Attribution 4.0 International License. https://doi.org/10.1515/9783111389929-018

As such, Powers' "metafictional noodling" serves a different purpose than Stone's polishing. On the one hand, Stone's polishing aims to refine or enhance reality, akin to the attractive cover of a book where surface sheen matters most, and all flaws must be smoothed over. Even his confession that "the woman on the page reduced all actual women to pale, insufficient reminders of the full-throated real"[11] espouses the belief that art transcends reality; it appears to promote a Platonic idealism where actual shadows are but mere glimpses of a higher form. However, through this, Powers critiques not only the realist tradition but also aestheticism and its ideals of beauty, which still rely on a hierarchical approach. On the other hand, the narrator's polishing has a counterintuitive effect: rather than enhancing the text, it continually draws attention to its status as a work-in-progress, highlighting its limited, flawed, and imperfect nature. This mirrors Thassa's "living watercolor," which eschews the pursuit of perfection and embraces deviations and irregularities in the plot. Even the very notion of plot—as a sequence of events or narrative structure—is challenged.

Thassa's compositing is more generous, incorporating a myriad of diverse and random scenes, people, thoughts, and images. It challenges hierarchical understandings of art and reality.[12] Rather than polishing its surface, Thassa aims to do the opposite—make every bump more visible. The story unfolds without adhering to any particular logic, and the conventional notions of beginnings and endings are brought into question. Thassa's choice of film as her medium allows her to move "beyond representation": "I love film; I just love it. I love putting the shots together. I love dubbing the sounds. Anything! I could play with the editing softwares all day long."[13] In contrast to Schiff's science show, Thassa's film embodies another example of "creative nonfiction." One important distinction lies in the absence of a definitive ending: while Schiff's show must conclude with a clear message, Thassa's camera can capture an endless sequence of shots, reflecting the boundless potential of the "living watercolor" to assume infinite forms. Moreover, the ending itself does not neatly resolve all conflicts; rather, it intertwines the two

---

[11] Ibid., p. 37.
[12] "Does her introduction of fiction into a purportedly nonfictional essay constitute the betrayal it seems? Or does Thassa's 'creativity with the facts' bring daily experience to life in a measure otherwise impossible? Just as she grafts animation onto filmed scenes of Chicago's less-visible citizens, she admits to having rearranged temporal order and geographical locations to boost the emotional impact of her 'nonfiction.' Her revelation is so disturbing, we realize, because Russell has unconsciously expected clear demarcations of any shift from the actual to the possible, and she has erased them. Yet the text we are reading relies on the same kind of categorical transgression" (Hamner, Predisposed Agency, p. 433).
[13] Powers, *Generosity*, p. 52.

notions—the finite and the infinite—in an endless spiral, reminiscent of the infinite marks that separate the narrative fragments. Similarly, the novel concludes with a circular image of the young boy and his bird, a motif that echoes its initial appearance at the beginning. Thus, most events are woven together like the two strands in a double helix, perpetually intertwining and evolving.

In contrast, the TV show featuring Kurton engages in precisely the kind of polishing or editing described—they omit Kurton's "wistful, penitent mood" because it does not align with the otherwise optimistic persona and the main plot of the episode: genetic enhancement.[14] The show adheres strictly to a single script, promising transparency rather than exposing the limits of vision, as if everything could be known. Moods, being qualities of feeling at a particular time, are inherently elusive and evasive. To "cut out" a mood also implies a disregard for the body, suggesting that Kurton's happiness hinges on the eradication of other feelings deemed negative—a concept akin to "emotional hygiene" as described by Guy Winch.

Powers' book achieves the opposite—it plays with the theme of visibility in order to assert the relevance of literature and advocates a generosity of feeling that encompasses both the positive and negative. On the one hand, it suggests that feelings like happiness are indescribable, especially since Thassa's happiness is never described, only narrated. On the other hand, the text employs literary synesthesia to convey a sense of joy, both in narrating Thassa's happiness and in describing Stone's cheerful breakfast scene. In this way, literature grants access to what is opaque, convoluted, and profuse—not by rendering it visible, but by imbuing it with language that is evocative in a multisensory manner. Words do not merely depict images; rather they intertwine to form a fabric that heightens embodied awareness.

At one point, Russell loses his temper in class during a debate on the relevance of comic books versus literature. One student, also known as the Joker, argues that "the best comics must be better than any print-only book. It kind of follows: pictures plus words gives you more to work with than just words alone."[15] In response, Russell asks: "What about interiority? [...] Complex levels of concealed thought? Things that aren't material or visible. What about getting deep inside people's heads?"[16] When his arguments fail to persuade, Stone erupts: "Let's all just drown out in shiny consumer shit," prompting the Joker to retort, "Only the

---

[14] Interestingly enough, even the notion of genetic enhancement relies on the same concept of cutting, replacing, or "editing." The crew implements such major changes, prompting Tonia to resign. Additionally, the show blends science with mysticism, as Tonia reads a passage from Kurton's Moleskin notebook written by a Christian mystic.
[15] Powers, *Generosity*, p. 89.
[16] Ibid.

mind can turn shit into shiny."[17] This brief exchange highlights several intriguing facets. Firstly, the Joker's remark encapsulates elements of self-help culture, suggesting that the mind should transform negativity into positivity and optimism —one should practice emotional hygiene. In other words, "shit" is not allowed to exist. However, Powers' novel takes a different approach: it acknowledges the existence of such language and incorporates it into the narrative, even if it is vulgar. Additionally, the term "shit" holds multiple meanings, including nonsense, foolishness, or trivial talk.[18] Hence, the Joker's comment also implies that only the extraordinary matters—the "shiny" amidst the mundane.

Once again, the metaphor of polishing is invoked here, as the student marvels at the imaginative prowess of genius to enhance reality, infuse meaning into nonsense, and transform a wasteland into bright visions. Simultaneously, through Russell's voice, the narrative critiques the visually-driven culture and the consumerist empire of shallow and flashy entertainment. Thus, polishing also alludes to marketing and advertising practices within this context. However, the novel's critique delves even deeper. First, it refrains from engaging in this form of polishing, remaining generous toward "shit," too. What's more, it exposes the shininess of the mundane, the ordinary miracles, through Thassa's joy, as well as the foolishness of the shiny, of entertainment industry products and popular shows where reactions are manufactured. So, there is no linear progress from "shit to shiny," but rather a contamination and intertwining of the two, as the novel provides a more generous perspective.

Additionally, the book offers a more nuanced critique than Russell's presumption, which perpetuates the emphasis on the visual. "[G]etting deep inside people's heads"[19] serves as another means of reinforcing the ideal of transparency, envisioning telepathic forms of communication and access to hidden thoughts and knowledge. In contrast, the novel suggests that the power of literature lies not solely in the conceptual and imaginative use of the words, but in the generous ways in which they raise embodied awareness—redirecting attention back to the body rather than away from it. However, this is not merely an attempt to manipulate the audience on a visceral level, as Tonia experiences when she hears the sound of the show's introduction. Through their generosity, books dismantle the illusion of control, oversight, or mastery, pulling readers in different and opposing directions. The notion of manipulation ultimately fails due to the unpredictability and

---

17 Ibid.
18 Shit, *Merriam-Webster*.
19 Powers, *Generosity*, p. 89.

generosity of differing worldviews. Additionally, the focus on material things often overlooked, demonstrates how the mind need not "turn shit into shiny."

Thassa's remark about "maybe you believe too much in words"[20] does not necessarily indicate her agreement with her peers; rather, it suggests that Russell may be overlooking something in his defense of literature—something that is beyond words. Thassa's words "make it okay to find pleasure in *nothing* at all—trading folk songs with the mailman or mapping the trees of the new South Side."[21] In other words, this pleasure can be found in the trivial, in what might otherwise be dismissed as "shit," but is in fact an integral part of life itself. Her joy resonates with Russell's desire to craft a story that "breaks free" and "invents itself out of meaningless detail and thin air."[22] This apparent "nothingness" carries profound meaning—it demonstrates that the "things that aren't material or visible"[23] can still make their presence felt in a book, but not simply by representing them through words.

Powers' novel subtly suggests the limitations of representation on several occasions. For instance, the narrator refrains from transcribing Thassa's story of ascent toward the Tiffany dome in Chicago, or provides only a trivial description of her performance at Oona's show: "In a canny elision, Powers gives only hints of Thassa's triumphant performance."[24] The narrator focuses solely on people's reactions, seemingly unable to articulate the story or the performance in words. Moreover, when Thassa repeatedly utters "I'm happy for"[25] three times in a row, it becomes apparent that her feelings may no longer be genuine, having already changed. Similarly, Stone refuses to express his love in words, because they are "hindering as fur on fish."[26]

In conclusion, the relevance of literature lies not solely in words or language per se, but rather the ways in which they coalesce, leaving gaps and resonating with multiple meanings—embracing the seemingly meaningless details that are often omitted in the polishing process. These seemingly insignificant details resonate with the body, exemplified by the recurring motif of the "secret quickening in [the] hands."[27] This motif is first introduced at the beginning of the novel, as a

---

20 Ibid., p. 90.
21 Ibid., p. 82; emphasis added.
22 Ibid., p. 129.
23 Ibid., p. 89.
24 McInnerney, Why Is She Smiling?
25 Powers, *Generosity*, p. 227.
26 Ibid., p. 206.
27 Ibid., p. 5.

dark-haired boy calms his yellow bird. Everett Hamner also discusses this scene, highlighting its significance:

> Darwin readers will remember that the Galapagos finches were especially critical to his discovery of natural selection. How are human personhood and meaningful agency reshaped by the realization that we are animals, and therefore as much the products of environmental and genomic factors as any other species? With the image of a finch, Powers suggests that we accept our biological boundaries not as the manacles of fate but as prerequisites to slow revision.[28]

The symbol of the American goldfinch embodies ideas of agency, as the bird is placed back in its cage once the boy feels seen. At the same time, this serves as an illustration of a seemingly trivial detail holding multiple layers of meaning: it condenses notions of life, livelihood, and generosity towards the nonhuman. The notion of quickening also alludes to the first movements of life, suggesting that novels are brought to life by such imperfect details. Darwin's encounter with a goldfinch led to his evolutionary insights, just as Newton's apple contributed to his insights on gravity. On the one hand, the novel challenges the reduction of the nonhuman to a mere tool of scientific genius. On the other hand, it redirects attention to the nonhuman realm and underscores the importance of human-nonhuman interaction. Human exceptionalism is contested by creating a space for the nonhuman to thrive—a generosity that literature exemplifies.

Aside from the boy with the goldfinch, the hand motif recurs in at least three additional instances throughout the novel: the man in Thassa's video whose sweeping hand motion causes the water to flow; Russell Stone's trembling hands before his first class; and the frozen motion of the pen, pausing in midair as Russell's hand "just hovers"[29] over the pages of his notebook. These instances introduce necessary pauses, however brief, and are imbued with agency. The shaking, quickening, and hovering hands carry manifold meanings, bringing together nature, art, the vulnerability of the body, and the act of handwriting. This generous imagery resonates with multiple layers of meaning, highlighting the relevance of literature as a form of embodied awareness.

Introducing writing as handwriting, and framing art as flowing from the hand, the novel not only recalls a rich historical tradition, such as the handwritten manuscripts of medieval times with their illuminated initials, but also emphasizes the body as the origin of art and inspiration, rather than solely the mind or human imagination. Writing is portrayed as originating from the body, not just the brain.

---

28 Hamner, Predisposed Agency, p. 434.
29 Powers, *Generosity*, p. 5.

It is akin to handmade craftwork, but with words as the medium. Each piece of writing is unique, shaped by factors such as the handwriting style, size, angle, color, or spacing—a characteristic often overlooked in the digital age where handwriting is regarded as anachronistic. This disinterest in writing represents a significant loss in the digital era, a blind spot underscoring the materiality of both reading and writing, rather than focusing solely on their cognitive aspects.

Despite the notion that all books seem to follow a limited set of plots, as expressed in the novel—"everything ever written derives from one of only twenty-four possible plots"[30]—each book remains distinctive. While books might use the same letters of the alphabet, just like with handwriting, it is the combination, contexts, and details that set them apart. As the novel shows, even a seemingly simple sequence of letters, such as "Jen,"[31] can convey multiple meanings simultaneously. The sound of the word "Jen" evokes associations with concepts like genie (wishful thinking), genius (brilliance and imagination), generosity, or gene/genome (heredity). This implicitly reflects on how genome editing might function, as changing one aspect could impact others due to the interconnectedness of the various agents at play. In this light, the statement that "[a]ll writing is rewriting,"[32] takes on added significance.

Accordingly, it is not solely the author who "makes" the writing come alive, but rather the myriad nonhuman things that populate it: the goldfinch, the worn marble steps, the winter air, the table, the boiling teapot, the raisin muffin, the coffee beans, the winter strawberry, a book, Atlas. However, this is not merely an exercise in encyclopedic realism aimed at creating a "reality effect" by listing objects.[33] Nor is it a commentary on the dichotomy between realism and idealism, as Powers' use of literary synesthesia moves beyond such binaries. For instance, the recurring reference to Atlas embodies this generous embrace of realms: nothing is purely physical, nor purely ideal. Atlas evokes both the geological features of the "Atlas Mountains"[34] and the mythological figure punished to bear the weight of the heavens on its shoulders.[35]

---

30 Ibid., p. 39. This idea is debated in class based on Harmon's book. Some of these plots include: "Personal Sacrifice for Moral Belief," "Passion Disrupts Judgment," "Audacious Experiment. Choose your own adventure!" These plots are broken down even further, with Russell ultimately concluding that there are only two: "the future arrives to smack around the past, or the past reaches out to strangle the future" (ibid., p. 40).
31 Happiness as Jen is described as a "scientific hallucination" (ibid., p. 216); the numerous Jens are only pretenders.
32 Ibid., p. 37.
33 Barthes, *Rustle of Language*, p. 141. In this context, it is also worthwhile to take a look at speculative realism and object-oriented ontology as a possible influence on Powers' work.
34 Powers, *Generosity*, p. 12.

The novel's conclusion has sparked extensive debate due to its ambiguity, presenting what appears to be two distinct endings. On the one hand, it challenges the conventional notion of denouement, of finding closure or resolution, by leaving the narrative open-ended and suggesting the possibility of multiple potential outcomes. On the other hand, it concludes with a highly symbolic scene that provides a sense of finality.[36] The novel is brought to a close with the meeting between the narrator and Thassa, blurring the lines between extradiegetic and intradiegetic realms. They both "sit and watch the Atlas go dark,"[37] echoing a sentence previously written by Stone in midair during his conversation with Candace: *"They sit and watch the Atlas go dark."*[38] In this case, "they" is replaced with "we," implying a shift in empathy. Additionally, the sentence in the conclusion is no longer italicized, suggesting that it has come alive through the act of rewriting. The significance of this sentence may allude to the release from the heavy burden of striving for happiness. As the mountains and celestial spheres of Atlas recede from view, the narrative makes space for simple, serendipitous moments. This act of rewriting differs from editing or polishing in that it does not necessarily imply the creation of a better version.

The second ending is not superior, it merely presents another universe in which Thassa may briefly come to life, as evidenced by the "small shared joy"[39] the novel concludes with. This "small shared joy" not only marks the end the novel but also perpetuates itself in an infinite feedback loop, once again challenging the notion of closure. This phrase holds the key to the various meanings of generosity depicted in the novel. Books themselves serve as prime examples of lively agents capable of eliciting such joy. Reading, too, exemplifies this "small shared joy"—not only between the reader and the author but also between the reader and the physical book, the characters within its pages, and the lively agents and

---

35 The mention of Atlas could also serve as a critique of Ayn Rand's *Atlas Shrugged* and her interpretation of Objectivism, which views "man as a heroic being, with his own happiness as the moral purpose of his life, with productive achievement as his noblest activity, and reason as his only absolute" (*Ayn Rand*, p. 351). In contrast, the novel critiques this notion of heroism by challenging the humanist worldview underlying it.
36 As Heinz Ickstadt has contended: a "narrative that seemed a tale of catastrophe and closure is opened up to the possibility of an alternative telling, or at least toward the reader's awareness of such a possibility. It is only when seen from the end, that the function of fiction and the power of story-telling to create, revoke, and re-create meaning become visible through Powers' 'asynchronous messaging.' [...] There is, as always, the structural strain between a plotline tending toward closure and another pushing toward openness" ('Asynchronous Messaging,' p. 37f).
37 Powers, *Generosity*, p. 322.
38 Ibid., p. 164; emphasis in original.
39 Ibid., p. 322.

nonhuman elements that animate it. In this respect, the novel is less pessimistic than commonly perceived, although it does not promote blind optimism either. This joy does not appear contrived but rather illustrates a simple, serendipitous moment that becomes possible once the burden of pursuing happiness dissipates with the disappearance of Atlas.

Similar to Toby in Margaret Atwood's *MaddAddam*, Thassa chooses to "preserve a last bit of agency by committing suicide."[40] And akin to Toby's fate, Thassa appears to be redeemed through rewriting: "She is redeemed in a second ending, in which the narrator writes Thassa back to life and has her return to Algeria, where her daughter is born."[41] However, both novels also redefine life writing—not as the story of a single protagonist, but as a literal writing of life understood in all its diversity, encompassing not just human experience but all forms of life. Thus, the emphasis is not solely on the personal redemption of these women, but on the concept of life persisting in various forms—including, or especially, as a book. In other words, writing does not need to be infused with life, as Graham P. Harmon's title implies; it is already alive.

The novel's examination of Harmon's *Make Your Writing Come Alive* critiques the notion of the writer as a naturally gifted genius, highlighting the laborious effort required in the writing process. Simultaneously, it exposes the growing sense of uncertainty and the existence of confining scripts while writing: Harmon's book promotes a scientific approach to writing, where plots are numbered and quantified, reducing writing to primarily an erudite activity. In the end, the novel exposes and criticizes this perspective, despite also engaging with it—for instance, it has been labeled a "cerebral"[42] novel. While advocating affective writing and reading, even if it appears to paradoxically lack in it, Powers' novel intentionally draws attention to the importance of reading as a space for human-nonhuman encounters. Reading is portrayed as a communal endeavor, with a flow of ideas resembling the presence of the genies described by Gilbert: nonhuman agents that interact with readers, enriching their experience.

---

40 Scherr, Emergence, p. 133.
41 Ibid.
42 Charles, Book World.

14 Conclusion: A Kinship of Posthumanity

This book underscores the unique contribution that the humanities—particularly literary studies—can offer to a transdisciplinary knowledge of life. This is especially relevant in a world dominated by natural sciences, which often espouse a biotechnological perspective on life. My analysis delves into a wide range of issues pertinent to the Anthropocene era and the age of the Internet. It explores how contemporary US-American self-help culture, science communication, and speculative novels intersect and shape each other thematically and structurally. For instance, they all employ life writing as a rhetorical device, albeit with distinct approaches and outcomes. Life writing has emerged prominently even in unexpected genres primarily focused on science, such as TED talks and speculative fiction. The second chapter provides an exploration of this phenomenon: from the sentimentalist rhetoric of the American neoconfessional with its redemptive narrative, to the utilization of confession in science communication with its empathic script, and finally to the autobiographical lens through which literature—and reading as a therapeutic activity—is viewed.

Self-help culture in the United States is often associated with the myth of rugged individualism and the ideology of positive thinking. However, this perspective represents only one facet of a broader narrative that is more adaptable and pervasive. Even self-help literature itself appears to critique this narrow viewpoint. Morgan Scott Peck, for instance, exposes the fallacy of perpetual happiness perpetuated by societal institutions, stating, "For motives of profit, the lies of materialism and advertising suggest that if we're not happy, comfortable, and fulfilled, we must be eating the wrong cereal or driving the wrong car."[1] Peck further challenges the illusion of rugged individualism, asserting: "If I think with *integrity* at all, I have to recognize immediately that my life is nurtured not only by the earth and the rain and the sun but also by farmers, publishers and booksellers, as well as by my children, wife, friends, and teachers—indeed, by the entire fabric of family, society, and creation. I am not solely an individual."[2]

The concept of integrity recalls the TED talk delivered by Pamela Meyer, which both begins and concludes this book. In "How to Spot a Liar," Meyer emphasizes:

> We wish we were better husbands, better wives, smarter, more powerful, taller, richer—the list goes on. Lying is an attempt to bridge that gap, to connect our wishes and our fantasies

---

1 Peck, *Road Less Traveled*, p. 32.
2 Ibid., p. 59f; emphasis added.

about who we wish we were, how we wish we could be, with *what we're really like*. And boy are we willing to fill in those gaps in our lives with lies.[3]

Meyer presents a critique from within, challenging the pervasive nature and rationale of self-improvement in US-American culture. Simultaneously, she raises one of contemporary rhetoric's most contentious questions: "what we're really like." Who constitutes this "we"? TED talks often utilize "a high incidence of inclusive 'we' with present tense [which] is used to indicate universal human qualities [...] or shared experiences."[4] Moreover, one of the most prevalent modals employed in TED talks is "can,"[5] likely due to "the spirit of 'can-do' and problem solving"[6] that underlies TED's optimism. In essence, TED creates a platform embodying the ethos of "Yes We Can."[7]

TED speakers aim to *"humanise* their intellectual experience,"[8] fostering "an ease and intimacy" with their ideas that leads to immediate identification with audience members.[9] On the one hand, TED serves as a platform for promoting "civic desire": "the desire to develop a culture of care with others, to engage in conversation about *our collective future*, with strangers as well as familiars, in a way that opens up to the development of a non-hegemonic commonness necessary for collective action in a democracy."[10] On the other hand, an analysis of TED talks also reveals the limitations of human-centric discourse and the inadequacy of developing a "community of feeling"[11] if it excludes the nonhuman and reinforces human superiority.

The three analytical chapters are divided into three parts. The first part has been focused on TED talks as a scientific strand of self-help. It examines TED talks and other media (online courses, podcasts, and social media content) where science is communicated to the public. Influenced by American self-help culture, TED talks do not only disseminate knowledge but also contribute to identity building. They do not need to inhibit emotional involvement to seem scientific,

---

[3] Meyer, How to Spot a Liar, 00:03:36; emphasis added.
[4] Scotto di Carlo, Patterns, 131 f.
[5] Ibid., p. 133. This is highlighted in Scotto di Carlo's analysis, where she identifies the most frequent modal verbs used in a selected corpus of TED talks, which are: can (51,08 %) and could (13,05 %).
[6] Elmer, Public Humanities, p. 111.
[7] President Barack Obama's campaign and the 2008 presidential election victory speech became famous precisely for the chant: "Yes We Can."
[8] Scotto di Carlo, Patterns, p. 140; emphasis added.
[9] Howard, Ideas Worth Spreading?, p. 74.
[10] Pfister, Technoliberal Rhetoric, p. 195; emphasis added.
[11] Ibid., p. 194.

quite the contrary. TED talks develop both trust and suspicion, authenticity and authority, as they include both personal stories and theoretical knowledge. In this respect, they do not reinforce only the principle of objectivity: "The word *objective*, according to the *Random House Dictionary*, means 'free from personal feelings.' Yet ironically, we need feeling in order to reflect on the external or 'objective' world. Taking feelings into account as clues and then correcting for them may be our best shot at objectivity."[12] Similarly, TED talks work with the notion of empathy as a new principle to suggest the authority of a "controlled tool of observation"[13] and humanize their content.

Their aesthetics of individualism and their focus on vision champion a humanist approach to matters of life. Consequently, their discourse on success, mindfulness, and happiness ends up popularizing a *duty to be alive* that primarily centers on the human and its future survival. They have become "very sophisticated in the techniques of deep acting; they suggest how to imagine and thus how to feel."[14] In other words, they can be particularly persuasive because they create powerful expectations about these topics. For instance, success comes across as the confidence of the individual who works hard, has genius ideas, and utterly believes in them. Mindfulness also implies a lot of self-control and the development of positive feelings, such as gratitude, love, or happiness. Besides positive feelings, happiness also relies on intrinsic motivation and finding flow. Thus, they all foster a community of feeling that relies on the exclusion and censoring of unwanted feelings. Discipline, "emotional hygiene,"[15] and faith in a higher power—this is all it takes to accomplish anything. This implies that acts of failure, distraction, or unhappiness are mainly the faults of the individual self who lacks willpower, creativity, or patience—even if they are usually associated with the information overload of contemporary digital culture.

The constant "surveillance of our feelings"[16] may become a form of social control disguised as self-improvement. Quantifying practices of measuring time and bodies should presumably cultivate enough self-vigilance to spur change and find fulfillment. Mindfulness entails becoming an inner scientist on the lookout for new data to combat the bad habits ingrained in the body; in this process, new brainwave technologies and forms of ranking purportedly assist in achieving clarity of vision. The body becomes so transparent that it almost vanishes—and

---

12 Hochschild, *Managed Heart*, p. 31; emphasis in original.
13 Lunbeck, Empathy, p. 266.
14 Hochschild, *Managed Heart*, p. 49.
15 Winch, Why We All Need.
16 Hochschild, *Managed Heart*, p. 228.

happiness as flow even relies on an out-of-body experience. Consequently, creativity is mainly defined as a tool used to transcend the body.

This community of feeling is justified as a means of becoming fully human. It emerges as a redemptive script focused on saving humanity while disregarding individual struggles. "We are faced with the task of educating ourselves to be fully human."[17] Indeed, TED talks play a role in this task, as they also shape a new duty to be alive. Paradoxically, even if they reinforce an ethic of life, they also rely on the principle of *memento mori*—reminding the audience of the inevitability of death. In this case, *memento mori* serves as a vigilant reminder urging people to choose life, to find happiness in the present moment, while death is portrayed as something to be feared and avoided at all costs.

As such, TED talks embody a shift from *I* to *we*, seemingly challenging the narcissism of contemporary digital culture. However, alongside the narcissist, American culture has also produced "another form of false self: the altruist, the person who is overly concerned with the needs of *others*."[18] Similarly, the novels examined in this book introduce the concept of "dangerous altruism" in order to raise a sense of alarm particularly to this narrative—where under the premise of a common "we" lies the ambitions of an "I," where the narcissist and the altruist are the same person. In other words, an analysis of contemporary dystopian literature sheds light on how the pursuit of *the greater good*, such as the survival of the human species, can be used to justify the restriction of civil liberties, including bodily privacy, while overlooking the interests of the nonhuman. In this case, they challenge the assumption that empathy inevitably leads to prosocial behavior, prompting questions about who empathizes, with whom, and for whose benefit.

In the novels, the stereotype of the mad scientist undergoes an update to highlight precisely this tension: powerful, privileged men endeavor to rescue the suffering populace. These novels offer commentary on the traditional trope of the scientific genius, portraying them not only as mad scientists but also as salesmen (such as Joshie in *SSTL*), artists (like Crake in *MaddAddam*), and narcissists hungry for public attention (such as Kurton in *Generosity*). These scientists present their projects in altruistic terms and adhere to a redemptive narrative. In various ways, they epitomize the apogee of humanism, espousing the belief in the superiority of human reason while striving to prolong human life.

The second part of each analytical section delves into contemporary speculative novels that engage with these themes; they offer a critical perspective on self-help culture and reframe scientific questions. These novels highlight the limita-

---

17 Peck, *Road Less Traveled*, p. 26.
18 Hochschild, *Managed Heart*, p. 195; emphasis added.

tions of vision and underscore the importance of other senses and of feeling alive. In other words, they interrogate the rhetoric of self-help culture by scrutinizing some of its most prominent expectations, which are also perpetuated in TED talks. Certain expectations become evident in the novels' critical reception as well—precisely because they emerge as anthropocentric preferences while reading. For instance, they challenge the focus on vision, which is often tied to the human intellect's power. These novels not only introduce other senses but also demonstrate their interconnectedness, illustrating how this mixing is essential for reimagining our relationship with the nonhuman.

Instead of emphasizing human genius, these novels redirect attention to a multisensory engagement with the nonhuman. In Gary Shteyngart's *Super Sad True Love Story*, smells take on significance, offering a fresh perspective on life. In a society dominated by the äpparat, where lives are defined by ratings, rankings, and numbers, smells disrupt this paradigm. They convey the fragility of life —a vulnerability shared with the nonhuman realm. Animals such as the otter, the elephant, and rhesus monkey puncture the narrative of human superiority and embody vitality. Whether the otter with its "salmon breath"[19] or the elephant with its large trunk and ears, their presence in the novel and vivid descriptions evoke what it means to feel alive and acquire the privilege of merely existing.

In Margaret Atwood's *MaddAddam* trilogy, sounds mediate a new form of interaction with the environment. In a society where the vision of a single human almost wipes out humanity, the "insight of interbeing" depends on an insight of intersenses. For instance, Toby's encounter with the pigs culminates with the image of a "songbird made of ice,"[20] which evokes both the clarity and brevity of melting ice, serving as a reminder of life's fragility. In this context, *memento mori* takes on a different connotation; it highlights the vulnerability of life and fosters an intimacy with loss. Life and death are not distinct but part of the same cycle, and feeling alive encompasses both beauty and grief, heralding its eventual passing.

In Richard Powers' *Generosity: An Enhancement*, touch also holds significance. In a sensationalist society where feelings are trained on TV shows, the novel presents an ordinary breakfast scene. Russell Stone's moment of happiness is not encoded in DNA or an extraordinary event. Rather, it is a simple interaction with the air, the teapot, the coffee beans, and a strawberry—a *spongy* strawberry. Similarly, Thassa's filming does not adhere to a grand script but captures a watercolor of blended senses. In short, these examples underscore the importance of feeling

---

[19] Shteyngart, *Super Sad*, p. 247.
[20] Atwood, *MaddAddam*, p. 224.

and experiencing the nonhuman through multiple senses, not just observing it from afar. If vision continues to be revered as the master sense and deemed "the noblest of the senses,"[21] it perpetuates the script of human exceptionalism.

The third part of each analytical section concludes by reflecting on the role of reading in our contemporary age, continuing the discussion initiated in the second part by examining the relevance of literature. Here, the aim is to question the conventional belief that "[w]orks of literature *open windows in our minds* and can change our consciousness,"[22] a notion particularly prominent in the genre of science fiction, which has long been perceived in visionary terms. However, as demonstrated in this book, contemporary speculative novels challenge this expectation of imaginative world-building, which often upholds a humanist perspective. Scientific innovations, technological breakthroughs, and futuristic visions typically capture readers' attention first. Yet, it is precisely this viewpoint that the mad scientists depicted in the novels also adopt.

If literature and science are inseparable, then changes are also possible by reimagining what reading means—an essential task for literary scholars. In other words, if books are approached solely as intellectual or visionary material, it perpetuates the belief in the superiority of the mind in society as well. The body remains marginalized or reduced to mere data, aligning with the perspectives of consumer capitalism and biotechnological approaches to life. For societal change to occur, there is a need to challenge our perception of books as well—not merely as data to be dissected, but as active nonhuman agents in their own right. These novels illustrate how both books and bodies are subjected to similar treatment. "Surveillance turns human bodies into 'discrete flows' which are then 'reassembled into distinct 'data doubles' which can be scrutinized and targeted for intervention' (606). The monitored body becomes a cyborg, a 'flesh-technology-information amalgam'."[23] Similarly, literary critics are urged to reconsider their reading practices—not as acts of surveillance, but as thoughtful engagements with the nonhuman.

As such, this book highlights the novels' most profound critique through their utilization of literary synesthesia—or, their ability to make readers aware of the material and sensory aspects of reading. They use literary synesthesia not to transcend biological confines, but to celebrate them; instead of suggesting mystical insights, they capture ordinary moments of feeling alive; and instead of glorifying human genius, they foster connections with the environment and draw attention

---

21 Jay, *Downcast Eyes*, p. 21.
22 Grace, Consciousness and Conscience, p. 223.
23 Wrobel, Negotiating Dataveillance, par. 11.

to the haptics of reading. This approach provides a more nuanced critique of Western civilization, challenging visions of human enhancement that have permeated various forms of media. Such a critique extends beyond bioethical concerns to encompass a critique of Western culture, which has elevated scientific knowledge while gradually marginalizing the role of the body and promoting a future-oriented mindset where survival and progress are equated. This critique is artpolitical, aiming to integrate aesthetics and politics without reducing texts to didactic tools or mere objects of beauty disconnected from broader societal contexts.

The mentioned novels challenge the expectation that probing and imagining unknown worlds is more important than exploring our everyday surroundings, such as our kitchens. They question the notion that books are merely data to be compiled and dissected, akin to a silent alphabet of letters. Instead, they redirect attention to the trivial, the ordinary, the seemingly insignificant cuts, and the easily dismissed aspects of life—to the "fading light [which] is us, and we are, for a moment so brief it can't even register on our äppärät screens, beautiful."[24] These novels illustrate how writing emanates from the hand—words are material, carrying not only meaning but also sounds, smells, tastes, and tactile impressions. In doing so, they challenge the metaphor of digging into a text. Words, like bodies, are sensitive to such acts, and textual immersion becomes a unique way to access some of its truths rather than merely surrendering to the text's ideology.

Practices of reading extend beyond introspective exercises, although they are often perceived as such. Instead, they broaden attention to include the nonhuman world. Reading intensifies not only the experience of oneself but also enhances knowledge of the external environment. Accordingly, these novels also challenge the expectation of emancipated selfhood—the strong belief in the characters' (and the readers') need for inner transformation. Typically, this transformation involves emotional labor aimed at creating a happier self, one that overcomes traumas and seeks redemption, often through confessional writing. In this context, the diaries and journals of the novels' protagonists are expected to serve as a means of finding catharsis. However, simultaneously, the novels' scenes of "self-descriptive reminiscence" do not primarily focus on shaping human subjectivity but rather portray the self as a *thing* in a world of things.

To be a thing generates a strong critique of the humanist notion that attributes imagination and creativity solely to the human mind. These novels question the narrow view that links humanity exclusively to its capacity for thought and reasoning. Instead, they redefine the concept of creativity. Creativity is portrayed not as a mystical ability of the human mind, nor as an inner, cerebral trait, but rather as an

---

24 Shteyngart, *Super Sad*, p. 203.

interaction with the nonhuman world. In this case, the artist is not exclusively human; instead, creativity pertains to life—the myriad ways in which things interact. It is the unique interaction between the self, a paintbrush, and a canvas, or between a person, their hand, a piece of paper, and a pen. Creativity, then, is not confined to the mind but becomes an external dance with the nonhuman—a choreography of gestures, elements, and things coming together, being alive.

Instead of seeking signs of human exceptionalism, these novels strengthen the importance of the nonhuman world. Animals are not merely included in the narratives to make a statement about human identity; rather they serve to foster a kinship of posthumanity. This kinship hinges on a multisensory awareness of the environment, prompting a reevaluation of the concept of empathy. Unlike in self-help culture, where empathy is often part of a sentimentalist rhetoric, or in scientific discourse, where it serves as a "controlled tool of observation,"[25] the novels present empathy in a different light. While books facilitate introspection and empathy, their lesser recognized achievement lies in promoting a kinship of posthumanity, showing the myriad ways in which the self is embodied and embedded in a rich environment of humans and nonhumans.

Jay David Bolter pointed out that "the future of humanism becomes a question of the future of the humanities."[26] Yet, as this analysis shows, the humanities are also precisely those academic disciplines that can afford to challenge humanism, to think beyond the human. If the "proper study for the posthuman condition is the complex human interaction with non-human agents,"[27] then practices of reading do precisely that. This does not mean that they merely "escape" humanism either. As Kate Soper also argues, "the most persuasive of the posthumanist discourses are those which are prepared to recognize and talk about the lurking humanism of the forms of questioning of the nature and limits of the 'human' that are opened up through the posthumanist project."[28]

Rather, these novels function like the "intimate outsider" of society—both immersed in and outside of it. In this context, can art be envisioned outside capitalism? Can it offer meaningful tools not only to critique the system but also to propose relevant alternatives? Can literature write its way out of the logic of profit and commodification? The suggested answer appears to be: both yes and no. Literature provides, even if only as brief moments of rupture and rapture, the necessary spaces to think beyond an economic totality.

---

25 Lunbeck, Empathy, p. 266.
26 Bolter, Posthumanism, p. 7.
27 Braidotti, Contested Posthumanities, p. 23.
28 Soper, Humanism, p. 375.

If the cultural directive is "Whatever you do, don't tell the truth of what it's like to be alive,"[29] literature defies that directive. It not only portrays the awareness of the self but also demonstrates how literary weaving is "an act both of life and of death."[30] Paradoxically, the ability to remain vulnerable, dependent, and affective subjects ensures survival—even when future survival takes the form of a book. As such, these novels advocate the importance of reading and writing, not merely as noble, humanist pursuits showcasing the power of imagination, but as practices that immerse individual selves in a network of embodied affects. Books serve as more than just an antidote to the fear of death; they offer intimate contact with death and loss. Being alive is not synonymous with only wonder, but also entails an intimacy with loss. Books do not merely reinforce the power of language, but they often highlight its failure. They strive to address the unsaid, express the unspeakable, and do so through slippages, failings, messes, and ruptures.

Future research could extend this investigation into various areas such as exploring instances of language failure, examining how literature defines life, and exploring whether this synesthetic aesthetic is present in other novels and genres too. This area remains largely unexplored and warrants further documentation. Additionally, future studies could explore alternative techniques and literary devices that emphasize the material and sensuous aspects of reading. There is also a need to develop new approaches to reading, practicing postcritique while remaining politically engaged, without assuming that an intimate engagement with a text necessarily maintains "political detachment."[31] It is crucial to emphasize the aesthetic mode of literature's political work and to recognize the political implications of aesthetics, as demonstrated by the analysis of TED talks. Furthermore, it would be worthwhile to investigate whether TED's aesthetics of individualism influence the communication of other scientific topics, a dimension that requires further research.

> We remain haunted by residues of the animal, plant, and mineral being that we have attempted to slough off. Our species-centrism has made us deaf to the call of these other forms of life upon us, bad readers and historians of the strange archives of animal-plant-fungal-bacterial mixing that, in fact, describe who and what we are and who and what we come into being with.[32]

It is precisely these archives that deserve more attention in our contemporary age, and literature generously offers avenues for exploring them.

---

29 Cain qtd. in Cording, New Book.
30 Olney, Memory, p. 874.
31 Lanzendörfer/Nilges, Literary Studies after Postcritique, p. 495.
32 Yates, Improbable Shepherds, p. 415.

Bibliography

Aamodt, Sandra: Why Dieting Doesn't Usually Work. On: *TED* (08.01.2014), https://www.ted.com/talks/sandra_aamodt_why_dieting_doesn_t_usually_work [last access: 01.04.2023].
Abbott, H. Porter: Autobiography, Autography, Fiction: Groundwork for a Taxonomy of Textual Categories. In: *New Literary History* 19/3 (1988), pp. 597–616.
Abend, Pablo/Fuchs, Mathias (Eds.): *Digital Culture and Society: Quantified Selves and Statistical Bodies* 2 (2016).
About Dhar Mann. https://www.dharmann.com/about [last access: 16.12.2022].
Achor, Shawn: The Happy Secret to Better Work. On: *TED* (01.02.2012), https://www.ted.com/talks/shawn_achor_the_happy_secret_to_better_work [last access: 01.04.2023].
Adams, Henry: *The Education of Henry Adams*. Boston 1974.
Ahmed, Sara: *The Cultural Politics of Emotion*. Edinburgh 2004.
Ahmed, Sara: *The Promise of Happiness*. Durham 2010.
Al-Khalili, Jim: *Paradox: The Nine Greatest Enigmas in Physics*. New York 2012.
Anderson, Chris: TED's Nonprofit Transition. On: *TED* (28.03.2016), https://www.ted.com/talks/chris_anderson_ted_s_nonprofit_transition [last access: 01.04.2023].
Anderson, Chris: TED's Secret to Great Public Speaking. On: *TED* (19.04.2016), https://www.ted.com/talks/chris_anderson_ted_s_secret_to_great_public_speaking [last access: 01.04.2023].
Anderson, Tom: Benjamin Franklin: The Unlikely Father of Self-Help. On: *Blinkist Magazine* (17.01.2018), https://www.blinkist.com/magazine/posts/benjamin-franklin-father-self-help [last access: 01.04.2023].
Anker, Elizabeth S./Felski, Rita (Eds.): *Critique and Postcritique*. Durham/London 2017.
Anker, Elizabeth. *Orgies of Feeling: Melodrama and the Politics of Freedom*. Durham/London 2014.
Anselm, Saint: *Anselm of Canterbury: The Major Works*. Oxford 1998.
Appleton, Sarah A: Myths of Distinction; Myths of Extinction in Margaret Atwood's *Oryx and Crake*. In: Appleton, Sarah A (Ed.): *Once upon a Time: Myth, Fairy Tales and Legends in Margaret Atwood's Writings*. Newcastle upon Tyne 2008. pp. 9–24.
Archibald, Matthew E: *The Evolution of Self-Help. How a Health Movement Became an Institution*. Palgrave 2007.
Arias, Rosario: Life After Man? Posthumanity and Genetic Engineering in Margaret Atwood's Oryx and Crake and Kazuo Ishiguro's Never Let Me Go. In: Barfoot, C.C./Tinkler-Villani, Valeria (Eds.): *Restoring the Mystery of the Rainbow: Literature's Refraction of Science*. Amsterdam 2011, pp. 379–394.
Atwood, Margaret: *Oryx and Crake. A Novel*. New York 2003.
Atwood, Margaret: *The Year of the Flood*. New York 2009.
Atwood, Margaret: *MaddAddam*. New York 2013.
Baggini, Julian: Is There a Real You? On: *TED* (13.03.2014), https://www.ted.com/talks/julian_baggini_is_there_a_real_you [last access: 03.04.2023].
Bakhtin, Mikhail: *The Dialogic Imagination: Four Essays*. Austin 1981.
Banerjee, Supana: Towards 'Feminist Mothering': Oppositional Maternal Practice in Margaret Atwood's Oryx and Crake. In: *Journal of International Women's Studies* 14/1 (2013), pp. 236–247.
Barfoot, C.C./Tinkler-Villani, Valeria: Introduction: Restoring the Mystery of the Rainbow. In: Barfoot, C.C./Tinkler-Villani, Valeria (Eds.): *Restoring the Mystery of the Rainbow: Literature's Refraction of Science*. Amsterdam 2011, pp. 1–12.

Barnett, Emma: Mindfulness: The Saddest Trend of 2015. On: *The Telegraph* (08.01.2015), https://www.telegraph.co.uk/women/womens-life/11331034/Mindfulness-the-saddest-trend-of-2015.html [last access: 03.04.2023].

Barr, Marleen S: America and Books Are Never Going to Die: Gary Shteyngart's Super Sad True Love Story as a New York Jewish 'Ustopia.' In: Baxter, Gisèle M./Grubisic, Brett Josef/Lee, Tara. *Blast, Corrupt, Dismantle, Erase: Contemporary North American Dystopian Literature.* Waterloo 2014, pp. 311–327.

Barthes, Roland: *The Rustle of Language.* Berkeley 1989.

Bartlett, Steven: Malcolm Gladwell: Working from Home Is Destroying Us! The Diary of a CEO, episode 162. On: *YouTube* (21.07.2022), https://www.youtube.com/watch?v=mgEs61k2mxY [last access: 03.04.2022].

Basics: Session 1. On: *Headspace*, https://www.headspace.com. [last access: 09.03.2023]

Baudrillard, Jean: *The Consumer Society. Myths and Structures.* Thousand Oaks 1998.

Bauman, Zygmunt: *Consuming Life.* Hoboken 2013.

Beckwith, Sarah: Reading for Our Lives. In: *PMLA* 132/2 (2017), pp. 331–336.

Belknap, Geoffrey/Burdett, Carolyn/Dawson, Gowan/Moulds, Alison/Shuttleworth, Sally: Citizen Science: Sally Shuttleworth and her Team Interviewed by Carolyn Burdett. In: *19: Interdisciplinary Studies in the Long Nineteenth Century* 21 (2015), pp. 1–18.

Benesch, Klaus: Auto/Biography and Mediation. In: *Anglia: Zeitschrift für Englische Philologie* 129 (2011), pp. 563–656.

Benesch, Klaus: From a *Thing* into an *I Am:* Autobiographical Narrative and Metahistorical Discourse in Contemporary African American Fiction. In: *Presses Universitaires François-Rabelais* 18 (1998), pp. 7–21.

Benesch, Klaus: *Romantic Cyborgs: Authorship and Technology in the American Renaissance.* Amherst 2002.

Benesch, Klaus: Writing Grounds: Ecocriticism, Dumping Sites, and the Place of Literature in a Posthuman Age. In: Meikle, Jeffrey L./Orvell, Miles (Eds.): *Public Space and the Ideology of Place in American Culture.* Amsterdam 2009, pp. 435–453.

Benzinger, Elisabeth/Jauss, Hans Robert: Literary History as a Challenge to Literary Theory. In: *New Literary History* 2/1 (1970), pp. 7–37.

Bercovitch, Sacvan: *The American Jeremiad.* Madison 2012.

Berlant, Lauren: *Cruel Optimism.* Durham 2011.

Berlant, Lauren: *The Queen of American Goes to Washington City. Essays on Sex and Citizenship.* Durham 1997.

Best, Stephen/Sharon, Marcus: Surface Reading: An Introduction. In: *Representation* 108 (2009), pp. 1–21.

Bieger, Laura: *Belonging and Narrative: A Theory of the American Novel.* Bielefeld 2018.

Bilyeu, Tom: Jason Silva on Overcoming Anxiety and Finding Flow – Impact Theory. On: *YouTube* (07.02.2017), https://www.youtube.com/watch?v=UD40iEzGvaQ [last access: 03.04.2023].

Bolter, Jay David: Posthumanism. In: Craig, Robert T./Jensen, Klaus Bruhn/Pooley, Jefferson D./Rothenbuhler, Eric W. (Eds.): *The International Encyclopedia of Communication Theory and Philosophy.* Hoboken 2017, pp. 1–8.

Booth, Alison: Mid-Range Reading: Not a Manifesto. In. *PMLA* 132/3 (2017), pp. 620–627.

Bone, Jane: Environmental Dystopias: Margaret Atwood and the Monstrous Child. In: *Discourse: Study in the Cultural Politics of Education* 37/5 (2016), pp. 627–640.

Bosco, Mark S.J.: The Apocalyptic Imagination in Oryx and Crake. In: Bouson, J. Brooks (Ed.): *Margaret Atwood: The Robber Bride, The Blind Assassin, Oryx and Crake.* London/New York 2010, pp. 156–171.

Bostrom, Nick: Transhumanist Values. In: Bouson, J. Brooks (Ed.): *Ethical Issues for the 21st Century.* Bowling Green 2003, pp. 3–14.

Botta, Giuseppina: Faustian Dreams and Apocalypse in Margaret Atwood's Oryx and Crake. In: Detmers, Ines/Grimm, Nancy/Thomson, Katrin/Volkmann, Laurenz (Eds.): *Local Natures, Global Responsibilities: Ecocritical Perspectives on the New English Literatures, ASNEL Papers 15.* Amsterdam 2010, pp. 243–255.

Bouskill, Kathryn: The Unforeseen Consequences of a Fast-Paced World. On: *TED* (09.12.2019), https://www.ted.com/talks/kathryn_bouskill_the_unforeseen_consequences_of_a_fast_paced_world [last access: 03.04.2023].

Bouson, J. Brooks: Introduction: Negotiating with Margaret Atwood. In: Bouson, J. Brooks (Ed.): *Margaret Atwood: The Robber Bride, The Blind Assassin, Oryx and Crake.* London/New York 2010, pp. 2–17.

Bouson, J. Brooks: "It's Game Over Forever": Atwood's Satiric Vision of a Bioengineered Posthuman Future in Oryx and Crake. In: *The Journal of Commonwealth Literature* 39/3 (2004), pp. 139–156.

Bouson, J. Brooks: A "Joke-Filled Romp" Through End Times: Radical Environmentalism, Deep Ecology, and Human Extinction in Margaret Atwood's Eco-Apocalyptic *MaddAddam* Trilogy. In: *The Journal of Commonwealth Literature* 51/3 (2016), pp. 341–357.

Bowdon, Tom Butler: *50 Self-Help Classics: 50 Inspirational Books to Transform Your Life from Timeless Sages to Contemporary Gurus.* Boston 2003.

Braidotti, Rosi: The Contested Posthumanities. In: Braidotti, Rosi/Gilroy, Paul (Eds.): *Conflicting Humanities.* London/New York 2016, pp. 9–45.

Braidotti, Rosi: Posthuman Critical Theory. In: Banerji, Debashish/Paranjape, Makarand R. (Eds.): *Critical Posthumanism and Planetary Futures.* Berlin 2016, pp. 13–32.

Brenton, Malin J.: *Feeling Mediated: A History of Media Technology and Emotion in America.* New York 2014.

Brewer, Judson: A Simple Way to Break a Bad Habit. On: *TED* (03.02.2016), https://www.ted.com/talks/judson_brewer_a_simple_way_to_break_a_bad_habit [last access: 03.04.2023].

Briceño, Eduardo: How to Get Better at the Things You Care About. On: *TED* (01.02.2017), https://www.ted.com/talks/eduardo_briceno_how_to_get_better_at_the_things_you_care_about [last access: 04.04.2023].

Britannica, The Editors of Encyclopaedia: Rhesus Monkey. On: *Encyclopedia Britannica* (18.03.2020) https://www.britannica.com/animal/rhesus-monkey [last access: 04.04.2023].

Broderick, Damien: *X, Y, Z, T: Dimensions of Science Fiction.* Rockville 2004.

Broderick, Lisa: The Brain on Slowed-Down Time. In: *Psychology Today* (09.10.2021), https://www.psychologytoday.com/us/blog/where-physics-meets-psychology/202110/the-brain-slowed-down-time [last access: 04.04.2023].

Brooks, David: Should You Live for Your Résumé … or Your Eulogy. On: *TED* (14.04.2014), https://www.ted.com/talks/david_brooks_should_you_live_for_your_resume_or_your_eulogy [last access: 04.04.2023].

Brown, Brené: *Atlas of the Heart: Mapping Meaningful Connection and the Language of Human Experience.* New York 2021.

Brown, Brené: The Power of Vulnerability. On: *TED* (23.12.2010), https://www.ted.com/talks/brene_brown_the_power_of_vulnerability [last access: 04.04.2023].
Brown, Deborah/Ellerton, Peter: Philosophy and Critical Thinking. In: *edX*, https://www.edx.org/course/philosophy-and-critical-thinking [last access: 04.04.2023].
Brown, Helen: Generosity by Richard Powers: Review. In: *The Telegraph* (01.02.2012), https://www.telegraph.co.uk/culture/books/bookreviews/7093977/Generosity-by-Richard-Powers-review.html [last access: 04.04.2023].
Brydon, Diana: Atwood's Global Ethic: The Open Eye, The Blinded Eye. In: Kozakewich, Tobi/Moss, John (Eds.): *Margaret Atwood: The Open Eye*. Ottawa 2006, pp. 447–458.
Building Introspective Places. On: *TED*. https://www.ted.com/playlists/530/building_introspective_spaces [last access: 04.04.2023].
Bullen, Ross: 'Act Two for America': Narcissism, Money, and the Death of American Literature in Gary Shteyngart's Super Sad True Love Story. In: *Canadian Review of American Studies* 48/2 (2018), pp. 231–253.
Butler, Judith: *Gender Trouble: Feminism and the Subversion of Identity*. London 1989.
Butter, Stella: A Manifesto for Positive Aesthetics. Review of: Rita Felski, Uses of Literature, Malden, MA/Oxford: Blackwell 2008. In: *Journal of Literary Theory* (12.11.2009), http://www.jltonline.de/index.php/reviews/article/view/130/424 [last access: 04.04.2023].
Byrne, Rhonda: *The Secret*. Portland 2006. Cabanas, Edgar/Illouz, Eva: *Manufacturing Happy Citizens: How the Science and Industry of Happiness Control our Lives*. Cambridge 2019.
Cabanas, Edgar/Illouz, Eva: *Manufacturing Happy Citizens: How the Science and Industry of Happiness Control our Lives*. Cambridge 2019.
Cain, Susan: *Bittersweet: How Sorrow and Longing Makes Us Whole*. New York 2022.
Camblin, Justin: Book Review: The Happiness Effect. On: *David Prince* (04.08.2017), https://www.davidprince.com/2017/08/04/book-review-happiness-effect [last access: 04.04.2023].
Camus, Albert: *The Myth of Sisyphus and Other Essays*. New York 2012.
Carr, Michael: Mind-Monkey' Metaphors in Chinese and Japanese Dictionaries. In: *International Journal of Lexicography* 6/3 (1993), pp. 149–180.
Chakravartty, Anjan: Scientific Realism. In: *The Stanford Encyclopedia of Philosophy (2017)*, https://plato.stanford.edu/archives/sum2017/entries/scientific-realism/ [last access: 04.04.2023].
Chapman, Julia Marie/Whitlock, Janis Leann: Social Media Influencers: Followers' Perceptions and Self-Concept. In: *Conference Poster: Society for Personality and Social Psychology* (2019), https://www.researchgate.net/publication/341654621_Social_Media_Influencers_Followers%27_Perceptions_and_Self-Concept [last access: 04.04.2023].
Charles, Ron: Book World: Ron Charles Reviews 'Generosity' by Richard Powers. In: *Washington Post* (07.10.2009), https://www.washingtonpost.com/wp-dyn/content/article/2009/10/06/AR2009100603282.html [last access: 04.04.2023].
Ciobanu, Calina: Rewriting the Human at the End of the Anthropocene in Margaret Atwood's MaddAddam Trilogy. In: *The Minnesota Review* 83 (2014), pp. 153–162.
Clark, Kent: Myth of the Genius Solitary Scientist Is Dangerous. In: *The Conversation* (21.11.2017), https://theconversation.com/myth-of-the-genius-solitary-scientist-is-dangerous-87835 [last access: 04.04.2023].
Clarke, Bruce/Rossini, Manuela: *The Cambridge Companion to Literature and the Posthuman*. Cambridge 2017.
Clute, John: Science Fiction from 1980 to the Present. In: James, Edward/Mendlesohn, Farah (Eds.): *The Cambridge Companion to Science Fiction*. Cambridge 2003, pp. 64–79.

Colagrossi, Mike: Alan Watts Quotes That Will Change Your Perspective on Life. On: *BIG THINK* (13.03.2019), https://bigthink.com/thinking/alan-watts-quotes-that-will-change-your-perspective-on-life/ [last access: 04.04.2023].
Compagnone, Antonio: The Reconceptualization of Academic Discourse as a Professional Practice in the Digital Age: A Critical Genre Analysis of TED Talk. In: *Hermes – Journal of Language and Communication in Business* 54 (2015), pp. 49–69.
Conferences. On: *TED*, https://www.ted.com/about/conferences [last access: 04.04.2023].
Confess. In: *Merriam-Webster*, https://www.merriam-webster.com/dictionary/confess [last access: 04.04.2023].
Cooke, Grayson: Technics and the Human at Zero Hour: Margaret Atwood's Oryx and Crake. In: *Studies in Canadian Literature / Études en Littérature Canadienne* 31/2 (2006), pp. 105–125.
Cording, Jess: In New Book, NYTimes Bestselling Author Susan Cain Explores the Value of Bittersweetness in a World of Toxic Positivity. In: *Forbes* (09.09.2022), https://www.forbes.com/sites/jesscording/2022/09/09/nytimes-bestselling-author-susan-cain-explores-the-value-of-bittersweetness-in-a-world-of-toxic-positivity/?sh=69254f8511ce [last access: 04.04.2023].
Cowden, Shelley: Transcendental Meditation: Counter Culture Spirituality to Postmodern Commodity. In: *Man in India* 90/1 (2010), pp. 353–364.
Cox, James M: Autobiography and America. In: *The Virginia Quarterly Review* 47/2 (1971), pp. 252–277.
Crary, Jonathan: *Suspensions of Perception: Attention, Spectacle and Modern Culture.* Cambridge 1999.
Crary, Jonathan: *24/7: Late Capitalism and the Ends of Sleep.* London 2013.
Crossley, Nick: Habit and Habitus. In: *Body & Society* 19/2&3 (2013), pp. 136–161.
Csikszentmihalyi, Mihaly: *Flow: The Psychology of Optimal Experience.* Manhattan 1990.
Csikszentmihalyi, Mihaly: Flow, the Secret to Happiness. On: *TED* (06.02.2014), https://www.ted.com/talks/mihaly_csikszentmihalyi_flow_the_secret_to_happiness [last accessed: 04.04.2023].
Cuddy, Amy: Your Body Language May Shape Who You Are. On: *TED* (01.10.2012), https://www.ted.com/talks/amy_cuddy_your_body_language_may_shape_who_you_are/comments [last access: 04.04.2023].
Cutts, Matt: Try Something New for 30 Days. On: *TED* (01.07.2011), https://www.ted.com/talks/matt_cutts_try_something_new_for_30_days [last access: 04.04.2023].
Daniels, George H: The Process of Professionalization in American Science: The Emergent Period, 1820–1860. In: Rheingold, Nathan (Ed.): *Science in America since 1820.* New York 1976, pp. 63–78.
Dante, Alighieri: *Inferno.* London 2013.
d'Entreves, Maurizio Passerin: Hannah Arendt. In: *The Stanford Encyclopedia of Philosophy* (2022), https://plato.stanford.edu/archives/fall2022/entries/arendt/ [last access: 04.04.2023].
Daston, Lorraine: Objectivity and the Escape from Perspective. In: *Social Studies of Science* 22/4 (1992), pp. 597–618.
Daston, Lorraine/Galison, Peter: The Image of Objectivity. In: *Representations* 40 (1992), pp. 81–128.
Davis, Tchiki: What Is Savoring – and Why Is It the Key to Happiness? In: *Psychology Today* (03.07.2018), https://www.psychologytoday.com/intl/blog/click-here-happiness/201807/what-is-savoring-and-why-is-it-the-key-happiness [last access: 04.04.2023].
Day, Sean: Some Demographic and Socio-Cultural Aspects of Synesthesia. In: Robertson, Lynn C./Sagiv, Noam (Eds.): *Synesthesia: Perspectives from Cognitive Neuroscience.* Oxford 2005, pp. 11–33.
De Certeau, Michel: *The Practice of Everyday Life.* Berkeley 1984.

Defalco, Amelia: Maddaddam, Biocapitalism, and Affective Things. In: *Contemporary Women's Writing* 11/3 (2017), pp. 432–451.
Degrushe, Allison: YouTube Officially Revealed Its U.S. Top 10 Creators of 2021 – Take a Look! On: *Distractify* (01.12.2021), https://www.distractify.com/p/top-youtubers-2021 [last access: 04.04.2023].
Deleuze, Gilles: Postscript on the Societies of Control. In: *Winter* 59 (1992), pp. 3–7.
Desbiens-Brassard, Alexandre: Environmental Discourses in Atwood's *MaddAddam* Trilogy; Or, The Neoliberal Prometheus. In: *Studies in Canadian Literature / Études en Littérature Canadienne* 45/2 (2021), pp: 141–160.
Dewey, John: *Art as Experience.* New York 1980.
Diseases of Modern Life. On: *TORCH*, https://www.torch.ox.ac.uk/diseases-of-modern-life [last accessed: 04.04.2023].
Dixon, Alex: Kindness Makes You Happy… and Happiness Makes You Kind. In: *Greater Good Magazine* (06.09.2011), https://greatergood.berkeley.edu/article/item/kindness_makes_you_happy_and_happiness_makes_you_kind [last access: 04.04.2023].
Dolezal, Luna: Human Life as Digitised Data Assemblage: Health, Wealth and Biopower in Gary Shteyngart's Super Sad True Love Story. In: *Medical Humanities* 42/4 (2016), pp. 219–224.
Doss, Erika: Public Feeling, Public Healing: Contemporary Memorials and the Meditation of Grief. In: Fitz, Karsten/Harju, Bärbel (Eds.): *Cultures of Privacy: Paradigms, Transformations, Contestations.* Heidelberg 2015, pp. 35–57.
Double. In: *APA Dictionary of Psychology.* https://dictionary.apa.org/double [last access: 04.04.2023].
Douglass, Frederick: Narrative of the Life of Frederick Douglass, An American Slave. In: Baym, Nina (Eds.): *The Norton Anthology of American Literature.* New York ⁶2003, pp. 996–1065.
Drucker, Johanna: Why Distant Reading Isn't. In: *PMLA* 32/3 (2017), pp. 628–635.
Duckworth, Angela Lee: Grit: The Power of Passion and Perseverance. On: *TED* (09.05.2013), https://www.ted.com/talks/angela_lee_duckworth_grit_the_power_of_passion_and_perseverance/comments [last access: 30.09.2022].
Duffy, Patricia Lynne: Synesthesia in Literature. In: Hubbard, Edward M./Simner, Julia (Eds.): *The Oxford Handbook of Synesthesia.* Oxford 2018, pp. 647–671.
Dunlap, Allison: Eco-Dystopia: Reproduction and Destruction in Margaret Atwood's Oryx and Crake. In: *The Journal of Ecocriticism* 5/1 (2013), pp. 1–15.
Dunn, Elizabeth W./Norton, Michael I.: How to Make Giving Feel Good. In: *Greater Good Magazine* (18.06.2013), https://greatergood.berkeley.edu/article/item/how_to_make_giving_feel_good [last access: 04.04.2023].
Dweck, Carol: The Power of Believing That You Can Improve. On: *TED* (17.12.2014), https://www.ted.com/talks/carol_dweck_the_power_of_believing_that_you_can_improve [last access: 04.04.2023].
Eggers, Dave: *The Circle.* New York 2013.
Ehrenreich, Barbara: *Bright-Sided: How Positive Thinking Is Undermining America.* New York 2009.
Ellerton, Peter: Listen and Learn: The Language of Science and Skepticism. In: *The Conversation* (25.04.2012), https://theconversation.com/listen-and-learn-the-language-of-science-and-scepticism-6633 [last access: 04.04.2023].
Elmer, Jonathan: Public Humanities in the Age of the Ideas Industry and the Rise of the Creatives. In: *University of Toronto Quarterly* 85/4 (2016), pp. 109–117.
Emerson, Ralph Waldo: The American Scholar. In: Baym, Nina (Ed.): *The Norton Anthology of American Literature.* New York 2003, pp. 1135–1147.

Emerson, Ralph Waldo: Nature. In: Baym, Nina (Ed.): *The Norton Anthology of American Literature*. New York⁶ 2003, pp. 1106–1134.

Ensler, Eve: Happiness in Body and Soul. On: *TED* (04.03.2014), https://www.ted.com/talks/eve_ensler_happiness_in_body_and_soul [last access: 04.04.2023].

Epstein, David: Are Athletes Really Getting Faster, Better, Stronger. On: *TED* (29.04.2014), https://www.ted.com/talks/david_epstein_are_athletes_really_getting_faster_better_stronger [last accessed: 04.04.2023].

Ereshefsky, Marc: Species. In: *The Stanford Encyclopedia of Philosophy* (2022), https://plato.stanford.edu/entries/species/ [last access: 04.04.2023].

Etcoff, Nancy: Happiness and its Surprises. On: *TED* (09.06.2009), https://www.ted.com/talks/nancy_etcoff_happiness_and_its_surprises [last access: 04.04.2023].

Ette, Ottmar: Literature as Knowledge for Living. In: *MLA Journals: PMLA* 125/4 (2010), pp. 977–993.

Euritt, Alyn: *Podcasting as an Intimate Medium*. London 2022.

Federspil, Giovanni/Sicolo, Nicola: The Nature of Life in the History of Medical and Philosophic Thinking. In: *American Journal of Nephrology* 50/4–6 (1994), pp. 337–343.

Felski, Rita: *The Limits of Critique*. Chicago 2015.

Felski, Rita: Response. In: *PMLA* 132/2 (2017), pp. 384–391.

Felski, Rita: *Uses of Literature*. Malden 2008.

Ferrando, Francesca: Posthumanism, Transhumanism, Antihumanism, Metahumanism, and New Materialisms: Differences and Relations. In: *Existenz* 8/2 (2013), pp. 26–32.

Ferreira, Marie Aline: "Toward a Science of Perfect Reproduction?": Visions of Eugenics in Contemporary Fiction. In: Barfoot, C.C./Tinkler-Villani, Valeria (Eds.): *Restoring the Mystery of the Rainbow: Literature's Refraction of Science*. Amsterdam 2011, pp. 295–415.

Filip, Loredana: Be-Longing in TED Talks on 'What is Home?' and Contemporary Postcolonial Fiction. In: Flügge, Anna/Tommasi, Giorgia (Eds.): *Perspectives on Homelessness*. Heidelberg 2022, pp. 273–299.

Filip, Loredana: The Future of the Enhanced Self and Contemporary Science Fiction: TED Talks and Dave Eggers' The Circle (2013). In: *Current Objectives of Postgraduate American Studies* 20/1 (2019), pp. 24–39.

Filip, Loredana: Genetic Enhancement, TED Talks, and the Sense of Wonder. In: *Medial Humanities* 47 (2021), pp. 210–218.

Filip, Loredana: Insight: Making a Case for Self-Vigilance. On: *Vigilanzkulturen, Hypotheses* (29.03.2022), https://vigilanz.hypotheses.org/2935 [last access: 04.04.2023].

Filip, Loredana: Self-Help in Times of Corona: Vigilance vs. Positive Thinking? On: *Vigilanzkulturen, Hypotheses* (23.03.2020), https://vigilanz.hypotheses.org/31 [last access: 04.04.2023].

Filip, Loredana: Vigilance to Wonder: Human Enhancement in TED Talks. In: Baelo-Allué, Sonia/Calvo-Pascual, Mónica (Eds.): *Transhumanism and Posthumanism in Twenty-First Century Narrative*. New York 2021, pp. 71–84.

Fisher, Helen: The Brain in Love. On: *TED* (15.07.2008), https://www.ted.com/talks/helen_fisher_the_brain_in_love [last access: 04.04.2023].

Fitz, Karsten/Harju, Bärbel: Cultures of Privacy: An Introduction. In: Fitz, Karsten/Harju, Bärbel (Eds.): *Cultures of Privacy: Paradigms, Transformations, Contestations*. Heidelberg 2015, pp. 1–15.

Fitz, Karsten: "Privatizing" the White House: American Presidents and the Visual Aesthetics of Privacy. In: Fitz, Karsten/Harju, Bärbel (Eds.): *Cultures of Privacy: Paradigms, Transformations, Contestations*. Heidelberg 2015, pp. 117–143.

Fluck, Winfried: Surface Readings and Symptomatic Readings: American Studies and the Realities of America. In: Fluck, Winfried/Pease, Donald (Eds.): *Towards a Post-Exceptionalist American Studies*, *REAL* 30 (2014), pp. 41–65.
For Those Who Want to Break Out of Their Shell. On: *TED*, https://www.ted.com/playlists/362/for_those_who_want_to_break_ou [last access: 04.04.2023].
Foucault, Michel: *Discipline and Punish: The Birth of the Prison*. New York 1977.
Foucault, Michel: *The History of Sexuality. Volume 1: An Introduction*. New York 1978.
Foucault, Michel: Technologies of the Self. In: Gutman, Huck/Hutton, Patrick H./Luther, H. Martin (Eds.): *Technologies of the Self: A Seminar with Michel Foucault*. Amherst 1988, pp. 16–49.
Fox, Nick J/Alldred, Pam: New Materialism. In: Atkinson, P.A/Delamont, S./Hardy, M.A./Williams, M (Eds.): *The SAGE Encyclopedia of Research Methods*. London 2018, pp. 1–16.
Foy, Nathalie: The Representation of the Absent Mother in Margaret Atwood's Oryx and Crake. In: Kozakewich, Tobi/Moss, John (Eds.): *Margaret Atwood: The Open Eye*. Ottawa 2006, 407–419.
Franklin, Benjamin: *Autobiography of Benjamin Franklin: 1706–1757*. Auckland 2009.
Freitas, Donna: *The Happiness Effect: How Social Media Is Driving a Generation to Appear Perfect at Any Cost*. Oxford 2017.
French, Steven: *Science: Key Concepts in Philosophy*. London 2007.
Freud, Sigmund: *Psycho-Analytic Notes on an Autobiographical Account of a Case of Paranoia (Dementia Paranoides)*. Redditch 2014.
Friedman, Susan: Both/And: Critique and Discovery in the Humanities. In: *PMLA* 132/2 (2017), pp, 344–351.
Fuhrmann, Delia: Being Kind Makes Kids Happy. In: *Greater Good Magazine* (01.08.2012), https://greatergood.berkeley.edu/article/item/being_kind_makes_kids_happy [last access: 05.04.2023].
Fukuyama, Francis: *Our Posthuman Future: Consequences of the Biotechnological Revolution*. New York 2002.
Gallo, David: Underwater Astonishments. On: *TED* (04.03.2014), https://www.ted.com/talks/david_gallo_underwater_astonishments [last access: 05.04.2023].
Gannett, Lisa: The Human Genome Project. In: *The Stanford Encyclopedia of Philosophy* (2002), https://plato.stanford.edu/archives/sum2022/entries/human-genome/ [last access: 05.04.2023].
Garber, Marjorie: *A Manifesto for Literary Studies*. Seattle 2003.
García-Pinar, Aránzazu: Getting Closer to Authenticity in the Course of Technical English: Task-Based Instruction and TED Talks. In: *English Language Teaching* 12/11 (2019), pp. 10–22.
García-Pinar, Aránzazu: The Influence of TED Talks on ESP Undergraduate Students' L2 Motivational Self System in the Speaking Skill: A Mixed Method Study. In: *ESP Today: Journal of English for Specific Purposes at Tertiary Level* 7/2 (2019), pp. 231–252.
Garrard, Greg: Reading as an Animal: Ecocriticism and Darwinism in Margaret Atwood and Ian McEwan. In: Detmers, Ines/Grimm, Nancy/Thomson, Katrin/Volkmann, Laurenz (Eds.): *Local Natures, Global Responsibilities: Ecocritical Perspectives on the New English Literatures, ASNEL Papers 15*. Amsterdam 2010, pp. 223–242.
Garrett, Matthew: You Have to Read First. In: *American Literary History* 29/1, pp. 142–155.
Garten, Ariel: Knowing Thyself with a Brain Scanner. On: *TED* (26.11.2011), https://www.ted.com/talks/ariel_garten_know_thyself_with_a_brain_scanner [last access: 06.04.2023].
Gavenila, Euodia Inge/Renandya, Willy A./Wulandari, Mega: Using TED Talks for Extensive Listening. In: *PASAA: A Journal of Language Teaching & Learning in Thailand* 61 (2021), pp. 147–175.
Genette, Gérard. *Narrative Discourse: An Essay in Method*. New York 1983.

Gerald, Casey: Embrace Your Raw, Strange Magic. On: *TED* (17.01.2019), https://www.ted.com/talks/casey_gerald_embrace_your_raw_strange_magic [last access: 06.04.2023].
Gerund, Katharina/Paul, Heike. "Sentimentalism." In: Christine Gerhardt (Ed.): *Handbook of the American Novel of the Nineteenth Century*. Berlin/Boston, 2018, pp. 1–17.
Ghalleb, Ines: *The Interdisciplinary Mind: Modes of Evolution in Richard Powers' Novels*. Hildesheim 2021.
Gilbert, Dan: The Surprising Science of Happiness. On: *TED* (12.08.2013), https://www.ted.com/talks/dan_gilbert_the_surprising_science_of_happiness [last access: 06.04.2023].
Gilbert, Elizabeth: The Surprising Science of Happiness. On: *TED* (25.04.2014), https://www.ted.com/talks/elizabeth_gilbert_your_elusive_creative_genius [last access: 06.04.2023].
Gilman, Charlotte Perkins: The Yellow Wallpaper. In: Baym, Nina (Eds.): *The Norton Anthology of American Literature 1865–1914*. New York [6]1998, pp. 832–845.
Gilmore, Leigh: American Neoconfessional: Memoir, Self-Help, and Redemption on Oprah's Couch. In: *Biography* 33/4 (2010), pp. 657–679.
Ginsburg, Michal Peled: Narratives of Survival. In: *NOVEL: A Forum on Fiction* 42/3 (2009), pp. 410–416.
Giusti, Francesco: Passionate Affinities: A Conversation with Rita Felski. In: *Los Angeles Review of Books* (25.09.2019), https://lareviewofbooks.org/article/passionate-affinities-a-%20conversation-with-rita-felski/ [last access: 06.04.2023].
Gladwell, Malcolm: Choice, Happiness, and Spaghetti Sauce. On: *TED* (04.03.2014), https://www.ted.com/talks/malcolm_gladwell_choice_happiness_and_spaghetti_sauce [last access: 06.04.2023].
Goethe, Johann Wolfgang von: *Faust: Part One*. Oxford 1987.
Goodwin, Kim: Mansplaining, Explained in One Simple Chart. On: *BBC* (29.07.2018), https://www.bbc.com/worklife/article/20180727-mansplaining-explained-in-one-chart [last access: 06.04.2023].
Gossin, Pamela: *Encyclopedia of Literature and Science*. London 2002.
Grace, Daphne M: Cognition, Consciousness and Literary Contexts. In: *Beyond Bodies: Gender, Literature and the Enigma of Consciousness*. Amsterdam 2014, pp. 9–33.
Grace, Daphne M: Consciousness and Conscience: The Ethics of Enlightenment. In: *Beyond Bodies: Gender, Literature and the Enigma of Consciousness*. Amsterdam 2014, pp. 215–229.
Grace, Daphne M: Quests and Questions of Consciousness: Margaret Atwood's Post-Human Futures. In: *Beyond Bodies: Gender, Literature and the Enigma of Consciousness*. Amsterdam 2014, pp. 197–214.
Gratzke, Michael: The Rise and Fall of 'Emotional Capitalism': Consumerism and Materialities of Love in Dystopian Works by Thomas Melle, Leif Randt and Gary Shteyngart. In: Gratzke, Michael/Malinowska, Anna (Eds.): *The Materiality of Love: Essays on Affection and Cultural Practice*. New York 2018, pp. 101–117.
Greenberg, Sean/Murray, Michael J.: Leibniz on the Problem of Evil. In: *The Stanford Encyclopedia of Philosophy* (2016), https://plato.stanford.edu/entries/leibniz-evil/ [last access: 16.04.2023].
Greenblatt, Stephen Jay: Culture. In: Lentricchia, Frank/McLaughlin, Thomas (Eds.): *Critical Terms for Literary Studies*. Chicago [2]2010, pp. 225–233.
Greenblatt, Stephen Jay: *Renaissance Self-Fashioning*. Chicago 1980.
Gregoire, Carolyn: A Free Online Course on the Science of Happiness Is About to Begin. In: *Huffpost* (08.09.2014), https://www.huffpost.com/entry/why-nearly-100000-people_n_5761258 [last access: 06.04.2023].

Gretzky, Madison: After the Fall: Humanity Narrated in Margaret Atwood's *Maddaddam* Trilogy. In: *Margaret Atwood Studies* 11 (2017), pp. 41–54.

Griskevicius, Vladas/Kenrick, Douglas T./Neuberg, Steven L./Schaller, Mark: Renovating the Pyramid of Needs: Contemporary Extensions Built Upon Ancient Foundations. In: *Perspect Psychol Sci* 5/3 (2010), pp. 292–314.

Grobe, Christopher: *The Art of Confession: The Performance of the Self from Robert Lowell to Reality TV.* New York 2017.

Grobe, Christopher: On Book: The Performance of Reading. In: *New Literary History* 47/4 (2016), pp. 567–589.

Guignon, Charles/Varga, Somogy: Authenticity. In: *The Stanford Encyclopedia of Philosophy* (2020), https://plato.stanford.edu/archives/spr2020/entries/authenticity/ [last access: 21.04.2023].

Gutman, Ron: The Hidden Power of Smiling. On: *TED* (11.05.2011), https://www.ted.com/talks/ron_gutman_the_hidden_power_of_smiling [last access: 06.04.2023].

Haase, Felix: Death by Data: Identification and Dataveillance in Gary Shteyngart's Super Sad True Love Story. In: Gross, Andrew/Zappe, Florian (Eds.): *Surveillance | Society | Culture.* Bern 2020, pp. 85–101.

Haidt, Jonathan/Hood, Ralph W./Newberg, Andrew B./Vago, David R./Yaden, David Brice: The Varieties of Self-Transcendent Experience. In: *Review of General Psychology* 22/2 (2017), pp. 1–18.

Hall, Stuart: Encoding and Decoding in the Television Discourse. In: Morley, David (Ed.): *Essential Essays, Volume 1.* Durham 1973, pp. 1–19.

Hamann, Paul: Under Surveillance: Genetic Privacy in Margaret Atwood's *MaddAddam* Trilogy. In: *Journal of Literature and Science* 12/2 (2019), pp. 62–79.

Hamner, Everett: The Predisposed Agency of Genomic Fiction. In: *American Literature: A Journal of Literary History, Criticism, and Bibliography* 83/2 (2011), pp. 413–441.

Haraway, Donna: A Cyborg Manifesto: Science Technology, and Socialist-Feminism in the Late Twentieth Century. In: *Simians, Cyborgs and Women: The Reinvention of Nature.* New York 1991, pp. 149–181.

Harel, Naama: Constructing the Nonhuman as Human: Scientific Fallacy, Literary Device. In: Barfoot, C.C./Tinkler-Villani, Valeria (Eds.): *Restoring the Mystery of the Rainbow: Literature's Refraction of Science.* Amsterdam 2011, pp. 897–911.

Harju, Bärbel: Too Much Information: Self-Monitoring and Confessional Culture. In: Gross, Andrew/Zappe, Florian (Eds.): *Surveillance | Society | Culture.* Bern 2020, pp. 57–81.

Harju, Bärbel: Privacy Crisis: Architecture, Suburbia, and Postwar America. In: Fitz, Karsten/Harju, Bärbel (Eds.): *Cultures of Privacy: Paradigms, Transformations, Contestations.* Heidelberg 2015, pp. 95–117.

Harland, Paul W.: Ecological Grief and Therapeutic Storytelling in Margaret Atwood's Maddaddam Trilogy. In: *ISLE: Interdisciplinary Studies in Literature and Environment* 23/3 (2016), pp. 583–602.

Harrington, Anne: *The Cure Within: A History of Mind-Body Medicine.* New York 2008.

Harris, John: *Enhancing Evolution.* Princeton 2010.

Harris, Tristan: How a Handful Tech Companies Control Billions of Minds Every Day. On: *TED* (26.07.2017),https://www.ted.com/talks/tristan_harris_how_a_handful_of_tech_companies_control_billions_of_minds_every_day [last access: 06.04.2023].

Haselstein, Ulla/Gross, Andrew S./Snyder-Körber, Maryann: Introduction: Returns of the Real. In: Haselstein, Ulla/Gross, Andrew S./Snyder-Körber, Maryann (Eds.): *The Pathos of Authenticity: American Passions of the Real*. Heidelberg 2010, pp. 9–31.

Hauskeller, Michael: *Better Humans? Understanding the Enhancement Project*. Durham 2013.

Hawking, Stephen: Questioning the Universe. On: *TED* (11.01.2014), https://www.ted.com/talks/stephen_hawking_questioning_the_universe [last access: 06.05.2023].

Hawthorne, Nathaniel: Rappacini's Daughter. In: Baym, Nina (Eds.): *The Norton Anthology of American Literature 1820–1865*. New York ^{6}2003, pp. 1313–1333.

Hawthorne, Nathaniel: *The Scarlet Letter: A Romance*. London 1852.

Hayles, Katherine: *How We Became Posthuman: Virtual Bodies in Cybernetics, Literature, and Informatics*. Chicago 2008.

Heinke, Christine: Hillary & Bill, Jackie & Jack, Michelle & Barack – A Public Love: US American First Ladies in the Limelight. In: Fitz, Karsten/Harju, Bärbel (Eds.): *Cultures of Privacy: Paradigms, Transformations, Contestations*. Heidelberg 2015, pp. 143–167.

Hengen, Shannon: Moral/Environmental Debt in Payback and Oryx and Crake. In: Bouson, J. Brooks (Eds.): *Margaret Atwood: The Robber Bride, The Blind Assassin, Oryx and Crake*. London 2010, pp. 129–140.

Herbrechter, Stefan: *Posthumanism: A Critical Analysis*. London 2013.

Herbrechter, Stefan/Callus, Ivan: What's Wrong with Posthumanism. On: *Rhizomes: Cultural Studies in Emerging Knowledge* (2003), http://www.rhizomes.net/issue7/callus.htm [last access: 06.04.2023].

Herwig, Malte: Ironic Science: Some Remarks on Humanism, Science, and Literature. In: Barfoot, C.C./Tinkler-Villani, Valeria (Eds.): *Restoring the Mystery of the Rainbow: Literature's Refraction of Science*. Amsterdam 2011, pp. 167–186.

Hill, Graham: Less Stuff, More Happiness. On: *TED* (24.03.2014), https://www.ted.com/talks/graham_hill_less_stuff_more_happiness [last access: 06.04.2023].

Hill, Napoleon: *Think and Grow Rich*. Glendale 1937.

His Holiness the Karmapa: The Technology of the Heart. On: *TED* (24.03.2014), https://www.ted.com/talks/his_holiness_the_karmapa_the_technology_of_the_heart [last access: 06.04.2023].

Hochschild, Arlie Russell: *The Managed Heart: Commercialization of Human Feeling*. Berkeley 1987.

Hogan, Patrick Colm: Affect Studies and Literary Criticism. In: Rabinowitz, Paula (Ed.): *Oxford Research Encyclopedia of Literature*. Oxford 2016.

Honoré, Carl: In Praise of Slowness. On: *TED* (04.03.2014), https://www.ted.com/talks/carl_honore_in_praise_of_slowness [last access: 06.04.2023].

Hornung, Alfred: *Auto/Biography and Mediation*. Heidelberg 2010.

Howard, Shannon: Ideas Worth Spreading?: TED's Rhetorical Position in College Composition. On: *The CEA Forum* (2017), pp. 62–87.

How TED Works. On: *TED*, https://www.ted.com/about/our-organization/how-ted-works [last access: 06.04.2023].

How to Be a Better You. On: *TED*. https://www.ted.com/playlists/8/a_better_you [last access: 10.04.2023].

How to Protect Your Passions from Burnout. On: *TED*, https://www.ted.com/playlists/689/how_to_protect_your_passions_from_burnout [last access: 10.04.2023].

Höpker, Karin: Happiness in Distress – Richard Powers' Generosity and Narratives of the Biomedical Self. In: Kley, Antje/Kucharzewski, Jan D. (Eds.): *Ideas of Order: Narrative Patterns in the Novels of Richard Powers*. Heidelberg 2012, pp. 285–312.

Huehls, Mitchum: Four Theses on Economic Totality. In: *American Literary History* 30/4 (2018), pp. 285–312.
Ickstadt, Heinz: 'Asynchronous Messaging': The Multiple Functions of Richard Powers' Fictions. In: Kley, Antje/Kucharzewski, Jan D. (Eds.): *Ideas of Order: Narrative Patterns in the Novels of Richard Powers*. Heidelberg 2012, pp. 23–43.
Illouz, Eva: *Emotions as Commodities: Capitalism, Consumption and Authenticity.* London 2017.
Illouz, Eva: Romantic Love and Its Discontents: Irony, Reason, Romance. In: *The Hedgehog Review* 12/1 (2010), pp. 18–32.
Illouz, Eva: *Saving the Modern Soul: Therapy, Emotions, and the Culture of Self-Help.* Berkeley 2008.
Impact Theory. On: *Impact Theory*, https://impacttheory.com [last access: 10.04.2023].
Insight. In: *Merriam-Webster*, https://www.merriam-webster.com/dictionary/insight [last access: 10.04.2023].
INTO THE WILD (USA, 2007).
Iyer, Pico: The Art of Stillness. On: *TED* (26.11.2014), https://www.ted.com/talks/pico_iyer_the_art_of_stillness [last access: 10.04.2023].
James, David: Critical Solace. In: *New Literary History* 47/4 (2016), pp. 481–504.
Jay, Martin: *Downcast Eyes: The Denigration of Vision in Twentieth-Century French Thought.* Berkeley 1993.
Jennings, Hope: Anthropocene Feminism, Companion Species, and the Maddaddam Trilogy. In: *Contemporary Women's Writing*, 13/1 (2019), pp. 16–33.
Jennings, Hope: The Comic Apocalypse of The Year of the Flood. In: *Margaret Atwood Studies* 3/2 (2010), pp. 11–18.
Jensen, Robert: Whiteness. In: Whiteness, Stephen M./McIlwain, Charlton D. (Eds.): *The Routledge Companion to Race and Ethnicity.* London 2011, pp. 21–28.
Jha, Amishi: How to Tame Your Wandering Mind. On: *TED* (23.03.2018), https://www.ted.com/talks/amishi_jha_how_to_tame_your_wandering_mind [last access: 10.04.2023].
Journalism. In: *The New York Times Company*, https://www.nytco.com/journalism/ [last access: 10.04.2023].
Kahneman, Daniel. The Riddle of Experience vs. Memory. On: TED (01.03.2010), https://www.ted.com/talks/daniel_kahneman_the_riddle_of_experience_vs_memory [last access: 10.04.2023].
Keck, Michaela: Paradise Retold: Revisionist Mythmaking in Margaret Atwood's MaddAddam Trilogy. In: *Ecozon@* 9/2 (2018), pp. 23–40.
Kedrowicz, April/Taylor, Julie: Shifting Rhetorical Norms and Electronic Eloquence: TED Talks as Formal Presentations. In: *Journal of Business and Technical Communication* 30/3 (2016), pp. 352–377.
Keltner, Dacher/Simon-Thomas, Emiliana: Course Syllabus: GG101x: The Science of Happiness. On: *edX*, https://www.edx.org/course/the-science-of-happiness-3 [last access: 10.04.2023].
Keltner, Dacher: The Compassionate Instinct. In: *The Greater Good Magazine* (01.03.2004), https://greatergood.berkeley.edu/article/item/the_compassionate_instinct [last access: 10.04.2023].
Keltner, Dacher (host): Three Good Things (episode 1). In: *The Science of Happiness* (05.02.2018), https://greatergood.berkeley.edu/podcasts/item/3_good_things [last access: 10.04.2023].
Keltner, Dacher (host): Quieting Your Inner Critic (episode 2). In: *The Science of Happiness* (05.02.2018), https://greatergood.berkeley.edu/podcasts/item/quieting_your_inner_critic [last access: 10.04.2023].

Keltner, Dacher (host): Walk Outside with Inside Out's Pete Doctor (episode 5). In: *The Science of Happiness* (26.02.2018), https://greatergood.berkeley.edu/podcasts/item/walk_docter_inside_out [last access: 10.04.2023].
Keltner, Dacher (host): Krista Tippett on Being Grounded in Your Body (episode 6). In: *The Science of Happiness* (05.03.2018), https://greatergood.berkeley.edu/podcasts/item/krista_tippett_on_body [last access: 10.04.2023].
Keltner, Dacher (host): How Gratitude Benefits Your Brain (episode 7). In: *The Science of Happiness* (12.03.2018), https://greatergood.berkeley.edu/podcasts/item/gratitude_benefits_your_brain [last access: 10.04.2023].
Keltner, Dacher (host): How to Forgive Your Father (episode 13), In: *The Science of Happiness* (21.06.2018), https://greatergood.berkeley.edu/podcasts/item/forgive_your_father [last access: 10.04.2023].
Keltner, Dacher (host): Listen Like It's Your First Date (episode 18). In: *The Science of Happiness* (26.07.2018), https://greatergood.berkeley.edu/podcasts/item/listen_like_your_first_date [last access: 10.04.2023].
Keltner, Dacher (host): What to Do When You Feel Like a Failure (episode 40). In: *The Science of Happiness* (11.04.2019), https://greatergood.berkeley.edu/podcasts/item/erin_morrow [last access: 10.04.2023].
Keltner, Dacher (host): A Better Way to Talk to Yourself (episode 41). In: *The Science of Happiness* (06.06.2019), https://greatergood.berkeley.edu/podcasts/item/theresa_scott [last access: 10.04.2023].
Keltner, Dacher (host): How to Be Less Hard on Yourself (episode 54). In: *The Science of Happiness* (05.12.2019), https://greatergood.berkeley.edu/podcasts/item/how_to_be_less_hard_on_yourself [last access: 10.04.2023].
Kern, Chelsea Oei: Big Data and the Practice of Reading in Super Sad True Love Story. In: *Arizona Quarterly: A Journal of American Literature, Culture, and Theory* 76/3 (2020), pp. 81–105.
Killingsworth, Matt: Want to Be Happier? Stay in the Moment. On: *TED* (16.03.2014), https://www.ted.com/talks/matt_killingsworth_want_to_be_happier_stay_in_the_moment [last access: 10.04.2023].
Kirkpatrick, Kate: Is Shame an Emotion? In: *The Oxford Philosopher* (21.06.2017), https://theoxfordphilosopher.com/2017/06/21/is-shame-an-emotion/amp [last access: 10.04.2023].
Kley, Antje: Literary Knowledge Production and the Natural Sciences in the US. In: Knewitz, Simone/Klöckner, Christian/Sielke, Sabine (Eds.): *Knowledge Landscapes North America*. Heidelberg 2016, pp. 153–177.
Kloeckner, Christian/Knewitz, Simone/Sielke, Sabine: *Knowledge Landscapes North America*. Heidelberg 2016.
Kovach, Elizabeth: E-pistolary Novels and Networks: Registering Formal Shifts between Henry Fielding's *Shamela* (1741) and Gary Shteyngart's *Super Sad True Love Story* (2010). In: Löschnigg, Maria/Schuh, Rebekka (Eds.): *The Epistolary Renaissance: A Critical Approach to Contemporary Letter Narratives in Anglophone Fiction*. Berlin 2018, pp. 261–276.
Koziol, Slawomir: Crake's Aesthetic: Genetically Modified Humans as a Form of Art in Margaret Atwood's Oryx and Crake. In: *Critique: Studies in Contemporary Fiction* 59/4 (2018), pp. 492–508.
Koziol, Slawomir: From Sausages to Hoplites of Ham and Beyond: The Status of Genetically Modified Pigs in Margaret Atwood's MaddAddam Trilogy. In: *Papers on Language and Literature* 54/3 (2018), pp. 261–295.

Kozubek, Jim: How Gene Editing Could Ruin Human Evolution. In: *Time* (09.01.2017), https://time.com/4626571/crispr-gene-modification-evolution/ [last access: 11.04.2023].

Krznaric, Roman: Six Habits of Highly Empathic People. In: *Greater Good Magazine* (27.11.2012), https://greatergood.berkeley.edu/article/item/six_habits_of_highly_empathic_people1 [last access: 11.04.2023].

Kucharzewski, Jan D: *Propositions about Life: Reengaging Literature and Science.* Heidelberg 2011.

Kuhn, Thomas S: *The Structure of Scientific Revolutions.* Chicago 1970.

Ku, Chung-Hao: Of Monster and Man: Transgenics and Transgression in Margaret Atwood's Oryx and Crake. In: *Concentric: Literary and Cultural Studies* 32/1 (2006), pp. 107–133.

Kung, Szu-Wen: Critical Theory of Technology and Actor-Network Theory in the Examination of Techno-Empowered Online Collaborative Translation Practice: TED Talks on the Amara Subtitle Platform as a Case Study. In: *Babel: Revue Internationale de la Traduction/International Journal of Translation* 67/1 (2021), pp. 75–98.

Kurzweil, Ray: Get Ready for Hybrid Thinking. On: *TED* (02.06.2014), https://www.ted.com/talks/ray_kurzweil_get_ready_for_hybrid_thinking [last access: 11.04.2023].

La Caze, Marguerite/Lloyd, Henry Martin: Editor's Introduction: Philosophy and the 'Affective Turn'. In: *Parrhesia* 13 (2011), pp. 1–13.

Lacombe, Michèle: Resistance in Futility: The Cyborg Identities of Oryx and Crake. In: Kozakewich, Tobi/Moss, John (Eds.): *Margaret Atwood: The Open Eye.* Ottawa 2006, pp. 421–432.

Lanzendörfer, Tim/Nilges, Mathias: Literary Studies after Postcritique: An Introduction. In: *Amerikastudien/American Studies* 64/4 (2019), pp. 491–513.

Latour, Bruno: Why Has Critique Run out of Steam? From Matters of Fact to Matters of Concern. In: *Critical Inquiry* 30 (2004), pp. 225–248.

Lee, Kristen: Has Mindfulness Become the New Kale? In: *Psychology Today* (05.01.2018), https://www.psychologytoday.com/intl/blog/rethink-your-way-the-good-life/201801/has-mindfulness-become-the-new-kale [last access: 14.04.2023].

Lee, Maurice S.: Deserted Islands and Overwhelmed Readers. In: *American Literary History* 26/2 (2014), pp. 207–233.

Levitin, Daniel: How to Stay Calm When You Know You'll Be Stressed. On: *TED* (30.09.2015), https://ed.ted.com/lessons/Ge4NK6fZ [last access: 14.04.2023].

Leys, Ruth: The Turn to Affect: A Critique. In: *Critical Inquiry* 37/3 (2011), pp. 434–472.

Li, Stephanie: Techno-Orientalism and the End of History in Gary Shteyngart's Super Sad True Love Story. In: Lavender, Isiah (Ed.): *Dis-Orienting Planets: Racial Representations of Asia in Science Fiction*, Jackson 2017, pp. 102–116.

Lightman, Alex: The Rise of the Citizen Scientist. In: Goertzel, Ben/Orban, David/Sirius, R.U. (Eds.): *Best of H+ Magazine*, CreateSpace Independent Publishing Platform 2013, pp. 13–21.

Love, Heather: Close but not Deep: Literary Ethics and the Descriptive Turn. In: *New Literary History* 41 (2010), pp. 371–391.

Lovelace, Christopher T.: Synesthesia in the Twenty-First Century: Synesthesia's Ascent. In: Hubbard, Edward M./Simner, Julia (Eds.): *The Oxford Handbook of Synesthesia.* Oxford 2018, pp. 409–440.

Ludewig, Julia: TED Talks as an Emergent Genre. In: *CLCWeb: Comparative Literature and Culture* 19/1 (2017), pp. 1–9.

Lunbeck, Elizabeth: Empathy as a Psychoanalytic Mode of Observation. In: Daston, Lorraine/Lunbeck, Elizabeth (Eds.): *Histories of Scientific Observation.* Chicago 2011, pp. 255–275.

Malewitz, Raymond: Some New Dimension Devoid of Hip and Bone': Remediated Bodies and Digital Posthumanism in Gary Steyngart's Super Sad True Love Story. In: *Arizona Quarterly: A Journal of American Literature, Culture, and Theory* 71/4 (2015), pp. 107–127.

Mann, Dhar: Bully Makes Fun of Nerd, Lives to Regret His Decision. On: *Facebook* (09.07.2019), https://www.facebook.com/watch/?v=381055202764606 [last access: 14.04.2023].

Mann, Dhar: Homeless Mom Collects Cans for Cash, Stranger Changes Her Life Forever. On: *Facebook* (27.07.2020), https://www.facebook.com/watch/?v=1045431879193132 [last access: 14.04.2023].

Mann, Dhar: My Life is like a Movie. On: Dhar Mann, https://www.dharmann.com/about [last access: 04.04.2023].

Mann, Dhar: Rich Dad Humiliates Poor Dad He Then Gets Instant Karma. On: *Facebook* (19.03.2020), https://www.facebook.com/watch/?v=680929632446691 [last access: 14.04.2023].

Mann, Dhar: Rich Man Destroys Shelter, He Lives to Regret It. On: *Facebook* (14.04.2022), https://www.facebook.com/watch/?v=1232619340888775 [last access: 14.04.2023].

Mann, Dhar: Spoiled Son Refuses to Get a Job, He Instantly Regrets His Decision. On: *Facebook* (28.05.2021), https://www.facebook.com/watch/?v=196139705693570 [last access: 14.04.2023].

Mann, Dhar: Spoiled Wife Fires Housekeeper, Instantly Regrets It. On: Facebook (14.09.2020), https://www.facebook.com/watch/?v=2717714831845347 [last access: 14.04.2023].

Mann, Dhar: Woman Is Getting Evicted from Her Home, You'll Never Believe What Happens Next. On: *Facebook* (22.11.2019), https://www.facebook.com/watch/?v=1204133649785725 [last access: 14.04.2023].

Manson, Mark: *Everything Is F*cked: A Book About Hope.* New York 2019.

Marks, Peter: Pleeblands, Compounds and Paradice: Utopian and Dystopian Spaces in Oryx and Crake. In: Marks, Peter (Ed.): *Literature and Politics: Pushing the World in Certain Directions.* Newcastle upon Tyne 2012, pp. 214–224.

Marx, Kate: Dystopian (Non)Fiction? Shteyngart, McCarthy and the Fall of the Animal Kingdom. In: *eSharp: Electronic Social Sciences, Humanities, and Arts Review for Postgraduates* 25/1 (2017), pp.1–11.

Maslow, Abraham Harold: *Motivation and Personality.* New York 1954.

Matthews, Samantha: Autobiography. On: *Oxford Bibliographies* (24.07.2013), https://www.oxfordbibliographies.com/display/document/obo-9780199799558/obo-9780199799558–0023.xml [last access: 16.04.2023].

McAdams, Dan P.: American Identity: The Redemptive Self. In: *The General Psychologist* 43/1 (2008), pp. 20–27.

McClanahan, Annie: Bad Credit: The Character of Credit Scoring. In: *Representations* 126/1; Special Issue: *Financialization and the Culture Industry* (2014), pp. 31–57.

McCrary, Jessica Edens: Changing the Subject: A Theory of Rhetorical Empathy. In: *South Atlantic Review* 86/2 (2021), pp.80+.

McGee, Micky: *Self-Help, Inc.: Makeover Culture in American Life.* Oxford 2005.

McGonigal, Kelly: How to Make Stress Your Friend. On: *TED* (04.09.2013), https://www.ted.com/talks/kelly_mcgonigal_how_to_make_stress_your_friend/comments [last access: 16.04.2023].

McInerney, Jay: Why Is She Smiling? In: *The New York Times* (01.10.2009), https://www.nytimes.com/2009/10/04/books/review/McInerney-t.html [last access: 16.04.2023].

McMahon, Darrin M.: Happiness, the Hard Way. In: *The Greater Good Magazine* (01.05.2009), https://greatergood.berkeley.edu/article/item/happiness_the_hard_way [last access: 16.04.2023].

Mead, Elaine: The History and Origin of Meditation. On: *Positive Psychology* (27.05.2019), https://positivepsychology.com/history-of-meditation/ [last access: 16.04.2023].

Mendlesohn, Farah: Introduction: Reading Science Fiction. In: James, Edward/Mendlesohn, Farah (Eds.): *The Cambridge Companion to Science Fiction*. Cambridge 2003, pp. 1–15.

Merikle, Philip M.: Toward a Definition of Awareness. In: *Bulletin of the Psychonomic Society* 22/5 (1984), pp. 449–450.

Meyer, Pamela: How to Spot a Liar. On: *TED* (11.03.2014), https://www.ted.com/talks/pamela_meyer_how_to_spot_a_liar [last access: 16.04.2023].

Michelson, Jared: Preaching as Confession. On: *Mere Orthodoxy* (16.03.2021), https://mereorthodoxy.com/preaching-as-confession/ [last access: 16.04.2023].

Miller, Arthur: *Death of a Salesman*. London 1989.

Mohr, Dunja M.: When Species Meet': Beyond Posthuman Boundaries and Interspeciesism – Social Justice and Canadian Speculative Fiction. In: *Zeitschrift für Kanada-Studien* 37 (2017), pp. 40–64.

Moi, Toril: *Revolution of the Ordinary: Literary Studies after Wittgenstein, Austin, and Cavell*. Chicago 2017.

More, Max: The Extropian Principles 2.5. In: *The Extropian Principles* (1993), http://www.aleph.se/Trans/Cultural/Philosophy/princip.html [last access: 16.04.2023].

Moretti, Franco: *Distant Reading*. London/New York 2013.

Moretti, Franco: Franco Moretti: A Response. In: *PMLA* 132/2 (2017), pp. 686–689.

Morin, Alain: Toward a Glossary of Self-Related Terms. In: *Frontiers in Psychology* 8/280 (28.02.2017), pp. 1–9.

Mosca, Valeria: Crossing Human Boundaries: Apocalypse and Posthumanism in Margaret Atwood's Oryx and Crake and The Year of the Flood. In: *Other Modernities* 9 (2013), pp. 38–52.

Moss, John: Haunting Ourselves in Her Words. In: Kozakewich, Tobi/Moss, John (Eds.): *Margaret Atwood: The Open Eye*. Ottawa 2006, pp. 1–7.

Murphy, John M.: "A Time of Shame and Sorrow": Robert F. Kennedy and the American Jeremiad. In: *The Quarterly Journal of Speech* 76 (1990), pp. 401–414.

Musk, Elon: The Future We're Building – and Boring. On: *TED* (30.04.2017), https://www.ted.com/talks/elon_musk_the_future_we_re_building_and_boring [last access: 16.04.2023].

Nadeem, Nahla: Stories That Are Worth Spreading': A Communicative Model of TED Talk Narratives. In: *Narrative Inquiry* 31/2 (2021), pp. 434–457.

Nagel, Thomas: What Is It Like to Be a Bat? In: *The Philosophical Review* 83/4 (1974), pp. 435–450.

Narkunas, Paul J.: Between Words, Numbers, and Things: Transgenics and Other Objects of Life in Margaret Atwood's Maddaddams. In: *Critique* 56 (2015), pp. 1–25.

Nayak, Annika: Over Half a Million People Signed Up For this Free Princeton Course on the Science behind Buddhist Meditation Practices. I Took It and Came Away with a Better Understanding of Myself. On: *BusinessInsider* (05.04.2021), https://www.businessinsider.com/guides/learning/coursera-princeton-buddhism-modern-psychology-review [last access: 16.04.2023].

Nelson, Deborah: *Pursuing Privacy in Cold War America*. New York 2002.

Néry, Guillaume: The Exhilarating Peace of Freediving. On: *TED* (04.12.2015), https://www.ted.com/talks/guillaume_nery_the_exhilarating_peace_of_freediving [last access: 16.04.2023].

Ngai, Sianne: *Our Aesthetic Categories. Zany, Cute, Interesting*. Cambridge 2012.

Ngai, Sianne: *Ugly Feelings*. Cambridge 2007.

Nguyen, Chi-Duc/Boers, Frank: The Effect of Content Retelling on Vocabulary Uptake from a TED Talk. In: *TESOL Quarterly* 53/1 (2019), pp. 5–29.

Northover, Alan: Strangers in Strange Worlds: Margaret Atwood's MaddAddam Trilogy. In: *Journal of Literary Studies* 33/1 (2017), pp. 121–137.
Norton, Michael: How to Buy Happiness. On: *TED* (24.04.2012), https://www.ted.com/talks/michael_norton_how_to_buy_happiness [last access: 16.04.2023].
Olney, James: Memory and the Narrative Imperative: St. Augustine and Samuel Beckett. In: *New Literary History* 24/4 (1993), pp. 857–880.
O'Malley, Glenn: Literary Synesthesia. In: *The Journal of Aesthetics and Art Criticism* 15/4 (1957), pp. 391–411.
Osborne, Carol: Mythmaking in Margaret Atwood's *Oryx and Crake*. In: Appleton, Sarah A. (Ed.): *Once upon a Time: Myth, Fairy Tales and Legends in Margaret Atwood's Writings*. Cambridge 2008, pp. 25–46.
Packnett, Brittany Cunningham: How to Build Your Confidence—and Spark It in Others. On: *TED* (25.11.2008), https://www.ted.com/talks/brittany_packnett_cunningham_how_to_build_your_confidence_and_spark_it_in_others [last access: 16.04.2023].
Paddington, Tad: On the Hand-Crafting of Genius. In: *Psychology Today* (18.08.2012), https://www.psychologytoday.com/intl/blog/smarts/200811/on-the-hand-crafting-of-genius [last accessed: 16.04.2023].
Parks, Acacia C.: I Want to Be Happier! What Should I Read? In: *Psychology Today* (18.08.2012), https://www.psychologytoday.com/intl/blog/the-science-self-help/201208/i-want-be-happier-what-should-i-read [last access: 16.04.2023].
Parser, Eli: *The Filter Bubble: How the New Personalized Web Is Changing What We Read and How We Think*. London, 2011.
Passion. In: *Merriam-Webster*, https://www.merriam-webster.com/dictionary/passion [last access: 20.04.2023].
Passion. On: *Thesaurus*, https://www.thesaurus.com/browse/passion [last access: 20.04.2023].
Paul, Heike: *The Myths That Made America: An Introduction to American Studies*. Bielefeld 2014.
Paul, Heike: Tacit Knowledge, Public Feeling, and the Pursuits of (Un-)Happiness. In: Adloff, Frank/Gerund, Katharina/Kaldewey, David (Eds.): *Revealing Tacit Knowledge: Embodiment and Explication*. Bielefeld 2015, pp. 197–222.
Peale, Norman Vincent: *The Power of Positive Thinking*. Denver 1952.
Peck, Morgan Scott: *The Road Less Traveled and Beyond: Spiritual Growth in an Age of Anxiety*. New York 1998.
Perkel, Jeffrey M.: The Power and Possibilities of Genome Engineering. In: *CRISPR-Cas: Engineering a Revolution in Gene Editing* (26.09.20149), https://www.science.org/do/10.1126/resource.2375822/full/horizon_crispr-cas9_booklet_2014_01_28.pdf [last access: 20.04.2023].
Persson, Ingmar/Savulescu, Julian: *Unfit for the Future: The Need for Moral Enhancement*. Oxford 2012.
Pfister, Damien Smith: Technoliberal Rhetoric, Civic Attention, and Common Sensation in Sergey Brin's 'Why Google Glass?' In: *Quarterly Journal of Speech* 105/2 (2019), pp. 182–203.
Piep, Karsten: "You're Going to Make Us All Happy": Orientalist Appropriations of the Berber Woman in Richard Powers's Generosity. In: *Critique: Studies in Contemporary Fiction* 60/1 (2019), pp. 49–57.
Pierson, Richard/Puddicombe, Andy: Headspace. On: YouTube (2017), https://www.youtube.com/watch?v=8QsdrphXX2s [last access: 20.04.2023].
Pink, Dan: The Puzzle of Motivation. On: *TED* (25.08.2009), https://www.ted.com/talks/dan_pink_the_puzzle_of_motivation [last access: 20.04.2023].

Poe, Edgar Allan: The Man of the Crowd. In: Baym, Nina (Eds.): *The Norton Anthology of American Literature.* New York ⁶1998, pp. 1561–1567.

Poe, Edgar Allan: The Murders in the Rue Morgue. In: *The Complete Poems and Stories of Edgar Allan Poe.* New York 1946.

Poe, Edgar Allan: The Tell-Tale Heart. In: *The Works of Edgar Allan Poe: Tales* 1. Philadelphia 1906.

Pope, Tara Parker: How to Be Happy. In: *The New York Times,* https://www.nytimes.com/guides/well/how-to-be-happy [last access: 20.04.2023].

Potts, Rick: Living in the Anthropocene: Being Human in the Age of Humans. In: *American Indian Magazine* 14/4 (2013), pp. 27–31.

Powers, Richard: *Generosity: An Enhancement.* New York 2010.

Prince Ea: Disrespectful Son Rejects Mom, Lives to Regret It. On: *Facebook* (20.07.2020), https://www.facebook.com/watch/?v=2601241666809585 [last access: 20.04.2023].

Prince Ea: Employee Teaches Boss a Lesson. On: *Facebook* (3 Feb. 2020), https://www.facebook.com/watch/?v=601525933756638 [last access: 20.04.2023].

Prince Ea: Flight Attendant Teaches Racist Traveler a Lesson. On: *Facebook* (19.06.2020), https://www.facebook.com/watch/?v=987405251692852 [last access: 20.04.2023].

Prince Ea: The Janitor Got the Last Laugh. On: *Facebook* (16 Dec. 2021), https://www.facebook.com/watch/?v=616316819609194 [last access: 20.04.2023].

Prince Ea: Professor Teaches Spoiled Students a Lesson. On: *Facebook* (13.07.2020), https://www.facebook.com/watch/?v=567327727269514 [last access: 20.04.2023].

Prince Ea: Stop Wasting Your Life. On: *Facebook* (10.06.2019), https://www.facebook.com/PrinceEa/videos/435397637256907/ [last access: 20.04.2023].

Programs and Initiatives. On: *TED,* https://www.ted.com/about/programs-initiatives [last access: 20.04.2023].

Puddicombe, Andy: All It Takes Is Ten Mindful Minutes. On: *TED* (11.01.2013), https://www.ted.com/talks/andy_puddicombe_all_it_takes_is_10_mindful_minutes [last accessed: 20.04.2023].

Quotes (DEAD POETS SOCIETY). On: *IMDb,* https://www.imdb.com/title/tt0097165/quotes/ [last access: 20.04.2023].

Rajnerowicz, Kazimierz: Nine Types of Advertising Appeals That Actually Work. On: *Tidio* (17.08.2022), https://www.tidio.com/blog/advertising-appeals/ [last access: 20.04.2023].

Ramirez-Duran, Daniela: Savoring in Positive Psychology: 21 Tools to Appreciate Life. On: *Positive Psychology* (05.02.2021), https://positivepsychology.com/savoring/ [last access: 20.04.2023].

Ramirez, Jesse J.: Contemporary Cultures of Privacy, or Rethinking the 'Privacy Panic': Shoping, Sexting, Surveillance, Copyright. In: Fitz, Karsten/Harju, Bärbel (Eds.): *Cultures of Privacy: Paradigms, Transformations, Contestations.* Heidelberg 2015, pp. 275–289.

Rand, Ayn: *The Ayn Rand Lexicon: Objectivism from A to Z.* München 1988.

Raschke, Debrah: No Magical Fish: The Apocryphal Book of Tobit in Atwood's MaddAddam Trilogy. In: *The Explicator* 78/2, pp. 88–92.

Raschke, Debrah: Margaret Atwood's MaddAddam Trilogy: Postmodernism, Apocalypse, and Rapture. In: *Studies in Canadian Literature* 39/2 (2014), pp. 22–44.

Raskopoulos, Jordan: How I Live with High-Functioning Anxiety. On: *TED* (26.07.2017), https://www.ted.com/talks/jordan_raskopoulos_how_i_live_with_high_functioning_anxiety [last access: 20.04.2023].

Rehearsals. On: *TED,* https://www.ted.com/participate/organize-a-local-tedx-event/tedx-organizer-guide/speakers-program/prepare-your-speaker/rehearsals [last access: 20.04.2023].

Ricard, Matthieu: The Habits of Happiness. On: *TED* (04.03.2014), https://www.ted.com/talks/matthieu_ricard_the_habits_of_happiness [last access: 20.04.2023].
Richard St. John. On: *TED*, https://www.ted.com/speakers/richard_st_john [last access: 20.04.2023].
Richard Williams, On: *Forbes*, https://www.forbes.com/profile/richard-williams/?sh=31447b5c6a07 [last access: 20.04.2023].
Ringo, Rano/Sharma, Jasmine: Reading a Feminist Epistemology in Margaret Atwood's MaddAddam. In: *Elope* 17/1, pp: 111–124.
Robbins, Mel: *The Five Second Rule: Transform Your Life, Work, and Confidence with Everyday Courage*. New York 2017.
Ronay-Csicsery, Istvan Jr.: Marxist Theory and Science Fiction. In: James, Edward/Mendlesohn, Farah (Eds.): *The Cambridge Companion to Science Fiction*. Cambridge 2003, pp. 113–124.
Rosen, Christine: The Confessional Culture. In: *Humanities* 32/1 (2011), pp. 1–8.
Rowland, Lucy: Speculative Solutions: The Development of Environmental and Ecofeminist Discourse in Margaret Atwood's MaddAddam. In: *Studies in Canadian Literature* 40/2 (2015), pp. 46–68.
Rua, Paula López: The Manipulative Power of Word-Formation Devices in Margaret Atwood's Oryx and Crake. In: *Revista Alicantina de Estudios Ingleses* 18 (2005), pp. 149–165.
Russell, Cameron: Looks Aren't Everything. Believe Me, I'm a Model. On: *TED* (16.01.2013), https://www.ted.com/talks/cameron_russell_looks_aren_t_everything_believe_me_i_m_a_model [last access: 20.04.2023].
Rutledge, Gregory: Shteyngart's Super Sad True(th): The Äppärät, A 'Work[ing] of Art' in an Internet Age of Digital Reproduction. In: *College Literature: A Journal of Critical Literary Studies* 47/2 (2020), pp. 366–397.
Sagiv, Noam: Synesthesia in Perspective. In: Robertson, Lynn C./Sagiv, Noam (Eds.): *Synesthesia: Perspectives from Cognitive Neuroscience*. Oxford 2005, pp. 3–10.
Sandel, Michael: *The Case against Perfection: Ethics in the Age of Genetic Engineering*. Cambridge 2007.
Sanders, Valerie: Life Writing. On: *Oxford Bibliographies* (25.10.2018), https://www.oxfordbibliographies.com/display/document/obo-9780199799558/obo-9780199799558-0151.xml [last access: 20.04.2023].
Sartre, Jean Paul: *Being and Nothingness*. New York 1992.
Sartwell, Crispin: *Political Aesthetics*. New York 2011.
Sawyer, Andy: Science Fiction: The Sense of Wonder. In: Berberich, Christine (Ed.): *The Bloomsbury Introduction to Popular Fiction*. London 2014, pp. 87–107.
Sayre, Robert F.: Autobiography and the Making of America. In: *The Iowa Review* 9/2 (1978), pp. 1–19.
Schäfer, Heike: The Pursuit of Happiness 2.0: Consumer Genomics, Social Media, and the Promise of Literary Innovation in Richard Powers' Novel. In: Kley, Antje/Kucharzewski, Jan D. (Eds.): *Ideas of Order: Narrative Patterns in the Novels of Richard Powers*. Heidelberg 2012, pp. 263–284.
Scheick, William J.: An Intrinsic Luminosity: Poe's Use of Platonic and Newtonian Optics. In: *Southern Literary Journal* 24/2 (1992), pp. 90–105.
Scherr, Alexander: The Emergence of 'Genomic Life Writing' and 'Genomic Fiction' as Indicators of Cultural Change: A Case Study of Richard Powers' Novel Generosity: An Enhancement (2009). In: *REAL: The Yearbook of Research in English and American Literature* 32 (2016), pp. 121–141.
Schmidt, Peter: Menippean Satire in the Digital Era: Gary Shteyngart's *Super Sad True Love Story*. In: Davis, Evan R./Nace, Nicholas D. (Eds.): *Teaching Modern British and American Satire*. New York 2019, pp. 277–285.

Schwartz, Barry: The Paradox of Choice. On: *TED* (22.01.2014), https://www.ted.com/talks/barry_schwartz_the_paradox_of_choice [last access: 20.04.2023].

Scotto di Carlo, Giuseppina: Patterns of Clusivity in TED Talks: When 'You' and 'I' Become 'We'. In: *Ibérica* 36 (2018), pp. 119–144.

Sedgwick, Eve Kosofsky: Paranoid Reading and Reparative Reading, or, You're so Paranoid You Probably Think This Essay Is About You. In: *Touching Feeling: Affect, Pedagogy, Performativity*. Durham 2002, pp. 123–151.

Selisker, Scott: The Novel and WikiLeaks: Transparency and the Social Life of Privacy. In: *American Literary History* 30/4 (2018), pp. 756–776.

Sennett, Richard: *The Fall of Public Man*. New York 1992.

Seyedlar, Mehdi Ordikhani: What Happens in Your Brain When You Pay Attention? On: *TED* (08.06.2017), https://www.ted.com/talks/mehdi_ordikhani_seyedlar_what_happens_in_your_brain_when_you_pay_attention [last access: 20.04.2023].

Shetty, Jay: About: Hi, I'm Jay Shetty. On: Jay Shetty, https://jayshetty.me/about-jay [last access: 10.04.2023].

Shetty, Jay: Find Your Flow. On: *Facebook* (04.08.2018), https://www.facebook.com/watch/?v=2104759739838480 [last access: 20.04.2023].

Shetty, Jay: If You Need to Focus, Watch This. On: *Facebook* (03.06.2018), https://www.facebook.com/watch/?v=2039223619725426 [last access: 20.04.2023].

Shetty, Jay: If You're Feeling Drained, Watch This. On: *Facebook* (20.02.2019), https://www.facebook.com/watch/?v=351844132331799 [last access: 20.04.2023].

Shetty, Jay: Jealous Boy Dumps Girlfriend Instantly Regrets It. On: *Facebook* (20.10.2020), https://m.facebook.com/watch/?v=270699054189863 [last access: 20.04.2023].

Shetty, Jay: Jealous Girl Instantly Regrets Decision. On: Facebook (23.10.2020), https://www.facebook.com/watch/?v=346713959902563 [last access: 20.04.2023].

Shetty, Jay: Poor Mom Teaches a Rich Mom a Lesson. On: Facebook (27.04.2019), https://www.facebook.com/watch/?v=589920261418062 [last access: 20.04.2023].

Shit. In: *Merriam-Webster*, https://www.merriam-webster.com/dictionary/shit [last access: 20.04.2023].

Shteyngart, Gary: *Super Sad True Love Story*. New York 2010.

Silverman, Gilian: Reading in the Flesh: Anthropodermic Bibliopegy and the Haptic Response. In: *Johns Hopkins University Press* 24/2 (2021), pp. 451–475.

Simon, Herbert A.: Designing Organizations for an Information-Rich World. In: Greenberger, Martin (Ed.): *Computers, Communication, and the Public Interest*. Baltimore 1971, pp. 37–72.

Sinek, Simon: How Great Leaders Inspire Great Action. On: *TED* (04.05.2010), https://www.ted.com/talks/simon_sinek_how_great_leaders_inspire_action [last access: 20.09.2022].

Sister True Dedication: Three Questions to Build Resilience – and Change the World. On: *TED* (06.12.2021), https://www.ted.com/talks/sister_true_dedication_3_questions_to_build_resilience_and_change_the_world [last access: 20.04.2023].

Smilek, Daniel/Callejas, Alicia/Dixon, Mike J./Merikle, Philip M.: Ovals of Time: Time-Space Associations in Synaesthesia. In: *Consciousness and Cognition* 16/2 (2007), pp. 507–519.

Smith, Larry: Why You Will Fail to Have a Great Career. On: *TED* (13.03.2014), https://www.ted.com/talks/larry_smith_why_you_will_fail_to_have_a_great_career [last access: 20.04.2023].

Snow, Charles Percy: *The Two Cultures and the Scientific Revolution*. New York 1959.

Soper, Kate: The Humanism in Posthumanism. In: *Comparative Critical Studies* 9/3 (2012), pp. 365–378.
Spahr, Clemens: Re-Learning to Read: Gary Shteyngart and the Commodification of Reading Practices. In: *Amerikastudien/American Studies: A Quarterly* 64/4 (2019), pp. 549–565.
Spengemann, William/Lundquist, L.R.: Autobiography and the American Myth. In: *American Quarterly* 17/3 (1965), pp. 501–519.
Spiegel, Michael: Character in a Post-national World: Neomedievalism in Atwood's Oryx and Crake. In: *Mosaic* 43/3 (2010), pp. 119–134.
Spivak, Gayatri Chakravorty: Can the Subaltern Speak? In: Grossberg, L./Nelson, C. (Eds.): *Marxism and the Interpretation of Culture.* London 1988, pp. 271–313.
Stableford, Brian: Science Fiction before the Genre. In: James, Edward/Mendlesohn, Farah (Eds.): *The Cambridge Companion to Science Fiction.* Cambridge 2003, pp. 15–31.
Staels, Hilde: Oryx and Crake: Atwood's Ironic Inversion of Frankenstein." In: Kozakewich, Tobi/Moss, John (Eds.): *Margaret Atwood: The Open Eye.* Ottawa 2006, pp. 433–446.
Staughton, John: How Are Mushrooms More Similar to Humans than Plants? On: *ScienceABC* (13.01.2016), https://www.scienceabc.com/nature/how-are-mushrooms-more-similar-to-humans-than-plants.html [last access: 21.04.2023].
Steindl-Rast, David: Want to Be Happy? Be Grateful. On: *TED* (27.11.2013), https://www.ted.com/talks/david_steindl_rast_want_to_be_happy_be_grateful [last access: 21.04.2023].
St. John, Richard: Success Is a Continuous Journey. On: *TED* (15.06.2009), https://www.ted.com/talks/richard_st_john_success_is_a_continuous_journey [last access: 21.04.2023].
Stein, Karen F: Problematic Paradice in Oryx and Crake. In: Bouson, Brooks (Ed.): *Margaret Atwood: The Robber Bride, The Blind Assassin, Oryx and Crake.* London 2010, pp. 141–155.
Sternbergh, Adam: How Podcasts Learned to Speak. On: *Vulture* (18.03.2019), https://www.vulture.com/2019/03/the-great-podcast-rush.html [last access: 21.04.2023].
Storey, Françoise/Storey, Jeff: History and Allegory in Margaret Atwood's Oryx and Crake. In: *Cycnos* 22/2 (2006), http://epi-revel.univ-cotedazur.fr/publication/item/653 [last access: 21.04.2023].
Strange, Adario: This Fake TED Talk about Nothing Might Be the Best You've Ever Seen. On: *Mashable* (12.06.2016), https://mashable.com/video/fake-ted-talk [last access: 21.04.2023].
Strauss Clara/Lever, Taylor Billie/Gu, Jenny/Kuyken Willem/Baer Ruth/Jones Fergal/Cavanagh, Kate: What is Compassion and How Can We Measure it? A Review of Definitions and Measures. In: *Clinical Psychology Review* 47 (2016), pp. 15–27.
Sugimoto, Cassidy/Thelwall, Mike/Larivière, Vincent/Tsou, Andrew/Mongeon, Philippe/Macaluso, Benoit: Scientists Popularizing Science: Characteristics and Impact of TED Talk Presenters. In: *PLOS ONE* 8/4 (2013).
Sutherland, Sharon/Swan, Sarah: Margaret Atwood's Oryx and Crake: Canadian Post-9/11 Worries. In: Ciano, Cara (Ed.): *From Solidarity to Schisms: 9/11 and After in Fiction and Film from Outside the US.* Amsterdam 2008, pp. 219–235.
Talks to Help You Find Your Purpose. On: *TED*, https://www.ted.com/playlists/313/talks_to_help_you_find_your_pu [last access: 21.04.2023].
Talks to Help You Manage Stress. On: *TED*, https://www.ted.com/playlists/315/talks_to_help_you_manage_stres [last access: 21.04.2023].
Talks to Help Practice Patience. On: *TED*, https://www.ted.com/playlists/353/talks_to_help_practice_patienc [last access: 21.04.2023].

Tayler, Christopher: Generosity by Richard Powers. In: *The Guardian* (20.01.2010), https://www.theguardian.com/books/2010/jan/02/richard-powers-generosity-fiction-review [last access: 21.04.2023].

Taylor, Charles: *The Ethics of Authenticity.* Cambridge 1992.

Taylor, Jill Bolte: My Stroke of Insight. On: *TED* (28.08.2013), https://www.ted.com/talks/jill_bolte_taylor_my_stroke_of_insight [last access: 21.04.2023].

Taylor, Steve: Empathy: The Ability That Makes Us Truly Human. In: *Psychology Today* (24.03.2012), https://www.psychologytoday.com/intl/blog/out-the-darkness/201203/empathy-the-ability-makes-us-truly-human [last access: 21.04.2023].

TED Conferences. On: *LinkedIn*, https://www.linkedin.com/company/ted-conferences/about [last access: 21.04.2023].

TED Content Guidelines. On: *TED*, https://www.ted.com/about/our-organization/our-policies-terms/ted-content-guidelines [last access: 21.04.2023].

TED Science Standards. On: *TED*, https://www.ted.com/about/our-organization/our-policies-terms/ted-science-standards [last access: 21.04.2023].

TED Talks as the Seven Deadly Sins. On: *TED*, https://www.ted.com/playlists/611/ted_talks_as_the_seven_deadly_sins [last access: 21.04.2023].

Teitell, Beth: Lucky Girl Syndrome Is a Hot New Self-Help Craze. One Woman Put it to the Test in Boston. In: *The Boston Globe* (06.02.2023), https://www.bostonglobe.com/2023/02/06/metro/lucky-girl-syndrome-its-hottest-self-help-craze-youve-never-heard-does-it-work [last access: 21.04.2023].

Tell, David: Rhetoric and Power: An Inquiry into Foucault's Critique of Confession. In: *Philosophy & Rhetoric* 43/2 (2010), pp. 95–117.

The Most Popular Science Talks. On: *TED*, https://www.ted.com/playlists/181/the_most_popular_science_talks [last access: 21.04.2023].

The Most Popular Talks of All Time. On: *TED*, https://www.ted.com/playlists/171/the_most_popular_talks_of_all. [last access: 21.04.2023].

The Science behind the Smell of Books, Explained by Preservation. On: *Libraries of University of Colorado* (01.05.2020), https://www.colorado.edu/libraries/2020/05/01/science-behind-smell-books-explained-preservation [last access: 21.04.2023].

Time Flies: U.S. Adults Now Spend Nearly Half a Day Interacting with Media. On: *Nielsen* (2018), https://www.nielsen.com/de/insights/2018/time-flies-us-adults-now-spend-nearly-half-%20a-day-interacting-with-media/ [last access: 21.04.2023].

Tomkins, Jane: *Sensational Designs: The Cultural Work of American Fiction, 1790–1860.* Oxford 1985.

Tommasi, Giorgia: Technology and Privacy: A Narrative Perspective. In: Fitz, Karsten/Harju, Bärbel (Eds.): *Cultures of Privacy: Paradigms, Transformations, Contestations.* Heidelberg 2015, pp. 245–258.

Trapp, Brian: Super Sad True Melting Pot: Reimagining the Melting Pot in a Transnational World in Gary Shteyngart's Super Sad True Love Story. In: *MELUS: The Journal of the Society for the Study of the Multi-Ethnic Literature of the United States* 41/4 (2016), pp. 55–75.

Travis, John: Making the Cut: CRISPR Genome-Editing Shows its Power. In: *Science* 350/6267 (2015), pp. 1456–1457.

Trice, Laura: Remember to Say Thank You. On: *TED* (04.03.2014), https://www.ted.com/talks/laura_trice_remember_to_say_thank_you [last access: 21.04.2023].

Trost, Matthew: AMA: TED's Chris Anderson Answers Reddit's Questions Right Here. On: *TED* (25.01.2010), https://blog.ted.com/teds_chris_ande_3/ [last access: 21.04.2023].

Tutorial 2: How to Develop Empathy and Define UX Problems. On: *CareerFoundry*, https://careerfoundry.com/en/tutorials/ux-design-process-for-beginners/ux-problems-definition/ [last access: 21.04.2023].

Tyler, Christopher W.: Varieties of Synesthetic Experience. In: Robertson, Lynn C./Sagiv, Noam (Eds.): *Synesthesia: Perspectives from Cognitive Neuroscience.* Oxford 2005, pp. 34–44.

Uchida, Yukiko/Ogihara, Yuji: Personal or Interpersonal Construal of Happiness: A Cultural Psychological Perspective. In: *International Journal of Wellbeing* 2 (2012), pp. 354–369.

Uicheng, Kanokrat/Crabtree, Michael: Macro Discourse Markers in TED Talks: How Ideas are Signaled to Listeners. In: *PASAA: A Journal of Language Teaching & Learning in Thailand* 55 (2018), pp. 1–31.

Urban, Tim: Inside the Mind of a Master Procrastinator. On: *TED* (06.04.2016), https://www.ted.com/talks/tim_urban_inside_the_mind_of_a_master_procrastinator [last access: 21.04.2023].

Van Dam, Nicholas T/van Vugt, Marieke K/Vago, David R./Schmalzl, Laura/Saron, Clifford D./Olendzki, Andrew/Meissner, Ted/Lazar, Sara W./Kerr, Catherine E./Gorchov, Jolie/Fox, Kieran C./Field, Brent A./Britton, Willoughby B./Brefczynski-Lewis, Julie A./Meyer, David E./: Mind the Hype: A Critical Evaluation and Prescriptive Agenda for Research on Mindfulness and Meditation. In: *Perspectives on Psychological Science* 3/1 (2017), pp. 36–61.

Vials, Chris: Margaret Atwood's Dystopic Fiction and the Contradictions of Neoliberal Freedom. In: *Textual Practice* 29/2 (2015), pp. 235–254.

Vincent, David: Privacy and Surveillance in the Nineteenth Century. In: Fitz, Karsten/Harju, Bärbel (Eds.): *Cultures of Privacy: Paradigms, Transformations, Contestations.* Heidelberg 2015, pp. 15–35.

Vincenty, Samantha: Oprah Explains What an 'Aha Moment' Really Means. On: *Oprah Daily* (10.09.2019), https://www.oprahdaily.com/life/a29090436/aha-moment-meaning/ [last access: 21.04.2023].

Vinge, Vernor: The Coming Technological Singularity: How to Survive in the Post-Human Era. In: *NASA. Lewis Research Center, Vision 21: Interdisciplinary Science and Engineering in the Era of Cyberspace* (1993), pp. 11--22.

Vint, Sherryl: Science Fiction and Posthumanism. On: *Critical Posthumanism* (24.05.2016), https://criticalposthumanism.net/science-fiction/ [last access: 21.04.2023].

Vision. On: *Merriam-Webster,* https://www.merriam-webster.com/dictionary/vision [last access: 21.04.2023].

Waldinger, Robert: What Makes a Good Life? Lessons from the Longest Study on Happiness. On: *TED* (23.12.2015),https://www.ted.com/talks/robert_waldinger_what_makes_a_good_life_lessons_from_the_longest_study_on_happiness/c [last access: 21.04.2023].

Waldman, Ezra: Privacy as Trust. In: Fitz, Karsten/Harju, Bärbel (Eds.): *Cultures of Privacy: Paradigms, Transformations, Contestations.* Heidelberg 2015, pp. 167–187.

Wasihun, Betiel: Surveillance and Shame in Dave Eggers' The Circle. In: *On_Culture: The Open Journal for the Study of Culture* 6 (2018), http://geb.uni-giessen.de/geb/volltexte/2018/13898/ [last accessed: 21.04.2023].

Wetzel-Sahm, Birgit: Negotiating the Right to Be Let Alone: The Constitutional Right to Privacy and the Cultural Practice of the US Supreme Court. In: Fitz, Karsten/Harju, Bärbel (Eds.): *Cultures of Privacy: Paradigms, Transformations, Contestations.* Heidelberg 2015, pp. 187–209.

What Is Compassion? In: *Greater Good Magazine,* https://greatergood.berkeley.edu/topic/compassion/definition [last access: 21.04.2023].

What Makes You Happy? On: *TED*, https://www.ted.com/playlists/4/what_makes_you_happy [last access: 21.04.2023].

Whitman, Walt: *Leaves of Grass: First and 'Death-Bed' Editions*. New York 2004. Who Are You? On: *TED*, https://www.ted.com/playlists/354/who_are_you [last access: 21.04.2023].

Willmetts, Simon: Digital Dystopia: Surveillance, Autonomy, and Social Justice in Gary Shteyngart's Super Sad True Love Story. In: *American Quarterly* 70/2 (2018), pp. 267–289.

Wilson, Sharon R.: Frankenstein's Gaze and Atwood's Sexual Politics in Oryx and Crake. In: Kozakewich, Tobi/Moss, John (Eds.): *Margaret Atwood: The Open Eye*. Ottawa 2006, pp. 397–406.

Winch, Guy: Why We All Need to Practice Emotional First Aid. On: *TED* (16.02.2015), https://www.ted.com/talks/guy_winch_why_we_all_need_to_practice_emotional_first_aid [last access: 21.04.2023].

Wingrove, Peter: Academic Lexical Coverage in TED Talks and Academic Lectures. In: *English for Specific Purposes* 65 (2022), pp. 79–94.

Wingrove, Peter: How Suitable Are TED Talks for Academic Listening? In: *Journal of English for Academic Purposes* 30 (2017), pp. 79–95.

Wisker, Gina: Imagining Beyond Extinctathon: Indigenous Knowledge, Survival, Speculation – Margaret Atwood's and Ann Patchett's Eco-Gothic. In: *Contemporary Women's Writing* 11/3 (2017), pp. 412–431.

Wolf, Gary: The Quantified Self. On: *TED* (16.03.2014), https://www.ted.com/talks/gary_wolf_the_quantified_self [last access: 21.04.2023].

Wolter, Ingrid-Charlotte: Science as Deconstruction of Natural Identity: Arthur Conan Doyle's 'When the World Screamed' and Margaret Atwood's Oryx and Crake. In: Detmers, Ines/Grimm, Nancy/Thomson, Katrin/Volkmann, Laurenz (Eds.): *Local Natures, Global Responsibilities: Ecocritical Perspectives on the New English Literatures, ASNEL Papers 15*. Amsterdam 2010, pp. 257–271.

Wood, Michael: Never Say Die. In: *The New York Times* (06.08.2010), https://www.nytimes.com/2010/08/08/books/review/Wood-t.html [last access: 21.04.2023].

Wooden, John: The Difference between Winning and Succeeding. On: *TED* (11.03.2014), https://www.ted.com/talks/john_wooden_the_difference_between_winning_and_succeeding [last accessed: 21.04.2023].

Wright, Robert: Buddhism and Modern Psychology. On: *Coursera*, https://www.coursera.org/course/psychbuddhism [last access: 22.04.2022].

Wright, Robert: *The Moral Animal. Why We Are the Way We Are: The New Science of Evolutionary Psychology*. New York 1994.

Wright, Robert: *Why Buddhism Is True: The Science and Philosophy of Meditation and Enlightenment*. New York 2017.

Wrobel, Claire: Negotiating Dataveillance in the Near Future: Margaret Atwood's Dystopias. In: *Commonwealth Essays and Studies* 43/2 (2021), par. 1–27.

X, Malcolm, with Haley, Alex: *The Autobiography of Malcolm X: As Told to Alex Haley*. New York 1965.

Yates, Julian: Improbable Shepherds: Multispecies Polities and the Afterlife of Pastoral in Margaret Atwood's Maddaddam Trilogy. In: *Criticism* 62/3 (2020), pp. 411–432.

Your Fat Friend: The Bizarre and Racist History of the BMI. On: *Elemental* (15.10.2019), https://elemental.medium.com/the-bizarre-and-racist-history-of-the-bmi-7d8dc2aa33bb [last access: 22.04.2023].

Yuksel, Peri: TED Talks Complement Self-Directed Learning (and Entertain Students). In: *Transformations: The Journal of Inclusive Scholarship and Pedagogy* 28/1 (2018), pp. 96–103.

Yu, Ning: Synesthetic Metaphor: A Cognitive Perspective. In: *Journal of Literary Semantics* 32/1 (2003), pp. 19–34.

Zappe, Florian/Gross, Andrew S.: Introduction. In: *Surveillance | Society | Culture*. Bern 2020, pp. 9–23.

Zappe, Florian: Gazing Back at the Monster – A Critical Posthumanist Intervention on Surveillance Culture, Sousveillance and the Lifelogged Self. In: *Surveillance | Society | Culture*. Bern 2020, pp. 39–55.

Zerilli, Linda M. G.: The Turn to Affect and the Problem of Judgment. In: *New Literary History* 46/2 (2015), pp. 261–286.

Zimbardo, Philip: The Psychology of Time. On: *TED* (22.06.2009), https://www.ted.com/talks/philip_zimbardo_the_psychology_of_time [last access: 22.04.2023].

Zinn, Jon-Kabat: *Coming to Our Senses.* New York 2005.

Zinn, Jon-Kabat: *Full Catastrophe Living.* New York 1991.

Zinn, Jon-Kabat: *Wherever You Go There You Are.* New York 1994.

List of Figures

Figure 1: Image for TED's playlist on "Who Are You?" accompanied by the caption: "What makes you, well, you? Get to know yourself a bit better with this collection of thought-provoking talks." © TED. Attribution 4.0 International (CC BY 4.0), https://www.ted.com/playlists/354/who_are_you [last access: 06.05.2024] —— **52**

Figure 2: Image for the TED playlist "How to Be a Better You" accompanied by the caption: "Ready for a change? These well-researched (and heartfelt) talks offer ideas and inspiration for all aspects of your life, from creativity to vulnerability, from competitive sports to collaborative games." © TED. Attribution 4.0 International (CC BY 4.0), https://www.ted.com/playlists/8/a_better_you [last access: 06.05.2024] —— **84**

Figure 3: Image for TED's playlist on "Talks to Help You Manage Stress." © TED. Attribution 4.0 International (CC BY 4.0), https://www.ted.com/playlists/315/talks_to_help_you_manage_stress [last access: 06.05.2024] —— **145**

Figure 4: Word cloud generated by MonkeyLearn after the guidelines of Basics Session 1, Headspace, https://monkeylearn.com/blog/word-cloud-generator/ [last access: 06.05.2024] —— **158**

Figure 5: Image for the playlist "What Makes You Happy?" accompanied by the caption: "Everyone wants to be happy. But how, exactly, does one go about it? Here, psychologists, journalists, Buddhist monks and more gives (*sic*) answers that may surprise." © TED. Attribution 4.0 International (CC BY 4.0), https://www.ted.com/playlists/4/what_makes_you_happy [last access: 06.05.2024] —— **215**

Figure 6: "Evidence of the Cultural Construal of Happiness." From: Uchida & Ogihara, 2012, Attribution 4.0 International (CC BY 4.0), featured in *The Science of Happiness* online course, https://www.edx.org/learn/happiness/university-of-california-berkeley-the-science-of-happiness [last access: 06.05.2024] —— **219**

Figure 7: Mihalyi Csikszentmihalyi's answer to the question "How does it feel to be in flow?" in "Flow: The Secret to Happiness," TED talk (00:13:48). © TED. Attribution 4.0 International (CC BY 4.0), [last access: 06.05.2024] —— **231**

Figure 8: Mihalyi Csikszentmihalyi's chart for flow in "Flow: The Secret to Happiness," TED talk (00:15:30). © TED. Attribution 4.0 International (CC BY 4.0), https://www.ted.com/talks/mihaly_csikszentmihalyi_flow_the_secret_to_happiness?language=en [last access: 06.05.2024] —— **232**

Index

Aamodt, Sandra 50, 159
– "Why Dieting" 159
Achor, Shawn 39, 86, 102
– "The Happy Secret to Better Work" 39, 86
acknowledgment 63–64, 205, 238, 261
Adams, Henry 31
– The Education of Henry Adams 31
aesthetic
– attachments 62, see also postcritique
– gratification 59
– needs 65
– pleasure 183
aesthetics
– and politics 5, 75, 135, 137, 187, 276, 278, see also artpolitical
– critical posthumanist 68
– of individualism 2, 42, 56, 160, 221, 234, 272, 278, see also TED talks
– positive 63
– postmodern 75, 177, see also sentimentalist
– synesthetic 127, 137–138, 187, 196, 251, 278, see also literary synesthesia
aestheticism 63, 71, 262
affect 66–68
– and cognition 61–62
– and its waning 177
– and literary studies 62
– and politics 61
– negative 223
– of aliveness 68, 75–76, 125, 183, 207, see also literary synesthesia
– theory 5, 61, 71
affective
– detachment 177–178
– relations 3
– subjects 278
– turn 61
agency 17, 72, 117, 123, 126, 131, 156, 177, 187, 236, 244, 247–248, 266, 269
– as control 27, 72
– granting/mediating 68, 77, 244
– individual 67
– of the text 64

– posthuman 199
– source of 28
– suspended 77
aging 21, 48, 135, 181, 198
alienation 2, 21, 73, 174, 243
altruism 217, 220, 255
– dangerous 101, 133, 176, 221–222, 237, 240–241, 258, 273
American
– dream 19, 111
– jeremiad 41
– scholar 22
Anderson, Chris 39, 40, 44–46, 105, 156, 163
– "TED's Nonprofit Transition" 40
– "TED's Secret to Great Public Speaking" 44–46
animatedness 63, 75–76
Anthropocene 143, 187, 270
anthropocentric 7, 64, 72, 77, 128, 138, 178, 185–187, 199, 205, 274
– non- 204
– post- 64, 188
anthropocentrism 129, 186, 234
anthropomorphic 192
anthropomorphism 68, 72, 123, 186–187
anxiety 30, 62, 82, 149, 198, 225, 232
– age of 152
Arendt, Hannah 21
artpolitical 135, 276
Atwood, Margaret 2, 8, 73, 110, 118, 133, 143, 170, 171–199, 200–209, 221–222, 237, 246, 255–257, 269, 274
– MaddAddam Trilogy 2, 8, 118, 133, 143, 170, 171–199, 200–209, 237, 246, 257, 269, 274
authenticity 1, 6, 15, 20, 23–24, 26, 36, 40, 47, 64, 82, 134, 218, 242, 272
– age of 24
– ethics 24
– the pursuit of 23
autobiography 3, 18–20, 23, 27, 62, 180, 248
– as self-help 20
– and life writing 20
– and self-vigilance 30

autobiographical
- lens 271
- narratives 242
- self 251
automatic 166, 190, 228, 230
automatism 28, 45, 77, 230
automaton 192
Atlas 255, 267–269
attention
- economy 147
- management 147, 157
awe 36–38, 56, 69, 167, 184, 222, 225, 229, 259
- walk 217, 225–226

Baggini, Julian 53–54, 165
- "Is There a Real You" 53–54, 165
beauty 54, 134, 183, 195–197, 201, 209, 253, 262, 274, 276
belonging 65, 83, 126, 129, 204
Benesch, Klaus 10, 17, 19, 21–22, 25, 48, 54–55, 76
Berlant, Lauren 34, 47, 62
- Cruel Optimism 47
body 2, 5, 10, 21, 26, 28–29, 30, 44, 48, 53, 62, 76–77, 86, 98, 99–100, 104, 107–109, 111, 114–116, 120–124, 126–127, 134–135, 138–139, 156–159, 163, 167–171, 177, 181, 188–192, 198–199, 204–206, 227, 229, 233, 235–236, 239–242, 251–252, 263–266, 272–273, 275–726
- and control 30
- and dualism/dichotomy 239
- and habits 28–29, 158
- and (im)mortality 10, 21, 120, 134
- and its vanishing 229, 272
- and technology 121
- as capital 4
- as data 4, 98, 107–109, 111, 121, see also Quantified Self
- language 44, 99–100
- that speaks 26
- scan 157–158, see also Cartesian dualism, see also corporeality, see also embodiment, see also materiality, see also mind over matter, see also vulnerability

Bouskill, Kathryn 166
- "Unforeseen Consequences" 166
bioethics 8, 55, 276
biohacking 22
biopower 107
bird(s) 71, 194–195, 249–250, 263, 266, 274
Brewer, Judson 144, 159, 162
- "How to Break" 159
Brin, Sergey 38, 45
- "Why Google Glass" 38, 45
Brooks, 50, 102–104
- "Should You Live" 103–104
Brown, Brené 50, 103, 139
- "Power of Vulnerability" 103
Buddha 54, 160
Buddhism 53, 151–152, 163–165
Buddhist 148, 151, 169, 215, 227

capitalism 2, 28, 48, 74, 89, 104, 109, 115, 137, 147, 174, 215, 275, 277
- techno- 204
capitalist 2, 48, 63, 109, 137, 175, 178, 181, 237
Cartesian
- division 135
- dualism 28
- perspectivalism 5
catharsis 23, 95, 219, 236, 276
cautionary 8, 173
caution 246, 258
chaos theory 33
citizen
- scientist 21–22, 160, 224
- science 22
Clear, James 28
- Atomic Habits 28
colonialism 187, see also postcolonial
colonialist 222
commodification 2, 126, 175, 189–190, 237, 239, 277
- of feelings 2, 175, 239
- of the female body 189–190, 237
commodified 19, 130, 177, 215, 238, 241
commodity 2, 7, 41, 123, 137, 148, 177, 220, 239, 253
- happiness as 2, 239
- life as 220
- mindfulness as 148

- TED as   41
- the self as   123
communication
- of science   2, 10, 31, 57
- digital   2
communal   85, 207, 221, 269
community   6, 22–23, 41, 57, 70, 74, 85, 89, 113–115, 118, 130, 172, 180, 195, 199, 204, 208, 218, 221, 244
- of feeling   271–273
compassion   15, 18, 64, 95–96, 103, 180, 194, 206, 217, 219–221, 243
- self–   219, 221–225
compositing   251–252, 254, 262
confession(s)   1, 3–4, 6, 15–17, 20–23, 25–26, 29, 31–32, 36, 40, 46, 50–51, 55, 57, 59, 63, 89, 95, 101, 114, 116–117, 120, 125, 181, 217–219, 221, 225, 228–230, 250, 252–253, 256, 262, 270, 276
- and privacy   23
- and power   26
- and reading   59, 63
- and self-help culture   17–18, 95, see also sentimentalism
- and science (communication)   16, 31–32, 35–37, 270
- and the digital age   23
- as didactic tools   3, 20, 56
- as empowerment   18
- as marketing strategies   3, 17
- as redemptive   24, 26, 276
- as rhetorical tools   16, 18, 35
- as tools of surveillance   18
- in TED   46, 57
- of happiness   50
- pseudo-   24
confessional
- culture   15, 18–19, 24, 27, 32, 117, 219
- mode   17
- neo-   26, 242, 270
- practices   23
- process   34
- society   1
- space   93
- speech   3, 6, 19, 26, 32
- style   46–47
- work   217
- writing   17, 24, 248, 251, see also life writing
confidence   1, 51, 83–85, 87, 89, 91, 93–94, 99–100, 154, 245–246, 252, 272
- building   83–85
- over   176
- self–   1, 42, 65, 245–246
conscious   25
- attention   226
- control   30
- self–   245, 254
- sub   45, 182
- un   165, 168, 183
consciousness   45, 48, 56, 84, 149, 151, 168, 171–172, 180–181, 193, 196–197, 222–223, 227–229, 232, 234, 275
- altered   168, 171, 196–197, 222–223
- eco-   172
- higher form of   232, 234
- self-   199, 227, 246, 250, 257
- space- and place-   76
consumer   4, 17, 28, 147, 174–175, 263, 275, see also capitalism
consumerism   1, 48, 148, 175, 181
consumerist   133, 138, 264
corporeal   55, 69, 76–77, 121, 123, 135, 159, 200, 257
corporeality   111, 122, 190, 206
Crary, Jonathan   5, 76
creative nonfiction   237, 245, 249, 251, 253, 259, 262
creativity   42, 48, 84, 90, 93, 102, 112, 162, 176, 206, 228, 239, 245, 253, 262, 272–273, 276–277
crisis
- and literary studies   7, 177
- climate   143
- economic   116, 131
- of humanities   2, 59, 65
- privacy   23
critical
- eco-   257
- solace   59, 67, 183, 185
- vigilance   62, 75, see also postcritique
Csikszentmihalyi, Mihalyi   35, 165, 227–231, 257, see also flow
Cuddy, Amy   99–100, 236, see also power posing, see also body language

Index

Cutts, Matt 98
– "Try Something New" 98
cybernetics 10
cyborg 54–55, 275
– art 200

Darwin, Charles 31–32, 99, 160, 213, 266
Daston, Lorraine 32–33, 35–36, 38, see also objectivity
death 21, 48, 67, 102–103, 107–110, 125–26, 128, 166, 183, 194, 198, 202, 208–209, 247, 273–274, 278
– drive/wish 182, 243
– of privacy 22–23
– of the subject 165, see also body and (im)mortality, see also life
description 56, 66–68, 114, 167, 183–185, 192, 195–196, 199, 203, 205, 227, 230, 246–247, 256–57, 265, 274
– re- 60
– thin 66, see also Love, see also James
de Certeau, Michel 17
Derrida, Jacques 188, 200
detach(ed) 30, 33, 35, 47, 51, 145, 150–152, 179, 224, 229, 248, 251
detachment 61–62, 146, 165, 171, 177–78, 224, 278
Dewey, John 4, 9, 28–29, 64–65, 69
diary 20, 116–121, 130, 135–136, 179, 202, see also confession, see also journal, see also life writing
diaries 22, 72, 120, 136, 261, 276
disidentification 53, 56, 165
discipline 3, 15, 26, 34, 81, 90, 98, 107, 118, 157, 190, 227–228, 272
– self- 90–92, 100, 144, 151, 160
DNA 10, 46, 58, 202, 237, 274
Duckworth, Angela Lee 91
– "Grit" 91
Dweck, Carol 91, 144, 154
dystopia 8, 69, 117, 173–174, 190–191
dystopian 172–173, 175, 182, 196, 273
– narratives 58
– perspectives 106
– transparency 163

ecocritical 257

ecocriticism 172
ecological 172–173, 186, 206, 257
economic totality 115, 277
Eggers, Dave 163
egotism 191, 243
egotistic 133, 188
elephant 124, 131, 274
Emerson, Ralph 22, 181, 191, see also American scholar
emodity 2, 47
embodied 206, 277–278
– awareness 74, 126–127, 139, 198, 200, 202, 205, 257, 263–264, 266
– dis- 121–122, 134–135, 198
– experiences 206
– life 107
– subject 5, 270, see also body
embodiment 5, 76, 198
emotion(s) 1–2, 5, 9, 22, 27, 29, 46–47, 50, 61–62, 68–70, 75, 90, 116, 134, 138–139, 148, 156, 160–162, 206, 216–217, 232–233, 236
– and technology 5
– individual 1
– in TED 47, 50
– lack of 192
– management 27, 100, 216, 224
– negative 50, 62, 232
– positive 222, 225–226, 232
emotional 2–5, 27, 34, 36–37, 56, 61, 63–64, 66, 74–75, 95, 100, 108, 138, 148, 151, 178, 180, 182–183, 191, 216, 224, 236, 243, 257, 262, 271
– contagion 47
– depth 178
– first-aid 49, 153
– hygiene 154, 263–264, 272
– labor 2, 276
– moods 61
empathy 3, 15, 18, 34–35, 48, 63–64, 66, 123, 132–133, 139, 180–81, 187, 192–194, 196, 216, 221, 224, 241, 243–244, 247, 261, 268, 272–273, 277
– age of 216
– and knowing others 18, 187
– and reading 16, 63–66
– as sympathetic identification 15, 34

– as psychoanalytic mode of observation 34–35, 193, 272
– as humanizing force 3, 15, 34, 180, 272
empathic 1, 34, 139, 187, 206, 243, 259, 261, 270
empowerment 15, 18, 85, 117
Enlightenment 3, 155, 204, 222
enlightenment 27, 56, 155, 158, 164, 168
Ensler, Eve 214, 236
– "Happiness in Body and Soul" 236
Ellerton, Peter 33
epistemological 62, 162, 206
epistemology 3, 60
– eye-centered 60, *see also* ocularcentrism
– onto- 3
Etcoff, Nancy 214, 232–234
– "Happiness and Its Surprises" 232–234
ethics 1, 24, 66, 82, 103, 121, 155, 247
– posthuman 187, 189, *see also* bioethics
expectation 5, 9–11, 18, 24, 32, 51, 70, 94, 129, 137, 160, 215–216, 229, 244, 272, 274–276
– horizon of 5
– reader 5, 9, 69, 129, 137, 177–178, 186, 275–276
experience(s) 9–10, 16, 30, 33, 35, 40–42, 46–48, 50, 53, 56–57, 64, 67, 72–75, 77, 89, 101, 114, 122–123, 136, 139, 152, 155, 165, 167–168, 171, 183, 186, 189, 192, 198, 202, 206–207, 217–218, 222, 224–231, 234–236, 243, 247, 249, 254, 258–259, 262, 269, 271, 273, 276
– human 57, 64, 186, 269
– immersive 61–62, 65, 75
– of reading 61–66, 178, 202
– ordinary/everyday 9, 165
– of feeling alive 9, 75, 129, 198
– of happiness 81
– synesthetic 71–73, 75, 197, 207, *see also* literary synesthesia
– TED 40–41
– transcendent 47, 222–223

Facebook 3, 36, 93, 96, 155, 216
feeling(s) 2, 6, 22–23, 25, 46–47, 61–63, 65, 67, 75, 87, 90–91, 97, 99, 119, 122, 125, 133–134, 150–151, 157, 161, 165, 167, 174, 182–183, 185, 189–190, 192, 196, 205, 214, 217, 221–228, 231, 232, 235, 239, 241–246, 250, 259, 263, 265, 271–275
– alive 9, 75, 122, 129, 188, 195–196, 199, 207, 255–256, 274–275, *see also* affect of aliveness
– happy 40
– positive 152, 272
– rules 27
– that humanize 34, *see also* affect, *see also* commodification of feelings, *see also* emotions
Felski, Rita 60–63, 65, 67
– Uses of Literature 60
– The Limits of Critique 62
Ferenczi, Sándor 34
filter bubble 147
flow 35, 94, 165, 222, 226–236, 257, 272–273, *see also* Csikszentmihalyi
Foucault, Michel 6, 18, 26, 31–32, 41, 64, 69, 176
Frankenstein 54, 183, 188, 191
Franklin, Benjamin 18, 20–21, 27–31, 48, 81, 97
– The Autobiography 20, 27, 29, 81
– and vigilance 29
free will 46, 248
Freitas, Donna 1, 15–16, 93
– Happiness Effect 1, 15–16, 93
Freud, Sigmund 34, 36, 109, 164–165, 232
Freudian 63, 83, 165

Garten, Ariel 155, 160–163, 167, 198
– "Know Thyself" 160–163
gaze(s) 25, 51–52, 123–124, 151–152, 183, 190, 195, 199, 214, 250
– animal 123, 195
– male 190
– play of 25, 97, 195, 247, 249–250,
gender 59, 92, 97, *see also* patriarchy, *see also* sexism
gene 58, 175, 237, 244, 267
– editing 58
– happiness 237, 239, 247
genetic 113, 181, 191, 237, 239, 244
– data 4, 45, 107, 248
– engineering 8, 58, 191, 254

- enhancement   237, 239, 263
generosity   176, 178, 220, 238, 240, 243–245, 254–255, 259, 261, 263–268
generous   218, 240–241, 245, 257–259, 262, 264, 266–267
genius   22, 38, 41–42, 56, 70, 83, 90–91, 93–94, 110, 160, 162, 228, 230–231, 234, 240, 244–245, 254, 258, 264, 266–267, 269, 272–274, 276
Gerald, Casey   50, 103
- "Embrace"   103
Gilbert, Dan   35, 214, 218
- "The Surprising Science of Happiness"   35, 218
Gilbert, Elizabeth   47, 244–245, 269
- "Your Elusive Creative Genius"   244–245
Google   45, 88, 155, 161
gratification
- aesthetic   59
- delayed   95, 170
- instant   93–97, 101
gratitude   35, 103, 119, 133, 152, 170, 198, 214, 217, 225, 235, 241, 272
- letters   35, 217
- journals   35, 217
Greater Good   176
- magazine   176, 216, 220
- podcast   156, 176, 223, 235
- Science Center   96, 216
grief   67, 129, 206, 208, 236, 274
Grobe, Christopher   17, 24, 46, 75
Gutman, Ron   98–99, 101, 103, 214, 236
- "Hidden Power"   98–99, 101, 103, 214, 236

habit   27–29, 49, 100, 105, 113, 132, 151, 153, 159, 164, 215–216, 228, 238
- bad   27–28, 97, 158–159, 272
- denigration of   28
- formation   27–28, 98, 151, 215–216
Happify   2, 215
happiness   1–2, 10, 27, 40–41, 48–50, 75, 81–82, 84, 86, 95, 102, 119, 146, 152–155, 162, 170, 182, 213–221, 223, 227–228, 230, 232–233, 235–237, 239, 241–244, 247, 253–258, 263, 267, 270, 272–274
- and money   100
- as emodity   2, 239

- as mission   101
- as a social goal   27, 102
- duty   1, 234, 242, 272
- effect   93–94, see also Freitas
- enhancing   156–157, 225
- lack of   108
- pursuit of   61, 111, 151–152, 237, 239, 255, 268–269
- scientific study of   35, 154–155, 170, 213–221, 223, 226, 228, 232–233, 235
- synthetic   218
- un-   109, 151, 232, 242, 272
Harju, Bärbel   3, 22–23, 26, 29, 34
Harrington, Anne   26, 30, 34, 45, 86, 92, 143, 149
- The Cure Within   26, 30, 34, 45, 86, 92, 149
health   30, 48–49, 91, 99, 101, 107–109, 112, 115, 122, 149, 201, 215–216, 220–221
hippie   109, 196, 227, 242
Hochschild, Arlie   1–2, 11, 27, 99, 272–273
- Managed Heart   1–2, 11, 27, 99, 272–273
home   83, 96, 112–113, 126, 128–129, 130, 161, 167, 182–183, 207, 214, 220, 223, 225, 229, 236
Human Genome Project   10, 237
human
- enhancement   7, 21, 46, 54–55, 57–58, 223, 276, see also transhumanism
- exceptionalism   97, 128, 254, 266, 275, 277
- imagination   59, 162, 266
- nature   7, 19, 22, 55, 103, 155, 176, 257
- subject(ivity)   107, 123, 177–178, 191, 276
- nonhuman interactions   10, 19, 72, 124, 128, 130, 171, 178, 184–186, 196–197, 259, 266, 269
humanism   59, 66, 97, 178, 204, 245, 273, 277, see also transhumanism, see also critical posthumanism
humanist   5, 7, 9, 38, 45, 56, 59, 64–67, 69, 76, 146, 156, 171, 174, 186–187, 193, 199, 222, 234, 268, 272, 275–276, 278
humanistic   38, 66, 68, 192
- psychology   24, 234, see also Maslow
humanity   3, 8, 15, 18, 21, 48–49, 58, 64–65, 101, 103–104, 129, 132, 137, 143, 149, 163, 166, 171–172, 174, 182, 186, 189, 202, 205–

        207, 221, 223, 234, 236, 238–239, 257,
        273–274, 276
– saving   101, 104, 205, 273
– shared   3, 143, 166, 234
– the future of   58, 223, 257
humanities   6–7, 9, 59, 61, 63–64, 110, 175,
        177, 180, 201, 254, 270, 277
– crisis of   2, 59, 65
– digital   60–61
– as posthumanities   7, 277

idealism   262, 267
ideas
– worth spreading   6, 39
– as patterns of information   45
Illouz, Eva   2, 34, 47, 61, 82, 90, 102, 138, 151–
        152, 164–165, 215, 224
imagination   38, 45, 59, 68–69, 71, 92–93,
        146, 162, 169, 171–172, 200, 205–206, 208,
        245, 249, 258, 266–267, 276, 278
immersion
– textual   75, 129, 138, 276
immigrant   85, 111, 119
– myth   20, 111
immigration   122
immortality   10, 21, 111–112, 121, 124–126, 129,
        134–135, 240
influencers   17, 82, 113
insight   35, 37–38, 48, 57, 68, 70, 90, 146,
        161–162, 169, 185, 196, 231, 250, 257, 274
– as second sight   161
– epistemic   60
– of interbeing   170–171, 178, 182, 186, 188,
        192–193, 274
– mystical   171, 196, 230, 275
– scientific   51, 53, 56–57, 217
interspecies   196, 206–207
intimacy   1, 3–4, 34, 36, 47, 63, 114, 116, 126–
        127, 179, 207, 222, 251, 271
– tyrannies of   23
– with loss   67, 125, 183, 274, 278
intimate
– outsider   8, 118, 137, 179, 248–249, 261, 277
– public   34, 47
intimization of science   6, 32
introspection   30, 51–52, 64, 151, 216, 221,
        250, 277

– age of   216
inward (turn)   23–24, 82, 84, 120, 131, 139,
        144, 153, 196, 225
Iyer, Pico   144, 146
– "Art of Stillness"   146

Jacob's ladder   84, 230, 257
James, David   11, 67, 120, 183, 185, 248, see
        also critical solace
Jha, Amishi   154
– "How to Tame"
journal   8, 22, 35, 106, 120–121, 126, 179, 202,
        204–205, 217, 242, 251, 254, 276, see also
        confession, see also diary, see also auto-
        biography
justice   17, 41, 87, 95–96, 101, 172, 176
– in-   27, 30, 85, 92, 175, 187
– multispecies   173, 188

Kahneman, Daniel   214, 235
– "The Riddle of Experience"   235
Kelly, Pat   43–44, 46
– "Thought Leader"   43–44
Keltner, Dacher   96, 156, 216–217, 219, 223–
        226, 235
Killingsworth, Matt   154
– "Want to Be Happier"   154
kinship   128, 138, 277
Kley, Antje   32, 35, 37, 60
Kohut, Heinz   34
knowledge   4, 6, 32–33, 38, 41–43, 46, 52,
        56, 62, 64, 83, 85, 132, 162, 170–171, 193,
        205–206, 238, 252, 255, 264, 272, 276
– and its limits   35, 196, 204, 246
– as a motivation for reading   60
– dissemination   3, 39–40, 43, 56–57, 205,
        216, 271
– expert/specialist/scientific   6, 32, 36, 58, 173,
        187, 276
– failure of   131
– humanization of   3
– lack of   70
– of life   9, 270
– ordinary   9
– production   10, 58–60, 68, 261
– self-   30, 107–108, 151, 162
– tacit   111, 135, 149, 213

– transdisciplinary   270, see also literature as life science

Law of Attraction   38
Levitin, Daniel   144, 150, 169
– "How to Stay Calm"   150
life   20, 21, 48–49
– and choice   23
– and death   21
– extension   21, 122, 125
– science   9, 77
– writing   6, 8, 10–11, 19–20, 59, 77, 106, 113, 249, 269, 270, see also death, see also body (im)mortality
Love, Heather   66–67
literary   9, 22, 53, 60, 67, 71, 73, 82, 101, 105, 117, 126, 129, 132, 135, 137, 171, 177, 184, 186, 199, 253–254, 261, 278
– absorption   66, 68, 76
– criticism   19, 59–60, 171
– debates   4
– devices/techniques   18, 70, 278
– genre   15, 172
– history   130
– knowledge   131
– naturalism   67–68
– scholars/critics   62, 65–66, 77, 131, 275
– studies   7, 16, 59, 62, 66–67, 74, 177, 270
– texts   11, 60–61, 76, see also literary synesthesia
literature   5, 7–8, 16, 58–62, 64–68, 74–76, 82, 127, 129, 131–139, 177, 187, 189, 199, 200–209, 236–237, 254, 261–269, 270, 275, 277–278
– and its role/relevance   2, 8–9, 11, 58–60, 74–75, 171, 177, 237, 250, 263, 265–266, 275
– and science (debates)   3, 251, 275
– as a life science   9, 77
– contemporary   71, 236, 273
– knowledge of   9, 131
Lucky Girl Syndrome   38

Mann, Dhar   95–96, 101
Manson, Mark   57
– Everything Is F*cked   57

mastery   88, 98, 148–149, 228, 231, 257, 264
– of habit   28
– of the mind   145
– self-   151–152, 157, 165, 224
materiality   46, 58, 73, 121, 135, 183, 189, 192, 203–204, 237, 267
McAdams, Dan   26–27, 56, 104, 236
McGonigal, Kelly   50, 101, 104–105
– "How to Make Stress"   101, 104–105
Moi, Toril   62–64
media   36, 237, 276
– consumption   147
– digital   245
– intimate   4
– mass   239, 246
– new   32, 36, 207
– online   2
– public   1, see also social media
memento mori   21, 81, 98, 102, 273–274
memoir   15, 20, 22, 41, 251
metafictional   128, 261–262
Meyer, Pamela   1, 3–4, 39, 270–271
– "How to Spot a Liar"   1, 3–4, 39, 270–271
mimesis   60
mindfulness   10, 48, 105, 143–170, 171–172, 178, 182, 188, 193, 196, 204, 207–208, 217, 222, 224–226, 230, 272
mind
– control   30, 162, 168–169
– over matter   28–29, 42, 227
– power   38, 45, 57, 86, 157–158, 166, 171, 193, 196, 228
Mohr, Monja   59, 72–73, 172, 178, 187–188, 195
molecular   10, 56, 107, 198
monkey   97–98, 128, 227, 274
monster   97, 183, 186, 191
monstrosity   186
monstrous   182, 192
motivation   42, 48–49, 60, 65, 83, 87–88, 108, 132, 219, 222, 246
– for reading   60
– intrinsic   88, 231, 272
– self-   83, 147
motivational   41, 84, 95
– force   38, 87
– industry   39, 87

– language   48
– speakers   17, 28, 30, 82, 93–95, 100, 147
– tools   46
mourning   121, 128–129, 207, 243, see also grief
multisensory   73, 123, 134, 185, 192–193, 196, 200, 207, 252, 256, 263, 274, 277
mundane   129, 197, 209, 264
myth   150, 177, 200, 220, 255–256
– cultural   8
– of Icarus   134
– of progress   19–20
– of the androgyne   138
– of the Garden of Eden   199
– of individualism   20, 213, 270
– of productivity   81
– of the unbiased observer   33
– making   180
mythic   40
mythical   182, 195, 199, 258

narcissism   24, 244, 273
narcissist   273
narcissistic   240, 253
narrative
– voice   96, 181
Néry, Guillaume   167–169, 234
– "Exhilarating Peace"   167–169
neoliberal   7, 59, 108, 143, 152, 174, 176
neuroscience   53
neuroscientist   55–56, 62, 150, 154, 159
new
– materialism   3, 7, 169
– materialist   3, 186
Ngai, Sianne   9, 28, 61, 63, 75–77
– Ugly Feelings   9, 28, 61, 63, 75–77
nirvana   47, 57, 164
Norton, Michael   214, 219–220
– "How to Buy Happiness"   220
nostalgia   119, 121, 127, 134, 183

objectivity   32–37, 39–40, 61, 67, 98, 146, 224, 272
ocularcentric   37, 60, 66
ocularcentrism   68, 246, 252
olfactory   73, 123, 127

optimism   2, 11, 47, 63, 109, 218, 264, 269, 271
– as a vision   57
– cruel   47, see also Lauren Berlant
– norm   11
optimistic   42–43, 57, 99, 185, 201, 208, 263
organic   54, 186
Orientalism   125, 242
otter   115, 122–124, 274

Packnett, Brittany   84–85, 100
– "How to Build Your Confidence"   84–85, 100
panopticon   25, 117, 190, see also surveillance
pastoral   209
pathology   63, 71, 246
patriarchy   97
patriarchal   40, 204, 220
Paul, Heike   1, 20, 40–41, 215, 243
perfect   53, 58, 84, 93, 137, 172–173, 191–192, 238–239, 261
– im-   125, 262, 266
perfection   19, 21, 134, 175, 182, 238, 246, 262
– im-   19, 21, 103, 189, 204
perfectionism   49
personal
– development   179
– fulfillment   82, 223
– growth   43, 48–50, 55, 154
– transformation   15, 23–24, 46
Pink, Daniel   86, 88, 231
– "Puzzle of Motivation"   86, 88
plasmaticness   28, 77
Plato   164, 169, 262
pleasure   63, 73, 81, 97, 99, 174–175, 183, 201, 207–208, 213, 226, 232–234, 259, 265
podcast   2, 17, 32, 36–37, 83, 96, 147, 156, 271
– Greater Good   156, 176, 216–217, 219, 223, 235
– On Purpose   96
polishing   202, 238, 254, 261–265, 268
politics   5, 48, 51, 61, 75, 135, 186–187, 213, 218, 276, see also aesthetics and politics
postcolonial   106–107, 111, 222
postcritical   63, 67, 73
postcritique   4, 62–63, 278, see also Felski
posthuman   9, 64, 76, 109, 171–173, 186–187, 189, 199, 203–204, 208, 277
posthumanism   3, 7, 9–10, 21

posthumanist   57, 66, 68, 70, 171, 173, 186, 205–206, 277
power
– of suggestion   30, 45
– of positive thinking   30, 45, 47, 63, 86
– relation(ships)   11, 18, 26, 187, 192
– to choose   56
Powers, Richard   8, 92, 101, 110, 114, 117–118, 133, 175–176, 189, 201–202, 207, 221–222, 237–260, 261–269, 274–275
– Generosity: An Enhancement   8, 101, 110, 114, 117–118, 133, 175–176, 189, 201–202, 207, 221–222, 237–260, 261–269, 274–275
Prince Ea   95–96, 101–102
privacy   1, 3, 15, 23, 72, 115, 117, 122, 136, 145–146, 161, 163, 190–191, 202–203, 221, 273
– and oversharing   1
– and its loss/death   22–23
procrastination   92, 94–95, 97–98, 102
psychology   30, 32, 34, 36, 48–49, 104, 144, 163, 170, 190, 216, 227, 233
– evolutionary   164–165, 232, 258
– humanistic   24, 28, 234
– positive   1, 35, 63, 175, 216–217, 226
psychoanalysis   34, 63, 143, 151–152, 165, 232
Puddicombe, Andy   50, 144, 150–151, 157
– "All It Takes"   144, 150–151, 157

quantified self   29–30, 74, 93, 98, 107–108, 116, 155
quantum mechanics   33

racism   7, 74, 85, 187, 242
rags-to-riches   51, 81, 93
rapture   21, 106, 183, 185, 188, 277
Raskopolous, Jordan   149
reading   4, 5–6, 9, 16, 57–58, 59–77, 106, 110, 121, 127, 130–139, 175, 199, 200–209, 245, 248, 250, 253, 256, 259, 268–269, 270, 275–278
– and confession   63, 248
– and its experience   62–63, 65–66, 178
– close   11, 66
– critical   62, 66, 130, 172, *see also* postcritique
– distant   60–61
– haptics of   73–74, 276
– materiality of   121, 267, 278

realism   253–254
– literary   67, 172, 261, 267
– scientific   32–33
– speculative   267
realist   177, 261–262
reception theory   5, *see also* horizon of expectation
redemption   21, 26–27, 41, 101, 103–104, 137, 181–182, 186, 208, 223, 239, 269, 276
redemptive   24, 26, 104–105, 115, 137, 181, 236, 242
– narrative/script   34, 43, 56, 96, 104, 188, 270, 273
– self   26
research
– as assemblage   3
– gap   43
– method   34–35
resilience   46, 86, 105, 154, 169
response-ability   188, 199, 206–207
responsibility   15, 96–97, 180
– individual/personal   27, 82, 89, 91, 102, 105, 160, 239, 255
– shared   57, 181
Ricard, Matthieu   144, 151
– "Habits of Happiness"   151
Robbins, Mel   97
Robbins, Tony   10
Romantic   30, 69, 71, 184, 199
– anti-   194
Romanticism   71, 104, 183
Rousseau, Jean Jacques   24
– Les Confessions   24
rumination   151, 153, 227
– self-   30, 97, 226

Sartre, Jean Paul   18, 25, 118, 139, 250
– and shame   25, 250
savoring   170, 225–226, 258
self-help
– and its scientific strand   51, 100, 271
– culture   2–3, 8, 10–11, 15–18, 23, 26–30, 34, 38, 43, 55, 58, 65, 84–86, 94, 97–98, 106, 108, 129, 145, 152, 157, 174–175, 181, 216–217, 220, 222, 238, 241, 245–246, 258, 264, 270–271, 274, 277
– rhetoric   84, 118, 170, 174, 218

self-made man   20, 82, 89, 83, 101, 109, 111
sensation without mediation   45, 72, see also technoliberalism
sentimentalism   18
sentimentalist   3, 18, 270, 277
sense
– of community   57, 89, 221, 244, see also dangerous altruism
– of smell   124
– of wonder   36–38, 56, 63, 68, 122, 184, 229, see also science fiction
– of touch   138, 184, 192, 257
– of sight   184, 190
scanning   130, 132–133, 139
science
– authority   6, 35–36, 40, 46–47, 51, 216, 272
– fiction   9, 37–39, 41, 68–70, 172, 184, 204, 223, 240, 257, 275
– wars   3, 33, see also communication of science, see also life science
science fictional
– estrangement   73
– expectation   9, 129
scientist   32–33, 41, 63, 70, 148, 175, 188, 191, 201, 221, 228, 239–240, 273
– inner   159–160, 171, 221, 272
– mad   70, 172, 273, 275, see also citizen scientist, see also neuroscientist
scripted(ness)   247, 249, 250
self
– actualization   24, 27, 65, 234
– awareness   23, 30, 62, 64, 98, 100, 102, 160–161, 167, 229, 233–234, 261
– control   29, 58, 65, 82, 90, 97, 100, 108, 144, 148–149, 151–152, 157–158, 199, 215, 228, 231, 272
– enhancement   222
– esteem   85, 219, 233–234
– examination   51, 151, 251
– fashioning   11, 259
– improvement   23, 36, 42–43, 45, 48, 55, 58, 81, 83, 89, 93, 105, 157, 175, 219, 222–223, 234, 238–239, 254–255, 271–272
– monitoring   22–23, 52, 100, 160, 215, 224, 234, 247, 250
– reflection   18, 53, 124, 216, 226, 250
– reliance   30, 85, 118, 181
– tracking   30, 108, 215
– transcendence   84, 151, 157–158, 214, 222–227, 232, 257, 259
– vigilance   30, 51–52, 56, 97, 152, 230, 233–234, 245–246, 272
self-care   30, 50, 109
self-descriptive reminiscence   11, 116, 120, 180, 245, 248, 276
sexism   7
Seyedlar, Mehdi Ordikhani   162–163, 198
– "What Happens in Your Brain"   162–163
Shetty, Jay   30, 94–96, 101
Shteyngart, Gary   7, 82, 106–139, 175–176, 201, 222, 232, 240, 245, 256, 274, 276
– Super Sad True Love Story   7, 82, 106–139, 175–176, 201, 222, 232, 240, 245, 256, 274, 276
Silva, Jason   227
Sinek, Silva   86–88
– "How Great Leaders"   86–88
Singularity   21, see also transhumanism
Sister True Dedication   168–170
– "Three Questions"   169–170
Sisyphean   255–256
Sisyphus   52, 255
skepticism   36, 77, 121, 196, 244, 246, 250, 253
– epistemological   164
smell(s)   4, 57, 71–72, 124, 126–127, 159, 168, 192–193, 197, 199–200, 207, 225, 258–259, 261, 274, 276
Smiles, Samuel   10, 29
– Self-Help   29
Smith, Larry   50, 90–93, 102–103
– "Why You Will Fail"   90–93
social media   17–18, 24, 82–83, 93–95, 106, 112–113, 117, 147, 254, 271
solitude   30, 32, 145, 171, 208, 219
sonorous   67, 198
sound   57, 69, 71, 136, 185, 193–198, 200, 207, 225, 252, 259, 262, 264, 267, 274, 276
speciesism   7, 187, see also anthropocentrism
speculation   39, 41, 200
speculative   9, 30, 41, 173
– fiction/literature/novels/writing   2, 5, 8, 58–59, 74, 77, 106, 169, 172, 270, 273, 275
– realism   267, see also dystopia, see also science fiction

Steindl-Rast, David   50, 152, 214
- "Want to Be Happy"   152
storytelling   96, 116, 179–180, 200, 202, 205, 208
St. John, Richard   89–93, 100, 103
- "Success"   89–93, 100
sublime   54, 151, 258
- mathematical   56
- technological   5
success   10, 20, 27, 38, 41, 48–49, 51, 81–93, 95, 98–103, 105–106, 110–111, 113, 118, 126, 138, 224, 227, 230, 272
surveillance   1, 5, 8, 18, 25–26, 117, 136, 190, 249–250, 272, 275
- self-   97, 249
- studies   1
- technologies   23, see also panopticon, see also privacy
survival   21, 70, 108, 111–112, 119, 128, 133, 156, 166–167, 169–170, 172, 180, 185, 199, 206–208, 223, 237, 255, 276, 278
- future   103, 143, 171, 207, 272, 278
- human   9, 166, 171, 273
- of the species   9, 57, 143, 165, 171, 273
- scenes   9, 70, 76, 119, 193–195, 197, 209
- struggle/quest for   9, 58, 116, 185, 195, 258
suspicion   62, 66, 181, 249, 272
- hermeneutics of   62
synesthesia   70–71
- literary   5, 9, 11, 66, 68, 70–77, 121, 135, 137–138, 184, 186–188, 193–194, 199, 200, 205, 209, 236, 251, 258, 263, 267, 275
- time-space   184

tactile   123–124, 127, 134, 257, 276
taste   57, 119, 124, 159, 207, 259, 261, 276
Taylor, Jill Bollte   47, 55–57, 196
- "My Stroke of Insight"   47, 55–57
technoliberal   6, 45
technoliberalism   7
technology   1–2, 4–5, 11, 21, 30, 34, 37, 40, 44, 46, 48, 54–55, 121, 124, 130, 146, 155–156, 161–162, 174, 190, 275
- and emotion   5
- bio   201, 206
- digital   130
- of the self   34, 64

TED
- and education   42, 46
- archive   50
- genre   6, 41–43, 46, 101
- history   39–40
- playlists
- "How to Be a Better You"   49–51, 83–105, 150
- "How to Overcome Your Fears"   50
- "Survivor's Wisdom"   49–50
- "Talks to Help Practice Patience"   144–145, 150
- "Talks to Help You Manage Stress"   144–145, 150
- "The Most Popular Science Talks"   39, 49, 55, 88, 159, 214,
- "The Most Popular Talks of all Time"   1, 43, 49–50, 55, 86, 88, 214
- "What Makes You Happy"   49–50, 214–236
- "Who Are You"   49, 52–53, 165, 235
telepathic   45, 161, 163, 264
telepathy   45–46
texture   57, 123, 259
The Karmapa, His Holiness   152–153
- "Technology of the Heart"   152–153
therapeutic   22, 24, 34, 120, 148, 180, 207, 225, 250, 270
therapy (culture)   3, 34, 175, 216, see also psychotherapy
thingness   10, 189, 204
Thoreau, Henry David   20, 38, 50, 145, 219
Tippett, Krista   156–157, 169
transcendental   53, 134, 145
Transcendentalist(s)   19, 145, 199
transhumanism   10, 18, 21, 110, see also human enhancement
transhumanist   21–23, 55, 101, 204
transparency   4, 60, 72, 115, 132, 160–161, 163, 191, 198, 256, 263–264
transparent   1, 98, 192, 272
- citizen   45
- eye-ball   191
trauma   26, 120, 164, 180, 182–183, 218, 224, 244, 247, 250, 276
- post-traumatic growth   104, 154
Tristan, Harris   155, 166
- "How a Handful"   155

tyranny
– of positivity   108, 217

universal   59, 89, 138, 191, 228, 235, 254, 271
universality   32, 221–222, 236
upward mobility   27, 48, 81, 84, 95, 134
Urban, Tim   97–98, 102
– "Inside the Mind"   97–98, 102
ustopia   173, 191, 209, 255, *see also* dystopia, *see also* utopia
utopia   173, 185, 191
– anti-   173, *see also* ustopia, *see also* dystopia
utopian   19–20, 41, 57–58, 85, 125, 173, 176–177, 187, 191, 208

ventriloquism   60
ventriloquist   188
Victorian   29, 146–148
vigilance   8, 29, 45, 62, 64, 66, 68, 127, 150, 194, 198–199, 208, 233, 249, 258
– critical   62, 75
– lack of   2, 65, 174, *see also* self-vigilance
vigor   81, 109, 122, 147–148, 152
visceral   73, 127, 136, 159, 205, 226, 236, 264
visibility   17, 49, 68, 190, 263
visual sense   4, 136, 162, 194, 235, 246, *see also* ocularcentrism
visualization   38, 61
vitalism   148
vital   16, 89, 108, 128, 148, 166, 169–171
vitality   11, 102, 122, 133, 148, 170, 185, 192, 199, 209, 274

Vitruvian man   55
voyeurism   15
voyeuristic   190, 247
vulnerability   15, 25, 47, 49, 57, 84, 103, 106, 111, 114, 121, 125–127, 129, 188, 194, 196, 241, 246, 266, 274
– in-   81, *see also* body (im)mortality

Waldinger, Robert   50, 214, 220–221, 233–234
– "What Makes a Good Life?"   220–221
wealth   81, 99, 102, 107, 112–113, 115, 128, 175, 218, 220–221
white privilege   135
whiteness   127, 134–135
Whitman, Walt   21–22, 253, 258
Winch, Guy   45, 153–155, 263, 272
– "Why We All Need"   153–155, *see also* emotional hygiene
Wooden, John   91–94, 100
– "Difference"   92
Winfrey, Oprah   26–27, 239
Wright, Robert   29, 151, 163–165, 230

yogi   30, 144–145, 158
youth   53, 107, 115, 122, 124–125, 127, 201, 246

Zerilli, Linda   61–62
Zinn, Jon Kabatt   148–149, 160, 165, 168
– Coming to Our Senses   160
– Full Catastrophe Living   149
– Wherever You Go There You Are   165

www.ingramcontent.com/pod-product-compliance
Lightning Source LLC
Chambersburg PA
CBHW051536230426
43669CB00015B/2615